# A Valley of Vision

# A Valley of Vision

## The Heavenly Journey of Abraham ben Hananiah Yagel

*Translated from the Hebrew, with an Introduction and Commentary, by*
*David B. Ruderman*

*upp*
University of Pennsylvania Press
Philadelphia

*Publication of this book has been aided by grants from the Frederick W. Hilles Publication Fund of Yale University, the Lucius N. Littauer Foundation, and the Louis and Minna Epstein Fund of the American Academy for Jewish Research.*

Library of Congress Cataloging-in-Publication Data
Jagel, Abraham ben Hananiah dei Galicchi, 16th/17th cent.
  [Ge ḥizayon. English]
  A valley of vision: the heavenly journey of Abraham ben Hananiah Yagel / translated from the Hebrew, with an introduction and commentary, by David B. Ruderman.
    p. cm.
  Translation of: Ge ḥizayon.
  Includes bibliographical references.
  ISBN 0-8122-8168-3
  1. Judaism—Fiction. 2. Judaism—Works to 1900. I. Ruderman, David B. II. Title.
PJ5050.J33G413 1989
892.4'32—dc20                                                    89-40400
                                                                    CIP

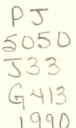

*For my other parents,*
*Rosalyn and Perry Sklersky*

# Contents

# *Acknowledgments*

As any translator of a premodern text well knows, one's work is fraught with numerous unanticipated challenges and difficulties. Completing the task requires the good counsel and expertise of wise and generous colleagues. I was blessed by the invaluable assistance of David Fink, who reviewed my entire translation at its initial stages and prodded me to work harder to improve my unfinished effort. As the work neared completion, Moshe Idel generously offered his time and valuable insights in reviewing the entire work. The introduction and text were also read (in their entirety or partially) by Steven Fraade, Elliott Horowitz, Giuseppe Mazzotta, and Benjamin Ravid. David Altshuler, Richard Cohen, Geoffrey Hartman, and Ivan Marcus read the introduction. I have profited immensely from all of their suggestions; the remaining deficiencies are, of course, my own responsibility.

A small part of my introduction, primarily the biographical sections and the section on the Siamese twins, is based on my book *Kabbalah, Magic, and Science: The Cultural Universe of a Sixteenth-Century Jewish Physician* (1988). My thanks to Harvard University Press for allowing me to "borrow" this material. My remarks on the Jewish gambler and my translation of his speech originally appeared in (the now defunct and most lamented) *Orim: A Jewish Journal at Yale*, 3 (1987): 110–24, in an essay titled "Memoirs of a Jewish Gambler." Part of my translation of "Job's Story" will soon appear (in a somewhat different form) in the anthology *Rabbinic Fantasies: Imaginative Narratives from Classical and Medieval Hebrew Literature*, edited by M. Mirsky and D. Stern (Jewish Publication Society, Philadelphia, 1990). A preliminary sketch of my introductory remarks was first published as "Some Literary and Iconographic Influences of the Renaissance and Baroque on Abraham Yagel's *Gei Ḥizzayon*" (in Hebrew), *Tarbiz*, 57 (1988): 271–79.

I wish to thank the Library of the Hebrew Union College–Jewish Institute of Religion in Cincinnati, Ohio, for permission to publish my translation of HUC MS. 743. I acknowledge the kindnesses of the staffs of Yale University Library, the Library of the British Museum, the Bodleian Library at Oxford, and the National and University Library of the Hebrew University in Jerusalem, especially its Institute for Microfilms of Hebrew

Manuscripts, where much of the research on this book was completed. I am also grateful to Yale University and the Institute for Advanced Study at the Hebrew University in Jerusalem (where I served as a fellow in 1987) for their generous support of my work.

I benefited greatly from the editorial assistance of Zachary Simpson and Ruth Veleta of the University of Pennsylvania Press. It remains only to express my gratitude to my wife, Phyllis, and to my children, Noah and Tali, for their love, their support, and their patience.

Orange, Connecticut
Rosh Hashanah, 5750

# 1. Introduction

Confined to a dark cell in the municipal prison of Mantua, Italy, around the year 1578, Abraham ben Hananiah Yagel brooded restlessly upon the course of his short life of twenty-five years. Having been blessed with exceptional scholarly and literary talents, he had never been capable of fully utilizing them. Instead of the serenity of books, of research and reflection he so keenly sought, and the material security upon which such a state depended, his life was in complete disarray.

Several years earlier, Yagel and his family had been forced to leave his birthplace in the territories of Venice and had settled in the vicinity of Mantua in search of more tranquil surroundings. Then his father suddenly died, leaving his son a small pawn bank for which he had neither experience nor inclination to manage. It seemed that every decision he took and every partnership he sought to form brought him more misfortune and misery. He first entered a rather uncommon arrangement with a female associate named Rina who proved to be most irritable and unreliable, leaving him penniless and totally dependent on her every whim and demand. Having sheltered her illegally in his home during a period of severe plague, he had incurred the wrath of the authorities and the local populace alike. To make matters worse, a rival banking clan, the Almagiati family, continually slandered him and would not desist until he had lost his entire estate and was thrown into this very prison.

So Yagel sat despondently and wallowed in his self-pity, relieved only by the solitude of the bare walls of his dungeon sanctuary. Suddenly, however, he was aroused in a dream by the soul of his father, who offered not only solace and counsel but the thrilling adventure of a heavenly journey in which he would meet other souls with other stories and who would instruct him on the ultimate purpose of his life and on the sublime mysteries of the divine universe.

Such was the dismal reality Yagel so graphically depicted in his *Gei Ḥizzayon* (*A Valley of Vision;* cf. Isaiah 21:1). Through his narration of these events, he hoped to unburden himself of the unpleasant circumstances of his most recent past and to solicit the reader's sympathetic response to his unjust fate. He would also set the stage for the artistic scenario of his miraculous deliverance, that dream odyssey through which he expected to elicit the fascination of his audience with his narrative from beginning to end. Whether or not the vicissitudes he described had actually transpired in precisely the way he claimed they had, Yagel intended to exploit fully a common literary motif of spiritual liberation from the fetters of corporeal imprisonment (i.e., the soul's release from its bodily captivity) in order to present his own story and his own religious message in the most imaginative way possible. By so doing, he composed a work unique among Jewish writers of his and previous generations. And for the modern reader, he left a remarkably entertaining narrative as well as a revealing window through which to observe some of the cultural and social concerns of Italian Jewry of the late sixteenth century.

## Yagel and the Context of Jewish Life in Late Sixteenth-Century Italy

That such an author would have chosen this literary form of self-expression is indeed a remarkable fact in itself, for Abraham Yagel's primary interest was not literature but natural history and medicine. His most important works, the unpublished *Beit Ya'ar ha-Levanon* (*House of the Forest of Lebanon;* cf. 1 Kings 10:17, 21) and *Be'er Sheva* were massive encyclopedias of the sciences of his day.[1] He was also an avid letter writer, corresponding especially with patients seeking his medical care.[2] He also composed a plague tract,[3] an elementary religious catechism which he audaciously adapted for Jewish usage from a Catholic manual,[4] and a small volume in praise of women,[5] all published during his lifetime.

Above everything else, however, Yagel saw himself as a skillful physician. Moreover, the intellectual elite of the Jewish community of north-central Italy knew him both in this capacity and as an authority on astron-

---

[1]*Beit Ya'ar ha-Levanon* is found in MSS. Oxford Bodleian Reggio 8–10 listed as nos. 1303–1305 in A. Neubauer, *Catalogue of the Hebrew Manuscripts in the Bodleian Library,* 2 vols. (Oxford, 1886, 1906). *Be'er Sheva* is found in MS. Oxford Bodleian Reggio 11 listed as no. 1306 by Neubauer.

[2]This correspondence is found in a work entitled *Bat Rabim (Daughter of Many),* MS. Moscow Günzburg 129 (Hebrew University and National Library Jerusalem, Microfilm 6809; hereafter cited as Jerusalem microfilm).

[3]*Moshi'ah Hosim* (Venice, 1587).

[4]*Lekah Tov* (Venice, 1595).

[5]*Eshet Hayil* (Venice, 1605).

omy and astrology. His illustrious contemporary Menahem Azariah da Fano even acknowledged him as "unique in our generation in the knowledge of the spheres" and as an "expert in all fields of learning."[6] Yagel's medical title thus provided him a certain professional status and intellectual authority among his coreligionists, an achievement that he earnestly sought and that partially compensated for the incessant economic difficulties which plagued him throughout his life.

Those difficulties, which he partially describes in *Gei Ḥizzayon,* were not entirely his own making and reflect to a large extent the general deterioration of the status and physical well-being of the Jewish community in the second half of the sixteenth century. Fifteen fifty-three, the year in which Abraham Yagel was born, marks a watershed in the history of the Italian Jewish community. In that year, the pope decreed that all copies of the Talmud be burned throughout Italy. Only two years later the infamous anti-Jewish edict *Cum nimis absurdum* sweepingly reversed the relatively tolerant papal policy toward Jews during the heyday of the Renaissance. In the emotionally charged atmosphere of the Counter-Reformation, Pope Paul IV (1476–1559) and his successors imposed restrictive legislation which led to the increased impoverishment, ghettoization, and expulsion of Jews, especially within the papal states themselves. These setbacks were accompanied by severe conversionary pressures: the enforcement of compulsory Christian preaching in synagogues; the proliferation of the *domus cate-chumenorum,* an institution designed to facilitate the large-scale conversion of Jews to Christianity; and the intensified Christian harassment of Jews, including the censorship of Hebrew books and the wide diffusion of anti-Judaic literature.[7]

[6]Menahem Azariah da Fano, *Asarah Ma'amarot,* MS. Strasbourg 3973 (Jerusalem microfilm 2867), J. Landauer, *Katalog der hebraishen, arabischen Mss.* (Strasbourg, 1881), p. 67, n. 47, chap. 29, fol. 125b. On Fano and his relationsip to Yagel, see below.

[7]On the decline of Jewish life in the second half of the sixteenth century, see, for example, K. Stow, *Catholic Thought and Papal Jewry Policy 1555–1593* (New York, 1977); idem, "The Burning of the Talmud in 1553 in the Light of Sixteenth Century Catholic Attitudes toward the Talmud," *Bibliothèque d'humanisme et Renaissance,* 34 (1972): 435–59; D. Carpi, "The Expulsion of the Jews from the Papal States during the Time of Pope Pius V and the Inquisitional Trials against the Jews of Bologna" (in Hebrew), in *Scritti in memoria di Enzo Sereni,* ed. D. Carpi and R. Spiegel (Jerusalem, 1970), pp. 145–65; R. Bonfil, "Some Reflections on the Place of Azariah de Rossi's *Me'or Einayim* in the Cultural Milieu of Italian Renaissance Jewry," in *Jewish Thought in the Sixteenth Century,* ed. B. Cooperman (Cambridge, Mass., 1983), pp. 23–48; D. B. Ruderman, "A Jewish Apologetic Treatise from Sixteenth Century Bologna," *Hebrew Union College Annual,* 50 (1979): 253–76; and their bibliographical references.

These measures stood in sharp contrast to the relatively benign treatment of Jews by church and secular authorities throughout the previous centuries. Jewish loan bankers had initially been attracted to northern and central Italy because of the generous privileges offered them by local governments eager to attract adequate sources of credit for themselves, for local businesses, and especially for small loans to the poor. As a result of the granting of such privileges to individual Jews in the thirteenth, fourteenth, and fifteenth centuries, small Jewish communities grew up throughout the region, totally dependent on the recipients of these legal contracts (*condotte*), who also carried the primary burden of paying taxes to the authorities. By the sixteenth century, Jewish merchants and artisans joined these communities until eventually the moneylenders were no longer in the majority. In the relatively tolerant state of Jewish political and economic life up until the mid-sixteenth century, the cultural habits and intellectual tastes of Italian Jews were stimulated by their proximity to centers of Italian Renaissance culture. A limited but conspicuous number of Jewish intellectuals established mutually fructifying liaisons with their Christian counterparts to a degree unparalleled in earlier centuries.[8]

The legislative measures of the mid-sixteenth century thus threatened to undermine the significant progress of Jewish-Christian rapprochement during much of the Renaissance. Along with the worsening political atmosphere by the late sixteenth and early seventeenth centuries, there was also a general decline in Jewish banking activities. As capital became more readily available to the Christian population, fewer merchants and artisans availed themselves of the services of Jewish loan bankers. The latter's clients were increasingly the urban poor, who offered greater risks and more modest profits. With increased restrictions on Jewish moneylending, with the constant pressures to reduce the interest rate, and with the inevitable uncertainties involved in reclaiming the full value of loans, Jewish banking operations suffered accordingly. Some banks were forced to close; others competed fiercely for the diminished revenue available.[9]

[8]On Jewish life in Renaissance Italy, see the standard surveys by C. Roth, *The Jews in the Renaissance* (Philadelphia, 1959); M. A. Shulvass, *Jews in the World of the Renaissance* (Leiden and Chicago, 1973); A. Milano, *Storia degli ebrei in Italia* (Turin, 1963); R. Bonfil, *Ha-Rabbanut be-Italyah bi-Tekufat ha-Renesance* (Jerusalem, 1979) [Translated into English by J. Chipman, *Rabbis and Jewish Communities in Renaissance Italy* (Oxford and New York, 1989)]; and D. B. Ruderman, *The World of a Renaissance Jew* (Cincinnati, 1981). On Jewish intellectual life in the period, see D. B. Ruderman, "The Italian Renaissance and Jewish Thought," in *Renaissance Humanism: Foundations, Forms, and Legacy*, 3 vols., ed. A. Rabil, Jr. (Philadelphia, 1988), I, pp. 382–433.

[9]For an overview of Jewish loan banking in Italy, see the surveys mentioned in the previous note and L. Poliakov, *Jewish Bankers and the Holy See*, trans. M. L. Kochan (London,

Abraham Yagel's intellectual world, his activity as a physician, and his accomplishments as a religious thinker and a fiction and scientific writer thus emerged in a context of declining political fortunes and diminished economic resources for the entire Italian Jewish community. And his own economic situation was even more precarious than that of most other Jews. Above all, he knew intimately and acutely the treacherous business world of moneylending. Prominent and relatively affluent Jewish loan bankers constantly interacted with Yagel as patrons of his specialized learning, as patients in his medical practice, and as supporters or competitors during his own brief but tempestuous career in banking.

## The Biography of Abraham Yagel[10]

Yagel was born in the small town of Monselice, located south of Padua and north of Rovigo in the area of the terra firma (the mainland possessions of the Venetian government).[11] That his birthplace was Monselice can be inferred from the way he usually signed his name: "Abraham b. Hananiah Yagel of the Gallico family of Monselice." Although almost nothing is known about his father or family origins, it is obvious that Gallico was his real family name and that he took the name "Abraham Yagel" (Abraham will rejoice) from the Hebrew liturgy of the afternoon service for the Sabbath.[12]

Nothing is known of Yagel's early childhood in Monselice. He seems to have reached Luzzara, near Mantua, sometime in the early 1570s with his father, and perhaps with at least one brother. In a fragmentary work written in this period, he refers to his father as still living.[13] In *Gei Hizzayon,* begun

Henley, and Boston, 1977). For the Mantuan region, the location of Yagel's bank, see S. Simonsohn, *History of the Jews in the Duchy of Mantua* (Jerusalem, 1977), pp. 196–317.

[10]For a more detailed exposition of Yagel's biography, see D. B. Ruderman, *Kabbalah, Magic, and Science: The Cultural Universe of a Sixteenth-Century Jewish Physician* (Cambridge, Mass. and London, 1988), chaps. 1–2, from which this shorter version is taken.

[11]On this region's Jewish population, see C. Roth, *History of the Jews of Venice* (Philadelphia, 1930), chap. 8. Yagel reveals his birthdate, 1553, on two occasions, the first in a letter written in 1613 on his sixtieth birthday, and the second in a 1623 letter to Hananiah Rieti, found in *Bat Rabim,* no. 67, fols. 106b–108b; 174a.

[12]On the Gallico family in Italy, see the interesting testimony of Solomon Graziano, who cites Mordecai Dato that this family was one of the famous four families to be exiled from Jerusalem when the Second Temple was destroyed. See E. Zimmer, "Biographical Details concerning Italian Jewry, from Abraham Graziano's Handwritten Notes" (in Hebrew), *Kiryat Sefer,* 49 (1974): 442.

[13]*Bat Rabim,* fol. 195b.

in 1578, however, he states that his father was no longer alive; he also recalls his father's death in *Beit Ya'ar ha-Levanon,* a work he began as early as 1579.

It is possible that Yagel arrived in Luzzara as early as 1571–72, when Venice temporarily expelled many Jews, who then sought refuge in the Mantovano.[14] In *Gei Ḥizzayon,* he provides a detailed account of several years of his troubled life beginning sometime in the mid-1570s. He carefully reconstructs his protracted negotiations with his unreliable business part- ner Rina, her unwelcome visit to Luzzara during the time of the plague of 1575–76, and the suffering he experienced due to her visit. He also relates in great detail the slanderous and insidious actions of his chief rivals, the Almagiati sons; the involvement of some of Mantua's most distinguished Jews in the controversy; his temporary escape from Luzzara and eventual return; his final capture in the home of a Christian citizen of Mantua; and his ultimate imprisonment in the city jail.

Besides this testimony, some additional data on this early period are available. Yagel indicates in passing some members of his family, especially a brother and a mother-in-law. The colophon of a poem written by Yagel's friend Mordecai Dato reveals the identity of Abraham's wife as Dina, the daughter of Batsheva Fano and Hosea (Salvatore) da Colonia.[15] The latter was a banker in the area of Viadana and Luzzara.[16] Yagel had apparently married Dina soon after his arrival in Luzzara in the 1570s and sometime after his father had died.[17] Yagel's notebook contains a copy of a 1567 public announcement clarifying Hosea's estate.[18] During the height of Yagel's financial problems, Batsheva had become ill, perhaps because of the plague, and may have died soon afterward. Yagel's brother also died at about this time, leaving some children who remain unnamed in the sources. The only additional information about Yagel's sojourn in Luzzara is a passing refer- ence to a patient in 1581 and to an undated conversation with a Christian traveler.[19]

---

[14]See Simonsohn, *Jews in Mantua,* p. 28; Roth, *Jews in the Renaissance,* pp. 88–92; and B. Ravid, "The Socioeconomic Background of the Expulsion and Readmission of Venetian Jews 1571–1573," in *Essays in Modern Jewish History: A Tribute to Ben Halpern,* ed. F. Malino and P. C. Alpert (Rutherford, N.J., 1981).

[15]MS. London British Museum 6469, add. 22094 (Jerusalem microfilm 5043), fol. 62a; M. Margoliouth, *Catalogue of the Hebrew and Samaritan Manuscripts in the British Museum,* II (London, 1965), p. 261. On Dato and his relationship with Yagel, see below.

[16]On Hosea, see Simonsohn, *Jews in Mantua,* pp. 224–26. His father was the banker Abraham b. Angelo da Colonia, who had also been a banker in Viadana and other cities.

[17]Some of the notices in Simonsohn refer to Batsheva as a widow and guardian of Dina.

[18]*Bat Rabim,* no. 6, fols. 9a–10a. The document is signed by three rabbis in Ferrara: Barukh Uziel Ḥasachetto, Raphael b. Yohanan Treves, and Aaron b. Israel Finzi.

[19]The sick woman is recorded in *Beit Ya'ar ha-Levanon,* pt. 1, chap. 15. He mentions the

We know considerably less about Yagel's life and career following the period described in *Gei Ḥizzayon*. Throughout the remaining years of the sixteenth century and into the first decade of the seventeenth, he visited a number of Italian communities, mostly in the vicinity of Mantua and Modena, including Pesaro,[20] Revere,[21] Ferrara,[22] Carpi,[23] Correggio,[24] Reggio,[25] and Modena.[26] He seems to have left Luzzara by the early 1580s, settling eventually in the town of Rubeira, in the province of Reggio Emilia. He was in Rubeira as early as 1585, and in 1593 he was given the right, in the absence of Christian physicians, to care for both Christian and Jewish patients.[27] Although he retained ownership of his property in Luzzara and

---

traveler in *Be'er Sheva*, MS. Oxford Bodleian Reggio 11 (Neubauer catalogue no. 1306), pt. 2, chap. 21, fol. 72b.

[20]In a letter of January 1582 asking the leaders of the yeshiva in Pesaro to assist the wife of Judah Moscato because her husband has been called away and cannot provide for her, Yagel mentions that he was in their city some years earlier; *Bat Rabim*, fol. 177a (the later folios contain no item numbers). As late as 1619 he inspected a manuscript by Yohanan Alemanno in Pesaro (fol. 118b).

[21]In *Be'er Sheva*, pt. 2, chap. 22, fol. 78a, he mentions spending a summer evening in the home of Judah da Revere, where he saw a copy of Abraham Farissol's geographic work. On the latter see Ruderman, *The World of a Renaissance Jew*, chap. 11. In *Beit Ya'ar ha-Levanon*, pt. 1, chap. 7, fol. 13a, he refers to Judah's medical skills in curing infections on women's breasts. There he places him in Zittone, near Ferrara.

[22]In June 1587 Yagel served as a tutor in the home of Joseph Fano outside Ferrara; MS. London Montefiore 462, no. 73, fol. 43b. See J. Boksenboim, *Iggrot Melamdim* (Tel Aviv, 1985), p. 89.

[23]In 1590–91 in Carpi Yagel copied some selections from the work of Joseph ibn Shraga, the Spanish kabbalist; *Bat Rabim*, fol. 153a.

[24]In January 1605 Yagel was in the home of "the nobleman da Revere" (Judah?) in Correggio, where he inspected a letter of Israel Sarug, the disciple of Isaac Luria and teacher of Menahem Azariah da Fano; *Bat Rabim*, no. 61, fols. 94a–95b.

Even earlier, in 1603, Count Camillo of Correggio appointed Yagel with another Jewish associate, David Ricchi (or Ricco), to manage the city mint and to print a variety of local coins. On this appointment, see S. M. Bondoni and G. Busi, eds., *Cultura ebraica in Emilia-Romagna* (Rimini, 1987), p. 581; V. Mioni and A. Lusuardi, *La zecca di Correggio: Catalogo delle monete correggesi, 1569–1630* (Modena, 1986), pp. 104–8. My thanks to Dr. Busi for this information. Cecil Roth, in his *Jews in the Renaissance*, p. 105, had already mentioned this fact without documenting it.

David Ricchi was involved in another partnership with Antonio Bulbarini to mint coins at Correggio, signed on 11 March 1613 (Bondoni and Busi, p. 581). In August of the same year, in a Hebrew letter written by Yagel, he describes the sentencing of his former associate at the mint and Ricchi's near death by hanging for an unspecified crime (see *Bat Rabim*, fols. 184b–185a). Ricchi apparently was charged for a crime related to his minting duties.

[25]In *Beit Ya'ar ha-Levanon*, pt. 4, chap. 31, fol. 75b, he mentions having seen a ferocious wild animal in Reggio in 1601. He probably frequented Reggio on account of his relationship with Menahem Azariah da Fano, who lived there.

[26]He was in Modena in August 1613, in 1617, and in 1620; *Bat Rabim*, fols. 184b–185a; no. 64, fols. 102b–105a; no. 68, fols. 108b–112a.

[27]From Rubeira in 1585 Yagel criticized a sermon of the rabbi of Modena and corre-

received some income from renting it out, his major occupation was that of a physician and a tutor in the home of some affluent Jewish banking families. Thus, during this period, he corresponded with a number of distinguished Jewish patients who obviously valued his medical opinion highly.

He also established close ties with some of the most influential Jewish bankers in the region, especially Joseph Fano, the most powerful and politically well-connected Jew in Reggio Emilia. Yagel visited Fano at his summer home outside Ferrara in 1587 and dedicated his small catechism for young children, *Lekah Tov* (*Sound Learning;* cf. Proverbs 4:2), to him in 1595.[28] Some years earlier in 1587, he dedicated his plague tract, *Moshi'ah Hosim* (*Savior of Those Who Take Refuge;* cf. Psalms 17:7), to another banker, Or Shraga Sanguini of Venice. Yagel also nurtured a long-term relationship with the Modena banking family of Sassuolo. As early as 1604, he carried on an intense correspondence with Daniel Modena over the illness and eventual death of Daniel's son.[29] The family employed him, at least periodically, as either a tutor or physician over the next ten years.[30]

Yagel's period of residence in the Reggio area coincided with that of the famous kabbalist Menahem Azariah da Fano, who lived in Reggio in the 1580s and returned there in the first decade of the seventeenth century.[31] The two were on intimate terms and corresponded frequently. Yagel's ties with Fano were not only intellectual or spiritual. In 1605, Yagel dedicated his third small book, *Eshet Hayil* (*A Woman of Valor*), a short commentary

---

sponded with Mordecai Dato later that year. The privilege granted to Yagel in 1593 is found in the Archivio di Stato, Rome, Fondo camerali I: Diversorum del Camerlengo, filza 407, fol. 158b. Yagel also corresponded with a number of people from Rubeira in 1600; *Bat Rabim,* nos. 47, 52, fols. 61b, 86b.

[28]On Fano, see C. Roth, "Josef Da Fano, il primo ebreo italiano nobile," *La Rassegna Mensile di Israel,* 14 (1948): 190–94. Cf. Simonsohn, *Jews in Mantua,* p. 32, nn. 114 and 115. He is referred to in some contemporary chronicles; see Giovanni Battista Spaccini, *Cronaca modenese,* ed. G. Bertoni, T. Sandonini, and P. Vicini, *Monumenti de storia patria delle provincie modenesi, XVI and XVII* (Modena, 1911), XVI, 332, where the duke attempts to pressure Fano to convert. See also Lodovico Vedriani, *Historia dell'antichissimi citta di Modena* (Modena, 1667), p. 609, where he recounts that Fano was wounded while playing cards. On *Lekah Tov,* see S. Maybaum, *Abraham Jagel's Katechismus Lekah-tob* (Berlin, 1892).

[29]His correspondence with Daniel is found in *Bat Rabim,* fols. 118a–b, 183b.

[30]Genealogical information on the Modena family is found in the beginning of MS. Bologna University 2206 (Jerusalem microfilm 27795) and MS. Cambridge 40/32 (Jerusalem microfilm 15877).

[31]The latest and most complete account of Menahem's life is R. Bonfil, "New Information on R. Menahem Azariah da Fano and His Age" (in Hebrew), in *Perakim be-Toledot ha-Hevra ha-Yehudit . . . le-Professor Ya'akov Katz* (Jerusalem, 1980), pp. 98–135.

on Proverbs 31, to Rachel, the wife of Hezekiah ben Isaac Foa, who was the wealthy brother-in-law of Menahem Azariah. This gesture was an obvious expression of his attempt to establish an economic relationship with a very well-to-do family that also supported Fano's mystical and intellectual pursuits.[32]

Yagel lived in the same region of Modena, Reggio, and Sassuolo during the remaining years of his life. An interesting portrait of Yagel in his later years was written by the wealthy banker, Raphael ben Bezalel Modena of Sassuolo, who probably employed Yagel as a teacher, personal physician, and adviser.[33] Modena relates that in 1614 he was invited to participate as godfather (*sandek*) in the ritual circumcision ceremony of his sister's newborn infant in Luzzara. Modena's brother-in-law, Elḥanan Yedidiah Rieti, and Rieti's father, Hananiah Eliakim Rieti, were also the trustees of the property that Yagel still owned in Luzzara. Yagel apparently accompanied Modena on the trip from Sassuolo to Luzzara either as his employee or, more likely, as a personal friend of the Rieti family with ties to the community of Luzzara.[34]

On their way home to Sassuolo after the ceremony, Modena and Yagel were stopped by four armed robbers outside Reggio, taken captive, and held for a ransom in the mountains overlooking Reggio. Because of the banker's obvious prominence, the Jewish communities in Modena, Luzzara, Sassuolo, Reggio, Mantua, and Ferrara recited prayers and mobilized their resources to secure their release. The kidnappers eventually sent Yagel to the city of Modena to bargain for the freedom of his valuable patron. The duke's militia finally intervened, surprised the captors, and liberated Modena. Modena and Yagel were then received with great fanfare as they were led on horses through the streets of Modena together with the captured criminals.

Modena's description of these events continually emphasizes the banker's importance not only to the six Jewish communities that sought his

---

[32]On Hezekiah Foa, see Simonsohn, *Jews in Mantua*, p. 510; M. Ghirondi and H. Neppi, *Toledot Gedolei Yisrael ve-Geonei Italyah* (Trieste, 1853), p. 110; Bonfil, "New Information," pp. 105–6.

[33]See note 29 above.

[34]The event is preserved in three manuscripts: MS. Budapest Kaufmann A557/14 (Jerusalem microfilm 12688), MS. Bodleian Mich. 186 (listed as no. 2061/2 in Neubauer, *Hebrew Manuscripts in Bodleian*), and MS. Warsaw 680. I have consulted the Budapest manuscript, which was also published by M. Stern, "Zur Berichte des Raphael aus Sassuolo" (Hebrew title "Megillat Nes"), in *Festschrift . . . D. Hoffman* (Berlin, 1914), Hebrew section, pp. 267–80; German, pp. 460–62.

release but even to the duke himself. At the same time, Yagel's portrait is most uncomplimentary: he is referred to as only "Abraham Yagel Gallico"; he appears to be only a servant and lowly companion of Modena; and he is deemed so unimportant that he is quickly released to negotiate the terms of the banker's ransom. It is hazardous to infer too much from this portrait.[35] It seems likely, however, that Yagel, who had recently passed his sixtieth birthday, was dependent on Modena for his economic support and that Modena treated him with little respect despite his age and his status as a learned physician and scholar.

The last documents regarding Yagel's life, written by Yagel in 1623 from San Martino (probably San Martino dall'Argine, near Gazzuolo in the Mantovano), seem to confirm this same portrait.[36] The fact that Yagel had left the Modenese region to return to the Mantovano suggests, at the very least, the economic instability of his life even after the age of seventy. In the first of a series of letters to Hananiah Rieti of Luzzara,[37] he acknowledges his economic situation and the poor business deals he had made over the years: "Behold I am seventy years old and my strength has waned. I no longer am able to go out and come as before. I am without money today because of the excessive expenditures in which I became entangled during the past several months and because of my negligible income due to the rise of the price of food in this region. . . . For forty years I have been involved in these kinds of [financial] controversies."[38]

Yagel had written to Rieti about the status of his home in Luzzara, which the Rieti family apparently had managed for him over the years, sending him the rent to which he was entitled. He had first contacted Raphael Modena, his former employer in Sassuolo and the brother-in-law of Rieti's son, regarding certain income which he had not received but Modena had "responded to me as a mocker before his slaves."[39] In desperation, Yagel turned to Hananiah Rieti (then an old man who died later that year) and later to Rieti's son Elḥanan to recover the income he was due; in either case, his demands seem to have remained unfulfilled.

The fact that this correspondence represents the final documentation of Abraham Yagel's life is in itself bitter testimony that Yagel's financial

[35]Cf. Simonsohn, *Jews in Mantua*, p. 712: "It is doubtful whether a scholar like Gallico would spend his last days as a servant, even if we give a wide interpretation to the term."

[36]*Bat Rabim,* fols. 171a–172a, 174a–175a.

[37]On Hananiah Rieti and his son, Elḥanan Yedidiah, see Simonsohn, *Jews in Mantua*, p. 731, and the sources he cites.

[38]*Bat Rabim,* fol. 174a.

[39]Ibid., fol. 171a.

problems plagued him to the very end. Framed by the painful feud with the Almagiatis in the 1570s and this last controversy with the Rietis in 1623, Yagel's career was marked throughout by financial failures, unreliable business partnerships, periodic anxiety, and severe loss of time. His experience provides a rare glimpse of the more unsavory business world of his Jewish contemporaries. His research and writing and his scientific and kabbalistic pursuits provided him the most fulfilling liberation from his constant economic concerns.

## Yagel's Standing Among the Intellectual Elite of His Community

In sharp contrast to the figure Yagel cut among his business associates was the intellectual stature he attained among the educated leadership of the Jewish community. An examination of his primary personal and intellectual ties, based mainly on the evidence of his own writing and correspondence, allows us to situate Yagel within a well-defined intellectual and literary circle of Italian Jewry and to ascertain his singular role within that circle.

Abraham's closest friend was surely Hananiah Finzi, a rabbi who lived in Gazzuolo, Dosolo, Viadana, and Mantua.[40] He apparently read the manuscripts of Yagel's many compositions and encouraged him greatly in his writing. Both Yagel's and Finzi's writing testify to the special friendship the two developed over the years, "a covenant of love connecting us" in Yagel's words.[41]

Yagel's most illustrious colleague was Menahem Azariah da Fano, already mentioned in relation to his sister, to whom Yagel dedicated his short book on women. Fano's connections with Yagel were based on intellectual grounds as well. On several occasions he solicited Yagel's advice on medical and astronomical matters including the diagnosis of two ill patients.[42] In *Beit Ya'ar ha-Levanon* Yagel records an extremely involved discussion between Fano and himself on astronomical matters.[43] What is interesting about this prolonged inquiry is not the specific issues discussed

[40]On Finzi, see Simonsohn, *Jews in Mantua*, pp. 30, 50, 226–28, 236, 357, 622, 708–9, 724. Finzi also had close ties with Menahem Azariah da Fano. He was one of the publishers of Fano's edition of the Roman High Holy Days prayer book, and he served with Fano in 1601 in Viadana in distributing the moneys owed Jewish refugees from Milan.

[41]The line is from *Be'er Sheva*, pt. 2, chap. 11, fol. 38b. See also *Beit Ya'ar ha-Levanon*, pt. 1, introduction, fol. 2b; pt. 4, chap. 100, fol. 230a; *Bat Rabim*, no. 44, fol. 78a; no. 77, fol. 199a.

[42]*Bat Rabim*, nos. 39, 40, fols. 72b–74a; nos. 41, 45, fols. 74b–75b, 80a; no. 59, fol. 93a.

[43]*Beit Ya'ar ha-Levanon*, pt. 2, chaps. 25, 26, and 29.

but the manner in which Fano sought to gain from Yagel "scientific" corroboration of specific statements in the kabbalistic literature. Yagel also displayed considerable fascination in finding correlations between natural and kabbalistic wisdom. Fano was the major Italian kabbalist in Yagel's day, and his writings evince little interest in sources and ideas outside the realm of mythical kabbalah, especially that associated with the doctrines of the school of Isaac Luria in Safed.[44] Thus the mutual respect between Yagel, the physician and astrologer, and Fano, the pure kabbalist, is all the more intriguing. It reveals a broader interest in natural and astrological learning on Fano's part, to the extent that this learning enhanced his kabbalistic insights. It also indicates Yagel's ability to assimilate kabbalistic texts and concepts into his broader intellectual vision. Despite their apparent differences, the two shared a common intellectual and spiritual agenda.

Another of Yagel's close associates was Mordecai Dato, the kabbalist, preacher, poet, and messianic enthusiast.[45] Dato not only dedicated a poem to Abraham's wife, Dina; he also composed one in honor of Yagel himself.[46] Yagel often cited Dato's opinions and even solicited his view, in one instance, on the subject of metempsychosis.[47] Like his relationship with Fano, Yagel's friendship with Dato was based on mutual respect and admiration, despite the obvious dissimilarities in their intellectual interests and literary accomplishments. Yagel showed little personal interest in messianic activity; Dato's and Fano's involvement in Lurianic kabbalah is nowhere reflected in Yagel's writing.

The key to the intellectual basis of the two men's friendship is found in a series of letters in the 1570s from Dato to another kabbalist, Ezra Fano, the teacher of Menahem Azariah da Fano, about the relationship between the kabbalah and other sources of knowledge.[48] In Dato's view, it was a

[44]This is the view of M. Idel, "Major Currents in Italian Kabbalah (1550–1650)," in *Italia Judaica*, 2, ed. S. Simonsohn and G. Sermoneta (Rome, 1987), pp. 256–57. See also A. Altmann, "Notes on the Development of Rabbi Menahem Azariah Fano's Kabbalist Doctrine" (in Hebrew), in *Studies in Jewish Mysticism Presented to Isaiah Tishby* (Jerusalem, 1984), pp. 241–67.

[45]On Dato, see Y. Jacobson, "The Messianic Doctrine of Mordecai Dato" (in Hebrew), Ph.D. diss., Hebrew University, 1982); R. Bonfil, "One of the Italian Sermons of R. Mordecai Dato" (in Hebrew), *Italia*, 1 (1976): 1–32; I. Tishby, "The Image of R. Moses Cordovero in a Composition of R. Mordecai Dato" (in Hebrew), *Sefunot*, 7 (1962–63): 121–161; reprinted in *Studies in Kabbalah and its Branches* (in Hebrew), (Jerusalem, 1982), pp. 131–86. All three authors provide useful bibliographies.

[46]MS. London British Museum 6469, ad 22094, fol. 60b.

[47]*Bat Rabim*, no. 73, fol. 116b. See also nos. 54 and 55, respective fols. 183a, 255a; *Eshet Ḥayil* (Venice, 1605), p. 5b.

[48]Bonfil discusses this correspondence from MS. Parma 130 in "Italian Sermons of Dato," p. 6, and more fully in his *Rabbanut*, pp. 189–90.

positive step for the kabbalah to seek external substantiation from other sources: "I have known that they, the kabbalah and the reason, ride coupled in my response, for this is an external supposition that nature, the senses, and philosophy acknowledge it [the kabbalah]. Thus I have no doubt proclaiming . . . that the words of the *Sefer ha-Zohar* [*The Book of Splendor;* the classic kabbalist text of thirteenth-century Spain] are kabbalah [i.e., revealed tradition]."[49] Dato cautioned that one should not expect to find a rational explanation for everything in the kabbalah; nor should one establish an equivalency between naturalistic and kabbalistic truth, since the latter is clearly superior to the former. Nevertheless, he was convinced that naturalistic explanations can often buttress kabbalistic insight.[50] No doubt Yagel shared the same conviction. He too considered his naturalistic investigations as confirming kabbalistic truth. And despite his own proclivity for the study of the sciences, he clearly acknowledged the priority of the Jewish mystical tradition in establishing all truth.[51]

Besides these three primary associates, Yagel was acquainted with or knew of several other prominent figures of Italian Jewish culture. He was on intimate terms with Judah Sommo Portaleone, the well-known dramatist and stage director of Mantua.[52] Yagel was also familiar with the opinions and writings of the great rabbi and preacher Judah Moscato and probably knew him personally.[53] Whether he had personal contact with the other luminary of Italian Jewry, Azariah de' Rossi, the historian and author of the *Me'or Einayim,* is impossible to say. It is clear, however, that Yagel consulted Azariah's work on several occasions and quoted it without acknowledging its author.[54] Finally, an author who died years before Yagel was born but who exerted an enormous influence on his thought was Yohanan Alemanno, the kabbalist-philosopher, physician, and magical writer. Yagel repeatedly cited his works; he even owned a manuscript of Al-

[49]In Bonfil, *Rabbanut,* p. 189. Dato employs here both meanings of the term "kabbalah": as a designation of the Jewish mystical tradition in particular and as revealed tradition in general.

[50]Ibid., p. 190.

[51]This is more fully discussed below and in Ruderman, *Kabbalah, Magic, and Science,* especially chap. 9.

[52]On their meeting in Sommo's home, see Ruderman, *Kabbalah, Magic, and Science,* chap. 8.

[53]See, for example, *Moshi'ah Hosim* (Venice, 1587), p. 18a; *Be'er Sheva,* pt. 2, chap. 4, fol. 21b. Moscato acted as arbitrator in Yagel's feud with the Almagiatis. Yagel once assisted Moscato's wife when she was in need of economic support. See *Bat Rabim,* fol. 177a.

[54]Yagel used Azariah's chapter on the history of the Hebrew language when composing his own in *Gei Hizzayon* (on this, see below). He also consulted Azariah on the suitability of reading Ben Sira (on this, see my *Kabbalah, Magic and Science,* chap. 7), and also copied a section of his discussion of the crimes of Herod in *Bat Rabim,* fol. 144b.

emanno's collected notations, to which he occasionally appended his own comments.[55]

In sum, Yagel knew personally the leading cultural figures of his generation or was at least acquainted with their writings. Those who knew him apparently welcomed Yagel into their circle and enormously appreciated his professional and intellectual achievements, which supplemented their own. This reception stands in sharp contrast to the shabby treatment he received from the Jewish bankers he describes in *Gei Ḥizzayon* and from Raphael Modena and the Rieti family much later. His relationship with his scholarly colleagues obviously enhanced his sense of self-esteem and positively reinforced his belief in the inherent value of his own writings.

## Judaism and Scientific Knowledge: The Unifying Vision of Yagel's Mental Universe

Yagel's appeal to these Jewish scholars was based on more than his mere mastery of the scientific and medical literature of his day. It rested on the fact that he creatively wedded his secular knowledge to his own religious tradition. He could not claim originality in his mastery of new scientific sources and methods; his knowledge of contemporary "science"—a typical blending of classical medicine and natural philosophy with astrology and the occult arts—was shared by a relatively large number of contemporary Christian savants. But he distinguished himself as a Jewish religious thinker in arguing more boldly and consistently than others that these disciplines could be inextricably linked to the sources of Judaism. Thus he sought to reshape Jewish culture by underscoring the religious value of comprehending the natural world, by reformulating kabbalistic tradition in the language of sixteenth-century scientific discourse so as to promote it as the highest form of human knowledge, and by advocating the legitimacy of the magical arts as the ultimate expression of human creativity in Judaism. His intellectual agenda was also related to an apparent psychological need of demonstrating the significance of the Judaic legacy for European civiliza-

[55]This fact has already been noted by M. Idel in "The Magical and Neoplatonic Interpretations of the Kabbalah in the Renaissance," in *Jewish Thought in the Sixteenth Century,* ed. B. Cooperman (Cambridge, Mass., 1983), pp. 224–27, and in "Major Currents in Italian Kabbalah," p. 247. In the latter work he mentions some fifteen references to Al-emanno's works in Yagel's writing. There are clearly more. See, for example, *Beit Ya'ar ha-Levanon,* pt. 4, chaps. 45, 53, 57, 67, 73, 74, 83–86, 88–91; *Bat Rabim,* fols. 126a, 126b, 181b; *Eshet Ḥayil,* p. 7a.

tion, especially during a period of increasing anti-Jewish agitation and cultural isolation. For Yagel, Jews since Solomon's time had always demonstrated a keen interest in naturalistic learning; they had always excelled in the occult and medical arts; and their unique kabbalistic heritage allowed them to penetrate the mysteries of the universe in a manner unattainable by the best of the natural philosophers. Accordingly, they were the best "scientists," well suited to assume a significant role within a culture that increasingly valued their virtues. And Yagel found confirmation of the continuing validity of "the wisdom of Israel" in the fact that some Christian scholars were attracted to the study of Judaism, especially its occultist and esoteric roots.[56]

Nevertheless, the elaborate intellectual edifice Yagel had labored to erect was soon to totter on the brink of disaster, through no fault of his own. The marriage between kabbalah and science eventually broke asunder as a result of historical forces unforeseeable by him. By the end of Yagel's life, the Lurianic kabbalah had helped to inject a new spiritual mood of prayer, ritual, and piety, especially in Italy's proliferating Jewish confraternities. The focus of this kabbalah was ritualistic activism rather than theosophic speculation. Its primary concern was to enrich the religious and spiritual needs of the Jewish community rather than its purely intellectual ones. And it emphasized the singularity of Judaism at the expense of speculative syncretism with other religions and cultures. Almost simultaneously, the mechanical and mathematical sciences of the seventeenth century were slowly discarding their occultist character and gradually moving in a direction that increased the distance between kabbalistic theosophy and scientific explanation. Yagel's efforts to redefine Judaism in an occultist and scientific key were soon to become hopelessly obsolete. His ambitious intellectual plan that had taken him almost a lifetime to conceive and explicate was virtually unnoticed by later generations.

When Yagel completed his first literary work, the *Gei Ḥizzayon,* he had only begun his distinguished medical career and his voluminous scientific writing. *Gei Ḥizzayon* is certainly a youthful indulgence, stimulated by an ugly taste of "the real world" and fed by a literary precocity and an adventurous and audacious spirit. As the work of a twenty-five year old, it lacks the vast erudition and mature insight of Yagel's later writing. Nevertheless, it would be wrong to view his heavenly journey with anything less than the seriousness it deserves. It is a book which already adumbrates Yagel's

[56]These themes are more fully treated in Ruderman, *Kabbalah, Magic, and Science.*

ultimate vision of the unity of all knowledge, his fascination with the natural world, his interests in magic and astrology, and his commitment to the primacy of the kabbalah in penetrating the sublime mysteries of the divine creation. Like his other writings, its creativity lies in its extraordinary integration of the wisdom and artistry of contemporary European culture with traditional Jewish modes of culture and thought. And like his later works, it is imbued with a deep sense of religiosity and an unwavering faith in the ultimate justice of God's mysterious ways in both the natural and human realms. Together with his entire corpus, it is a work of Jewish advocacy, an argument for the uniqueness and continued legitimacy and relevance of Judaism in a culture of growing complexity and spiritual upheaval.

Indeed, one might even argue that *Gei Ḥizzayon* as Yagel's first book was also his best. In reality, Yagel's ambitious encyclopedias were never completed despite the extraordinary efforts of their indefatigable author. Nor were the imaginative playfulness and bold experimentation of this narrative ever replicated in the scholarly tomes Yagel later produced. And nowhere else can one find so succinct a summary of the author's message as in the ultimate vision of this work's final pages. It is to this composition specifically that we now turn.

## A Brief Synopsis of *Gei Ḥizzayon*

Part 1 opens as Abraham Yagel is awakened by the soul of his deceased father while incarcerated in the municipal prison of Mantua. The father allays his fears of speaking with a dead person, asks him to explain the circumstances which led to the imprisonment, and invites him to roam the heavens with him to see all the "hosts" who will meet them. After a long speech by the father on the human soul, the quest for wisdom, the supreme purpose of life, and the evils of usury, the two finally begin their ascent, at which time Yagel opens his long account of his life from the time his/father had died. He relates how he struggled to manage the pawn bank his father had left him in Luzzara and how he tried to arrange a partnership with Madame Rina.

Abraham's speech is interrupted by the sudden appearance of two souls reading from the book of Isaiah: the first, an elementary school teacher, who had neglected his students, and who was now obliged to instruct the second, an incessant gambler. Both relate their life stories; the gambler especially offers a spirited and playful defense of his addiction.

Abraham then resumes his life story, explaining the circumstances surrounding the unfavorable arrangement he had concluded with his new
partner. He is again interrupted by the loud sound of two other souls,
which occasions the father's long discourse on "dying before one's time."
When the father concludes his homily, the first of the two souls proceeds to
tell his life story. He had been a rhetorician employed by a tyrannical king
and was placed in captivity for unintentionally killing the king's dog. There
he was called by Satan, who led him on a visit to Gehenna. He returned to
warn the king and his household to repent of their evil ways and died soon
after. The second soul then relates his story of unrequited love, jealousy,
murder, and horrific revenge. He relates how his burning love for the wife
of his friend ultimately led him to take his friend's life while on a hunting
expedition, disguising his crime as the work of a ferocious wild animal. The
woman eventually learned of the murder of her beloved husband, successfully plotted her retribution by offering him her bed at an appointed
time, drugging him, and then violently piercing out his eyes. He eventually
died, whereas she took her own life.

The father elaborates upon the moral lessons derived from these two
stories. In the course of his remarks, he presents his strong advocacy of the
belief in metempsychosis. Abraham then takes up his story again, relating
how Madame Rina had reneged on all her promises to him; how he had
turned to the Almagiati family to salvage his banking operation; and how in
the time of a plague Madame Rina had precipitously entered Luzzara
seeking his protection and led to his incurring the wrath of his neighbors
and fellow citizens.

Abraham interrupts his speech when the souls of Siamese twins fly
toward them in a terrifying manner. The father explains that these are the
souls of twins who had died three years earlier in Venice. Before allowing
the souls to speak, the father presents a long digression on the nature of the
soul, on the difference between Jewish and gentile souls, and on the
Noahide commandments. The twins then offer an elaborate discussion of
the material, astral, and moral causes of their condition. When they conclude, Abraham resumes his account, describing his treacherous dealings
with the Almagiati brothers and his futile efforts to extricate himself from
his damaging commitments to Madame Rina.

He is interrupted by the biblical character of Job. Father and son
initially discuss whether Job was actually a real person and decide that he
was. Job then relates the extraordinary story of a maiden who was sold into
slavery, was enticed to sleep with her master, but then confessed the
husband's seduction to his wife. The wife in turn proceeded to entrap her

husband by plotting a supposed encounter between him and the innocent girl while secretly substituting herself for the damsel in the husband's bed. In the end, the husband repents and the girl is rewarded for her virtue. Abraham's father expands on the moral lessons of this story, including a discourse on divine justice and on the ability of Israel to overturn the force of its constellation.

Abraham returns to his life story, relating this time how the Almagiati brothers plotted successfully to humiliate him and throw him into prison. Yagel sought out arbitrators to effect an honorable compromise but the Almagiati would accept nothing less than his utter ruination. He eventually pauses to listen to the stories of two more souls: a maiden of exceptional industry, faithfulness, and virtue who is eventually rewarded for her efforts; and a "hard-spirited woman who never saw goodness in her lifetime." The second woman was the daughter of a rich merchant who had lost his fortune. She subsequently married a young man who was captured by pirates. She sought to ransom him but lost her money and sold herself into slavery. When her husband learned of her fate, he took his own life. She in turn was seduced by her master, was eventually released, and in her shame and grief took her own life as well. The contrasting stories afford Yagel's father the opportunity to expound on the many lessons to be learned from the women's behavior. The father again digresses to explain his conviction that the souls of human beings can even enter the bodies of animals through metempsychosis.

Yagel resumes his account of his downfall at the hand of the Almagiati brothers and Madame Rina. Yagel valiantly tried to defend himself against the vituperations of his adversaries. His personal papers were confiscated by the authorities, and eventually he was ambushed, falsely accused of having a dagger in his possession, and thrown into prison. When Yagel concludes his impassioned defense of his past actions, a caravan of angels approaches them. The father then proceeds to offer his son some instruction in the heavenly secrets, indicating that this sapience is beyond the reach of human intelligence and only available through "the splendor of the Torah and the kabbalah." While offering the promise of a future heavenly journey, he abruptly concludes his remarks as Yagel is awakened by the sound of the rooster.

Part II opens in the same jail cell, as Yagel laments his fate by identifying with the sentiments expressed in Psalm 120, which begins: "A song of ascents. In my distress I called to the Lord." He eventually falls asleep and sees a vision of three women approaching him in the company of his father. He describes the appearance of each of the women, who are sisters. Yagel is initially frightened to stand in the presence of these noble figures but is reassured by his father to ascend again, this time to the field where the women are sitting.

The first woman presents an opening discourse in which she rebukes Yagel for misusing the psalm to apply to his own personal experience. The second woman then advises Yagel to seek instruction from the movement of the heavenly bodies and proceeds to explicate a rabbinic passage describing the relation between the sun and the moon. In the course of her remarks, she explores the meaning of the concept of Fortuna, to which the first woman also adds her own insights. The third woman then offers the longest monologue, objecting to her younger sister's claim regarding the power of the heavenly constellations. She states emphatically that a Jew has the ability through his moral action to overcome the influence of the stars, that God's actions are thoroughly just, and that humans should not impute any imperfection to him. She further underscores the finitude of human understanding and cautions him not to be misled by the philosophers and astrologers who minimize the significance of human action in averting the heavenly decree.

The women then depart for the hill of frankincense on the summit of the mount of myrrh.[57] The father explains the symbolic meaning of each of the sisters: the first represents the study of philosophy; the second is the science of astrology; and the third is the divine science, the knowledge of the Torah and the kabbalah, the most perfect of the sciences. Yagel asks his father whether he should understand these figures as allegories or as spiritual beings in their own right. His father explains that they are indeed celestial beings who descend from above to teach mere mortals the secrets of the Divine.

Father and son take the path leading to the hill of frankincense, and on the way Yagel attempts to conclude his narration of the events leading to his final incarceration. After being called to Mantua, he found himself in the company of a non-Jew who invited him to eat at his table, a civil crime then unknown to him. He was subsequently arrested and thrown into prison at the instigation of the Almagiati brothers. Before finishing his narration, he and his father encounter five men engaged in argument about a rabbinic passage. The five stand at the foot of the mountain, incapable of ascending to the hill of frankincense. The oldest of them elucidates each of their human imperfections that prevent their ultimate ascent. As Yagel and his father turn away from the men, the father sermonizes about the example of

---

[57]The terms are borrowed from Song of Songs 4:6.

their human frailties and the ultimate superiority of Torah wisdom over that of the philosophers. The son responds by offering his final lament about his own failure, proclaiming his own innocence and the guilt of his detractors.

The two ascend the mountain before them, where they encounter another noblewoman at the summit. From her two breasts flow fresh water, which creates a mighty river below and which nourishes all life along its banks. This woman represents "the science of language," who teaches the seventy languages to all peoples on the earth. She then offers a long discourse on Hebrew as the holy tongue, and also on Latin, Greek, Arabic, and several European languages.

When the woman concludes her speech, Yagel and his father pass a small stream called "the passage of love" and approach a palace in the middle of the hill of frankincense, where they are met by the third sister who escorts them into the palace. They enter a large hall of pure marble and behold the symbolic images on three of the walls: that of a man, a very high tree, and a third which goes unmentioned. The fourth wall is translucent, reflecting the images of the other three. Their mentor then proceeds to discant on the primary meaning of the palace: the harmony of the universe, and the concatenation of the divine, celestial, and material worlds. She offers them an elaborate explanation of the ten divine *sefirot* and how they precisely correspond to the ten spheres of the celestial world. She then demonstrates how these same ten creative principles manifest themselves in the natural world and even within the human body itself, represented by the figure on the first wall. The tree on the next wall, she explains, similarly suggests the universal correspondence of each plane of existence. It is the Tree of Life, the Torah, whose commandments offer men divine reward and eternity. The fourth wall represents the next world, the divine retribution for the achievements of this world.

The woman leads the two men into a great parlor where they rejoin the other two sisters. The latter wish to offer further instruction, but their older sister informs them that the night is over. Yagel awakes in his bed as morning arrives.

## *Gei Ḥizzayon* as a Jewish Work

In the single reference to *Gei Ḥizzayon* in his other writings, Yagel calls it "our sermon or homily" (*derushainu*), as if to suggest that the work could be subsumed under the traditional Jewish genre of rabbinic discourse or sermon.[58] Indeed, anyone perusing the text will quickly note its ethical and didactic tone, its generous quotations from rabbinic and kabbalistic literature, and its preoccupation with the grand themes of Jewish religious thought: the suffering of the righteous, the purpose of human existence as prescribed by the Torah, the ethics of family and business relationships, the pursuit of wisdom, and more. No doubt Yagel intended that his readership would see his composition as a distinctly Jewish work; its innovations in style and content would appear less conspicuous when embedded in a multitude of rabbinic citations and moral exhortations.

In fact, the two most distinctive features of the work—its utilization of Italian novelle and other folktales in religious teaching and its elaborate description of a heavenly journey—were not without precedent in Jewish literature. "Moralistic storybooks," as Joseph Dan calls them,[59] already appear in Hebrew literature in the early Middle Ages. The earliest, the *Midrash Aseret ha-Dibrot* (*The Homily on the Ten Commandments*), purports to be a rabbinic discourse on the Ten Commandments but is actually a collection of stories, each exemplifying a single commandment and followed by a short homily that makes the message of the story explicit.[60] Nissim ibn Shahin's *Ḥibbur Yafeh me-ha-Yeshu'ah* (*An Elegant Composition on the Deliverance*), written in the eleventh century, is a similar collection of narratives, many based on oriental folktales, which were Judaized to illustrate specific moral themes. Like Yagel, the author of this work was not adverse to including tales of a sexual nature in his compendium.[61] The medieval composition called *The Exempla of the Rabbis,* by Moses Gaster, constitutes an even larger miscellany of such moralistic fables.[62] Later collections written in Yiddish circulated widely among the Jews of Eastern Europe.[63]

Even more obvious is the Jewish provenance of the literature of heav-

[58]*Be'er Sheva,* pt. 2, chap. 6, fol. 25a.

[59]J. Dan, "Ethical Literature," *Encyclopedia Judaica* (cited hereafter as *EJ*), 16 vols. (Jerusalem, 1972), 6: 924.

[60]On this work, see J. Dan, *Ha-Sippur ha-Ivri bimai ha-Beinayim* (Jerusalem, 1974), chap. 7.

[61]On this work, see ibid., chap. 8; S. W. Baron, *A Social and Religious History of the Jews,* 18 vols. to date (New York, 1952–83), 6: 184–85; Nissim Ben Jacob Ibn Shahin, *An Elegant Composition Concerning Relief After Adversity,* trans. by W. M. Brinner (New Haven, 1977).

[62]M. Gaster, *The Exempla of the Rabbis,* 2nd ed., intro. by W. G. Braude (New York, 1968); Dan, *Ha-Sippur ha-Ivri,* chap. 9.

[63]For another overview, see J. Dan, "Fiction Hebrew," *EJ,* 6: 1261–71.

enly journeys. Whether he intended it or not, Yagel's choice of this narrative form placed him in a hallowed line of writers beginning with Isaiah and Ezekiel and culminating in the visionaries of the mystical *Hekhalot* texts of the early Middle Ages. The Jewish apocalypses of Hellenistic Judaism are especially replete with heavenly ascensions attributed to such biblical figures as Adam, Enoch, Abraham, Levi, Isaiah, Zephaniah, and Barukh. The narrator is led to the highest reaches of heaven, often portrayed as a heavenly temple resting on a holy mountain reminiscent of the earthly one. The ascent usually confers superhuman or angelic status on the person privileged to undertake it. He is offered glimpses of the heavenly throne, converses with angels, and learns the nature and the fate of souls after death. The journey often suggests the parallel odyssey of the soul after death or Moses' ascent to Sinai. In either case, the narrative focuses on a revelation of divine secrets, the resolution of the contradictions between life and death, and the ultimate comprehension of divine justice. Medieval Hebrew works such as *Gedulat Moshe* (*The Greatness of Moses*), Moses' tour of heaven and hell, and the account of paradise in *Midrash Konen* follow similar lines.[64]

Judged by the standards of these elaborate heavenly tours, the ascent of *Gei Ḥizzayon* is most unspectacular. The narrator ascends with the soul of his father and with three angelic mentors to the mountain of myrrh and to the hill of frankincense. He eventually is ushered into a heavenly palace with walls of transparent crystal inlaid with gold and silver, the conventional materials of earlier ascents. As in the earthly temple, there are assorted figures or hangings on the walls. His final revelation comes after gazing on these remarkable figures.

In light of such a fecund tradition of Jewish descriptions of other worldly tours, it might be conceivable to argue that Yagel's narrative was

[64]On this literature, see A. F. Segal, "Heavenly Ascent in Hellenistic Judaism, Early Christianity and their Environment," *Aufstieg und Niedergang der Romischen Welt* (Berlin and New York, 1980), II.23.2., pp. 1333–94; M. Himmelfarb, "From Prophecy to Apocalypse: The Book of Watchers and Tours of Heaven," in A. Green, *Jewish Spirituality: From the Bible Through the Middle Ages* (New York, 1986), pp. 145–65; idem, *Tours of Hell: An Apocalyptic Form in Jewish and Christian Literature* (Philadelphia, 1985); idem, "Apocalyptic Ascent and the Heavenly Temple," *Society of Biblical Literature 1987 Seminar Papers,* ed. K. H. Richards (Atlanta, Georgia, 1987), pp. 210–17; D. L. Halperin, "Heavenly Ascension in Ancient Judaism: The Nature of the Experience," in ibid., pp. 217–32; J. D. Tabor, *Things Unutterable: Paul's Ascent to Paradise in Its Greco-Roman, Judaic, and Early Christian Contexts* (Lanham, Md., 1986); H. R. Patch, *The Other World According to Descriptions in Medieval Literature* (Cambridge, Mass., 1950). On heavenly journeys in Muslim literature, see M. Asin Palacios, *Islam and the Divine Comedy,* trans. and abridged by H. Sunderland (New York, 1926).

primarily indebted to this ancient Jewish genre, or as one scholar has put it: "His book is embedded in an ancient Jewish tradition and independent of the influence of the great Italian author [Dante]."[65] No doubt such a pronouncement might be appealing to certain Jewish readers of Yagel's work and surely would have pleased to no end Yagel, who, like other Jews of the Renaissance, searched passionately for Jewish roots for all his endeavors. He certainly would have preferred that his readers believe that he had been stimulated by an indigenous ancestral Jewish tradition rather than the external and superfluous inspiration of a Dante or any other "gentile" for that matter. Such a view may be appealing, but is highly questionable. There is no evidence whatsoever to suggest that Yagel was consciously drawing from an ancient Jewish genre when he composed his heavenly journey or, for that matter, when he put together his collection of exemplary stories. If he were aware of such antecedents, he nowhere alluded to them. On the other hand, there is clear evidence to suggest that Yagel consciously drew from external sources—especially certain Italian novelle and the Latin author Boethius (not Dante, as we shall see) in shaping his own narrative. That Jewish precedents for his choices existed is beyond doubt; that he consciously utilized them is most unlikely. In the opinion of Yagel, his choices were unique among Jewish writers and therefore would be judged as highly innovative. He had chosen to appropriate two kinds of literary sources into his Hebrew narrative with the knowledge that they did not come "from the well of Israel." Nevertheless, he believed that in his hands they would be profitably exploited in the teaching of Torah.

## *Gei Ḥizzayon* as an Early Modern Autobiography

Joseph Dan, in his brief discussion of *Gei Ḥizzayon,* singled out the autobiographical sections for special mention. In his opinion, Yagel's work was unique in that it apparently represents the first autobiography of a simple man who lacked literary, political, or historical pretensions, and who only wished to describe his insignificant internal world.[66] Dan's assessment of Yagel's autobiography has already been challenged for good reasons. Yagel's work may not have been the first of its kind.[67] More important,

[65]Dan, *Ha-Sippur ha-Ivri,* p. 205.

[66]Dan, *Ha-Sippur ha-Ivri,* pp. 217–21.

[67]I. J. Yuval, "A German Jewish Autobiography from the Fourteenth Century" (in Hebrew), *Tarbiz,* 55 (1986): 546.

Yagel was not "the simple man" Dan assumed; nor did he lack literary pretensions in shaping his autobiography, as I hope to amply demonstrate.

Dan's emphasis on the special quality of the autobiography, however, constitutes an appropriate point of departure for our own discussion. Yagel's reconstruction of a part of his life history was written about 1578 and represents one of the first comprehensive portraits of the self in early modern Hebrew literature. Only David Reuveni's diary and Joseph of Rosheim's memoir precede it; the autobiographies of Leon Modena, Isaac Min ha-Levi'im, Yom Tov Lipmann Heller, and Glueckel of Hameln follow it.[68] The appearance of Yagel's composition also coincides with the flowering of Renaissance autobiography, especially in Italy. Benvenuto Cellini's monumental *Life* was completed some twelve years earlier; Girolamo Cardano finished his *Book of My Life* only a year before his death in 1576, only three years before Yagel penned his own self-reflections.[69]

Depending on how strictly or loosely one defines autobiographies of the sixteenth and seventeenth centuries, Yagel's discussion of his self may or may not qualify as a legitimate candidate for inclusion in this genre. According to one definition, autobiography should be distinguished from memoirs, diaries, *ricordanze,* journals, and recollections since it involves the formulation of a coherent interpretation of the self at a particular point in time, usually toward the end of one's life. The author attempts to view his past in an effort to construe it as a whole.[70] Following these criteria, Yagel's

[68]*Sippur David ha-Reuveni,* ed. A. S. Aescoly (Jerusalem, 1940); Joseph of Rosheim, *Sefer ha-Mikneh,* ed. H. Fraenkel-Goldschmidt (Jerusalem, 1970); Leon Modena, *Sefer Ḥayyei Yehudah,* ed. D. Carpi (Tel Aviv, 1975), English trans. by M. Cohen, *The Autobiography of a Seventeenth-Century Venetian Rabbi: Leon Modena's Life of Judah,* with intros. by N. Z. Davis, H. Adelman, T. Rabb, and historical notes by B. Ravid and H. Adelman (Princeton, 1988); Isaac Min ha-Levi'im, *Sefer Medabber Tahapukhot,* ed. D. Carpi (Tel Aviv, 1985); Yom Tov Lipmann Heller, *Megillat Eivah* (Breslau, 1937); Glueckel of Hameln, *Die Memoiren der Glückel von Hameln,* ed. D. Kaufmann (Frankfurt am Main, 1896), English trans. by Beth-Zion Abrahams, *The Life of Glückel of Hameln, 1646–1724 Written by Herself* (New York, 1963).

[69]Benvenuto Cellini, *Vita de Benvenuto Cellini: Testo critico,* ed. O. Bacci (Florence, 1901), English trans. by J. A. Symonds, *The Life of Benvenuti Cellini* (Garden City, N.Y., 1961); Girolamo Cardano, *De Propria Vita Liber* in his *Opera Omnia,* 10 vols. (Lyons, 1663; reprint, New York, 1967), 1: 1–54, English trans. by J. Stoner, *The Book of My Life (De Vita Propria Liber)* (New York, 1962). Both these works are described in K. J. Weintraub, *The Value of the Individual: Self and Circumstance in Autobiography* (Chicago, 1978). See also J. Goldberg, "Cellini's 'Vita' and the Conventions of Early Biography," *Modern Language Notes,* 89 (1974): 71–83; M. Gugielminetti, *Memoria e scrittura: L'autobiografia da Dante a Cellini* (Turin, 1977).

[70]See T. C. Price Zimmerman, "Confession and Autobiography in the Early Renaissance," in *Renaissance Studies in Honor of Hans Baron,* ed. A. Molcho and J. A. Tedeschi (Dekalb, Ill., 1971), pp. 121–22; R. Pascal, *Design and Truth in Autobiography* (Cambridge, 1960), chap. 1. Cf. P. Delany, *British Autobiography in the Seventeenth Century* (London, 1969), pp. 1–2.

work is not a true autobiography: he wrote it at the beginning of his life; it covers only a span of several years; and it is organically linked to a larger aesthetic design, that of the description of heavenly journeys of the narrator. Nevertheless, the autobiographical sections of *Gei Ḥizzayon* should not be reduced to ordinary memoirs or recollections. Yagel's ruminations on his immediate past are more than *ricordanze;* they entail an interpretation of this past experience which attempts to clarify the meaning of the self. Yagel's long justification of his actions is analytic and introspective; it is also therapeutic in resolving a painful identity crisis. Accordingly, it can be compared meaningfully with other contemporary autobiographies, both Christian and Jewish.

The self-portraits of Cellini and Cardano, nevertheless, appear to have little in common with Yagel's composition. Besides the obvious difference in scale between the works of these famous Italians and that of Yagel, there is also the profound difference in motivation which informs each of the works. Cellini and Cardano both have high regard for themselves and their accomplishments. The recording of their past lives for posterity is an exercise in self-aggrandizement.[71] In contrast, Yagel's effort is self-deprecatory. He fully acknowledges his past mistakes and, as a penitent, seeks compassion from his father and ultimately his reader. Having entangled himself with the wrong business partners, having made several unwise decisions for which he paid dearly, and having been the victim of circumstances beyond his control, Yagel wrote to set the record straight, to salvage whatever he could of his personal honor, and to justify his actions to himself and others.

The major event that precipitated the crisis of Yagel's young life was undoubtedly his father's death. The choice of his father's soul as his heavenly companion and as the "confessor" for the penitent son is hardly fortuitous. Above all, the son needed to explain himself to his own father, particularly how he failed miserably with his inheritance, and how he disgraced the family name.

It is the Augustinian confession rather than the contemporary mode of Renaissance autobiography which is comparable to Yagel's composition. *Gei Ḥizzayon* is a deeply religious exploration of the self. Like the Christian confessional, Yagel's reconstruction of his past constitutes a formal self-examination, a systematic rehearsal of his transgressions, and an ultimate surrender of the self by acknowledging his complete dependence on God.[72] Yagel alleviates his guilt by confessing it and is ultimately consoled by a

[71]Cf. Weintraub, p. 117.

[72]On the Augustinian confession, see Weintraub, pp. 18–48; Zimmerman, "Confession and Autobiography"; P. Courcelle, *Les confessions de Saint Augustin dans la tradition littéraire*

higher revelation, a divine enlightenment that offers him a new perspective by which to view his life, and is thus radically transformed. In this sense, Yagel's exploration of the self represents a throwback to ancient and medieval forms of religious self-examination rather than the more secularized form of self-flattery employed by his Italian contemporaries.

Yagel would have viewed favorably the metaphor of autobiography as that of the physician who undertakes a self-examination to cure himself.[73] In this respect, but only in this respect, his autobiography shares a common perspective with that of Girolamo Cardano. Both Yagel and Cardano were erudite physicians; both had attempted to record the abundance of "divine signs" in nature by writing exhaustive encyclopedias of the sciences; and both shared a common fascination with the occult. In fact, Yagel not only quoted extensively from Cardano's scientific works but even praised him as a brilliant physician and naturalist.[74] Cardano's *Book of My Life* was first printed only in 1643 and was probably unavailable to Yagel during the writing of *Gei Ḥizzayon*. Nevertheless, their shared conviction that the pursuit of knowledge is the key to mastering life suggests an obvious similarity between their two compositions. Both men as physicians devoted their lives to searching for the divine clues hidden in nature, and both were comforted in their belief that they were blessed with special insights into mysteries other men could not fathom. Both of their endeavors to explore themselves were primary extensions of their self-proclaimed "scientific" quests to penetrate the ultimate reality of their complex worlds.[75]

If the difference between Yagel's work and other Christian autobiographies far outweigh their similarities, what can be said regarding his work in relation to other contemporary Jewish autobiographies, most notably Leon Modena's *Life of Judah*? According to Natalie Zemon Davis's most recent appraisal, Leon's composition represents a combination of confession, lament of calamities, and celebration of the author's achievements in preaching and writing. He understands his personal history by reference to traditional Jewish categories of collective suffering as a punishment and as a test. But beyond the religious need to confess, Davis also underscores Modena's concern for his family legacy as a powerful motivation in explor-

---

(Paris, 1963); and G. Misch, *Geschichte der Autobiographie,* 4 vols. (Frankfurt am Main, 1949–69), I², pp. 637–78.

[73]The metaphor is found as early as Origen. See Zimmerman, "Confession and Autobiography," p. 125; J. T. McNeill, *Mediaeval Handbooks of Penance* (New York, 1938), p. 7.

[74]On the influence of Cardano on Yagel, see Ruderman, *Kabbalah, Magic, and Science,* especially chaps. 4, 5, and 6.

[75]Cf. Weintraub's suggestive comments, especially pp. 164–65. On Yagel's "scientific quest," see Ruderman, *Kabbalah, Magic, and Science.*

ing his past life. In addition to the interplay between achievements, sins, and calamities that mark his book, Modena also reveals a distinctive contrast between his secret life as a Jew and his public posture in the Christian world. For Davis, Modena's protected inner space might suggest a distinctive Jewish construction, a double perspective in which to regard the self, in writing early modern autobiography.[76]

As we have seen, Yagel and Modena share a common concern in lamenting their misfortunes and in acknowledging their assorted transgressions before God. But Yagel has little to celebrate with respect to his past achievements, and he could not expect that any of his actions would be worthy of emulation by his progeny. The collective model of suffering may be implicit in his lament, but his is primarily an individual recitation of personal sins and failings. The divine exile was not a fundamental explanation of his calamity. His lack of experience in business and his bad choice of associates were more relevant. Unlike Modena, who enumerates his sins but experiences no change of heart, Yagel undergoes a definitive purgation and spiritual transformation. And also unlike Modena, there is no clear differentiation between protected Jewish inner space and public image in Yagel's writing. Yagel, of course, wrote only in Hebrew and never composed a work exclusively for Christian eyes. Nevertheless, he displays little inhibition in revealing his most glaring and embarrassing weaknesses to his reader. His self-portrayal is far from complimentary; he readily acknowledges that he was less the man than his father was. Admittedly, Yagel's work ultimately remained no more than a private document, read only by family and friends. Yet there is no indication that Yagel ever expected such a fate for his book, or that he intended that it would lack a wide readership. To vindicate himself, he would have preferred that his testimony become part of the public record.

In sum, Yagel's autobiography cannot be easily classified in relation to other contemporary Christian or Jewish works. It addresses exclusively only one horrendous period in the life of its author. And because of its inextricable connection and inevitable subordination to the overall literary design and religious message of the entire work, it diverges noticeably from other self-portraits written in the sixteenth and seventeenth centuries.

[76]Davis's essay titled "Fame and Secrecy: Leon Modena's *Life* as an Early Modern Autobiography" constitutes one of the introductory essays to Cohen, *The Autobiography of a Seventeenth-Century Venetian Rabbi,* pp. 50–70. It has been previously published in Italian as "Fama e riservatezza: La 'Vita' de Leone Modena come autobiografia della prima età moderna," *Quaderni storici,* 64 (1987): 39–60. Davis's essay is the first attempt, to my knowledge, to integrate Jewish autobiography of the early modern period into a general and theoretical context.

## The Influence of the Italian Novella Tradition

In addition to the autobiographical sections, the first part of *Gei Ḥizzayon* contains some nine novelle, or short stories, which are interspersed within the continuing dialogue between Yagel and his father's soul. There is no doubt that Yagel was influenced by the tradition of Boccaccio in utilizing this material and that he actually selected specific tales from Italian collections of his day, translated them, and adapted them for his own usage. This is not to say that Yagel was fully acquainted with the prolific tradition that Boccaccio had initiated and was in a position to select his samples from a vast array of novella collections. In reality, Yagel displays only a limited awareness of this genre and probably made his selections almost exclusively from one contemporary source, as we shall soon see.

Nevertheless, we should not minimize the significance of Yagel's borrowing from this tradition, despite his limited exposure. We have already mentioned previous Hebrew translations of folktales of oriental or Arabic origin. But this is the first time, to my knowledge, that a Jewish author appropriated the framework of an entire novella collection into his own Hebrew work, edited its materials judiciously to fit the needs of his audience, and employed them to illumine "the higher truths" of Judaism.[77]

To attain the loose structural unity he desired, Yagel adapted as his framing devices his own life situation, the circumstances leading to his prison sentence, and his subsequent visit by his father's soul. By situating each of his otherwise unrelated anecdotes within such a cornice or frame-tale, he hoped to lend some credibility and an air of reality to the fantastic stories to follow. Furthermore, the cornice provided the necessary direction and seriousness for the entire endeavor; it allowed Yagel the flexibility to insert long monologues, speeches, and comments into the narrative, to suppress the potentially scatological or scandalous nature of the tales, and to shift the emphasis of the stories from entertainment to religious and moral education.[78] The type of "disaster" cornice Yagel adopted was espe-

[77]On the novella tradition, see generally, R. J. Clements and J. Gibaldi, *Anatomy of the Novella: The European Tale Collection from Boccaccio and Chaucer to Cervantes* (New York, 1977); J. L. Smarr, *Italian Renaissance Tales* (Rochester, Mich., 1983); L. Di Francia, *Novellistica*, vols. 1–2 (Milan, 1924–25); I. Rodax, *The Real and the Ideal in the Novella of Italy, France, and England* (Chapel Hill, 1968). On the tradition in the sixteenth century, see G. Salinari, *Novelle del Cinquecento* (Turin, 1976); B. Porcelli, *La novella del Cinquecento* (Rome and Bari, 1973); G. B. Marchesi, *Per la storia della novella italiana nel secolo XVI* (Rome, 1887; M. Righetti, *Per la storia della novella italiana al tempo della reazione cattolica* (Teramo, 1921).

[78]On the cornice, see L. Graedel, *La cornice nelle racolta novellistiche del Rinascimento italiano e i rapporti con la cornice del Decamaron* (Florence, 1956); Clements and Gibaldi, pp. 36–48.

cially common among later *novellieri*. Some form of physical discomfort or a gloomy social context—a plague, a war, or the physical or psychological distress of one or more individuals—impels them to react by telling each other stories by which they learn to cope with their misfortunes.[79]

By the second half of the sixteenth century, in the atmosphere of Counter-Reformation Italy, Italian novella collections became increasingly pedagogic and moralistic in tone and content. *Novellieri* like Matteo Bandello, Giambattista Giraldi Cintio, Girolamo Parabosco, or Giovanni Francesco Straparola view their stories as case histories in teaching moral behavior. Virtue always wins and vice is punished. The wantonness described in previous collections is more and more limited, more stories end on a tragic rather than a comic note, and more fable or fairy tales replace familiar life settings. Following each tale, the editor often appends a little sermon against the vice just graphically depicted in his narrative. It is precisely this kind of novella collection that Yagel had in mind in shaping his own version.[80]

Yagel's major source for his own stories is a volume titled *La Piacevol Notte et Lieto Giorno*, composed by Nicolao Granucci (1522–1603) and published in Venice in 1574, only a few years before *Gei Ḥizzayon* was written. Granucci was a relatively minor writer who achieved limited success in compiling and publishing several novella collections in which the moralistic tone is especially dominant. Of the four works he published, the last two are the most well known: *L'Eremita, la Carcere e'l Diporto* (Lucca, 1569) and *La Piacevol Notte*. Neither work was highly original or well conceived. Granucci unimaginatively modeled his works after the better known *Diporti* of Parabosco and the *Piacevoli Notti* of Straparola.[81]

In *L'Eremita*, Granucci recounts a series of personal misfortunes highly similar to Yagel's own life situation: an injury to his leg "from an unknown hand," a false accusation, and a subsequent exile. He eventually returns to his native Lucca where he is incarcerated for several months. Upon gaining his freedom, he lives in the company of several noble persons

[79]See Clements and Gibaldi, pp. 44–48.

[80]On these later *novellieri*, see especially the works of Smarr, di Francia, Salinari, Porcelli, Marchesi, and Righetti listed in note 77 above.

[81]On Granucci, see Righetti, *Per la storia*, pp. 69–87; Di Francia, *Novellistica*, 2, pp. 111–20; A. Van Bever and E. Sansot-Orland, *Oeuvres Galantes des Conteurs Italiens*, 2 vols. (Paris, 1917–18), 2, pp. 242–54; T. Roscoe, *The Italian Novelists*, 4 vols. (London, 1825), 3, pp. 225–33. Brief discussions on Granucci are included in the anthologies of Porcelli and Salinari. G. Busi, in his important essay, "Sulla *Ge Ḥizzayon* (La valle della visione) di Abraham Yagel," in *Annali della facolta' di lingue e letterature straniere di ca' Foscari*, 23 (1984): 19, already noticed the parallel between Granucci and Yagel but failed to appreciate Yagel's great dependence on him.

whom he engages in conversation on a certain day, thus providing the framing device for his story collection. *La Piacevol Notte* is initially situated in Siena during the author's visit in 1568. From Siena, Granucci traveled to the small town of Pienza in search of some ancestors. Having met several individuals in the local monastery, he and his companions exchange a variety of stories which constitute the bulk of this collection.

Granucci is a most unstudied author and for good reason. As Letterio di Francia has clearly pointed out, Granucci's work was not only conventional and tedious, he had little inhibition in flagrantly "borrowing" from the most obvious of sources. In di Francia's judgment, "We are obliged to conclude that in the history of the Italian *novellistica*, the name of Granucci can only appear as the most dishonest plagiarist."[82] Whether or not such an assessment is too harsh, it is clear that Yagel did his own "borrowing" from someone less than a giant of the novella tradition. Our interest in Yagel's dependence on Granucci lies more in this Jew's ability to use what he had taken for his own didactic purposes than in the aesthetic quality of his sources. Yagel may have been an undiscriminating student of Italian literature but he was an innovative Jewish educator.

## Yagel's Reworking of Granucci's Novelle

One of the most dramatic tales Yagel borrows from Granucci's collection describes the horrific vengeance of the woman who blinds her husband's murderer before killing herself (section 30). The story had originally appeared in Apuleius's *The Golden Ass*.[83] In Granucci's version, a young man named Savinio falls in love with a beautiful woman named Clarice. She finds his personal habits revolting and decides to marry another man named Luceio. Although Savinio continues to desire Clarice secretly, he finds himself in a position to rescue her new husband from his enemies. Luceio is so grateful that he invites Savinio into his home, where he is treated as a brother. Finding himself in close proximity to the woman he desires, Savinio is more aroused and plots his friend's downfall. The two decide to hunt wild boar in the forest, and they mount their horses and depart. Suddenly, Savinio turns on his friend, attacking the horse and rider, and Luceio is murdered. Savinio prepares the dead man's wounds so as to give

---

[82]Di Francia, *Novellistica*, 2, p. 120.
[83]I have used the Loeb ed. trans. by W. Adlington and revised by S. Gasellee (Cambridge, Mass., 1965), bk. 8, pp. 344–64.

the appearance that the wild boar had killed his friend; he then kills the animal. Returning from the forest, Savinio explains his friend's unfortunate death and tries to console the heartbroken Clarice. A short time passes and Savinio crudely asks for her hand in marriage. She quickly discerns his deceit and plots her revenge. She invites him to her room, drugs him, and, while he sleeps, pierces his eyes with her needle. Since "death ends all misery," she then takes her life with her husband's sword.[84]

In Yagel's Hebrew composition, the story appears oddly out of place.[85] The challenge of using such a tale with hunting scenes and multiple murders to teach Jewish values was surely daunting. One scholar was so taken by the bizarre scene of the hunt in Yagel's narrative that he was convinced "that even at the end of the sixteenth century the sport of hunting in forests was still widespread among the Jews of Italy."[86] Italian Jews, of course, were generally not hunters, and certainly not hunters of wild boar. Yagel obviously took a liking to the ancient tale, and deemed it acceptable for Jewish tastes if several modifications were made. By translating it into Hebrew, he naturally introduced a biblical and rabbinic idiom more familiar and thus more palatable to Jewish readers, but additional changes were still required.

In Granucci's account, Savinio is hardly described. Yagel's character, who addresses him and his father in the first person, is an impious womanizer who neglects the study of Torah. He is so hostile to learning that he announces: "I would have held a sword at the entrance to the house of study, piercing anyone who might enter, and striking down anyone interested in a book."[87] In contrast, the man he eventually kills is "versed in intellectual and divine matters." His wife is a modest and dignified Jewish woman, totally committed to her husband, and scrupulous in her observance of the Jewish laws regarding mourning. When Yagel describes the hunt scene, he patently reveals a certain discomfort. He quickly passes over the details of the hunt and lets the boar kill the husband rather than allow his friend to become the murderer. However, when Yagel comes to discuss the mourning period of the woman, he cannot refrain from offering some passing and extraneous comments about a rabbinic dispute on the appropriate period a widow should wait before remarrying.[88] And most signifi-

[84]Nicolao Granucci di Lucca, *La Piacevol Notte et Lieto Giorno, opera morale* (Venice, 1574), pp. 140a–144a.

[85]See below, Part I, secs. 30–32, pp. 111–17.

[86]I. Zinberg, *A History of Jewish Literature,* 12 vols., trans. by B. Martin (Cincinnati and New York, 1969–75), 4, p. 126.

[87]See below, p. 112.

[88]See below, pp. 114–15.

cant of all is the father's long homily that immediately follows the story, in which he waxes eloquent on the nature of human sin, on breaking the yoke of heaven, and on the proper punishment to evildoers.[89] The connection between the story's plot and Yagel's moral is exceedingly weak but it did not deter him from using it. By allowing himself a little latitude regarding the details of the story, Yagel may have intended to shock his reader and reinforce his proper behavior. Alternatively, he may simply have enjoyed titillating him with the sordid details of the narrative. In either case, he assumed, it was just a story, not real life.

Granucci's novella of Federico and Giulia also finds its place in Yagel's narrative.[90] Granucci apparently based the novella on a similar narrative of Masuccio, which Yagel might also have consulted.[91] Granucci, like Masuccio, focused his story on the male character Federico, an honorable and virtuous youth who remained poor because of the whims of fortune. He was sent by his employers to Venice, where he boarded a ship to Alexandria. On the way, he was captured by pirates who sold him as a slave to a merchant in Constantinople. Before he had departed from Venice, he had fallen in love with Giulia, also a person of social standing, who was stricken with grief upon hearing of her lover's enslavement. Disguising herself as a man, she sailed to Constantinople in the hope of redeeming Federico. To her delight, she located him and negotiated a payment for his release. Before she could conclude the deal, however, a Sicilian sailor robbed her of all her funds, leaving her incapable of rescuing her young man. In desperation, she sold herself into slavery in order to gain his freedom. Nevertheless, the story ends happily, for she is able to escape from her master in a fishing boat with the assistance of certain sailors. Both lovers eventually return to their homeland and are greeted with great joy by their fellow citizens. Granucci ends the novella on a homiletical note, praising the great force of youthful love and the ardent desire of the soul to escape from its bodily prison in search of a higher truth.

Yagel's version of the story is considerably different, most notably in its tragic ending (which, incidently, is more similar to that of Masuccio) and in its focus on the unfortunate woman rather than on the man.[92] Yagel introduces this character together with another woman who first relates her

---

[89]See below, pp. 117–21.

[90]Granucci, *La Piacevol Notte,* pp. 129a–132a.

[91]I have used the edition of Masuccio Salernitano, *Il Novellino,* ed. R. di Marco (Bologna, 1968), pt. 4, novella 39, pp. 274–78. It is also found in the English translation of W. G. Waters as *The Novellino of Masuccio,* 2 vols. (London, 1985), 2, pp. 217–23.

[92]See below, secs. 86–89, pp. 183–93.

life story. The first woman is a paragon of virtue, supportive of her needy father, modest, diligent, and generous in all her activities. She is unquestionably "a woman of valor," a model of Jewish femininity, who is ultimately rewarded for her effort by meeting the perfect mate. He, in turn, willingly invites her into his home as his wife and offers to support her poor father. She graciously accepts and serves him as faithfully as she had served her father.

The second woman is then introduced; she is meant to provide a striking contrast to the first. She is "a hard-spirited woman who never saw goodness in her lifetime."[93] Her rich father lost all his wealth when rival merchants libeled him before the king. She sought a young man from a family of her father's enemies. After a secret liaison between them, he set off on a voyage, was captured by pirates, and was sold into slavery in Egypt. She followed him with the ransom money but was deceived by a "Canaanite" who took her money and sailed to Jaffa. Without seeking God's help, she sold herself into slavery and was seduced by her master, who then refused to marry her but forced her to remain as his concubine for a year. In the interim, her lover died in grief. When she was finally redeemed, she was married off to a man who also died, some two years later. In despair, she tried to take her own life but instead suffered the agony of a long and painful illness. She was finally punished for her sins when her soul entered the body of a mad dog.

Having offered his readers his study in contrasts, Yagel delineates seventeen moral and religious lessons to be learned from these two lives.[94] He includes the following in his tedious list: that God never deserts the righteous, that a father should scrupulously supervise his young daughter, that a person should keep his home physically and spiritually clean, that a person should not lose hope even in a time of great trouble and sorrow, that a man or woman should not be prevented from marrying the person of his or her choice, that women should not be trusted with money, and that no person should curse himself. Finally, the woman's fate in the dog's body provides Yagel the opportunity to lecture on his view of metempsychosis.[95] The transformation of an endearing story on the power of love into a case history of seemingly unending sins and omissions was now complete.[96]

[93]See below, p. 189.

[94]See below, pp. 193–99.

[95]On this theme in Yagel's writing, see below, and see Ruderman, *Kabbalah, Magic, and Science,* chap. 8.

[96]Before concluding this section on Granucci's influence on *Gei Ḥizzayon,* we might suggest two other instances of Yagel's apparent borrowing from him. The charming story

## Job's Story

The story that the biblical character of Job relates to Yagel and his father
(Part 1, section 71) is another good example of Yagel's type of Renaissance
storytelling in a Jewish key. The basic plot, that of a wife who takes her
maidservant's place in her own husband's bed, was well known to Italian
readers. The story had been told, for example, in Giambattista Giraldi
Cintio's famous novella collection called the *Ecatommithi* (*The Hundred
Tales*), first published in 1565.[97] A similar version had appeared even earlier
in *Le Porretane,* Sabadino degli Arienti's famous collection first published in
1483.[98]

   Both Italian writers situate their stories in Italy. Cintio describes the
relationship of a rich doctor of Ferrara with his voluptuous maid, Nigella.
Outsmarted by his wife, who orchestrates the change of partners, the
doctor begs his wife's forgiveness and sends the honest maid to Mantua
where she happily is rewarded in marriage to a blacksmith. In Sabadino's
version, the duke of Milan is attracted to a noblewoman of the same city.
His wife hears of his planned liaison with the woman in a castle in Pavia and

---

(Part 1, sec. 53) of the fool who inquires about the inappropriateness of nature's creating a small
plant for watermelons and a large tree for peanuts is taken from Granucci, *La Piacevol Notte,*
p. 165a. Moreover, Yagel's idea of the aforementioned virtuous woman (Part 1, sec. 87) being
nursed by a sheep in the absence of her mother may have been inspired by a similar account in
Granucci, p. 32a.

   The origin of the rhetorician's story (sec. 29) of his calling Satan and his descent and
return from Hell, while drawing on familiar themes in Christian and Jewish literature, is still
unknown to me. On the theme of the devil pact in European literature, see, for example, C.
Dédéyan, *La thème de Faust dans la littérature européenne,* 4 vols. (Paris, 1954–67); P. M. Palmer
and R. P. More, *The Sources of the Faust Tradition* (New York, 1936); H. Fisch, "The Pact with
the Devil," *Yale Review,* 69 (1980): 520–32. On the theme in Jewish sources, see most recently,
M. Idel, "The Jewish *Magus* from the Renaissance Period to Early Hasidism," in *Religion,
Science, and Magic,* ed. J. Neusner, E. S. Frerichs, P. V. McC. Flesher (Oxford and New York:
1989). On the literature of visitations to Hell, see Himmelfarb, *Tours of Hell,* and the earlier
literature she cites.

   [97] I have used the edition of G. Salinari, *Novelle del Cinquecento* (Turin, 1976), bk. 3, no. 9,
pp. 554–60; see also Busi, "Sulla *Ge Ḥizzayon*," p. 21.

   [98] I have used the edition of B. Basile (Rome, 1981), no. 26, pp. 229–37. The same motif is
found in other novella collections. For examples, see D. P. Rotunda, *Motif-Index of the Italian
Novella* (Bloomington, Ind., 1942), pp. 98, 126. Granucci also includes a story with the same
motif, titled "La novella di Alonzo re di Portogallo" (*La Piacevole Notte,* pp. 145a–149a). It
describes a king's attraction for a young damsel who resembles his wife. Through a switch of
partners, the queen ends up in bed with her husband who takes her to be his lover. Although
the basic outline of this tale parallels the Job story and may have inspired Yagel, those of Cintio
and Sabadino still approximate more closely the Hebrew version. An interesting parallel of the
same motif is also located in M. Gaster, *The Exempla of the Rabbis* (New York, 1968), p. 124.

surreptitiously changes places with her husband's mistress. When the husband is finally exposed, he recants, treats the young girl honorably, and restores her to her parents, after which she ultimately marries a more appropriate mate.

Yagel's version of the narrative is notably different from the Italian *novellieri* in three ways. First, the provenance of Yagel's story is no longer Italy but Egypt and Ethiopia. Second, his story focuses more on the virtue of the maidservant than of the crafty wife. Furthermore, when the husband's lechery is revealed, the maidservant's situation proves to be even more precarious than before. Instead of being rewarded for her honesty and temperance, her master harbors a grudge against her. Only through Job's intervention does she finally receive an appropriate reward by becoming the bride of the Ethiopian king. Finally, Yagel grafts onto his story the figure of Job, who performs a divine mission in rescuing the young maiden from her evil master.[99]

No doubt, the intercession of Job represents Yagel's most unusual interpolation in rewriting the familiar story. Especially bizarre is the way Yagel introduces Job into the narrative. After the narrator protests to his father that Job is an allegorical figure and not an actual person, Yagel presents a detailed discussion of the rabbinic sources regarding Job's authenticity,[100] and only after his son has finally been persuaded of Job's actual existence is the biblical figure introduced. Yet Job then relates to his readers a fantastic anecdote which obviously bears no relation to reality and following which Job and his questioners abruptly turn to consider such abstract theological questions as the rewards bestowed upon seemingly unvirtuous people like Haman and the influence of the constellations on the fate of the Jewish people.

The awkward coexistence of rabbinic commentary, entertaining narrative, and theological elucidation characterizes Yagel's work throughout. Even more extraordinary is the blurring of the boundaries between reality and fantasy and between the sacred and profane realms: Job, the supposedly real person and biblical character, becomes the mouthpiece for a totally worldly but fictional story. Why did Yagel find this story appropriate in the first place in conveying his message of the reward for moral virtue? And why the special link with Job? To attempt to answer these questions is perhaps to expect too much from the boldly conceived but somewhat imperfectly executed work the young Yagel had penned. No doubt the

[99]See below, pp. 161–67.
[100]See below, pp. 161–64.

combination of pieces he shaped was sometimes contrived, even forced. Yet, in his own mind, the remarkable mingling of the real and the fictional had its higher purpose. As with the other stories, Yagel believed that he could succeed in teaching Judaism through entertainment. He elevated the profane story by sanctifying it through the voice of a biblical figure revered in Jewish tradition, and thereby legitimated his use of this narrative for moral edification and spiritual insight.

### The Memoirs of a Jewish Gambler

At least two of the narratives Yagel employed in the first part of *Gei Ḥizzayon* appear to be based on sources outside the novella tradition. They are the speeches of the Jewish gambler (Part 1, section 18) and of the Siamese twins (Part 1, section 46) and they constitute two of the most fascinating sections of Yagel's book. Because they treat two major aspects of Renaissance Jewish life—gambling and the plague—in a most unusual and original manner, they each deserve close examination.

Yagel introduces the gambler after a short and relatively unimaginative speech by the soul of an elementary school teacher who "sometimes wrote books and documents for others in order to earn a living."[101] Since he had neglected the education of the young, he was guilty of the transgression expressed in the biblical verse: "Cursed be he who is slack in doing the Lord's work" (Jeremiah 48:10). The man had been assigned the punishment of wandering in the company of "unruly souls who had expired without delight, such as this man [the gambler] who died without learning except for the small amount [he had mastered] in his youth."[102]

His companion is none other than a compulsive gambler, obliged to receive heavenly instruction from the first soul in lieu of the education he had forfeited because of his lifelong preoccupation with games of chance. When pressed by his interlocutors, Yagel and his father's soul, to explain the reason for his excesses, the gambler responds that he had been taught to play by "one of the rhetoricians . . . a proud and insolent man." The witty and cunning speech of the "rhetorician" in praise of gambling then follows.

Although the specific source of Yagel's discourse on games of chance is not yet known to me, the general context of his remarks is quite apparent.

[101]See below, pp. 89–90.
[102]See below, p. 90.

Most obvious is the Jewish compulsion for gambling especially prevalent among Italian Jews. Rabbinic literature is replete with references to gamblers, especially compulsive ones. According to the Mishnah they are deemed morally contemptible and consequently disqualified from offering testimony and serving as judges. Throughout the Middle Ages, rabbis and communal leaders regularly denounced gambling and enacted communal legislation to limit, if not to prohibit, all games of chance. The rabbis were particularly aware of the deleterious psychological effects of gambling on the players and the negative image they projected within their communities.[103]

In Renaissance Italy, Jewish participation in gambling reached epidemic proportions, due apparently to the influence of the prevailing passion for games of chance within Christian society.[104] As early as 1416–18, Jewish communal ordinances appear in Bologna and Forlì prohibiting the playing of dice and card games.[105] In subsequent years and in a variety of communities, similar legislation was regularly passed, but to little avail. Despite the disinclination for such games shared by rabbis and lay leaders, especially noticeable in times of communal crisis, and despite their desire to eradicate the menace of gambling, the lure of the game was overpowering. In Cremona, for example, three rabbis proposed a ban on gambling in 1576 to avert the "divine decree" of a plague which threatened the physical well-being of the Jewish community. Their action proved so unpopular that it was eventually rescinded. In fact, their detractors not only questioned the proposition of a causal relationship between the evil of card-playing and the plague, they even challenged altogether the assumption that gambling was sinful and generally forbidden according to rabbinic law.[106]

---

[103]A convenient summary of the subject of gambling in rabbinic and medieval sources is found in L. Landman, "Jewish Attitudes Toward Gambling," *Jewish Quarterly Review*, n.s. 57–58 (1966–68): 298–318; 34–61. See also V. Kurrein, "Kartenspiel und Spielkarten in Jüdischen Schrifttum," *Monatsschrift für Geschichte und Wissenschaft des Judentums*, 66 (1922): 203–11; I. Rivkind, "On the History of Gaming in Judaism" (in Hebrew), *Horeb*, 1 (1934): 82–91 and 2 (1935–36): 60–66; I. Abrahams, *Jewish Life in the Middle Ages* (New York, 1969), pp. 388–98. Additional references can be found in S. W. Baron, *The Jewish Community*, 3 vols. (Philadelphia, 1948), 2, p. 207, n. 30.

[104]See, for example, Roth, *The Jews in the Renaissance*, pp. 26–27; idem, *Venice*, pp. 207–9; I. Abrahams, "Samuel Portaleone's Proposed Restrictions on Games of Chance," *Jewish Quarterly Review*, o.s. 5 (1892–93): 505–15.

[105]L. Finkelstein, *Jewish Self-Government in the Middle Ages* (New York, 1964), pp. 286, 291.

[106]On the Cremona incident, see M. Benayahu and G. Laras, "The Appointment of Health Authorities in Cremona in 1575" (in Hebrew), *Michael*, 1 (1972): 78–143.

Then in 1584, at the tender age of thirteen, the aforementioned Leon Modena composed a small essay on the subject of gambling. In the form of a dialogue between two fictional characters named Eldad and Medad, Modena presented arguments both in favor of and against gambling, ultimately reaching a negative judgment on the sport.[107] Nevertheless, as his autobiography graphically testifies, Modena, along with other members of his family, was seriously addicted to games of chance and suffered continually because of the huge sums lost at the gaming tables.[108] When certain rabbis of Venice ordered a ban against the playing of cards within the Jewish community in 1628, it was this same Modena who challenged the measure in an eloquent and learned rabbinic responsum. Modena's legal brief pointedly exposed the equivocal nature of rabbinic attitudes toward gambling and the unrealistic expectations of those who believed that the vice would simply disappear through such unenforceable and ineffectual legislation. Modena surely realized that gambling was undesirable on moral grounds; nevertheless, this alone could not deter any addicted gambler from visiting the gaming tables regardless of what measures the community took to curb his insatiable gambling appetite.[109]

Yagel's ruminations on gambling were written only a few years before Modena composed his youthful treatise on the subject. Lacking the seriousness of purpose and the moral assurance of the younger Modena, Yagel, though he recognized the excesses of the gambler, had little intention of scolding him about the moral depravities associated with the sport. On the contrary, he contended that what might appear on the surface as repugnant could easily be considered laudatory, even virtuous, if only one were to penetrate the ultimate meaning behind the cards and the dice.

Modena, through the mouthpiece of Medad, had advanced a number of positive points in favor of the sport, although he later refuted them. Medad minimized the extent of financial loss associated with such games. He argued that there were clearly more injurious ways of losing one's wealth, especially by lending money. Furthermore, gambling was a kind of index of a person's character; it sharpened his wits, and, by playing the

---

[107]For an English translation of this work, called in Hebrew *Sur me-Ra,* see H. Gollancz, *Translations from Hebrew and Aramaic* (London, 1908), pp. 161–219. The work was first published in 1595 in Venice.

[108]See H. Adelman, *Success and Failure in the Seventeenth Century Ghetto of Venice: The Life and Thought of Leon Modena 1571–1648,* unpublished Ph.D. diss., Brandeis University, 1985, pp. 224–33, 308–9, 645–47, 670–80, 935–37, 1072–77, and *The Autobiography of a Seventeenth-Century Venetian Rabbi,* index, "gambling."

[109]See Leon Modena, *She'elot u-Teshuvot Zikne Yehudah,* ed. S. Simonsohn (Jerusalem, 1956), n. 78, pp. 100–14.

game, by experiencing its peaks and valleys, a person might come to learn the lessons of life.[110]

Yagel's arguments in favor of gambling were more ingenious, indeed more outrageous. His speaker intended to demonstrate "that all human perfection is found in cards and dice."[111] Rather than being merely a game of sport, playing at cards or dice hints at higher truths, revealing the orderly structure of the universe and the majesty of the Creator. The game is ultimately a symbolic representation of the universe as a whole and therefore, remarkably, mastery of the rules of the game leads the initiate to glimpse the deepest meaning of human experience.

The notion that cards (and dice) were originally designed to remind human beings of the higher structure of the universe constitutes the principal assumption of the art of cartomancy, a "science" of divination well known in sixteenth-century Italy.[112] As early as 1540, Francesco Marcolini published in Venice a handbook for fortune-telling through the use of cards.[113] He was followed by a variety of Italian pamphleteers who similarly described the divinatory virtues of card games.[114] The better-known Pietro Aretino, in his political satire Le carte parlanti, published in 1543, made use of the idea that tarot and ordinary playing cards have symbolic meanings that can reveal the fates of their players.[115] Later occultists, including the well-known M. Eliphas Levi, constructed elaborate systems of correspondences between the cards and the arrangement of the universe. Levi, in particular, even underscored the connection between the four card suits and the four letters of the tetragrammaton, and that between the twenty-two tarots and the twenty-two letters of the "Kabbalist alphabet."[116]

Because of Yagel's strong interest in magic, kabbalah, and astrology,

[110]Gollancz, *Translations,* pp. 171, 177, 184, 202–4.

[111]See below, p. 92.

[112]See W. H. Willshire, *A Descriptive Catalogue of Playing and Other Cards in the British Museum* (London, 1876), especially the section on cartomancy (taken from the appendix of A. P. Buchan in S. W. Singer, *Researches in the History of Playing Cards* [London, 1816], pp. 357–62), pp. 146–60; P. Boiteau D'Ambly, *Cartes à Jouer et la Cartomancie* (Piccadilly and London, 1859); *Encyclopedia Italiana* (Milan, 1931–39), 9, pp. 250–51; C. P. Hargrave, *A History of Playing Cards and a Bibliography of Cards and Gaming* (Boston and New York, 1930), pp. 223–45, 378–80.

[113]Hargrave, p. 242; R. Cavendish, *The Tarot* (New York and London, 1975), p. 150; Wilshire, pp. 159–60.

[114]Wilshire, p. 160; Hargrave, p. 244.

[115]C. Cordié, *Opere di Pietro Aretino e di Anto Francesco Doni* (Milan and Naples, 1976), pp. 458–80, including bibliography and excepts from *Le carte parlanti.*

[116]Wilshire, pp. 148–50. On Levi, see T. Williams, *Eliphas Levi, Master of Occultism* (University, Alabama, 1975).

especially as they related to his medical practice, it comes as no surprise to discover that he displayed an obvious familiarity and understandable enthusiasm for the "science of the cards." Like other sixteenth-century naturalists, he was obsessed with correlations and connections in everything as revelations of the ultimate divine harmony of all things. The enthusiasm for unfolding the divine secrets in games of chance expressed in the gambler's speech was transparently his own.

Yagel was careful to label the rhetorician as a "wicked and deceitful man" and to point out that he had built "a formless building with empty stones." Nevertheless, he nowhere refutes his clever advocate of gambling. On the contrary, he peppers his speech with ample biblical and rabbinic citations, and even blatantly misquotes passages to substantiate his point.[117] It is the delightful combination of utter seriousness, playfulness, even blasphemous satire, together with the necessary modicum of pious condemnation, that marks the special quality of Yagel's literary creation.

One can only imagine how Yagel's contemporaries might have reacted to his seeming impropriety. They could not have helped being offended by his undisguised attempt to make light of their ineffectual measures to curb gambling and excoriate the compulsive gambler. Before their very eyes he had skillfully transposed a reprehensible sin into a sterling virtue and had accomplished this in a seemingly innocent and entertaining manner.[118]

### Out of the Mouths of Babes: The Speech of the Siamese Twins

Among the characters who engage Yagel and his father in dialogue in the first part of *Gei Ḥizzayon*, the Siamese twins are surely the most peculiar. Yet, in the case of the twins, Yagel was actually describing two real creatures rather than products of his own imagination.

Yagel's story was based on an ugly incident that took place in the Jewish ghetto of Venice on 26 May 1575. On that day, the daughter of Gabriel Ẓarfati, the wife of a Jew named Petaḥiah, gave birth to a creature with two heads and four hands but conjoined from the waist down.[119] The

[117]See the text below, pp. 92–97.

[118]In 1756, Raphael Yehiel Sanguinetti delivered a sermon in Fiorenzuola on a theme similar to that of Yagel's gambler. He described the Italian game *tre sette* and interpreted it allegorically. See MS. Jerusalem Ben Zevi 4031 (Jerusalem microfilm 17700); also MS. Budapest Kaufmann A 538/1 (Jerusalem microfilm 15177).

[119]The Hebrew sources describing the incident include Y. Boksenboim, *She'elot u-Teshuvot Mattanot ba-Adam* (Tel Aviv, 1983), pp. 28, 95–96; MS. Jerusalem National and

news of the strange birth quickly spread throughout the ghetto and beyond. The infants, apparently healthy at birth, became an instant sensation
to Jews and non-Jews alike. A stream of visitors inundated the family's
residence. Under constant pressure and exposure, the infants succumbed
some eight days later.[120]

The story of this bizarre spectacle did not end, however, with the death
of the twins. Instead of immediately burying the deceased children, the
father handed them over to the local *gemilut ḥasadim* (benevolent) society
"as a present."[121] The members of the society preserved them in a solution,
carried them from place to place, and displayed the corpse to anyone who
would pay a price to view it, until they had collected "a handsome sum." It
is not clear who was ultimately responsible for this profitable but uncons-
cionable capitalist venture—the parents, the heads of the confraternity, or
both parties.[122] Whatever the case, the perpetrators had sought to legitimate their actions by appeal to Jewish religious custom and apparently had
obtained approval from some questionable legal authorities.[123] Nevertheless, there were those among the Venetian rabbinate who could not countenance such an act, notably Rabbis Samuel Judah Katznellenbogan and
Raphael Joseph Treves, who composed responsa disapproving of the sodal-
ity's activity and calling for the immediate burial of the children in accordance with the dictates of Jewish law.

Largely as a result of the notoriety gained by the confraternity's hawk-
ing of the unfortunate children, news of the monstrous birth spread quickly
beyond Venice to other parts of Italy and to Germany. To both a popular
audience and a learned community of scholars fascinated by the new "science" of teratology, the data on the Jewish twins were of considerable

University Library Heb. 3428, no. 153; MS. Strasbourg Heb. 4085, fol. 291 (a responsum of
R. Samuel Judah Katznellenbogan), which, on the basis of Boksenboim's quotations (*Mattanot ba-Adam,* p. 28), seems identical with *Zerah Anashim* (Husiatyn, 1902), responsum 34,
pp. 50–54. The precise date of the birth is supplied by Yagel himself. See below, p. 147.

[120]The time of the death is reported by Katznellenbogan, MS. Strasbourg Heb. 4085;
the twins are reported to have died at slightly different times.

[121]As reported in MS. Jerusalem Heb. 3428 (Boksenboim, *Mattanot ba-Adam,* p. 28).

[122]MS. Jerusalem Heb. 3428 reports that the father handed over the corpse to the
confraternity. Katznellenbogan, MS. Strasbourg Heb. 4085, appears to suggest that the father
may have been unaware of the society's intentions (Boksenboim, *Mattanot ba-Adam,* p. 28):
"and perhaps without the knowledge of their father." For a similar example of displaying a
monstrous corpse for profit, see K. Park and L. J. Daston, "Unnatural Conceptions: The Study
of Monsters in Sixteenth- and Seventeenth-Century France and England," *Past and Present* 92
(1981): 20, 34–35.

[123]See Katznellenbogan, MS. Strasbourg Heb. 4085, and the responsum in *Mattanot ba-
Adam,* written by Rabbi Raphael Joseph Treves, according to Boksenboim.

interest.[124] Full descriptions and portraits of the twins are found in monster handbooks and they were also memorialized in contemporary German and Italian poems.[125] The coincidence of the twins' birth with the outbreak of the devastating plague of 1575 led many observers to consider their birth as a manifestation of divine displeasure with Venice and its inhabitants.[126]

The most important vehicle of dissemination about the monstrous birth was undoubtedly an anonymous fourteen-page pamphlet in Italian, first published by Giuseppe Gregorio of Cremona in Venice only two days after the twins' death, and reissued the next year in Bologna. The treatise, which includes a picture of the twins and two horoscopes summarizing the pertinent astrological data of the day of birth and the day of impregnation, is titled: *Discorso sopra gli accidenti del parto mostruoso nato di una Hebrea in Venetia nell'anno 1575 a di xxvi di Maggio*. The second edition emphasizes the Jewish provenance of the birth by providing the additional title: *Dove si ragiona altamente del futuro destino de gli Hebrei*.[127]

After describing the "monster," the author offers a detailed explanation of this phenomenon according to the conventional division of reality into three parts: material, heavenly, and divine. He first considers the immediate cause of the birth as understood by naturalists and physicians:

[124]On the study of monsters in the sixteenth and seventeenth centuries, see L. Thorndike, *A History of Magic and Natural Science,* 8 vols. (New York, 1929–41), 6, pp. 286–87, 488–91; J. Céard, *La nature et les prodiges; L'insolite au XVIe siècle en France* (Geneva, 1977); R. Wittkower, "Marvels of the East: A Study in the History of Monsters," *Journal of the Warburg and Courtauld Institutes* 5 (1942): 159–97; Park and Daston, "Unnatural Conceptions," pp. 20–54; A. J. Schutte, "Such Monstrous Births," *Renaissance Quarterly,* 38 (1985): 85–106.

[125]See, for example, Ulisse Aldrovandi, *Monstrorum Historia* (Boulogne, 1642), pp. 647–48; Johann Schenck, *Monstrorum Historia Memorabilis* (Frankfurt am Main, 1609), p. 7; A. Sonderegger, *Missgeburten und Wundergestalten in Einblatten und Handzeichnungen des 16. Jahrhunderts* (Leipzig and Berlin, 1927), pp. 22–23, which draws on a collection of J. J. Wick (1522–88) for the years 1560–87 in the Zentralbibliothek of Zürich.

[126]On the Venetian plague of 1575–77, see E. Rodenwalt, *Pest in Venedig 1575–77. Ein Beitrag zur Frage der Infektkette bei dem Pestepidemien West-Europas* (Heidelberg, 1953); P. Preto, *Peste e società à Venezia, 1576* (Vicenza, 1978); B. Pullan, *Rich and Poor in Renaissance Venice* (Cambridge, Mass., 1971), pp. 314–26.

[127]E. Morpurgo, "Bibliografia della storia degli ebrei nel Veneto," *Rivista israelitica,* 9 (1912); 226–27, lists the work as no. 662 in his bibliography and indicates that it was published first in Venice in 1575. A. Sapadin, "On a Monstrous Birth Occurring in the Ghetto of Venice," *Studies in Bibliography and Booklore,* 6 (1964): 153–58, discusses the second edition. I have consulted a copy of this edition in the library of the Hebrew Union College–Jewish Institute of Religion in Cincinnati. Morpurgo lists another pamphlet on the same incident (no. 663 in his list), titled *Nova et ridicolosa espositione del mostro nato in Ghetto con il lamento del suo padre per la morte di quello ecc.* (Venice, 1575), which I was unable to locate. Morpurgo adds that, according to this work, the father castigated himself for having failed to circumcise the twins. See also Busi, "Sulla *Ge Ḥizzayon,*" pp. 23–27.

either an excessive or insufficient amount of semen or unclean spermatozoa. Next he considers the astrological factors, concluding with the explanation of the ancient seers (*aruspici*) that such prodigies are omens of heavenly displeasure. He describes other recorded incidents of monstrous births both in ancient times and in the more recent past. He concludes with a vilification of the "perverse and obstinate *sinagoga*," the false Jewish interpretations of the prophecies of the book of Daniel, and the usurious practices of contemporary Jews. After predicting their final doom, he calls for the conversion of Jews to Christianity.

In contrast to their portrayal in the *Discorso,* the twins in Yagel's narrative are recovered from their miserable lot as pitiful oddities of nature, recast as majestic prophetic characters in a mysterious romance, and thus afforded a place in the annals of Hebrew literature. Relying primarily on the *Discorso* for his information, Yagel uses the incident to impart a religious message profoundly different from that of the Italian pamphleteer.

The twins make their entrance in a highly dramatic fashion.[128] While attached to each other, they fly toward Yagel and his father and whisper quietly to each other, "their voices sounding like a ghost out of the ground." Their initial pronouncements are prophetic. One predicts "a war or famine in the land or one of the remaining calamities threatening to come into the world." The prognostication is imprecise, but surely Yagel had in mind the disastrous plague of Venice, which immediately followed the death of the twins. The same child counsels immediate flight from the city but simultaneously contradicts himself by quoting the rabbinic statement, "If there is a plague in the city, remain where you are."[129]

The opening prophecy of doom is followed by a long discussion between Yagel and his father on the essence of the soul, how it comes into the world, and related issues, all triggered by the strange appearance of these infant souls.[130] Finally, father and son approach the twins and ask them the reason for their being attached. The first child is impatient with them and refuses to respond but the second calmly frames a long answer.

Following the structure of the *Discorso*'s argument, the infant divides his explanation into three parts corresponding to the order of the three worlds. He opens, however, with a strong religious emphasis. Since God is always just, any calamity is caused by human rather than by divine failing. He then draws a parallel between the biblical incident of the finding of a

[128]See below, p. 135.
[129]See below, p. 135. Cf. B. T. Babba Kamma 60b.
[130]See below, pp. 136–40.

slain body in a field (Deuteronomy 21) and the corpse of the Venetian twins. In both cases, those responsible for ruling the state were ultimately responsible for the welfare of their communities. Although the father's household bears partial responsibility for this disaster, the city's inhabitants and particularly their leadership are also culpable. The fact that the plague took the lives of so many Venetian citizens is tangible evidence of their punishment. That Yagel similarly blames the communal leaders in Luzzara and Mantua for his own misfortune is perhaps more than coincidental.

Following this opening, Yagel turns to the information supplied by his Italian source for most of the remainder of the infant's speech. The child describes some monstrous births earlier in the century; he also quotes verbatim the testimony of the medieval Arabic scholar Ibn Abi Ridjal (Aben Ragel) and of Xenophon regarding other monstrous children.[131] He paraphrases the *Discorso* on the heavenly cause of the birth, lifting the entire first half of its astrological calculations but curiously ignoring the entire second half.[132] His naturalistic explanations also generally follow the outline of the Italian pamphlet.[133] He repeats the primary reasons for the abnormality—the excess, scarcity, or filthiness of the sperm—but also includes a wealth of additional information drawn primarily from rabbinic sources and Yagel's own medical experience.[134] The scene closes with the children asking Yagel and his father for their prayers.

Yagel's fascination with the prophetic ability of young children proved to be lifelong. Some twenty years later, he responded to a query about an illustrious child prodigy named Nahman. And some forty years later, he again reflected on the birth of a young wonder child in Poland, in a manner strikingly reminiscent of his previous ruminations. This is not the place to treat those later reactions in detail.[135] Suffice it to say that in all three cases, he was fascinated by the phenomenon and treated such wonders seriously and credulously. His interest was spurred in part by the great importance

---

[131]See below, p. 146; *Discorso* (Bologna, 1576), p. 10 (my pagination).

[132]See below, pp. 147–48; *Discorso,* chap. 2.

[133]See below, pp. 149–53; *Discorso,* chap. 1.

[134]Yagel refers to the idea that the womb has seven sacs, three at each side and one in the middle. If the sperm enters at the right, the infant will be male; if it enters at the left, it will be female; and in the middle, it will be androgynous. For earlier Jewish sources for this idea, see J. Trachtenberg, *Jewish Magic and Superstitition: A Study in Folk Religion* (New York, 1939; reprint, New York, 1970), pp. 188, 303, n. 13.

[135]I have treated them in Ruderman, "Three Contemporary Perceptions of a Polish Wunderkind of the Seventeenth Century," *Association for Jewish Studies Review,* 4 (1979): 143–63; and idem, *Kabbalah, Magic, and Science,* chap. 5.

the motif of the child prodigy held in earlier Jewish literature, particularly as a divine seer of messianic redemption. But as his reading in the *Discorso* illustrates, Yagel was also attracted to "monster children" as subjects of contemporary science.

Like other naturalists of his day, Yagel was concerned with such bizarre phenomena of nature because of his desire to record and measure every abnormality so as to penetrate the order and regularity of the universe. Monsters such as the Siamese twins testified to the fecundity and multiformity of nature; they also functioned as portents of things to come. A knowledge of these signs permitted humans to acquire greater wisdom about the universe, but at the same time they dramatically indicated the finitude of human experience, for nature still chose to hide its face, to deceive mankind. Thus, accompanying the effort to explain monsters in a natural context was a chilling fear that not all had yet been explained. The monster might also present a sign, an omen, a celestial notice of the potential terror and instability of the yet unknowable future.[136]

Yagel, like many of his learned contemporaries, did not distinguish clearly between the universe as a religious subject and as a scientific one. The Siamese twins of Venice could be explained by material and astrological causes, but they were also prominent manifestations of divine wrath. And in the literary setting of *Gei Ḥizzayon,* they became remarkable mouthpieces for some of the divine truths Yagel hoped to impart to his readers.

### The Impact of Boethius and the *Consolatio* Genre

Beyond the inspiration of the novella tradition for Yagel's work is that of the Roman philosopher Boethius (475?–525). The profound influence of Boethius's *Consolation of Philosophy* on *Gei Ḥizzayon* is not readily discernable to the reader of the first part of the work. Yagel quotes from Boethius's work on several occasions, but no more than other works.[137] There is the obvious parallel of a fallen, virtuous man and tragic figure, who, through his suffering, becomes aware of a higher truth, and who, through a series of fictional instructors, is enlightened through his spiritual odyssey on high. But the first part lacks the clear structural unity and thematic coherence of Boethius's classic. It is broken up by Yagel's tedious autobiographical

---

[136]For an elaboration on these ideas, see my works cited in the previous note.
[137]See below, pp. 240, 260.

digressions and it lacks the serious tone of the *Consolation,* particularly in the graphic plots of the novelle. In fact, previous scholars who have studied Yagel's work have usually been struck by its resemblance to Dante, never mentioning Boethius in the first place.[138]

When Yagel introduces Lady Philosophy with the precise adornments of Boethius's famous mentor at the beginning of the second part, Yagel's indebtedness to the Latin work becomes more apparent.[139] The influence rests not only on the portrayal of Lady Philosophy but also on the entire structure of *Gei Ḥizzayon* and in the organic relationship between the book's seemingly disparate parts. The novella genre had provided Yagel with the kind of divertissements through which he could introduce his intial moral exhortations; but the *consolatio* genre afforded him the appropriate model in which to frame his deepest theological reflections.

Yagel was not the first Hebrew writer to be charmed by Boethius's well-read work. The book was translated into Hebrew at least three times and it was quoted occasionally by other Hebrew authors.[140] Contemporary Jewish writers who had read the *Consolation* include David Messer Leon, Joseph Taitaẓak, and Eliezer Ashkenazi.[141] A copy of the work even appears in the private library of a sixteenth-century Mantuan Jew.[142] Yet, in com-

[138]Thus Roth, *The Jews in the Renaissance,* pp. 105–6, and Dan, *Ha-Sippur ha-Ivri,* pp. 202–5, have characterized the work; but Busi, "Sulla *Ge Ḥizzayon,*" p. 20, already discounts any significant relationship to Dante.

[139]On Boethius and the influence of *The Consolation of Philosophy,* see especially S. Lerer, *Boethius and Dialogue: Literary Method in "The Consolation of Philosophy."* (Princeton, 1985); E. Reiss, *Boethius* (Boston, 1982); M. H. Means, *The Consolatio Genre in Medieval Literature* (Gainesville, Fla., 1972); H. R. Patch, *The Tradition of Boethius: A Study of His Importance in Medieval Culture* (New York, 1935); P. Courcelle, *La Consolation de Philosophie dans la tradition littéraire* (Paris, 1967). I have used the English translation of *The Consolation of Philosophy* of R. Green (Indianapolis, 1962).

[140]MS. Vatican Neofite 8/2 (Jerusalem microfilm 6160), translated by Samuel Benveniste in the fourteenth century; MS. Moscow Günzburg 180/3, translated by Azariah ben R. Joseph ibn Abba Mari, known as Bonafoux Bonfil Astruc in Lucca in 1423 (this manuscript has been published by S. J. Sierra [Turin and Jerusalem, 1967], titled, *Boezio De Consolatione Philosophae Traduzione ebraica di Azaria . . . Astruc 5183–1423*); MS. Paris héb. 895, translated by the same Astruc of the previous manuscript in Province, fifteenth century. The manuscripts are discussed by M. Steinschneider, *Die Hebraeischen Übersetzungen des Mittelalters und Die Juden Als Dolmetscher* (Berlin, 1896), pp. 466–67, and by Sierra in the introduction to his edition.

[141]Sierra, pp. 15–25, discusses Taitaẓak (based on J. B. Sermoneta, "Scholastic Philosophic Literature in Rabbi Joseph Taitaẓak's *Porat Yosef*" [in Hebrew], *Sefunot,* 2 (1971–77: 137–85) and Ashkenazi. Messer Leon quoted Boethius's *Consolation* in his commentary to Lamentations, MS. Paris 676, fol. 240b; in *Shevah Nashim,* MS. Parma 1395, fol. 107b; and in *Tehillah le-David* (Constantinople, 1557), p. 83a. My thanks to Professor Hava Tirosh-Rothschild for these references.

[142]Z. Baruchson, *Ha-Sifri'ot ha-Peratiyot shel Yehudei Ẓefon Italya be-shalhei ha-Renasance,* unpublished Ph.D. diss., Bar Ilan University, 1985, p. 282.

parison with the extraordinary popularity of the work and its enormous influence on the course of European literature, its impact on Jews was relatively limited. When Azariah ben R. Joseph ibn Abba Mari translated the *Consolation* in the early fifteenth century, he was clearly sensitive to the negative reaction his translation of the Latin classic might provoke, particularly among rabbis and those "commoners who pretend to be good and pious Jews in a [pseudo] piety of ignorance." Nevertheless, he argued, there was no cogent reason to reject works of gentile wisdom out of hand, for "one should accept the truth from whomever speaks it," as Maimonides did. Moreover, the real value of the book lay in its "enhancement of the belief in God's unity and His providence over all individual beings by way of [His just] rewards and punishments," a sentiment later shared by Yagel as well.[143]

Despite the strong endorsement of Mari, however, no Hebrew author seems to have been as deeply affected by the *Consolation* as Yagel was. His sojourn in the Mantuan jail certainly afforded him an emphathetic perspective from which he could appreciate the plight of Boethius. He could take comfort in the fact that his incarceration was perhaps a metaphor of a more profound detention, that of the soul trapped in the confining space of the material world. When no longer hindered by the corporeal senses, the author's soul would be free to wander the heavens and free to partake of a higher moral instruction and revelation sure to engender a spiritual conversion from despair to optimistic faith.[144] Or, as Girolamo Cardano, Yagel's contemporary, had put it: "In a prison is darkness, filthiness, solitariness, fetters, and all other kinds of miseries. But pray, what is this life, but an imprisonment of a man's mind, much worse than that of the body . . . Boethius wrote nothing better than what he wrote in prison."[145]

The prison motif, however, did not exhaust the value of Boethius's model for Yagel. The entire structure of the *Consolation* from beginning to end was also useful to him. Boethius's work can be divided into three natural divisions: the elegy of the narrator, the gentler remedies offered by his philosophic teacher, and, finally, her stronger remedies.[146] The book opens with an unashamedly emotional lament of the narrator over his tragic fall. Dame Philosophy is then introduced. She gives the narrator a chance to present his case. Accordingly, he justifies his political involvements and

---

[143]Sierra, p. 28.

[144]On the Neoplatonic origin of this metaphor, see P. Courcelle, "Tradition platonicienne et traditions chrétiennes du corps-prison," *Revue des études latines*, 43 (1965): 406–43.

[145]Girolamo Cardano, *His Three Books of Consolation Englished* (London, 1683), bk. 3, chap. 3, p. 147.

[146]I follow here the analysis of Means, *The Consolatio Genre*, pp. 18–30.

refutes the charges against him. She rebukes him for his lack of understanding of the ways of the world and then offers "gentler remedies," soft rhetorical persuasion not intended to cure but merely to strengthen the patient sufficiently so that the proper antidote can be offered at a later stage. Then, when he is sufficiently ready for the strong dosage of medicine, he is fed the most serious philosophical arguments regarding divine providence, free will, and the like. In the end, by silently assenting to his teacher's arguments, the narrator's state of good health is assured.

If it can be safely argued that such a division closely approximates the natural development of the *Consolation,* then the influence of Boethius on the structure of Yagel's work is all the more visible. Yagel too begins his work in despairing lament. His meeting with Lady Philosophy is postponed until later, but the soul of his father provides him his initial support and heavenly instruction. He also encourages Yagel to present his full case, to justify himself to the extent he is able, and to refute the charges against him. The father then introduces him to the "gentler remedies" of the heavenly teachers he meets. He is both entertained and edified by their stories as he regains his spiritual health and is readied for the heavier dosage of the "stronger remedies" to follow. By the time Lady Philosophy appears with her sisters, the wordy telling of his life story is nearly concluded, and he is ready to stand silently before a higher cast of heavenly characters who are more spiritually elevated than his father or any of the other souls he had previously encountered, and capable of leading him to the highest secrets of the heavenly divine palace.

The structural parallels between Boethius's and Yagel's books become even more distinct with the help of Seth Lerer's recent reading of Boethius. For Lerer, the movement of the *Consolation* is as follows: "The prisoner moves from silence, through vacuous oratory, through limited dialectic to philosophical demonstration, and finally to the silence of a reader engaging fully with intellectual texts."[147] As Lerer later puts it, the progression from "lethargic speechlessness" to rhetorical excess is necessary before he can be introduced to philosophical demonstration.[148] And when he speaks, it is "an eloquence without wisdom," for what he considers to be truths are merely "the facts, a bill of particulars in a case of law. This is not the *veritas* of the philosopher, but simply a record of human events . . . [it is written for] public remembrance, and for vindication in the court of men rather than in the eyes of God."[149]

[147]Lerer, *Boethius and Dialogue,* p. 9.
[148]Ibid., p. 96.
[149]Ibid., p. 103.

So too for Yagel. He is initially stunned by the appearance of his father. But when he is coaxed into speech he chatters endlessly as if he were defending himself in a law court. But after his final report to his father in the initial moments of his second journey, he ceases to talk about himself. He is more interested in knowing whether he can expect divine forgiveness, and then he is totally consumed by the teaching of his angelic mentors. What emerges, in Lerer's words, is "a process of turning away from the voices of men to the inner voice of the self or God."[150] Yagel finally reaches the stage Joseph Mazzeo calls "a rhetoric of silence."[151] By the end of his second night, Yagel the prisoner, like Boethius, "grows from a writer of complaint to a reader of moral fable. From his first, insecure autobiographical statements . . . towards a confident reading of mythological poetry."[152]

There is still one final parallel between Boethius and Yagel: the absence of an audience. As Lerer emphasizes, Boethius lived in a world where a literary public was disappearing. He was fully aware of his culture's decline and realized the near futility of his role as the last great philosopher of his generation. Boethius is the paradigmatic intellectual of a decaying world. He reads and writes within the closed confines of his study. There is no longer the possibility of dialogue; only monologue, a lonely voice in a barren wilderness of cultural decline and depravity.[153]

There is, of course, the risk of pushing our analogy too far. Nevertheless, whether Yagel realized it or not, his biography and the social setting of his writing mirrored those of Boethius. Yagel, too, eventually became a lonely man. Endowed with great intellectual gifts and with a broad cultural vision, he gradually found himself more unappreciated and ignored by his community as he grew older. His close relationships with Jewish intellectuals such as Menahem Azariah da Fano and Mordecai Dato are recorded early in his career but not later. Most telling is the fact that his major writings, including his *Gei Ḥizzayon,* were never published in his lifetime and never read by more than a handful of people. Might this suggest more than anything else his ultimate isolation from the cultural world of his Jewish contemporaries? His life work was the final chapter in a history of intellectual bridges between late Renaissance culture and Judaism. With the decline of the Aristotelian cosmos, the rise of Lurianic kabbalah, and the separation of mathematical science from magic and mystical theosophy,

[150]Ibid., p. 49.

[151]J. Mazzeo, "St. Augustine's Rhetoric of Silence," *Journal of the History of Ideas,* 23 (1962): 175–96.

[152]Lerer, *Boethius and Dialogue,* p. 166.

[153]Ibid., pp. 19–29.

Yagel, by the end of his lifetime, would have probably viewed his cultural universe as a decaying one. He, like Boethius, had lost his public readership; so he, too, wrote for himself.

We should emphasize, however, that the parallels between Boethius and Yagel extend only to the structures and social settings of their work. Yagel needed a literary paradigm and he found it in Boethius. But he did not require the Latin philosopher's message; he had his own. He might have agreed with many of the philosophical positions articulated in the *Consolation,* but they were insufficient in themselves. Indeed, they were merely philosophical! True illumination of the soul for Yagel could never be realized through the aid of philosophy alone. Thus, Yagel introduces his readers to the two sisters of Dame Philosophy: one representing the "science" of astrology and one representing the highest divine science of the Torah, identifiable with the Jewish esoteric tradition, the kabbalah.[154] The second sister allows Yagel to offer additional insight in a field he had mastered with great expertise. It is the third sister, however, who is the ultimate guide. She is the only one capable of making the final ascent, of interpreting the most precious divine secrets, and of even correcting her two inferior sisters who are incapable of ascending to the spiritual heights she has reached. In the final analysis, Boethius provided Yagel only a literary framework; he already possessed a theology from a higher authority.

### *Emblematica* and the Teaching of Judaism

When Yagel introduces Lady Philosophy to his readers, he is doing more than merely borrowing Boethius's famous mentor; he is visualizing her. Perhaps the most unique dimension of *Gei Ḥizzayon* is its utilization of iconographic symbols for Jewish instruction. There are no pictures accompanying the text of Yagel's book, but they could have been easily inserted if the author had ever succeeded in printing the work. Even if he had intended to use words alone, it is virtually certain that the visual object or scene he was conveying was still uppermost in his mind. Yagel's portrayals of Lady Philosophy, her two sisters, Fortuna, Cupid, the mother of all languages, as well as the visual symbols in the magical palace at the culmination of his journey, all suggest that he was fully aware of popular emblematic handbooks of his day and clearly knowledgeable in the art of devising symbolic images.

154See below, pp. 223–24.

In the sixteenth and seventeenth centuries, hundreds of emblem collections were printed throughout Europe. They offered a fixed expression and convenient reference for hundreds of concepts—political, moral, and religious. Artists, preachers and political leaders, in addition to a large reading public, found such compendia of visualized ideas to be useful instruments of learning and inspiration. As a moral and didactic medium, the emblem could reduce an intellectual concept to a sensible image, thereby imprinting upon the memory of the beholder a firmer and more lasting impression than that of an abstract idea.[155]

The emblem was usually composed of three parts: *inscriptio, pictura,* and *subscriptio.* The *inscriptio* was a motto or quotation which introduced the emblem. The *pictura* itself could depict one or several objects, persons, events, or actions, sometimes set against imaginary or real backgrounds. Beneath the *pictura* was the *subscriptio,* a prose or verse quotation from some learned source or the words of the emblematist himself.[156] Emblems may have originated from Egyptian hieroglyphics or from the Greek or Latin epigrams; they were embellished over time through the addition of much medieval material, and virtually standardized by the late sixteenth century in Western art, poetry, and rhetoric as decorative symbols, as mnemonic devices, and as an acknowledged part of the proper education of any literate European.

The most famous emblematic handbook was Cesare Ripa's *Iconologia.* First printed in Rome in 1593, it was reprinted in numerous editions in a variety of languages throughout the next two centuries. By the time Ripa published his work, there existed a fairly common agreement on the way in which most basic ideas could be effectively represented in a visual manner and this consensus is incorporated into his illustrations and texts. Whether Yagel actually studied an edition of Ripa or not, he obviously consulted handbooks similar to it and adapted their iconography to suit his own needs. Ripa's portrait of Lady Philosophy accompanied by the full text of Boethius would appear to have been the most probable source of inspiration for Yagel's own description.

[155]On emblem collections of the sixteenth and seventeenth centuries, see Cesare Ripa, *Baroque and Rococo Pictorial Imagery,* introd., trans., and comment. by E. A. Maser (New York, 1971); M. Praz, *Studies in Seventeenth Century Imagery,* 2 vols. (London, 1939; London, 2nd ed., 1964); R. J. Clements, *Picta Poesis: Literary and Humanistic Theory in Renaissance Emblem Books* (Rome, 1960); P. M. Daly, *Literature in the Light of the Emblem: Structural Parallels between the Emblem and Literature in the Sixteenth and Seventeenth Centuries* (Toronto, Buffalo, London, 1979); R. Klein, *Form and Meaning; Essays on the Renaissance and Modern Art,* trans. M. Jay and L. Wieseltier (New York, 1979).

[156]Daly, *Literature in the Light of the Emblem,* pp. 6–8.

As E. H. Gombrich has shown, in his well-known essay on philosophies of symbolism and their bearing on art, two primary traditions of understanding symbolic images were dominant in the sixteenth century: the Aristotelian and the Neoplatonic.[157] The distinction between the two might be expressed by the function each assigned the visual image: the first as representation; the second as symbolization. For the Aristotelians, the image was primarily a pedagogic device to hold the verbal definition of a concept together. Its aim was to sum up and to crystallize the qualities of a virtue previously discussed in moral theology so as to reinforce the virtue's meaning in the most striking and memorable manner possible. The art of assigning an image to represent a virtue or concept was thought to be a kind of rhetorical device, a mere decoration. Growing out of the tradition of medieval didacticism, with its heavy emphasis on the power of language, the image simply "stood for" something else whose essence had been previously conveyed by words. The visual image was simply a useful but dispensable substitute or supplement for concretizing and exemplifying what language had already explained. Ripa's rationalistic handbook of allegorical imagery was fed primarily by this tradition.

For the Neoplatonists, a totally different intellectual orientation prevailed, one that acknowledged the inadequacy of discursive speech and earnestly sought an alternative through the medium of the visual symbol. Symbolism constituted a kind of revelation for them whereby God imparted his ideas to the minds of men. Such a revelation, condensed into a visual symbol, was somehow nearer the realm of absolute truth than one explained by words; it was a more immediate path to knowledge and to ultimate truth. And by contemplating the visible, the beholder was in a position to gain some insight into the invisible. Since an emblem not only instructs but affects us, it is a magically potent instrument, actually imparting something of the power of the spiritual essence which it embodies. It functions as a kind of talisman, a means by which the inhabitants of the divine world visit the earth and assume visible form so as to impart knowledge and supernal power to human beings. The emblem, in this sense, can be subsumed under the category of supernatural omens and celestial spokesmen and be treated as part of the "science" of divination.

Yagel, of course, did not need the Neoplatonic interpretation of the emblem to enlighten him on the significance of celestial spokesmen. He

[157]E. H. Gombrich, "Icones Symbolicae: The Visual Image in Neo-Platonic Thought," *Journal of the Warburg and Courtauld Institutes*, 11 (1948): 163–92; reprinted and revised in *Symbolic Images: Studies in the Art of the Renaissance II* (Edinburgh, 1978).

already was intimately familiar with the traditions of Jewish *maggidim* (celestial spokesmen), angels, and demons, which were thought not only to exist but also to guarantee the only sure pipeline to divine knowledge available to mere human beings.[158] His fascination with all forms of magic sanctioned, so he believed, by his own religious tradition, his ultimate quest to penetrate the secrets of the divine world through kabbalistic theosophy, and his deep ruminations over the ultimate meaning of human existence allowed him to identify fully with the intellectual orientation and spiritual potency of Neoplatonic thought. Thus, his discovery of the Neoplatonic interpretation of the emblem must have come as a kind of revelation to him. The exciting coincidence that the emblems of the "gentiles" could be understood and appreciated in precisely the same manner as those extra-mundane personifications of the Jewish esoteric tradition was not to be taken lightly. It was further proof of the contemporaneity and relevance of Judaism within European culture of the sixteenth century. The visual symbol of the Christian handbook, so thought Yagel, could then be easily appropriated into a Jewish theological text since its actual meaning and function, as interpreted by the Neoplatonists, was fully compatible with traditional Jewish beliefs.

That this was precisely Yagel's intention in *Gei Ḥizzayon* is fully confirmed by his discussions of the emblems he presents. After describing the illustrations of the three majestic sisters with all their accessories at the beginning of the second book, he eventually offers his elaborate explanation of the visual symbols he had portrayed.[159] The three women appear generally as they would appear in any standard handbook. Lady Philosophy is virtually identical with her counterpart in Ripa's text except that the Greek *theta,* standing for theory, and the Greek *pi,* standing for practice in Ripa is replaced by the Hebrew *tav* for *tiḥeyeh* (you will live) and *tav* for *tamut* (you will die), alluding to the mark placed on the foreheads of the men in the prophet Ezekiel's vision.[160] The kind of philosopher Yagel prescribes is best exemplified by Maimonides. The portraits of astrology and divine science generally follow the lines of similar emblems, with the standard paraphernalia of cups and horns brimming with flowers or gold or the like.[161]

Yagel's interpretation of the ripped dress Lady Philosophy is wearing

[158]For literature on *maggidim* in the sixteenth century, see below, pp. 273–74.
[159]See below, pp. 257–72.
[160]See below, p. 257.
[161]See below, pp. 264–72.

generally follows Boethius; it alludes to the neglect and distortion of ancient philosophy by those who taught it after Plato's death. But this standard explanation does not fully satisfy Yagel. In his characteristic way, he inserts a rabbinic text which speaks of the heretics (*minim*) who corrupted the liturgy after the ancient rabbis had established it. He modestly suggests that the rabbis and Boethius were describing the same phenomenon.[162] Furthermore, when explaining the adornments of Lady Astrology, he takes pride in pointing out that the science of astrology originated with Abraham and Moses. Wherever the wisdom of the Jews can be correlated with that of the gentiles, Yagel is quick to point out the correlation.[163]

The most revealing part of his discussion follows the father's elucidation of the adornments of each of the sisters. Yagel then asks: "Tell me whether these women appear as allegories in the manner in which the ancient gentile writers often used them rhetorically in their poems as a mirror of everything . . . or are these three wise women actually noble women . . . or creatures or kinds of forces or spiritual beings appearing in the form of these ladies?"[164] In other words, should Yagel understand these emblems in an Aristotelian or Neoplatonic sense?

The father initially responds: "You asked a hard question and it is difficult for me to say." Nevertheless, his answer is immediately forthcoming and unambiguous. He fully acknowledges that separate spiritual beings exist which influence every science and field. He quotes the *Sefer ha-Aẓamim*, a Jewish magical text, attributed to Abraham ibn Ezra, on the creation of spirits and demons. And he not only mentions the frequent visitation of *maggidim*, but even suggests the procedures of making an incantation, locking the spirit in a sealed room, and visualizing it in the form of a teacher sitting behind a desk. Additional rabbinic testimonies are brought to substantiate the reality of such spiritual beings, including a Talmudic story regarding an evil spirit whom the rabbis were afraid to kill; instead, they removed its eyes.[165]

The last text allows Yagel to establish the correlation he is seeking. "The gentile rhetoricians" who draw the familiar emblem of Cupid with his eye closed probably had in mind the same incident related by the rabbis, argues Yagel. And if this coincidence is not enough to make his case, he is even ready to supply his own testimony based on personal observation of

---

[162] See below, p. 264.
[163] See below, pp. 265–66.
[164] See below, pp. 272–73.
[165] See the text below, pp. 273–76.

several noblemen who actually take magical oaths on a Cupid doll. The conclusion is thus indisputable: "Anyone who thinks that all this happened allegorically, that the ancients drew him [Cupid] this way to teach the hidden secrets of wisdom . . . thinks like any philosophic investigator who has not deepened his thought and investigation. Rather he understands only the books of Aristotle and his associates who only appeared recently, of whom the ancients never imagined."[166] The ancients, of course, include not only Plato and his associates but their ideological allies, the rabbis and kabbalists.

Yagel's employment of emblems for the spiritual edification of his Jewish readers was not without precedent among Christian clerics of the sixteenth and seventeenth centuries. The Jesuits, in particular, had produced an impressive emblematic literature as part of their missionary campaign.[167] According to Mario Praz, the emblems were well-suited to the Jesuits, since their graphic nature coincided with "the Ignatian technique of the application of the senses, to help the imagination picture to itself in the minutest detail circumstances of religious import, the horror of sins and the torments of Hell."[168] Even before the Jesuits, Georgette de Montenay had published the first devotional emblem book in 1571 entitled *Emblèmes ou devises Chrestiennes,* a clear reflection of Calvinist thinking of the previous decade.[169]

In contrast, Yagel's approach in using emblems for Jewish religious education appears to have remained unexploited by later Jewish writers.[170] A peculiar subgenre of literary Hebrew riddles, which first appeared in Italy about 1640 and which were recently explored by the late Dan Pagis, suggests some relation to Yagel's usage. This literary fashion, popular among Italian and Spanish-Jewish circles in Amsterdam for more than two centuries, consisted of an enigmatic picture together with a long and intricate Hebrew poem with concealed Italian or Spanish keywords and other en-

[166]See below, p. 276.

[167]Clements, *Picta Poesis,* pp. 101–4; W. B. Ashworth, Jr., "Catholicism and Early Modern Science," in *God and Nature: Historical Essays on the Encounter between Christianity and Science,* ed. D. C. Lindberg and R. L. Numbers (Berkeley and Los Angeles, 1986), p. 156.

[168]Praz, *Studies,* I:13, quoted in Clements, p. 101.

[169]Georgette de Montenay, *Emblèmes ou devises Chrestiennes,* reprint of 1571 edition, ed. J. Horden (Yorkshire, England, 1970).

[170]Emblems were employed, however, in the design of Jewish marriage contracts in seventeenth- and eighteenth-century Italy. See the interesting illustrations, for example, described by S. Sabar in "The Use and Meaning of Christian Motifs in Illustrations of Jewish Marriage Contracts in Italy," *Journal of Jewish Art,* 10 (1984): 47–63. My thanks to Professor Richard Cohen for the reference.

coding devices. These emblem riddles, which Pagis calls a typically baroque or mannerist product, became the core of riddling contests held at weddings and various other occasions.[171] These picture-riddles appear to have been utilized strictly for entertainment rather than for the more spiritual purpose Yagel had in mind. Yagel appears to have been the only Jew to enlist the literature of emblems in the cause of communicating the higher truths of the kabbalah.

## The Discourse of the Mother of All Languages

In addition to the emblems of the three sisters, I have mentioned earlier another feminine figure who appears prominently in the second part of *Gei Hizzayon*. She is the "science of language who speaks correctly in every one of the seventy languages."[172] Her debut before Yagel and his father at the summit of the mountain, on the final leg of their journey, is spectacularly conceived. Dressed in black, with purplish hair, the noble woman projects a most handsome appearance. Flowing from her two breasts is a stream of fresh water which feeds a mighty river. The river spawns a verdant valley teeming with pleasant trees and fragrant flowers, where children sip from its sweet waters along its banks. The image appears to be borrowed from the standard depiction of Grammatica as a woman with healthy breasts from which sweet milk flows,[173] but it is certainly embellished in Yagel's picturesque scenario.

The image affords Yagel the opportunity to present one of the longer discourses in his entire book, on the origin and history of language and, particularly, on the centrality and singularity of Hebrew. Yagel's contribution to the subject emerges in a period of heightened linguistic consciousness among Christians and Jews alike. The dominant views on language were based on long-held assumptions originating in the Bible and in classical traditions. Almost all students of language in the sixteenth century

---

[171]D. Pagis, *Al Sod Ḥatum* (Jerusalem, 1985); idem, "Baroque Trends in Italian Hebrew Poetry as Reflected in an Unknown Genre," *Italia Judaica II* (Rome, 1986), pp. 263–77.

[172]See below, pp. 297–313.

[173]See, for example, Cesare Ripa, *Della Novissima Iconologia* (Padua, 1625), p. 284: "et dalle mammele versera molto latte . . . Il latte, che gl'esce dalle mammelle, significa, che la dolcezza della scienza esce dal petto, et dalle viscere della Grammatica." Cf. also the image of the font of seventy languages flowing from the forehead of a man, found in the writing of Abraham Abulafia, the thirteenth-century Jewish mystic (described by M. Idel, *The Mystical Experience in Abraham Abulafia* [Albany, 1988], p. 97).

assumed that biblical Hebrew was the original tongue of humanity. It was considered to be God's language, a perfect means of communication where words precisely mirrored the things they represented. God's confounding the tongues at Babel precipitated a linguistic crisis, one paralleling the fall of man from God's grace. From one language emerged many, seventy or seventy-two in number. No language, even Hebrew, could claim any longer the privileged status of divinity and universality that the biblical tongue had once held.[174]

The primary goal of sixteenth- and seventeenth-century linguistic theory was to search for the roots of the *lingua humana* among the large number of inferior variants and dialects that Western culture had inherited from the condition engendered by Babel. The effort to recover the divine tongue was motivated by a larger epistemological and spiritual preoccupation, a nostalgic yearning to rediscover that original lost human state of unity, to be redeemed from a world of divisiveness, and to return to the blissful state at the moment of creation.[175]

If words once represented things, then the rediscovery of that original language was the key to unlocking the secrets of the universe. Comparative linguistics thus emerged as an effort to discover how the divine Hebrew tongue was scattered among so many dialects and languages. By identifying

[174]On sixteenth- and seventeenth-century views of language, and Hebrew in particular, see D. F. Lach, *Asia in the Making of Europe* (Chicago and London, 1977), vol. 2, bk. 3, chap. 11, especially pp. 501–10; D. C. Allen, "Some Theories of the Growth and Origin of Language in Milton's Age," *Philological Quarterly*, 28 (1949): 5–16; C. G. Dubois, *Mythe et langage au seizième siècle* (Bordeaux, 1970); P. Cornelius, *Languages in Seventeenth and Early Eighteenth Century Imaginary Voyages* (Geneva, 1965); *The Fairest Flower: The Emergence of Linguistic National Consciousness in Renaissance Europe*, International Conference of the Center for Medieval and Renaissance Studies, UCLA, 12–13 December 1983 (Florence, 1985); A. Borst, *Der Turmbau von Babel*, 4 vols. in 6 (Stuttgart, 1957–63), III, 1; D. S. Katz, "The Language of Adam in Seventeenth Century England," in *History and Imagination: Essays in Honor of H. P. Trevor-Roper*, ed. H. Lloyd Jones et al. (London, 1981), pp. 132–45; W. K. Percival, "The Reception of Hebrew in Sixteenth-Century Europe: The Impact of the Cabbala," *Historiographia Linguistica*, 11 (1984): 21–38. On earlier Jewish views of the Hebrew language, see A. S. Halkin, "The Medieval Jewish Attitude Toward Hebrew," *Biblical and Other Studies*, ed. A. Altmann (Cambridge, Mass., 1963), pp. 233–48. See also A. Schrieber, "Das Problem des Ursprung der Sprache in Jüdische Schriften," *Magyar Zsido Szemk*, 59 (1937): 334–49; S. Rosenberg, "Logic and Ontology in Fourteenth Century Jewish Philosophy" (in Hebrew), unpublished Ph.D. diss., Hebrew University, Jerusalem, 1974, pp. 164–67, 282–84; I. Twersky, *Introduction to the Code of Maimonides* (New Haven and London, 1980), p. 324, n. 1; and especially, M. Idel, *Language, Torah, and Hermeneutics in Abraham Abulafia* (Albany, 1988), chap. 1, for the views of Abulafia and Yohanan Alemanno. My thanks to Professor Idel for allowing me to consult the galleys of his new book.

[175]See especially Dubois, *Mythe et langage*, pp. 19–40.

the equivalencies between one language and another, the linguist attempted to recover that elusive unity presently hiding its face. The method of collecting alphabets, especially the more exotic ones, comparing etymologies, and identifying their Hebrew derivatives was widely employed by such Christian scholars as Guillaume Postel, Conrad Gesner, Claude Duret, Joseph Scaliger, and Isaac Casaubon, and by such Jewish scholars as Azariah de' Rossi, David Provenzali, Elijah Melli, Judah Moscato, and Abraham Portaleone.[176]

The biblical view competed with that of Aristotle and other later linguists who stressed the natural evolution of languages. According to this position, words were mere conventions for expressing things. Language could be subjected to a logical analysis stressing its regularities of structure, its basic grammar. This demystifying of language reduced its value to one of essential social communication. The myth of Babel, with its stress on the supernatural origin of language, was a theological assumption of no import for language study.[177]

Despite this more utilitarian approach toward linguistics, the biblical view was not easily dislodged. Hardly anyone questioned the assumption that Hebrew was once the mother language by which God created the universe. What was challenged, however, was the assumption that Adam actually spoke the same language as contemporary Jews, and that Jews could rightfully claim that they were still the guardians of the divine tongue of creation. A growing number of Christian scholars argued that Hebrew eventually lost its sacred character and privileged status during the Babylonian captivity. When the Jews mingled with their captors, primitive Hebrew was eventually lost as the Jews gradually forgot their ancestral language. Consequently, Ezra was obliged to translate the Bible into new characters upon the return of the Jews to their homeland. From that point on, these new characters become the basis of the Jewish language of the Diaspora. The script now in use among the Jews is not identical to its ancient Hebrew prototype. And if the Jews are no longer the heirs of the original divine tongue, then it might be located among some other peoples,

[176]On the Christian preoccupation with comparative linguistics, see especially D. C. Allen, "Theories of Language," pp. 8–9; M. T. Hodgen, *Early Anthropology in the Sixteenth and Seventeenth Centuries* (Philadelphia, 1964), pp. 304–6. For de' Rossi, see his *Me'or Einayim* (Vilna, 1864–66), chap. 57, pp. 453–66. He refers to David Provenzali's work *Dor ha-Pelagah* (no longer extant) on p. 456. Melli's work is referred to by Yagel below, p. 310. Moscato treats the subject in his commentary *Kol Yehudah* to Judah ha-Levi's *Kuzari*, 2: 68; and Abraham Portaleone in his *Shilte ha-Gibborim* (Mantua, 1512), pp. 8a–12b.

[177]See especially Lach, *Asia in the Making*, pp. 502–3; Dubois, *Mythe et langage*, pp. 97–110; and compare the earlier view of Maimonides in Twersky, *Introduction to the Code*, p. 324.

or perhaps any search for that first language is in vain. The best one can hope for is some artificial scheme of a universal language "scientifically" reconstructed by contemporary linguists.[178]

Yagel's treatise on language emerges in the context of these contemporary discussions, and particularly as a response to the argument of Hebrew's discontinuity with its primitive counterpart. His discussion also reveals a keen awareness of the significance of language in general within sixteenth-century Christian and Jewish culture. It is motivated by a desire to defend the chosen status of contemporary Hebrew, that cultivated by his coreligionists, and to demonstrate its direct linkage with the divine tongue spoken at Creation. But it is also related to his intrinsic interest in all languages, not only Hebrew, as part of the larger quest he shared with other physicians and naturalists of his day to discover signs of the divine unity in all corners of creation, in words as well as in things.[179]

Yagel is heavily indebted to his contemporary, Azariah de' Rossi, whose more lengthy discussion of the antiquity of the Hebrew language and its script appeared several years earlier. Yagel regularly borrows from de' Rossi's discussion without slavishly copying from it. His treatment of the antiquity and divine status of Hebrew, interspersed generously with rabbinic citations, draws heavily from de' Rossi.[180] Nevertheless, Yagel diverges from his primary source in three critical ways.

First, Yagel does not confine himself to a discussion of Hebrew. As he announces from the beginning, the emblem of the nursing mother represents the "science of all languages," not Hebrew alone. He is particularly interested in discussing the origin of Greek and Latin. In both cases, his primary source is Isadore of Seville's *Etymologiarum,* a source still popular among contemporary writers and well known to de' Rossi, who also quotes from it in another context.[181] In contrast to his discussion of Hebrew, Yagel stresses the social context of Latin and other languages. Their intrinsic beauty and order are not bestowed by divine fiat but through the artificial imposition of grammatical rules by learned men and by the establishment of exceptional standards of great writing. He also stresses the role political leaders play in consciously resolving to upgrade the quality of their language and culture by providing the proper social and educational conditions for its refinement. Yagel not only recognizes the rich traditions of the

---

[178]Cornelius, *Languages in Imaginary Voyages,* pp. 15–18; J. Knowlson, *Universal Language Schemes in England and France 1600–1800* (Toronto and Buffalo, 1975).

[179]On the collusion of linguists and doctors, see Dubois, *Mythe et langage,* p. 141.

[180]Specific references to Yagel's borrowings are found in the notes below, pp. 299–311.

[181]See the text and notes below, pp. 304–9.

Latin language; he is also sensitive to the extraordinary strides vernacular Italian had made in his day, "until it now has become as beautiful and exalted as Latin."[182] He is equally forthcoming in his praise of Arabic, Spanish, and German, emphasizing in each case the positive role governments have played in the elevation of their respective languages from a previous state of corruption and neglect. Yagel's genuine interest and appreciation of the beauty and intrinsic worth of languages other than his own plainly suggests his pleasurable exposure to the primary literatures of Western culture.

Second, while sharing the same point of view as de' Rossi, Yagel develops his own arguments and provides his own examples in promoting the uniqueness of the Hebrew language. As he does elsewhere, in the case of language, he strongly injects astrological causation into his discussion. Hebrew's uniqueness, he argues, is attributable to the special dosage of supernal power with which it is bestowed. He also provides an original touch with his enthusiastic endorsement of rabbinic Hebrew, its continuity with that of the Bible, and its sheer splendor and perfection. He especially waxes eloquent over the beauty of the Hebrew prose Judah the Patriarch employed in the writing of the Mishnah.[183] Like de' Rossi, he is fascinated by comparative philology, particularly in devising supposed Hebrew origins for Italian words, but offers his own list independent of that used by de' Rossi.

Finally, Yagel concludes his remarks with an original discourse on the mystical role of the Hebrew language. Freely quoting from *Sefer ha-Zohar*, he underscores the eternality of Hebrew, the perfection derived from its enunciation, and the potential dialogue with the hosts of Heaven engendered by communicating in the holy tongue.[184] The climactic peroration of his eloquent spokeswoman poignantly reminds his reader of the mysterious setting in which the entire oration began. The symmetry between the opening and closing of the woman's speech is thus artistically realized.

### The Underlying Message of *Gei Ḥizzayon*

Having established how Yagel appropriated the genres of the novella, the *consolatio,* and the *emblematica* for the purpose of teaching his religious

[182]See below, p. 306. On the *questione della lingua,* see R. A. Hall, *The Italian "Questione della lingua": An Interpretative Essay* (Chapel Hill, 1942); B. Migliorini, "La questione della lingua," in *Problemi ed orientamenti critici di lingua e di letteratura italiana,* ed. A. Momigliano (Milan, 1949).

[183]See below, p. 307; cf. Judah ha-Levi, *Sefer ha-Kuzari,* 3: 67.

[184]See the text below with specific citations, pp. 311–13.

message, we are finally left with the task of delineating that message. When
Yagel, in the company of his father's soul, is escorted into the heavenly
palace at the summit of the holy mountain, he has reached not only the
culmination of his journey but the crowning moment of spiritual enlightenment. As we have seen, his final destination is the majestic room of four
walls, each painted with a very special emblem: one, the figure of man, one,
the image of the Tree of Life, one, unmentioned, and one translucent wall
reflecting the images of the other three and signifying the world to come.
Here the eldest sister instructs him in "the chapter headings" of the intention of the artist who designed the room. She is most explicit in first
announcing the essence of this instruction:

> Come with me so that I might show you the concatenation of the
> worlds and their interconnection in my treasure house, and how man
> is like the example of this great building. He is fitting and ready with
> respect to his form to receive a good emanation of all the worlds, so
> long as he acknowledges that his ways are according to the Torah,
> through which God instructs him. In this manner, he will become a
> living creature through his own resources, loved above and pleasing
> below, and greater than the ministering angels. During his lifetime,
> when he is still imprisoned in the tresses of matter, he will behold God
> while still in his flesh. . . . Likewise, at his death, his mind, spirit, and
> soul will ascend . . . to cling to eternal life.[185]

The treasure house appears to represent a kind of magical palace, a
talismanic building which enables those in it to receive the divine emanation it attracts. The fact that man "is like the example of this great building,"
capable of receiving an emanation of all the worlds so that he will be greater
than the angels and capable of beholding God while "still in his flesh,"
suggests as well the magical capacity of certain human beings who have
reached this height of illumination through the guidance of the Torah. A
Jew, equipped with the higher wisdom of the kabbalah, is capable of
attaining the status of a magical operator, a divine magus. Stated differently, when a person gazes at the image of the "treasure house," he is
reminded of his own innate ability to bring down the divine effluvia
through the agency of kabbalistic sapience. For he "is like the example of
this great building," that is, the building symbolizes for him the unique

[185]See below, p. 314.

power available to him through the spiritual resources of the Jewish esoteric tradition.[186]

That the very first idea the woman articulates represents the secret of "the concatenation of the worlds and their interconnection" underscores the primary significance of this concept for Yagel. Moreover, the elaborate discussion of the *sefirot* that immediately follows, which demonstrates that every process in the highest level of creation (that level known only to the kabbalists) has its analogue in the lowest levels as well—in the heavens, in the material world, and even in the various parts of the human body— reinforces the same principle. As Yagel's entire scientific corpus manifestly reveals, Yagel shared the passion of many sixteenth-century Christian naturalists for demonstrating the interconnectedness of all knowledge. He enthusiastically searched for signs in nature to correlate with other signs in order to classify, integrate, and thus reaffirm the essential divine unity. Yagel's tour de force of correlative speculation in his final discourse on the *sefirot,* his triadic linking of naturalistic, astrological, and kabbalistic knowledge, constitutes the ultimate realization of that quest.[187]

The ideal of interconnectedness, however, also held specific Jewish implications for Yagel. His intellectual task, as he might have defined it, was to integrate Jewish knowledge with the sources of other traditions and other disciplines. By harmonizing Jewish and non-Jewish learning, whether on the basis of observation of the physical world or on the basis of books, no matter how alien and dissimilar the association might appear, he would narrow the cultural distance separating Judaism from Western civilization. By demonstrating that the ideas and cultural signatures of his own tradition resembled those in the larger world of nature and in European culture, he hoped to gain cultural respect and social acceptance for himself and for his oft-beleaguered community.

The insights of the Jewish tradition, especially its esoteric ones, were in no way inferior to those of other cultural legacies, including those of Christianity; on the contrary, they were plainly superior. Jews long before had loudly proclaimed the superiority of their own unadulterated traditions; but especially in Yagel's era, such boastful claims may have fallen on attentive ears. The more the Jew could assemble his own signs, publicize them, and reveal their relatedness with other signs, the more acceptable he

---

[186]On Yagel's awareness of Guilio Camillo's magical *theatro* and his other magical preoccupations, see Ruderman, *Kabbalah, Magic, and Science,* chap. 7.

[187]This theme in Yagel's writing is treated more fully in Ruderman, *Kabbalah, Magic, and Science.*

imagined Judaism might be rendered in a larger intellectual and more cosmopolitan community. Indeed, so Yagel believed, only the Jews held the keys to unlocking the mysteries of God's creation; only through the kabbalah could a person become a true magus, privileged to comprehend and to control the most powerful forces of the cosmos. Despite all the correlations the naturalist and astrologer could establish, each one's knowledge was insufficient without that of the kabbalist. In Yagel's eyes, the kabbalah, as the most elevated occult philosophy, was finally to receive the status to which it was entitled: the ultimate guide and teacher of all mankind.

The theme of interconnectedness serves an additional function in Yagel's narrative. It provides an answer, the only possible answer for Yagel, to the problem of theodicy and the suffering of the righteous. Knowledge is useless if it cannot offer some comfort, some reassurance about the precariousness, continual anguish, and seeming absurdity of human experience. If the highest form of creation is intimately linked to the lowest, if God is intimately involved with each and every creature, no matter how insignificant, there is hope that life has value and that man is not solely left to his own resources. When human beings comprehend the secret of the interconnectedness of all the worlds, they will not despair; they will take comfort in the fact that the universe is indeed purposeful and sympathetic to creative human endeavor. As it was for Boethius, such knowledge is Yagel's key to redemption.

Related to the theme of the meaning of suffering and divine justice is Yagel's curious preoccupation with the notion of transmigration of souls, a theme he treats extensively both in *Gei Ḥizzayon* and in his later writings. For Yagel, in contrast to other contemporary Jews, transmigration was a principal doctrine of Judaism. He was even willing to allow for the transmigration of human souls into animal bodies, on the condition that the concept was not taken literally but was seen only as the acquired animal characteristics that were observable in the visage of human beings, or as a temporary purgation of limited duration in which no contamination of the sinful soul by the animal body occurred. Yagel's carefully constructed view was informed by a variety of sources—Neoplatonic, kabbalistic, naturalistic, and even Catholic.[188] Like so many other profound secrets of God's creation, Yagel considered the doctrine of metempsychosis to be part of that sanctified body of knowledge available exclusively to the initiate in kabbalistic theosophy and true "science." Since life was not futile, though it

[188]For a full discussion of these sources, see Ruderman, *Kabbalah, Magic, and Science,* chap. 8.

often seemed to be, human suffering must represent a form of purgation; and since divine justice permeates the universe, there must exist a life beyond earthly existence. Thus the notion of the transmigration of souls seemed neither distasteful nor inappropriate in a dark physical and moral universe which desperately required the reassurance of God's supreme justice.

The sublime and compelling image of the dream palace as the culmination of Yagel's heavenly odyssey underscores the author's sober reaffirmation of life and his irrepressible optimism in facing the future. Ultimately, his argument maintained that there was more to human experience than the stark reality he had graphically depicted. Earthly existence was surely painful and, though he had temporarily left it behind, he could not escape from it. In that real world, good men such as Yagel constantly struggle to make ends meet. Despite their most earnest efforts, they are often deceived and cheated by their closest associates. They are also brutalized by physical illness and disease, by political unrest, and by religious discrimination. In that world, Jews often earn their living as usurers despite the despicable nature of the profession.[189] And in that world, a scholar and physician can suffer intolerable indignities despite the nobility of his calling.

Only in an imaginary world are women treated as celestial princesses, as oracles of divine wisdom clothed in radiant splendor. In the real world, women have a different function: to serve faithfully and diligently the men they love. They are taught to stay at home, to keep the house clean, to obey their father's and husband's whims and wills, to suckle their young, and never to involve themselves in "the ways of the world" without the consent and advice of men.[190] Women who deviate from their "proper station," like the girl who attempted to redeem her lover and subsequently ruined her life,[191] and like the indecisive and unreliable Madame Rina, bring ruin to themselves and to all who come in contact with them. In the usual network of social relationships in which Yagel functioned, women fulfill themselves by living vicariously through the lives of their male partners. Only in the fantasy of the supernal palace are women's roles inverted, whereby they teach men the highest truths of the Torah.

Nevertheless, the radiance of the heavenly palace fortifies the author and his readers with the comforting reassurance that beyond the plane of one's physical existence lies a deeper and more substantial reality. Beyond

[189]See Yagel's specific comments on the evils of usury below, pp. 81–83.
[190]Yagel's portrait of the ideal woman is found in his *Eshet Ḥayil* and in the story of the virtuous woman below, pp. 184–89.
[191]See below, pp. 189–93.

the misery of an unsuccessful business practice lies the spiritual delight of books and scholarship. Beyond the physical misery of this mundane world is the spiritual exultation of the next. Beyond the shabby way men and women relate to each other in ordinary life lies the promise of what might transpire in an extraordinary life. Beyond the precarious status of a beleaguered community is its potential glory as the spiritual mentor of Western civilization. A Jew and his dreams; a human document of despondent wretchedness and soaring transcendence.

## A Final Reflection: *Gei Ḥizzayon* and the Baroque Sensibility

To readers of seventeenth-century literature, our characterization of Abraham Yagel's work might certainly recall a number of prominent themes of the so-called baroque style of literature and art. Any hesitation in employing the term to describe *Gei Ḥizzayon* might be justified in view of the term's ambiguous nature and the wide range of meanings assigned to it by literary and art historians.[192] One might be even more reluctant to invoke such a general cultural category to describe Jewish literature of the period simply because the term "baroque" has almost never been associated with the history of Jewish culture.[193] Indeed, only recently have Jewish historians attempted to consider the applicability of such related categories as "Renaissance"[194] or "early modern"[195] for demarcating distinctive cultural epochs in Jewish history.

[192]The literature on the baroque mentality is enormous. On the history of the term in scholarship prior to 1946, see R. Wellek, "The Concept of Baroque in Literary Scholarship," *Journal of Aesthetics and Art Criticism,* 5 (1946–47): 77–109, reprinted with a postscript in *Concepts of Criticism* (New Haven and London, 1963), pp. 69–127. Some recent works which proved particularly helpful to me in conceptualizing this section include: J. R. Martin, *Baroque* (New York, 1977); F. J. Warnke, *Versions of Baroque: European Literature in the Seventeenth Century* (New Haven and London, 1972); M. J. Hanak, "The Emergence of Baroque Mentality and Its Cultural Impact on Western Europe after 1550," *Journal of Aesthetics and Art Criticism,* 28 (1970): 315–26; C. Calcaterra, "Il problema del Barocco," in *Problemi ed orientamenti critici di lingua e di letteratura italiana,* ed. A. Momigliano, vol. 3 (Milan, 1949), pp. 405–501; W. Sypher, *Four Stages of Renaissance Style: Transformations in Art and Literature 1400–1700* (Garden City, N.Y., 1956); and P. N. Skrine, *The Baroque: Literature and Culture in Seventeenth Century Europe* (New York, 1978).

[193]The one major exception is the interesting essay of G. Sermoneta, "Aspetti del pensiero moderno nell'Ebraismo tra Rinascimento e eta barocca," *Italia Judaica II: Gli ebrei in Italia tra Rinascimento e eta barocca* (Rome, 1986), pp. 17–35. However, neither Sermoneta nor any other writer in the volume defines precisely what he means by the term "baroque" in relation to Jewish culture.

[194]See, for example, D. Ruderman, "The Italian Renaissance and Jewish Thought," *Renaissance Humanism: Foundations and Forms,* ed. A. Rabil, Jr., 3 vols. (Philadelphia, 1987), 1: 382–433.

[195]See, for example, J. Israel, *European Jewry in the Age of Mercantilism 1550–1750* (Oxford, 1985).

Nevertheless, Yagel's carefully conceived literary work, although written in Hebrew and addressed particularly to Jewish concerns, has much in common with some of the more important features of the baroque style. To the extent that such a style permeated the literary and artistic consciousness of the period roughly spanning from the late sixteenth to the mideighteenth centuries, it provides a useful index to the structure of that consciousness and to the prevailing attitude toward experience among writers and artists of the European world. If Yagel's book can meaningfully be associated with the baroque style, it would provide a striking illustration of a shared and deeply felt Jewish identification with some of the larger cultural sensibilities of the age.

Most art and literary historians have long discarded the notion originally articulated by Jacob Burckhardt that the baroque constituted nothing more than a particular style that revealed the decadence of the High Renaissance, an art that was extravagant, heavily ornate, and bombastic.[196] Rather, it has been more recently designated as a cluster of more or less related styles, which in its earlier phases contains significant survivals of the styles of a previous period, namely the Renaissance, and which in its later phases anticipates the later era of Neoclassicism.[197] Baroque writers and artists were particularly fascinated by the relationship between appearance and reality. The naturalism and visual realism of the Renaissance era was now qualified by a fundamentally metaphysical view of the world. A crisis of confidence in the precise relationship between the visible and ineffable realities informs the baroque mentality, a turning away from the world of appearances in search of a deeper truth within the inner life. The baroque artist is obsessed with the contradictory nature of human experience. He feels isolated by the deceptive appearance of the material world, plagued with metaphysical doubt, profoundly convinced that life is no more than a dream, a stage on which masked actors conceal the real truth, and that a transcendent reality must lie beyond the immediate. He holds the conviction that ultimate meaning in life is not gained in the world of senses, in the vanity of human desires and aspirations, but in the liberation of the self by embracing the overarching unity of the cosmos.

Allegory is essential to the baroque mood. Baroque writing and painting often contain allegorical and emblematic meanings. Familiar objects of visible reality are to be viewed as emblems of a higher, invisible, and more

[196]His view is discussed by H. Woelfflin, *Renaissance und Barock* (Munich, 1888), p. 10, and by Wellek, p. 77.
[197]See especially Warnke, p. 1.

penetrating reality. Allegory underscores the baroque consciousness of the coexistence of two planes of existence—the worldly and transitory, the celestial and eternal.

Beyond the glitter and ornamentation of this earthly existence, thus, lies a darker and more introspective side to the baroque mentality: a disillusionment with human achievement, a pessimistic mood of withdrawal, of disenchantment and brooding anxiety, a concerted effort to escape in order to deflect one's gaze from the vicissitudes of earthly existence. Only in moments of intense passionate experience, in losing oneself in mystical union, and in the divine revelation of spiritual values can the artist gain the ultimate resolution of the contradictions of his mundane life and the final consolation for his tortured soul.

Yagel's narrative, with its introspective and searching features, its obsession with the apparent contradiction between external appearance and inner reality, its allegorical mode, and its depiction of the author's deeply felt need to escape to a higher metaphysical plane of existence, patently reflects the baroque sensibility. *Gei Ḥizzayon* is a baroque vision in a kabbalistic key. It is a work anchored in a specific Jewish reality but which displays a close affinity to the mood and literary style of baroque culture, especially that of post-Tridentine Catholicism, and to the mind-set of Jesuit Counter-Reformist writing and art.[198]

Ironically, *Gei Ḥizzayon* is also a product of the Counter-Reformation in another, more profound sense. One of the more negative effects of Catholic reform was the erection of the ghetto system throughout the Italian Jewish communities at the end of the sixteenth and early seventeenth centuries. For Jews, the baroque sense of isolation and internalization was thus reinforced in a most tangible way by those ghetto walls—by that sense of abrupt closure and demarcation from the cultural and material world of their Christian contemporaries.[199] *Gei Ḥizzayon* is the vision of a Jew, writing in the age of the ghetto, who shares with baroque writers a similar attitude toward the dual reality of human existence but who perceives that reality from a particular Jewish focus. As a Jew living in late sixteenth-

---

[198]See especially, R. Wittkower and I. B. Jaffe, eds., *Baroque Art: The Jesuit Contribution* (New York, 1972).

[199]For a recent imaginative discussion of the impact of the ghetto on Jewish culture, see R. Bonfil, "Change in Cultural Patterns of Jewish Society in Crisis: The Case of Italian Jewry at the Close of the Sixteenth Century," *Jewish History*, forthcoming, and see also the cogent remarks of B. Ravid in his excursus, "The Venetian Ghetto in Historical Perspective," in *The Autobiography of a Seventeenth-Century Venetian Rabbi*, pp. 279–83.

century Italy, Yagel could appreciate better than any Christian the stark contrast between the alienation of his shabby, putrid, and confining ghetto dwelling and the exhilaration of the radiant, dazzling, and spacious kabbalistic palace of his spiritual odyssey. In this sense, Yagel's Hebrew composition vividly shows a most peculiar face of the baroque mentality.

## An English Translation of *Gei Ḥizzayon*

There are only two extant manuscripts of *Gei Ḥizzayon:* one located at the Hebrew Union College in Cincinnati and the other at the British Museum in London.[200] The Cincinnati manuscript consists of 94 leaves in an Italian cursive script of the sixteenth century. It is written in the same handwriting as Yagel's other works, *Beit Ya'ar ha-Levanon, Be'er Sheva,* and his collection of letters and other notices entitled *Bat Rabim,* which are all clearly in the hand of their author. The leaves of the title page, the indexes, and the first page of the text are missing, but the rest of the manuscript is intact and generally legible.

The British Museum manuscript was written close to the date of the original manuscript since it bears a censor's mark of 1600.[201] The copyist obviously considered the autobiographical sections to be unnecessary and omitted them. The manuscript consists of 128 leaves, also in an Italian cursive script of the sixteenth century, but not written by Yagel. The manuscript includes an index of 168 sections of Part II, followed by an index of 100 sections of Part I.[202] The manuscript was owned by the great nineteenth-century book collector, Joseph Almanzi, who inspected the work in 1846.[203]

Alexander Mani published the first part of *Gei Ḥizzayon* in Alexandria, Egypt, in 1880. He utilized a manuscript in the private collection of Rabbi Judah Bibas in Hebron, which subsequently disappeared from sight.[204] However, a comparison of the printed text with the Cincinnati manuscript yields the obvious conclusion that the latter is identical with the manuscript

[200]MS. Cincinnati Hebrew Union College–Jewish Institute of Religion 743 and MS. London British Museum 875, add. 26,963 (G. M. Margoliouth, *Catalogue of the Hebrew and Samaritan Manuscripts in the British Museum,* 4 vols. [London, 1965], 3, p. 170).

[201]On fol. 128b.

[202]These indexes were apparently included in the Cincinnati manuscript as well (although they are now missing), since in the printed edition of Mani, based on the Cincinnati manuscript, the editor included the first index for Part I.

[203]On Almanzi and his library, see *EJ,* 2: 660–61.

[204]On Judah Bibas, see *EJ,* 4: 813; cf. Busi, "Sulla *Ge Ḥizzayon,*" p. 29, n. 11.

Mani used in his edition. The manuscript contains a number of marginal comments which are duly noted in Mani's edition. Because of the absence of its initial leaves, the Cincinnati manuscript was never properly identified. The identification is now certain.

This new edition of Abraham Yagel's work is based on Mani's edition and the Cincinnati manuscript. Where Mani's reading is questionable, I have consulted the Cincinnati manuscript. For the second part of the book, I have relied exclusively on the Cincinnati manuscript, using the London manuscript to check any illegible or unclear words. I have translated the entire text of *Gei Ḥizzayon* with the exception of a few marginal comments in the second half which were partially illegible or which contained extraneous material and clearly interrupted the flow of the text.[205] I have also introduced my own subtitles into the text to aid the reader of this relatively long work. Although a more detailed index of both parts appears in the original manuscript, its subdivisions are too numerous and wordy to be helpful to the modern reader. While I have indicated these original divisions in the text by bracketed numbers, inclusion of their titles would have confused and distracted rather than aided in reading the text.

I have attempted to identify all biblical, rabbinic, and medieval Hebrew and other sources in my notes. Since Yagel, in the style of sixteenth-century Hebrew, often uses biblical and rabbinic idioms for his own self-expression, I have indicated their sources whenever possible. I have consulted the new Jewish Publication Society *Tanakh* for all biblical translations but have adapted them when necessary to conform to the apparent meaning Yagel assigned them. I also consulted the translations of the Babylonian Talmud and *Midrash Rabbah* published by the Soncino Press in adapting my own translations of Yagel's rabbinic sources. I have used the notes for further clarification, for discussion of issues not included in the introduction, and for additional bibliographical references related to the text. I have rendered a literal translation of the Hebrew text, adapting the text slightly in places to produce a more fluid and lucid English style. Where it was necessary to clarify a word or expression, or to fill in a cryptic phrase, I have indicated my addition by bracketing. Clauses occasionally marked off by parentheses belong to the original text; they are set off from the rest of the sentence in order to render as faithfully as possible a complex Hebrew syntax into English.

---

[205]These omissions are fully identified in the notes below. I also hope to publish a separate volume of the Hebrew text in the near future.

I am perhaps more aware than anyone else of my inadequacies in translating and annotating such a long and complex Hebrew text. My only hope is that I have allowed Yagel's work to be understood and appreciated by the English reader. Yagel never enjoyed the privilege of a large readership for *Gei Ḥizzayon*. It is my hope, some four hundred years later, that this extraordinary product of the symbiotic relationship between Italian and Jewish culture of the late sixteenth century will now find that readership it so fittingly deserves.

# 2. *A Valley of Vision*,[1]
# Part I: The First Night

## The Initial Appearance of the Soul of Yagel's Father

[1] In a dream, in a night vision, while [I was] asleep upon [my] bed during my imprisonment, a voice called in my ears.[2] The voice was the voice of Jacob,[3] like the voice of my father, may his memory be blessed. He appeared to me and said:[4] "What are you doing here and who are you to be here?[5] Are you really my son Abraham?"

I was stunned by the sound of the call[6] and almost lost my breath. I covered my face with the cloak that I wore, since I was afraid to look in any direction. But when he saw that I was frightened, stricken with terror,[7] he gave me strength by speaking to me in the pleasant voice in which he had spoken when he was living in this world: "Don't be afraid, Abraham, my

---

[1]The expression is from Isaiah 22:1. The scene of Isaiah's vision is Jerusalem, which is described here as a valley, a reflection of the city's topography as a valley surrounded by hills. The phrase, as used by Yagel for the title of his work, perhaps suggests the contrast between looking up at a vision and looking down, i.e., into an abyss; the latter vision is one of profundity and extraordinary depth.

[2]The line is constructed from a string of biblical phrases, included Job 33:15, Genesis 42:17, and 1 Samuel 15:14. The line also contains an additional phrase from Genesis 40:16: "In my dream, similarly," which I have not translated because of the redundancy.

[3]This phrase from Genesis 27:21 has engendered confusion among scholars who assumed that Abraham's father was named Jacob (and not Hananiah) on the basis of the line. J. Dan, for example, *EJ* 9:1267, concluded that the author of this work and the author of the other writings of Abraham Yagel (where Yagel refers to his father as Hananiah) might not be the same person. Such a conclusion is totally unfounded since Yagel refers to *A Valley of Vision* in his other writings. The phrase "the voice of Jacob" does not refer to the name of the author's father.

[4]Literally, "like the voice of Abraham's father. . . . He appeared to Abraham and said to him. . . ."

[5]Cf. Judges 18:3.

[6]See Jeremiah 14:9.

[7]See 2 Samuel 1:9.

son, for I am your father, the one who made you,[1] and I will not hurt you. A father's compassion for his son endures forever.[2] But, be silent and listen.[3] I will question you and you will inform me."

Upon hearing these words, I lifted my eyes and saw his image before me. I raised my voice and cried out in the bitterness of my soul and was overcome with emotion.[4] While raising my voice, weeping, and wailing, I sought to embrace him and kiss his hands. Yet I only embraced the air! Nothing met me. I continued to wail and cry until he said: "Why are you crying? Do you not know that I have gone the way of all the earth,[5] that a wind has swept me up?[6] My spirit and breath have expired.[7] I am without substance, stripped of everything, so that you cannot feel anything [when you touch me]. [2] After so much has happened to us [the souls of the dead], and the account of our actions has been handed over to God, our fate is to rise each month from our place [where the souls rest], and to roam the earth, its length and breadth,[8] in order to rescue the oppressed from the hand of the oppressor,[9] to serve on a mission for our Creator, and to be divinelike emissaries for Him, as it is written in the verse: 'to permit you to move about among these attendants [the angels].'[10] Now tell me about yourself and why you were placed in this building."

I answered: "My master, if you are God's emissary, you surely must know what happens on earth. Why do you ask me? Is it to remind me of the sorrows I have encountered? Is it to keep me from asking you my questions about the matters of that world to which you belong, or [about the] other subjects concerning the secrets of nature and creation which our blessed sages called *ma'aseh bereshit* and *ma'aseh merkavah?*"[11]

He replied: "My son, pay attention. Listen to the father who bore you. [3] Know that the deceased know nothing of the particulars that befall the inhabitants of the earth, as it is written: 'His sons come to him and he does

[1] See Deuteronomy 32:6.
[2] Cf. *Bereshit Rabbah,* 54:2, and elsewhere.
[3] See Deuteronomy 27:9.
[4] Cf. Song of Songs 5:4.
[5] Cf. 1 Kings 2:2.
[6] Cf. Ezekiel 3:12.
[7] Cf. Job 34:14.
[8] See Genesis 13:17.
[9] See Jeremiah 21:12.
[10] Zachariah 3:7.
[11] These terms originally referred to the biblical account of Creation and the prophetic description of the chariot-throne in the first chapter of Ezekiel and were adapted by the rabbis to designate esoteric speculations that were never to be studied in public and only by worthy individuals. See Mishnah Ḥagigah 2:1. Maimonides, in the introduction to his *Moreh Nevukhim,* describes these two areas as physics and metaphysics, respectively.

not know it.'[1] Even those three pumpkin seeds which we incidentally are able to recognize are not perceived clearly, nor are they known as they actually are.[2] The general rule is that the dead know if famine or drought or pestilence or war has been decreed on a state, city, or region, because they hear about it from behind the curtain[3] every New Year when the decree is issued. This is like the situation of the two spirits which our sages of blessed memory described in the chapter *Mi she-Metu*.[4] But the dead know nothing of particular matters related to worldly affairs and vanities. Why do they need this sorrow? It is sufficient that each sorrow has its hour[5] during its [the spirit's] imprisonment in the mire and filth of the body when living on earth. Since knowing such things offers no integrity nor happiness to their souls, they would not attempt to know them; if they did, they could know them through their cause, that is, through the disposition of the heavens and their constellations.[6]

"This is how I know that your twilight stars[7] are struggling in their orbits to cause you pain, and that [these troubles] came to you through financial matters. Tell me from beginning to end how these things developed with your enemies. But now, blessed be God, if you wish, let us roam together this night. You shall see all the hosts who will meet us. Come with a cry of joy![8] Do not let your heart be filled with fear or trembling, for I am your father, your maker, who will protect you from all evil afflictions and return you to your place before morning. Let us talk together intimately.[9] Tell me of [the] ways and paths [you have followed], and I shall also answer some of your questions and explain those matters that you [will be able to] understand.

## The Father's First Speech

[4] "Your soul possesses faith, intelligence, and wisdom, but as long as you are captive in the tresses of matter,[10] you will never be able to know

[1]Job 14:21.

[2]This may refer to pumpkin or squash seeds or even stomach worms. See E. Ben Yehudah, *Milon ha-Lashon ha-Ivrit* (Jerusalem and Tel Aviv, 1948), 2:831. Compare also the expression in Isaiah 17:6. I could not locate Yagel's precise source.

[3]That is, the curtain of heaven, a common rabbinic expression. See Babylonian Talmud (cited hereafter as B. T.) Ḥagigah 15a, Yoma 77a, and elsewhere.

[4]B. T. Berakhot 18b.

[5]For the expression, see B. T. Berakhot 9b.

[6]This is the first of Yagel's many references to astrological causation, a theme that he especially develops in the second part of this work.

[7]Cf. Job 3:9.

[8]Cf. Psalm 126:6.

[9]Cf. Psalm 55:15.

[10]Cf. Song of Songs 7:7.

anything clearly in all its dimensions, since your body and your corporeality oppress you. Your soul is most influenced by all that transpires in your body. How then can you understand profound matters while it [your soul] is captive in tresses? You surely know how the Holy One, blessed be He, responded to Moses, the man of God, whose body was pure and cleansed of all earthly matter. Despite this fact, when he requested to know God's ways, he was informed: 'Man shall not see me and live.'[1] [5] Rather God told him: 'You shall see My back,'[2] that is, you may know the connections of the worlds, as our sages, of blessed memory, declared: 'He showed Moses a knot [connection] of *tefillin* [phylacteries], etc.'[3] They wished to indicate by this that God showed him the connections of the worlds to each other, that is, how each is influenced by the other and affects the other, leading ultimately to the Creator of everything who understands all their actions.[4]

"He said to man that the fear of the Lord, the pursuit of His ways, and [the idea that] the law of the Lord is perfect, are all wisdom.[5] Through these precepts, a person may attain the goodness of God in the graciousness of his Temple[6] after separating himself from matter. Furthermore, to shun evil is understanding.[7] [Such directives are subsumed under] the negative commandments, and so are other matters forbidden for the sake of the general welfare and [the good of] human society. They include treating all persons leniently and showing them compassion, and not holding their every word and deed by the letter of the law, as the sages, of blessed memory, stated: 'Jerusalem was destroyed only because they gave judgments according to [the letter of] biblical law.'[8]

[6] "Therefore the rabbis and the sages of the world enacted laws and restrictions, as they stated: 'A judge can only treat what his eyes see.'[9] There is also a popular saying which goes: 'He gave laws and rules but He did not give [men] the ability to calculate and organize them.' Therefore, the punishment for one who breaks this rule [of transgressing God's limits] is

[1]Exodus 33:20.

[2]Exodus 33:23.

[3]B. T. Berakhot 7a.

[4]The theme of the interconnectedness of the three worlds is a major theme in all of Yagel's writings and figures prominently in the second part of *Gei Hizzayon,* where it constitutes the most profound secret mere mortals are capable of understanding. See the introduction above.

[5]This is an expansion of Job 28:28, including the insertion of Psalm 19:8.

[6]Psalm 27:4.

[7]The last phrase of Job 28:28.

[8]B. T. Babba Meziah 30b.

[9]B. T. Sanhedrin 6b.

greater than he can bear,[1] for a serpent will bite him.[2] And know that 'a serpent,' in this case, refers to time, for the ancient Egyptians depicted time as a tortuous serpent[3] with its tail in its mouth. Thus time passes and punishes those who break its law, as it is written: 'Now shall the new moon devour them with their portions.'[4] The new moon comes and goes and they utterly perish since the bites of this serpent and its comings and goings devour them.

[7] "One also is commanded to avoid anything that might harm his soul, such as anger, 'For anger rests in the bosom of fools,'[5] arrogance, and greed. Rather, he should be satisfied with only what is necessary. This state is called 'wealthy' in the language of the rabbis, as they stated: 'Who is wealthy? One who is happy with his portion.'[6] [One should also avoid] 'the throat,' that is, [one should] not eat his fill or clothe himself in elegant clothing.[7] Such gluttony not only causes difficult and long illnesses that require constant medical attention, but the soul becomes marred by materiality [as it is] unable to edify itself to appreciate desirable things, as Scripture states: 'The belly of the wicked shall want.'[8] With such excessive and gluttonous eating, men deprive their body and their soul. It is appropriate instead to do as the same verse indicates: 'The righteous [man] eats to satisfy his desire,' that is, the righteous [man] eats to maintain his body and health in order that his soul may be satiated with its ideas. A similar thought was expressed by a sage: 'One person eats in order to live, while another lives in order to eat. The ass and the [latter] person are equal in my estimation.'[9]

"A person should also distance himself from lusting after women, as the rabbis, of blessed memory, prohibited prolonged conversation with

---

[1]Cf. Genesis 4:13.

[2]See Ecclesiastes 10:8.

[3]For the expression, see Isaiah 27:1. Note how Yagel already refers to iconographic representations of abstract ideas, a usage more prevalent in the second part of his book. On the theme of time depicted as a snake or dragon biting its tail, see E. Panofsky, *Studies in Iconology: Humanistic Themes in the Art of the Renaissance* (Oxford, 1939; New York, 1967), p. 74. On Yagel's use of these "emblems," see the introduction above.

[4]Hosea 5:7.

[5]Ecclesiastes 7:9.

[6]Avot 4:1.

[7]See Isaiah 23:18.

[8]Proverbs 13:25. Yagel's fusion of medical and moral advice is most characteristic of his writing. On his training as a physician, see the introduction above.

[9]For variants of the same expression, see E. Blankstein, *Mishle Yisra'el ve-Umot ha-Olam* (Jerusalem, 1964), vol. 1, item 281.

them [women] in the first chapter of Avot.[1] They said this of a man's own wife; how much more of his fellow's wife! Anyone who prolongs his conversation with them [is guilty] since every person is formed from clay[2] and lewd passions gain the upper hand, as David stated: 'And in sin my mother conceived me.'[3] A person can easily have his passion aroused and damage his body, since several serious and harmful illnesses are contracted by men due to excessive lust, such as venereal discharge, fever in the kidneys, weakness of the limbs, etc. [8] For this reason, they [the rabbis] stated: 'And he brings evil on himself, etc. [when conversing with women].'[4] Besides this, he neglects the words of the Torah. Such unintentional neglect of study is reckoned deliberate until, ultimately, he dies with a stricken soul. He shall never see goodness and inherits hell and the nethermost pit.

"Therefore, my son, listen to my voice. Do not let your heart entice you to investigate what is above you. For the Ancient of Days [God] covered ancient matters from [His] creatures, and it is impossible to fathom their mystery and comprehend their truth.[5] You are still corporeal; it is therefore sufficient for you and those like you to walk in innocence and to distance yourself from distasteful things, as I told you. You should believe everything that has come down from our rabbinic tradition, from the orders of the Talmud and the sages of the world, with a pure mind, without doubt, and without hesitation. You should fear God, my son. Who are the kings [whom you should fear]? They are the rabbis.[6]

"This is the path you should follow to acquire knowledge. Then the mysteries of wisdom will be revealed to you daily according to your mind's capacity for wisdom. The heavens will influence you, and you will be renewed with a proper spirit, because one who comes to be purified is assisted [by heaven].[7] You will understand from study what is required of you, and your soul will acquire much integrity until [finally] your body returns to God, who bestowed it. Then, in plain sight,[8] all the hidden

[1]Avot 1:5.

[2]See Job 33:6.

[3]Psalm 51:7.

[4]Avot 1:5, slightly misquoted.

[5]Despite this pious declaration and others like it, Yagel's intention was indeed to penetrate the divine secrets to the fullest extent that he was capable. See the introduction above.

[6]See B. T. Gittin 62a.

[7]See B. T. Yoma 38b.

[8]Cf. Numbers 14:14; Isaiah 52:8.

things in life will be revealed to you, without any doubt. But now get ready to approach me, if you desire, to wander with me this evening so that we might talk and we might profit."

I asked: "My father, my master, please inform me how I will be able to roam since I have no wings to fly in heaven."

He responded: "This [your] body will remain here, on the bed in this building, in its place, while your soul comes with me; for without the body, it cannot be restrained from going."

I then replied: "My master, don't ask my soul to separate itself from this matter [body]. I am still young and it [my soul] has not yet acquired its complete refinement; moreover, I have young children. If the decree [of death] has arrived at the right time, remove all false judgment and I shall be ready. However, if it is not so and my time to die has not yet come, let my soul remain with me for some more days and years until the time of its passing away."

He then answered: "Do not be concerned, my son! I do not wish to separate it [your soul] from you at this time, but [I wish] only to roam [with you] and talk to you and to restore it [your soul] as it was before morning."

[9] I further inquired: "How can my soul speak to my master without a connection to the body? The bodily organs provide the capacity to speak; without them, how can it [the soul] make any long or short speech that can be properly heard?"

He answered: "You are like Ben Zoma on the outside.[1] What foolishness you speak! Why is it difficult for you to comprehend how your soul will speak, lacking bodily organs? It is not difficult for you to understand my clear speech in the holy tongue. I died on the earth; nevertheless, my soul speaks with you, although I possess no bodily organ."

I then responded: "This is actually not difficult for me to understand since I have read and learned that souls are given a garment with the likeness and form of the body when they are separated from the body. Souls utilize this garment as they use bodily organs. Since the garment is very thin and spiritual, I was incapable of touching or embracing you."[2]

---

[1]See B. T. Ḥagigah 14b. A statement of R. Joshua referring to the fact that Ben Zoma had passed beyond the limit of permitted research in his esoteric speculations.

[2]Yagel refers here to the Neoplatonic astral body, the starlike vehicle or garment of the soul, called, in the language of the kabbalists, *malbush*. Cf. D. P. Walker, "The Astral Body in Renaissance Medicine," *Journal of the Warburg and Courtauld Institutes,* 21 (1958):119–33. In *Beit Ya'ar ha-Levanon,* bk. 3, chaps. 4–7, Yagel discusses this concept based on its description

He retorted: "Your ears should listen to what comes out of your mouth![1] Just as the souls of the dead are given a garment, so too will it [a garment] be given to your soul."

I then asked: "What is the nature of this garment which will be provided to my soul until its return to my body in the morning?"

He answered: "A garment of translucent pure air. However, as long as you are still alive, you are incapable of understanding how this air is transformed into the soul's garment like matter. It is sufficient for you to realize that this matter was investigated by the ancient scholars who testified that when men lie on their beds and sleep, [their souls] depart from them. Every [soul] roams on high in its own way. Thus the [author of the *Sefer*] *Zohar* wrote on the portion *Va-Yeshev*, page 183.[2] Therefore, be strong and of good courage and do not be fainthearted. Come with me and I will [eventually] return you to your cell."

## A Discussion on the Quest for Wisdom and the Purpose of Human Life

I then declared: "I am ready for your command, and where you shall go, I shall go,[3] only guard my soul. But please inform me that your words are sincere since no man has the right to demand knowledge. It is sufficient for him to walk in innocence, as Scripture states: 'You must be wholehearted [innocent].'[4] [He should] direct his ways and actions by way of the Torah and the commandments. [10] What is the advantage of the wise man over the fool? All his days, the wise man is engrossed in wisdom and even at night his mind has no respite.[5] The fool, on the other hand, is preoccupied with idleness, never opening a book, and only practicing the commandments as women do them, learning them by rote.[6] Moreover, he protects

---

found in Cornelius Agrippa's *De occulta philosophia*, bk. 3, chap. 37, and tries to reconcile it with rabbinic and kabbalistic sources. On the notion of *malbush* in Lurianic kabbalah, see G. Scholem, *Kabbalah* (Jerusalem, 1974), pp. 150–51.

[1]Cf. Jerusalem Talmud (cited hereafter as J. T.) Berakhot, 2:4.

[2]This last quote and reference is found on the margin of the Cincinnati manuscript and was not included in the body of the text. See *Sefer ha-Zohar*, parshat Va-Yeshev, 1:183a.

[3]Cf. Ruth 1:16.

[4]Deuteronomy 18:13.

[5]Cf. Ecclesiastes 2:23.

[6]Cf. Isaiah 29:13. Note Yagel's interesting substitution of "women" for "men." If it is not a slip of the pen, it certainly is in consonance with his general attitude toward women.

himself from sin and falsehood [out of fear] from the punishment associated with the steps of evildoers, which is sufficient for him in this world. Only in the next world, when his soul is separated from him, will it acquire learning in the heavenly academy."

He responded: "I am truly surprised by these comments and by this question! How can you be so foolish as to ask it? Who does not know that the advantage of the wise man over the fool is like that of light over darkness?[1] The wise man, who labors in God's Torah and zealously desires His commandments, sees clearly how to protect himself from any blemish or inclination to sin, performs the commandments for their own sake, and knows the greatness of his Maker, as Maimonides, of blessed memory, wrote: 'The neglect of learning the principles [of faith] and, particularly, of knowing the First Cause, leads to deliberate sin. One who succumbs to it is called a heretic and idolator and has no place in the world to come.'[2] Notice how much he emphasized the neglect of study to which the fool, whom you mentioned, succumbs.[3]

[11] "We find that even a descendent of Noah [a non-Jew] is punished for not learning, as the rabbis, of blessed memory, state in chapter Ha-Hovel:[4] [in explicating the biblical verse] 'But you must restore the man's wife; since he is a prophet.'[5] [They ask:] 'But is it only the wife of a prophet who has to be restored, whereas the wife of another man need not be restored? [R. Samuel b. Naḥmani] said [in the name of] R. Jonathan: "Restore the man's wife" [surely implies] in all cases. For, as to your [Abimelech's] allegation: "Will you slay people even though they are innocent? He [Abraham] himself said to me: 'She is my sister!' and she [Sarah] also said: 'He is my brother!' " '[6] [You should know that] 'he [Abraham] is a prophet' who has already taught the world that when a stranger comes to a city, he is to be questioned regarding his wife, whether she is his wife or sister, or regarding food and drink.[7] From this we learn that a descendent of Noah [a non-Jew who observes the seven Noahide commandments, in this case, Abimelech][8] may be worthy of death if he had the opportunity to

[1]Cf. Ecclesiastes 2:13.
[2]Yagel appears to be summarizing the import of the opening paragraphs of the Sefer ha-Maddah, Hilkhot Yesodei ha-Torah, 1.
[3]Sefer ha-Maddah, Hilkhot Talmud Torah, 1.
[4]B. T. Babba Kamma 92a.
[5]Genesis 20:7. God addresses Abimelech, the king of Gerar, in a dream in regard to Abraham and Sarah.
[6]Genesis 20:4–5.
[7]The order of the Talmudic line is reversed in Yagel's version.
[8]See B. T. Sanhedrin 56a.

learn and did not do so [and thus committed a crime through his ignorance of the law].

"This is also what Zophar the Naamathite said to Job to explain [to him] the nature of his crime and sin, on account of which Job was afflicted through no apparent fault of his own. [He stated] that because [Job] did not acquire [the] human ability to learn and understand, he was justly afflicted, as the verse states:[1] 'But would that God might speak, and open his lips against you. He would tell you the secrets of wisdom' of which you did not concern yourself, 'for there are many sides to sagacity' in which you engaged. 'And know that God has overlooked for you some of your iniquity,' that is, He will forget your iniquity and not exact punishment for your sin.

"A wise man who labors in the Torah will understand the secret regarding the difference between one who serves his Maker out of love and one who serves Him out of fear. What is the fear and inner love whose secret is hinted to the discerning by the rabbinic statement: 'Do not be slaves who serve [12] their master in order to receive a reward, etc.'?[2] Even if the reward is spiritual, do not serve Him for such an ulterior reason. Rather, everything has a higher purpose, as the verse also suggests in stating: 'And the fear of heaven shall be upon you,' and as is clear to the kabbalists.

"With the exception of what constitutes the secret of Creation, the general order of nature endowed everything to work and function. No creature was created without a purpose. God did not form any creature, whether above or below, to sit and do nothing. Man was also born to work.[3] If he is meritorious, he labors in the Torah; if [he is] not, he works in an occupation.[4] Since he is an intermediary between the higher creations, the heavenly hosts, and between the lower ones established on earth, as the rabbis recall in *Bereshit Rabbah*,[5] it is therefore in his power to direct himself toward any goal he wishes. If [he elects] a higher goal—to stand in God's image, for which he was created (as the biblical verse states: 'Let us make man in Our image, after Our likeness'[6] and as David the king, may he rest in peace, said: 'Surely man walks as a mere image'[7])—he only will be able to achieve this by way of the Torah and [through] wisdom. He then will be as

[1]Job 11:6.

[2]Avot 1:3.

[3]Job 5:7.

[4]For the expression, see *Bereshit Rabbah,* 13:5, but compare Maimonides' formulation in *Sefer ha-Maddah,* Hilkhot Talmud Torah, 3:10–11.

[5]*Bereshit Rabbah,* 8:11.

[6]Genesis 1:26.

[7]Psalm 39:7.

the angels of God. He may also tarnish [God's] image and form and turn below, to be likened to the cattle upon a thousand hills.[1] But if he is meritorious and directs his thoughts to a higher purpose, as we have said, and [if] he labors in the Torah, he then will be given power to dominate over all created things. Moreover, he shall inherit the two worlds, this one and the next, as the rabbis stated at the end of tractate *Kiddushin*:[2] '[Have you ever seen [a] wild beast or a bird [with a craft? Yet] they are sustained without anxiety. Now, they were created to serve me while I was created to serve my master. Surely, then, I should make a living without anxiety, etc.' Yet if a person directs his goal to the vanities of this world and breaks the yoke of the Torah, he will then receive the yoke of the government and the yoke of earning a living, and will be unable to rest or remain calm.[3] In this labor of vanities, his days and years will be consumed and he will be unable to sit idle, as we have stated.

## On the Evils of Usury

[13] "In order to sustain this natural state, the holy Torah forbade the taking of interest, because the profit it generates is gained without work and effort, as Scripture states: 'With the sweat of your brow, you shall eat bread.'[4] Likewise, all the lawgivers of every nation prohibited it [this practice] since it provides no welfare to the state; on the contrary, it brings a loss to the state. If it were not for the fact that the great rabbinic codifiers had permitted interest [to be charged] to a stranger, as the biblical verse states, 'From a stranger you may take interest,'[5] I would argue that the simple meaning of the verse also forbids us [from taking interest] from him [the stranger] as long as we [the Jews] were living on our own land. This is for several reasons. First, since [imposing] interest is an activity lacking any utility to the state, as we have said, why should it be permitted when it engenders a loss or damage to the country in which we live? Aren't we required to pray for the welfare of the government? Moreover, didn't the biblical verse prohibit the destruction of any tree for food, even in time of war, to protect the welfare of the community?[6]

[1] See Psalm 50:10.
[2] B. T. Kiddushin 82a.
[3] See Avot 3:5.
[4] Genesis 3:19.
[5] Deuteronomy 23:21.
[6] See Deuteronomy 20:19. Yagel's explicit critique of Jewish moneylending on interest is especially interesting because of his own personal involvement in moneylending in Luzzara, described in the text below and in the introduction. His argument that usury is harmful to the

"When the verse speaks of lending interest to the stranger, it means a stranger who comes to your land from a distant place for reasons of trade and [who] is short of funds. In this case, you are permitted to lend him on interest, just as the merchants are accustomed to take profit through [bills of] exchange.[1] This practice is permissible for two reasons. First, the loan benefits him until his return to his own land. Moreover, it benefits your land since he will then return on other occasions to bring his merchandise. He then will say that if he requires funds, he will not be prevented from borrowing on interest until he has completed his business. Second, since he is a stranger from a distant land, what damage does it inflict to the welfare of your land by lending him on interest for any loan he makes? Notice then that the verse speaks only about the stranger we have described.

"If you argue, however, that the verse refers to strangers living among you, [you should recall] that the Torah already has forbidden them to dwell on the land unless they accept the seven Noahide commandments, as the Bible states: 'They shall not dwell on the land lest they make you sin against me.'[2] It also states: 'You shall show no mercy upon them,'[3] which was interpreted by the rabbis to mean: 'You shall not let them dwell on the land.'[4] If you insist that this stranger refers to the same one in whose land you dwell, [we would ask] who would be willing to permit something that leads to loss and damage to the country which is also your possession? As the saying goes: 'Don't cast dirt into the well which provides you water.'[5] This, then, is the first reason.

"The second reason is that the initial provocation for the series of calamities, exiles, and destructions [against the Jewish community] was [due to lending on] interest. It was also the reason for [the] slandering [of]

---

social order and is gained without honest labor mirrors the natural law arguments against usury promoted by the scholastic theologians. See J. T. Noonan, Jr., *The Scholastic Analysis of Usury* (Cambridge, Mass., 1957), pp. 37–60; Ruderman, *The World of a Renaissance Jew,* pp. 89–94. For a similarly negative view of usury by a sixteenth-century Italian Jewish banker, see Yeḥi'el Nissim da Pisa, *Ma'amar Ḥayyei Olam,* ed. G. Rosenthal (New York, 1962).

[1]Yagel here uses the word *cambio,* reminiscent of the scholastic distinction between a *mutuum* (loan) and a *cambium* (bill of exchange) which canon lawyers used to justify the reality of sixteenth-century Italian banking operations. Without this legal distinction, a large percentage of European business transactions would have been considered usurious. See Noonan, pp. 171–92, 311–39, and Ruderman, *The World of a Renaissance Jew,* p. 213, n. 40. Yagel's arguments here and above leave little doubt as to his familiarity with the scholastic discussions and his agreement with them.

[2]Exodus 23:33.

[3]Deuteronomy 7:2.

[4]B. T. Avodah Zarah 20a.

[5]B. T. Babba Kamma 92b.

the Jews in the places where they lived among all nations and peoples, as the author of the *Shevet Yehudah* wrote in the discourse of Thomas the king.[1] Observe this and take notice, and if they are the words of [merely] one individual, consider what the rabbis said: 'Among the dead whom the prophet Ezekiel revived, one remained dead since he was a lender on interest to gentiles.'[2] The rabbis also wrote explicitly and not by inference in the chapter *Elu ha-Lokin*[3]: 'He did not loan money on interest, even from a gentile, etc.,' and in *Nedarim*, chapter *Ha-Noder Min ha-Mevushal*,[4] [they wrote]: 'A sectarian [*min*] said to R. Judah: "Your face is like that of a moneylender or pig raiser." He replied: "Both of these are forbidden to Jews, etc."' If interest to a gentile had been permitted, the sectarian would have responded to R. Judah accordingly. Likewise, R. Judah would not have answered that the two are absolutely forbidden if it were not for the fact that they are similarly prohibited with respect to any place, any time, and any person.

"Let us return to our original intention [regarding the thought] that man was born to work.[5] If a person succeeds in removing the yoke of earning a living and places the yoke of Torah and wisdom upon himself, he will be happy. Wisdom fortifies the wise man in every respect so that he is loved above and cherished below.[6] Kings will seek his counsel, advisors and judges of the earth will judge him justly, and he will acquire secrets of the King of glory, since God's secret is available to those who fear him.[7] The world was created only to obey this person,[8] as it is well known. The rabbis similarly declared in the Jerusalem Talmud *Pe'ah*: 'All the earth does not equal one word of Torah.'[9]

---

[1]Yagel refers to the seventh chapter of Solomon ibn Verga's *Shevet Yehudah*, first published in 1554. See the critical edition of A. Shoḥat (Jerusalem, 1947), pp. 30–31: "A second reason for the hatred is that when the Jews came to my lord's kingdom they were poor and the Christians were rich. Now it is the opposite, since the Jews are clever and achieve their purposes with cunning. Moreover, they became very rich by lending on interest. My lord will note that three-quarters of all the lands and estates of Spain are all in the hands of the Jews, and this on account of the heavy interest." Quoted from the English translation of *Shevet Yehudah* by M. Meyer, in *Ideas of Jewish History* (New York, 1974), pp. 112–13.

[2]*Pirke de R. Eliezer* (Warsaw, 1852), 33, p. 79 (and D. Luria's commentary, n. 130).

[3]B. T. Makkot 24a. The rest of the paragraph is found in the margin of the Cincinnati manuscript.

[4]B. T. Nedarim 49b.

[5]Cf. Job 5:7.

[6]See B. T. Berakhot 17a.

[7]See Psalm 25:14.

[8]Cf. B. T. Berakhot 6b.

[9]J. T. Pe'ah 1:1.

"Furthermore, one who serves the King, recognizes Him and His greatness, and knows those things which give Him pleasure, is not similar to the one who merely observes His commandments. For the herald cries out[1] and the punishment is tied to the heel of those who violate His words, like the case of the fool who walks in darkness, obeying commandments taught by rote,[2] without any reason or intelligence. He is cursed since he did not learn, as the rabbis rebuked him in *Sukkah*,[3] because his sons and the members of his household [are required to] recite [the *Hallel* prayer] on his behalf [since he is unable to do so]. They also declared in [tractate] *Hagigah*[4] concerning the biblical verse: ' "And you shall come to see the difference between the righteous and the wicked, between him who has served the Lord and him who has not served Him," that the "righteous" is the same as he "who has served the Lord," while the "wicked" is the same as he "who has not served Him." He [Hillel] answered them: "He who has served Him" and "he who has not served Him" both refer to those who are perfectly righteous. But he who repeated his chapter [i.e., his lesson] one hundred times is not to be compared with he who repeated it one hundred and one times, etc.' The kabbalists also have a secret in interpreting the same passage regarding one who repeats his chapter one hundred times and is called 'he who has not served Him,' and the one who repeats his chapter 101 times and is called 'He who has served the Lord.' [They refer to the biblical verse]: 'But wisdom, where shall it be found?'[5] With either interpretation—according to our way[6] or according to the simple meaning of the verse—we have learned that one whose learning is insufficient is called 'one who does not serve Him.'

[14] "The commandments also possess a special virtue that provides some satisfaction to those who follow them, whether they perform a small amount or a lot, whether they perform them for their own sake and with conviction or not. The rabbis also declared on this subject: 'Commandments do not require intention.'[7] They also stated, 'God wanted to reward Israel . . . even the empty one among you will be filled with commandments and good deeds and with these, they will be rewarded for the next world.'[8]

[1]See Daniel 3:4.
[2]Cf. Isaiah 29:13.
[3]B. T. Sukkah 38a.
[4]B. T. Hagigah 9b, discussing the verse Malachi 3:18.
[5]Job 28:12. The *gematriah* (the numerical equivalent) of "where" (*me'ayin*) is 101. Thus the verse indicates that wisdom is found when one's chapter is repeated 101 times.
[6]Note that Yagel identifies himself with the esoteric interpretation of the passage.
[7]B. T. Rosh Ha-Shanah 28b.
[8]B. T. Makkot 23b.

"This is what makes the glory and majesty of our holy Torah superior in strength and vigor to other fields. In other disciplines, many people do not become wise; rather, one in a thousand gains refinement for his soul from the ideas he acquired from that learning. (Even so, it is apparent that through such study [of disciplines] other than [that of] the Torah the soul cannot acquire perfection.) In the meantime, [the rest of] the thousand, who lack the correct opinion and possess limited understanding of its [the discipline's] essential ideas and matters, remain like an ass. 'For man abides not in honor; he is like the beasts that perish. Such is the fate of them who are foolish, the end of those who instruct with their own talk.'[1] We may conclude with the verse: 'Their soul perishes in youth.'[2]

"This is not the case, however, for the children of the holy Torah, [who are] called by the name of Israel. Any man or woman who performs any commandment acquires some perfection for his or her soul so as not to perish when the body perishes. After the soul is purified in the river of fire[3] or in Hell, 'God truly does all these things'[4] according to His attribute of mercy, restoring it [the soul] to a second or third body in order that none of our souls will remain banished [from paradise].[5] And all of us will be reviewed in one review,[6] being like the host of angels visiting in His sanctuary. In any case, everything depends upon the greatness of one's action and one's learning.[7] Happy is the one who comes here with his learning in hand,[8] who is valued in that good world [the next world].

"It might appear contradictory to you what I stated initially, namely that it is sufficient for you to avoid evil, to do good, and not to wander in that which is above you. I meant to indicate that you should not wander after the stubbornness of your heart, nor request to know what is on high in the heavens and deep in the earth, nor what is the place of the world, like the philosophers' speculations. The latter struggle with this [idea] and still do not know if the world is subsumed under the definition of 'place'; for if they uphold such an idea, a surrounding matter will have to stand outside that which exists; but this is a falsehood.[9] There are also other such vanities

[1]Cf. Psalm 49:13–14.

[2]Job 36:14.

[3]Cf. *Sefer Zohar* 2:111b; 2:252b.

[4]Job 33:29.

[5]Cf. 2 Samuel 14:14. Yagel refers here to the doctrine of metempsychosis, a theme he returns to constantly in this work and in his other writings. See the introduction above.

[6]Cf. B. T. Rosh ha-Shanah 18a.

[7]Cf. Avot 3:16.

[8]B. T. Pesaḥim 50a, *Kohelet Rabbah*, 9:8.

[9]On the difficulties of understanding Aristotle's definition of space in relation to the world, and the extensive discussions of these difficulties in medieval philosophy, see H. Wolfson, *Crescas' Critique of Aristotle* (Cambridge, Mass., 1929), pp. 38–69.

which offer no perfection to the one who knows them nor can one resolve them in this lifetime. A similar thought was expressed by R. Abaye in the first chapter of *Gittin:*[1] 'Because a man does not know this rule of R. Isaac, is he therefore not to be counted a great scholar? If it were a rule established by logical deduction, we might think so, etc.' In a similar way, should we say that because someone does not understand, due to the greatness or depth of a concept, or due to his own limitations in comprehending any words of wisdom, that he has no place in heaven? On the contrary, it is madness and foolishness to request to understand such ideas and only a loss of time, 'for would you discover the mystery of God?'[2] It is sufficient for us to understand the words of the Torah and the words of our rabbis, of blessed memory, and to accept their words with a cheerful countenance, as I have said. Now leave, rise quickly, and come with me, for we shall go out to the field and speak together. I cannot stand here any longer because I have a long way to go before [reaching the place] where the sun does not shine on the inhabitants of the world, on those who dwell on this earth."

## The Beginning of the Ascent and the Beginning of the Son's Monologue

And I, in the meantime, girded my loins and went out from my body as a man exiting [from] a narrow place. A wind swept me and we went roaming to and fro together as flying birds. He directed me to tell him everything that had happened to me from beginning to end, including all the disputes with my enemies that eventually led to the situation of my imprisonment. I thus began:

[15] "You knew, my master, that after your separation from me I came to Luzzara, it being truly as its name, a light.[3] But now its splendor and its light turned away and it remained dark and gloomy, because without light, darkness comes.[4] And now it is like the city of Shechem, a place deserving of punishment.[5] All the people who came to live in this city were stricken, [either] physically or financially, from the day I came until the present.[6]

[1]B. T. Gittin 6b.

[2]See Job 11:7.

[3]Luzzara, a small town southwest of Mantua in the Mantovano. Yagel was born in Monselice in 1553 and arrived in Luzzara in the early 1570s. See the introduction above. Yagel alludes to the derivation of the name "Luzzara" from the Italian "luce," light.

[4]Cf. *Bereshit Rabbah,* 68:7.

[5]Cf. B. T. Sanhedrin 107a.

[6]Yagel's extreme statement undoubtedly was colored by his own financial troubles as well as by the frightening plague of 1575–76. See below.

God's hand was even upon those people who came to live there temporarily; they also were stricken and suffered the afflictions of the land. I was thus stricken initially, for after your coming to this city,[1] God's spirit swept you up and took you from me. I remained a young man without a teacher in business skills, for I had never assumed the responsibility of earning a living. I came here, and from the first day troubles and tribulations, consisting of human illnesses and injuries, surrounded [me] and hovered over my head. There was also a famine in the land, a lack of food and drink, when I came to the city. Thus I saw that I was unable to manage the bank alone and I searched for a person to assist me. However, I was unable to do so without the permission of his excellence, the duke, may his majesty be exalted.[2] I made a request of him two or three times[3] in a letter addressed to him, but matters were drawn out and he did not approve of me sufficiently to respond to my query and grant my request.

"The Holy One, blessed be He, who brings people pursued by fate to one inn in order to punish them together,[4] purposefully brought about a partnership [between me] and Madame Rina, the wife of Jacob de Lacairo, may the Lord preserve him.[5] According to the terms of the agreement, she was to pay for [her share] in advance by placing funds in the bank. Thus the partnership began, although these arrangements were known only to us.[6] She also saw fit to appoint a trustee to examine my expenses and to supervise the business. These are the principal terms which we drew up together."

## The Appearance of the First Two Souls

[16] But when I began to list the principal terms, I heard the voices of two souls speaking to each other and I stood up to hear what they were saying. Lo and behold, they were reading from the book of Isaiah from the portion: "Let me sing for my beloved a song of my lover about his

---

[1]This seems to contradict Yagel's earlier statement that he came to Luzzara after being separated from his father. Here he indicates that his father died only after they both had arrived in the town.

[2]Duke Guglielmo. On his relationship to his Jewish subjects, see Simonsohn, *Jews in Mantua*, pp. 25–31. The events that Yagel describes here are not mentioned in any of the archival documents, according to Simonsohn, p. 252.

[3]Cf. Job 33:29.

[4]Cf. B. T. Makkot 10b.

[5]I could not identify him. Simonsohn, p. 252, omits his name altogether.

[6]Since they had not been officially approved and were thus illegal.

vineyard."[1] These were their words, that is, what the first [soul] was saying to the other:

"You must know that the prophet likened the community of Israel to a vineyard. In the case of the vineyard, the more dry and unfertile the land on which it is planted, the choicest and superior will be the fruit it produces, pleasing God and man. Similarly, in the case of [the people of] Israel, the more they are in sorrowful straits, the more righteous they are, just as the rabbinic parable relates in *Hagigah:* 'Poverty befits Israel like a white band on a red horse.'[2]

"This is what the prophet said: 'My beloved had a vineyard on a fruitful hill,'[3] that is, a good and fertile place. But the person who initially planted the vineyard in that place planted the front line of the fertile field in a hidden corner [filled] with briars and thorns, stones and sand. When he later observed the beauty of the fruit and its excellence, he asked himself: 'If I can produce such fruit in a place neither hoed nor fertilized, what might it yield if I cleared the field of stones and removed the thorns from the vineyard?' So then 'he broke the ground and cleared it of stones, etc.'[4] Thus he hoped to make good and excellent vines because of the productivity of the land and because of the [added] fertilization. However, the opposite occurred, for it yielded wild grapes.[5]

"The vineyard of the Lord of hosts, the house of Israel,[6] is similar. While they [the people of Israel] were in Egypt, in the mud and furnace of calamities, they would call to God 'out of their straits'[7] and pray to Him. They also were deemed righteous in believing in His prophets, in Moses and in Aaron, a holy one of God, when God ordered them to 'cast away every man the detestible thing of his eyes, etc.'[8] They accepted upon themselves the covenant of their foreskins, as it is written: 'When I passed by you and saw you wallowing in your blood,'[9] and as the rabbis declared: 'Two bloods, the blood of the pascal lamb and the blood of circumcision.'[10] They also believed in Moses and followed him in the desert, as the verse

[1] Isaiah 5:1.

[2] See B. T. Hagigah 9b and the Tosafot on the same page, where a slightly different version appears. Cf. also *Vayikrah Rabbah,* 13:35.

[3] Isaiah 5:1.

[4] Isaiah 5:2.

[5] Cf. Isaiah 5:4.

[6] Cf. Isaiah 5:7.

[7] Cf. Psalm 118:5.

[8] Ezekiel 20:7.

[9] Ezekiel 16:6.

[10] *Mekhilta,* parshat Bo, 5:28.

states: 'I remembered you for the affection of your youth, your love as a bride, etc.'[1] However, after they left the furnace of exile and servitude for plenitude, it was said [of them]: 'Jeshurun waxed fat and kicked, etc.'[2] It was also said: 'I who lavished silver on her and gold which they used for Baal.'[3] This, then, is what the prophet said: 'And he hoped for justice' while they were dwelling in peace, 'but behold, injustice, for equity, but behold, iniquity!'"[4]

When these souls, who were coming toward us [as they discussed] this story, saw us, they became quiet. We approached them and greeted them and they returned our greeting. We said to them: "Please inform us of the deeds in which you labored in this world when you were living on the earth."

## The Schoolteacher's Story

[17] The first [soul], who had been interpreting the aforementioned portion [of the Torah], responded: "I was a teacher of young children all my life. I taught them with righteousness and faith to give priority to those things worthy of priority according to the order of study of Bible, Mishnah, and Talmud, in the way the rabbis stipulated in the chapter *Meshu'ah Milḥamah*:[5] 'Put your external affairs in order,' which is Bible; 'Get ready what you have in the field,' which is Mishnah; 'Then build yourself a home,' which is Talmud, etc.

"I would also instruct and guide them in morality and correct behavior. The teacher is further obliged to explain and to teach young children these matters, since this is also a part of the totality of Torah, as Maimonides, of blessed memory, explained so well in the first chapter of his commentary to the Mishnah, tractate *Pe'ah*, regarding the passage 'the study of Torah is equal to them all.'[6] He stated that all the commandments are divided into two parts. The first part includes the commandments that relate to man's soul, pertaining to his relationship with the Holy One, blessed be He, such as [the commandments] of fringes, phylacteries, the Sabbath, idolatry, and the like. The second part includes commandments

[1]Jeremiah 2:2.
[2]Deuteronomy 32:15.
[3]Hosea 2:10.
[4]Isaiah 5:7.
[5]B. T. Sotah 44a, where the rabbis interpret Proverbs 24:27.
[6]See Maimonides on Pe'ah 1:1.

pertaining to the value of human relationships, such as the prohibitions against theft, deceit, animosity, and revenge; or the commandment for loving one's neighbor, not harming him or standing idly by his blood; or [the commandment dictating] respect for parents and sages, who are parents of everyone. When a person performs the commandments pertaining to his soul's relationship with its Creator, he will be reckoned justly; God will reward him in the next world for doing them. When he performs the commandments pertaining to the betterment of society, he also will be reckoned justly in the next world. He will discover goodness in this world since he acted in a righteous manner with other human beings; moreover, when he behaves accordingly, others will emulate him, and he will receive credit for this as well.

"All the commandments pertaining to [the relationship] between man and his neighbor are subsumed under the [category] of acts of loving-kindness. Pay attention to them for thus you will find them. So [it was that] Hillel the elder, when asked by a heathen to teach him the Torah on one foot, said to him: 'What is hateful to you, do not do to your neighbor.'[1] When you investigate this matter, you will discover that the study of the Torah is weighted against everything, for in Torah study, man gains everything since Torah leads to action.[2]

"Therefore, you see, just as the teacher must instruct his students in Bible, Mishnah, and Talmud, he also must teach them good taste and opinion, civility and morality. With this [practice], he preserves the intention of the Torah, as I did with my pupils. However, since I sometimes wrote books and documents for others in order to earn a living, and I neglected the education of youth, I was guilty of [the crime expressed in the biblical verse]: 'Cursed be he who is slack in doing the Lord's work.'[3] Therefore, it was decreed in heaven that for all the time I lost in these pursuits, I would wander, neither resting nor being quiet. I would teach the unruly souls who had expired without delight, such as this man who died without learning except for the small amount [he had mastered] in his youth."[4]

[1] B. T. Shabbat 31a.
[2] This is the end of the summary of Maimonides' discussion.
[3] Jeremiah 48:10.
[4] The teacher's punishment seems excessive for merely taking on extra work to support himself. Certainly the teacher's "extracurricular" activities accurately reflected the reality of the Jewish teaching profession in fifteenth- and sixteenth-century Italy. For two examples of Jewish teachers who were underpaid and forced to seek other employment, including copying manuscripts and documents, see Ruderman, *The World of a Renaissance Jew,* chap. 2; A. Marx, "Glimpses of the Life of an Italian Rabbi of the First Half of the Sixteenth Century," *Hebrew*

## The Gambler's Speech

[18] The second [soul] then spoke: "I recall my sins today.[1] Know that my father, who had taken care of me and sent me to school, died during my childhood. When he died, I left my teacher and my studies as a child flees from books, and in place of books I took up cards and dice. But with them, I grew old and gray[2] and toiled all my life. I never let my soul rest, but instead I hurriedly recited prayers and petitions early in the morning and cut [them] short as R. Akiva did when he publicly prayed.[3] I would then go to a public meeting place to play with friends; there I would eat a little, drink a little, and sleep a little[4] in order not to lose much time. Nor did I find rest during Sabbaths and holidays, which are days of relaxation and rest to all the weary. Rather, I was distressed by the idleness. How I would praise the words of the rabbis in [tractate] *Ketubbot* that idleness leads to boredom![5] This was my fate, day and night, until time and chance followed their earthly course.[6] And now it has been decreed from heaven that I shall wander for as much time as I wasted playing cards and dice, traveling with elementary schoolteachers to learn wisdom and intelligence from them, so that, after all the sorrow I have encountered, I might stand on the threshold of God's courts[7] in the academy on high."

[19] We then requested of him: "Please tell us whether you had read or learned how to leave 'a lovely hind,'[8] to follow the error of frivolity, and instead of the wheat which you planted in your childhood,[9] to produce thistles and weeds[10] in your adolescence and in your old age. If you sinned in your adolescence, why did you not venture,[11] even once, to repent of your ways, since you were in that world which is the world of deed? Gray hairs are now scattered over you, but you have taken no notice."[12]

---

*Union College Annual*, 1 (1924): 605–16. See generally Bonfil, *Ha-Rabbanut be-Italyah bi-Tekufat ha-Renesans,* chap. 4.
[1]Cf. Genesis 41:9.
[2]Cf. I Samuel 12:2.
[3]B. T. Berakhot 31a.
[4]Cf. B. T. Berakhot 4b.
[5]B. T. Ketubbot 59b.
[6]Cf. Ecclesiastes 9:11.
[7]Cf. Psalm 84:11.
[8]Cf. Proverbs 5:19.
[9]Cf. Job 31:40.
[10]Cf. Mishnah Kilayim 1:1.
[11]Cf. Esther 7:5.
[12]Cf. Hosea 7:9.

He responded: "It was one of the rhetoricians who taught me to play, a proud and insolent man, Scoffer is his name.[1] He said to me: 'Know that all of human perfection is in cards and dice, since the one who prepared and ordered them was a most mighty man of God, a perfect and very wise man, knowledgeable and intelligent. He arranged them so that they would hint at all the creatures of heaven and earth as signs before one's eyes, revealing the majesty of his Creator.'"

We then requested of him: "Tell us his dreams and words."

He replied: "Since man is an intermediary being, resting on the earth while his head reaches the heavens, he received [from God] intelligence and knowledge to understand that which exists in the lower world and in the highest heaven.[2] Yet his intelligence is incapable of penetrating higher [than that] for the sake of his own glory and honor, 'since it is the glory of God to conceal a matter.'[3] Just as it is impossible for a blind person to appreciate light, so is it impossible for a mere mortal to evaluate directly the ideas which are above the heavens. 'Who has ascended heaven and come down'[4] to tell how the uppermost angels serve Him? [20] Thus the rabbis forbade this investigation, as they taught in chapter *Ein Dorshin:*[5] 'It is inappropriate for someone to come into the world who has observed three things: What is above, what is below, what is before and after, etc.' Thus, how good it would be if man's investigation would cease at His highest heavens and that he would know, by way of tradition, that there is one Creator of everything and that He is unique, rules over them [His creatures], and labors and acts with them as He wishes!

"What need does a person have to search for great things in order to know His ways and His actions? One who does not show respect to his Creator is called wicked, and it would have been fitting for him not to have come into the world. Rather it is sufficient for him to examine them [the subjects he is permitted to study], and at that point his research should end, as the rabbis wrote: '[on the biblical verse] "For this is your wisdom and your understanding in the sight of the peoples."[6] What wisdom is in the sight of the peoples? This is the calculations of the seasons, etc.'[7] Just as a

---

[1]Cf. Proverbs 21:24.

[2]A common Renaissance theme. See, for example, P. O. Kristeller, "The Philosophy of Man in the Renaissance," in *Renaissance Thought: The Classic, Scholastic, and Humanist Strains* (New York, 1961), pp. 120–39.

[3]Proverbs 25:2.

[4]Proverbs 30:4.

[5]B. T. Ḥagigah 11b.

[6]B. T. Shabbat 75a on Deuteronomy 4:6.

[7]In other words, the wisdom of the stars, up until the uppermost heavens but not exceeding them.

man who gains no intelligence or understanding is likened to a beast, and just as the rabbis also hinted regarding the [biblical] verse: 'But who never give a thought to the plan of the Lord,'[1] so it is for the one who seeks to know more than he is permitted to understand. His efforts are in vain, for he still is incapable of understanding despite all his effort, except as much as a fox can get from a harvested field.[2] These are the two extremes from which man should distance himself. Just as we find in the *Ethics*[3] that extremes are disgraceful while the middle road is always correct, similarly, regarding learning, these extremes are disgraceful and the intermediate path is correct and good.

"And now you shall see that, in cards, man's investigation is satisfied regarding all that he is permitted to consider.[4] That is because scholars know that the heavenly stars are divided into twelve signs [of the zodiac] and forty-eight figures. Similarly, one can find forty-eight figures in cards, since for every one of the four kings there are twelve pieces at his table[5] which correspond to the twelve signs.[6] The heavenly sphere is also divided into four parts. In every part one may observe a change in the world, depending on the position of the sun [in relation to that part], either with respect to the four seasons as cold or hot, summer or winter, or with respect to daily changes. Depending on how the four parts appear to rise on the horizon, whether crooked or straight, the days and nights will be shortened or lengthened. This manner is fixed and never changes; it is neither lengthened nor shortened either on the longest day of the year or on the shortest since three signs [regularly] shine on the horizon and three recede.[7]

"Similarly, you will notice how the cards are divided into the rule of four kings. Each one [king] can influence the player using it [the card] by providing him either a blessing or a curse from 'the children of his house,' which will prove valuable according to the nature and rules of the game. The player always derives a known account and equal number from the

[1] B. T. Shabbat 75a on Isaiah 5:12. The verse is applied to the person ignorant of the wisdom of the stars.

[2] Cf. B. T. Niddah 65b.

[3] Aristotle, *Nicomachean Ethics*, II,6. Note the clever way in which Yagel introduces the subject of card playing, i.e., as part of an excursus on the useful knowledge available and permissible to human beings.

[4] On the general context of the gambler's speech, see the introduction above.

[5] Cf. Song of Songs 1:12. On the twelve zodiac signs and forty-eight figures, cf. Abraham ibn Ezra, *Sefer Reshit Ḥokhmah*, eds. R. Levy and F. Cantera (Baltimore, 1939), p. 153.

[6] There appears to be a gap in the Hebrew text here, as Mani indicates, p. 8a.

[7] Mani correctly suggests that the numbers should read six and six (as appears below in the text), instead of three and three. Cf. David Ganz, *Neḥmad ve-Na'im* (Jesnitz, 1743), section 116, p. 39a.

cards; the number may appear good one time or bad another time. Just as there are always six constellations on the horizon and sometimes the day is long and sometimes short, so it is [with respect to cards]. Furthermore, if you pay attention to the players, you shall observe that the action of the cards is really the action of the stars. The stars sometimes raise a person from the dung heap[1] to the heaven but suddenly, 'He perishes forever, like his dung; Those who saw him will say: "Where is he?" '[2] The cards similarly raise him up, offering him bountiful success and victory so that 'He made its posts of silver.'[3] But immediately, 'You see it, then it is gone.'[4]

"What we have stated regarding success is also true regarding evil influence, since for a scholar, knowledge of a thing and its opposite are one.[5] Just as a person who is under an evil celestial influence is capable of 'cooling' the evil by his effort and wisdom, as Scripture states: 'Hide but a little moment, until the indignation passes,'[6] so the expert in card playing will detect a bad day and not enter into the snares of the game. 'He will deliver it, as he protects it; he will rescue it as he passes over,'[7] until the evil hours pass which are undesirable, and 'then the lame man will leap as a deer.'[8]

"These four kings on the cards also hint at the four elements upon which the world rests. They also recall the creation of the world through the passage of four ages, namely, those of gold, silver, copper, and iron.[9] Thus the king of shields[10] represents the world of gold when it was still new, when people did not act deceitfully against their neighbor nor did they lie to each other [while] sitting at the table together,[11] rather justice, justice they pursued.[12] The cow and the bear grazed and every man sat under his vine and under his fig tree.[13]

"The silver world arose after it, represented by the king of goblets.[14] The world then began to decline from its former majesty and goodness.

[1]Cf. Psalm 113:7.
[2]Job 20:7.
[3]Song of Songs 3:10.
[4]Proverbs 23:5.
[5]If you understand one thing, you can figure out its opposite. Cf. Aristotle, *Categories,* 10 (11B25). For the same expression, see below.
[6]Isaiah 26:20.
[7]Cf. Isaiah 31:5.
[8]Isaiah 35:6.
[9]On the four ages, see Ovid, *Metamorphoses,* Loeb ed. (Cambridge, Mass., 1946), bk. 1.
[10]Also called *danari.*
[11]Cf. Daniel 11:17.
[12]Cf. Deuteronomy 1:20.
[13]Cf. Isaiah 11:7, Micah 4:4, and elsewhere. Cf. Ovid, *Metamorphoses,* p. 9.
[14]Or *cuppe.*

The [God's] blessing no longer flourished as it had previously in the golden world. This is hinted at by the goblet, which has a receptacle [suggesting closure or finitude]. It is not round without beginning or end, as in the case of the king of shields [which are round]. Do not ask why the first days were better than these; it is simply because the first ones were like gold and these [later days] were like silver. This [latter] world began when Solomon died, for in his days the disc of the moon was filled, as the rabbis explained in *Midrash Rabbah* regarding the verse 'This month shall be to you.'[1] When he died, the kingdom of the house of David was divided and Shishak came upon Jerusalem and took away the treasures of silver and gold.[2] 'And he increased mourning'[3] in the world. Then the silver world, the rule of King Jove, the son of king Saturn, began. The golden bowl was crushed, and in its place stood the silver suggested by the goblet in the biblical verse: 'And put my goblet, my silver goblet.'[4]

"Afterward, the king of toil arose,[5] who lies in wait, and he took clubs[6] in his hand and copper replaced silver. The club signifies 'toil,' as the rabbis state: 'A club and whip fell from heaven.'[7] And it came to pass in the days of the king who came after him [referring to the king of spades]; in every place where it was stated 'and it came to pass' it signifies there was no distress.[8] He was a tyrannical king who lived by his sword.[9] This denotes the world of iron, which is more evil than that of all the other metals, for when it was created, all the trees trembled.[10] Thus in this world, 'the earth trembles' and 'the sun and moon withdraw their brightness.'[11] Moreover, there is no day which does not have a curse and each day's curse is more severe than that of

[1]*Shemot Rabbah*, 15:26, on Exodus 12:1. During his rule, Solomon reigned over the entire earth, but when he died, royal power diminished. This is like the moon whose light wanes after reaching a full disc. On Solomon's golden shields, see 1 Kings 14:26.

[2]See 1 Kings 14:25.

[3]Cf. Lamentations 2:5.

[4]Genesis 44:2. Cf. Ovid, *Metamorphoses*, p. 11.

[5]Or "strain." Ovid, p. 11, calls the third kingdom a brazen race, of sterner disposition.

[6]Or *bastoni*.

[7]This is a blatant misquotation of *Sifre Devarim* 40, p. 83 (Finklestein ed.). The original speaks of a piece of bread and a stick falling from heaven, i.e., God's mercy and severity of judgment together. Here the verse emphasizes only the latter quality. Both this quote and the next one suggest the author's playfulness in fabricating supposed rabbinic statements to legitimate the gambler's argument, a kind of "Purim Torah."

[8]The second part of the line refers to the phrase in the first part. The explanation is precisely the opposite of a rabbinic statement which indicated that every time the phrase "and it came to pass" appears, it signifies that there was distress. See B. T. Megillah 10b; *Bereshit Rabbah*, 42:3. To the reader familiar with rabbinic literature, the author's humor in deliberately fabricating the texts would have been obvious.

[9]Or *spada*.

[10]See *Bereshit Rabbah*, 5:9.

[11]Cf. Judges 5:4; Joel 2:10, 4:15.

the preceding one.[1] If it had not been for the doxology recited after the scriptural reading[2] and the [response of] 'Amen, may His name [be blessed],' after studying *aggadah* [rabbinic homily],[3] the world would not endure, as Scripture states: 'A land of thick darkness, as darkness itself,'[4] and as the rabbis declared in chapter *Eglah Arufah*.[5]

"King Nebuchadnezzar's dream also hinted at these four worlds. If he would have understood cards, he would not have needed Daniel to interpret it [his dream]. 'The head of fine gold'[6] was the kingdom of Assyria which, according to the opinion of Isaac Abravanel in his commentary on Daniel, began in the reign of Amraphel, the king of Shinar, and [continued] until Nebuchadnezzar.[7] This was the gold world suggested by the king of shields. After it, the Persian kingdom arose, which was more evil than the previous one; 'its breasts and arms were of silver.'[8] The third king was the kingdom of Greece, of copper, and the fourth king was mighty as iron. Notice the wonderful [coincidence] that just as the fourth kingdom is divided into two parts, Edom and Ishmael, similarly the design of the swords on the cards [of spades] depicts two spears, the head of one opposite the end of the other, [as the verse states]: 'They shall intermingle with the offspring of man but they shall not cleave one to another.'[9]

"This wicked man would have continued to speak deceitfully and to entice those who heard his words that praised the cards in such a manner. Yet where it is stated to be brief, I have no right to [speak] at length. May his mouth be stopped up with earth, for he torments me still and is about to shake me severely![10]

"He also would have tied a knot of lies and vanities around the dice, declaring that their inventor and organizer was a great wise man and prophet unlike anyone who arose in Israel or among the nations of the

[1]Cf. B. T. Sotah 49a, Mishnah Sotah 9:12.

[2]*Kiddushah de-Sidrah,* "the doxology of the order," now recited at the conclusion of the morning service which begins: "And a redeemer shall come to Zion." Cf. I. Abrahams, *A Companion to the Authorized Prayer Book* (New York, 1966), pp. 82–83.

[3]The line from the *kaddish* prayer (also a doxology), which originally functioned as the concluding prayer to public aggadic reading.

[4]Job 10:22.

[5]B. T. Sotah 49a. The same passage is quoted below in Part II, sec. 50.

[6]Cf. Daniel 2:32.

[7]Cf. Abravanel, *Ma'ayene ha-Yeshu'ah,* Ma'ayan 6 (Tel Aviv, 1960), p. 308, which is not the precise reference.

[8]Cf. Daniel 2:32.

[9]Daniel 2:43. On the Italian style of crossing or interlacing the marks on the suits of spades and clubs, see Wilshire, p. 23 and plate 9; W. G. Benham, *Playing Cards* (London and Melbourne, 1931), p. 9.

[10]Cf. B. T. Babba Batra 16a; Isaiah 22:17.

world. He was the same Balaam, the son of Beor, to whom the rabbis referred in interpreting the verse: 'There has not risen a prophet in Israel like Moses.' [They declared]: 'He rose only among the foreign nations. Who was he? Balaam.'[1] We have found in *Midrash Tanḥuma,* in the [biblical] portion of Noah, that 'Balaam began with dice, etc.'[2] He invented and established them [the dice] according to a science [regarding the number seven] greater than natural science and astronomy, for 'sworn are the rods and their point,'[3] which are always seven. Seven recalls the world's creation 'for in six days the Lord worked . . . and He rested on the seventh day.'[4] [The number seven] also hints at the seven nebulous stars, for, like them, good appears either in their coming or returning. [The number seven] is also suggested in the interpretation of the verse: 'Their king shall rise above Agag'[5] by the author of the *Akedat Yizḥak.* This [king] refers to David; when he arises, he [Agag] declines.[6]

"He further concluded that their material [of the dice], which is dry bones, and their play, which is spinning around a board or table, hints at the rolling of the bones of the dead and other things underground. He continued to talk more obscure nonsense about the excellent number seven, which Vergil called a perfect number because of its perfection. However, in reality, only six is a perfect number, as is clear to the mathematicians.[7] The author of the *Akedat Yizḥak* also praised [this number] on the Torah portion *Shemini.*[8]

"This, then, is the essence of his words which seduced me, caused me to give up all other things and activities, and focus my attention on cards, since I believed that all human perfection depended on them. This wicked and deceitful man enticed me with the pleasantry of his words to believe that falsehood could be substantiated. He built a formless building with empty stones[9] and he brought me to this point."

---

[1] See *Sifre Devarim,* end of 357, on Deuteronomy 34:10.

[2] *Midrash Tanḥuma* (Buber ed.), parshat No'aḥ, 217 (New York, 1946), p. 48. In *Beit Ya'ar ha-Levanon,* 4:12, Yagel again refers to the importance of dice, quoting ibn Ezra. He also attributes the invention of dice to Balaam.

[3] Habakkuk 3:9. "sworn" (*shevu'ot*) is taken to mean seven (*shevah*).

[4] Exodus 20:11; 31:17.

[5] Agag was the Amalak king mentioned in Numbers 24:7.

[6] Isaac Arama, *Akedat Yizḥak* (Pressburg, 1849), vol. 4, parshat Balak, 82, p. 113b. The numerical value of "Agag" is seven and of "David" is fourteen (double seven).

[7] Cf. V. F. Hopper, *Medieval Number Symbolism* (New York, 1938), pp. 36–37. Compare also the quotation of Philo, in Hopper, pp. 47–48. A perfect number is one whose divisors add up to the number itself. For example, the divisors of 6 are 1, 2, 3, and $1 + 2 + 3 = 6$.

[8] Isaac Arama, *Akedat Yizḥak,* vol. 3, parshat Shemini, 59, p. 22b.

[9] Cf. Isaiah 34:11.

### Resumption of the Son's Life Story

[21] Some time afterward, the souls left us and we returned to our talk. I began to relate the principal conditions [agreed upon] between us [between Madame Rina and Abraham Yagel]: "First, it was expected of me to take the initial profit of fifteen percent of the earnings for myself and to hand over to Madame Rina ten percent annually. [The latter sum] was to be free of any tax or other duty or any fixed or irregular expenditure. From the remainder, that is, from the five percent, I was to pay all the annual expenses of the bank, both fixed and additional outlays as they arose, as well as the expenses and salary of her trustee, other remaining expenditures, and direct and indirect damages. If anything else remained, I was expected to hand it over to her trustee since she wished to benefit him by giving both of us a present [to purchase] chickens and pigeons for slaughter."

My father then remarked: "If your stupidity and lack of understanding led you to provide all of this, how could you complain about this [arrangement]? Doesn't it state in Scripture that 'a man's folly subverts his way'?[1] You should have first consulted wise and understanding men; they would have instructed you in the strategy you should have chosen, since 'there is victory with a multitude of counselors.'"[2]

I responded: "Pay attention, my master, if my words seem sincere to you. I was then like a person sinking in the river. Even if a sharp sword had been held out to me, I would have taken hold of it, and would not have felt if it cut my hand, since all my body was like a sieve. I utterly had no support nor any escape. I was pressured to lend money; the ledger was open and I couldn't find a partner. I initially required permission from his honor, the duke, may his majesty be exalted. I had asked him twice to grant my request, but it was to no avail. As time passed, my troubles increased with each moment bringing new hurt and additional loss and expenditures. Thus from the outset, the terms [offered by] Madame Rina seduced and overcame me, couched in the pleasantness of her words. [She claimed] that money offers a solution and that I would never lack funds again. I also could utilize the money for other business ventures so that by increasing trade, benefits would increase. Thus the saying goes: 'Cling to a nobleman and they [his dependents] will bow down to you.'[3] Similarly, the popular expression states that one who touches honey will lick his fingers. Thus, with these expectations, the partnership began.

[1] Proverbs 19:3.
[2] Cf. Proverbs 11:14; 24:6.
[3] Cf. *Sifre Devarim*, 6; Rashi on Genesis 15:18, and elsewhere.

"However, according to my opinion, it began at the time when Saturn or Mars was dominant [in the skies], or any evil conjunction among those mentioned by Haly [Aben Ragel] in his book,[1] indicating a calamitous result for anyone who begins an activity [in this period]. I swear by God that from that day on, all my actions were cursed. How beautiful was the messenger of good tidings,[2] Adam Ḥazak, may he be protected,[3] who initially said to me: 'I heard about the partnership you concluded. May the Lord send you blessing in your barns.[4] But know that anyone who associates with her [Madame Rina] and touches her money [can be designated by the biblical verse]: "Write you this man childless, a man who shall not prosper in his days." '[5] And so it was. When it came time for the woman to provide a decent amount [of funds] for the bank, and we came to write up the papers between us, my hopes were dashed,[6] for she retreated from the pledges she had made to me on the first day. She now wanted to put in only what she had already deposited. She expressed herself fully and clearly to me that she no longer desired to be involved in this business venture and that I should not restrain myself from looking for someone else to take her place.

"Her decision was based on three reasons. First, [the response to] my third letter of request [to open the bank] which I had sent to the honorable duke had been delayed, since [it had been linked to his pending decision] on the general terms to be extended to the Jews. Second, she was no longer enthusiastic about the venture. Just as it is the nature of primal matter to desire a form and then to reject it immediately and desire another, so too is it the nature of women to want something and then to reject it. This matter confirmed for me all my life why the philosopher had likened the lecherous woman to primal matter. Indeed, all women are equal in this respect.[7] Third, the individual who was designated to divide the aforementioned profit of five percent was supposed to come and live in this city and assume

[1] Yagel was referring to Albohazen Haly filii Abenragel, *Libri de Judiciis Astrorum* (Basel, 1551). Yagel quoted this author on other astrological matters, including the Siamese twins he describes below. See Ruderman, *Kabbalah, Magic, and Science*, p. 199, n. 43.

[2] Cf. Isaiah 52:7.

[3] On Adam Forti (Ḥazak), see I. Sonne, *Mi-Pa'olo ha-Revi'i ad Pi'us ha-Ḥamishi* (Jerusalem, 1954), p. 211, where Forti is mentioned as having signed a letter with other communal leaders in Mantua, offering assistance to the Jewish community of Ancona in 1569.

[4] Cf. Deuteronomy 28:8.

[5] Jeremiah 22:30.

[6] Cf. Job 41:1.

[7] Yagel's general attitude toward women was more positive in his *Eshet Ḥayil* (Venice, 1605), a short commentary on Proverbs 31, which he composed for Rachel, the wife of the wealthy banker Hezekiah b. Isaac Foa. See his further thoughts on women below and see the introduction above, p. 64.

the responsibility[1] of supervising the gains and losses related to the monthly operations [of the bank]. When he realized, however, that there would be no profit to show for his labor, he changed his mind regarding these arrangements, and decided against coming to live here. Since Madame Rina had placed so much trust in his counsel, when he pulled out, she likewise desired to withdraw from the venture.

"These then are the factors which convinced her to change her mind. Although this is hardly a matter of hidden secrets, one might still ask what I initially had expected from such an arrangement and what had I envisioned in the end. She did tell me orally and even put it in writing that 'within a year, fixed like the years of a hired laborer,'[2] I would be expected to find a person to take her place who would be required to pay her back without any expectation of receiving any more from her. If, after the year, a replacement had not been found, she would appoint whomever she desired to collect the loans and pledges [to compensate] for all my expenditures, damages, and that which caused damage [to her]."

[22] In the meantime, we heard a thunderous, screaming voice and noticed two men flying toward us, telling each other the story of their lives. The first declared: "Woe to me for my pain and sorrow is greater than yours!" But the other responded: "My ruin is greater than yours, vast like the sea!"[3] I stood unnerved by the voices [of the men] opposite me.

But my father turned to me and said: "Don't be afraid, for I am with you. Don't be terrified since they cannot harm you in any way. If their countenances appear evil and scary at first, you should know that I recognize these two souls who departed the earth before their time. They wander until the time comes when they finally will be allowed to rest and enjoy the fruit of their labor."

## On "Dying Before One's Time"

[23] I asked: "How can man die before his time? Isn't his time decreed in the night that he was conceived and on the day he was born?[4] Doesn't man have a term of service on earth in which he can calculate his days and years as those of a hired servant[5] who is appointed for a year or two, or a week or

[1]Cf. Isaiah 9:5.
[2]Cf. Isaiah 21:16.
[3]Cf. Lamentations 2:13.
[4]Cf. Job 3:3.
[5]Cf. Job 7:1.

a jubilee? The poet wrote regarding the general duration of men's time [on earth]: 'The days of our years are seventy, etc.'[1] If one receives less than this time, it was because of a heavenly decree emanating from the star ruling him at the moment of his birth and conception. Both of them, that is, birth and conception, 'will be established together,'[2] as Hermes wrote and as ibn Ezra remarked in his commentary on *Shemot*.[3] The place [that determines] growth at birth, by which life is determined, is the place of the moon at conception as all the astrologers and [natural] philosophers conclusively establish in their writings. [The only difference between them] is that the astrologers claim that everything is the result of the reigning constellation, while the [natural] philosophers claim that it is the result of the nature of matter and its composition. Galen writes that from this [matter], the [evil] inclination emerges, as it states in the biblical verse: 'For He knows our [evil] inclination and remembers that we are dust.'[4]

"According to the natural strength and vitality of seminal drop, the strength or weakness of a child is determined, as Nahmanides alluded to in his *Iggeret ha-Kodesh,* when he commented on the passage where R. Isaac says: 'One who turns his bed to the north or south, etc.'[5] Depending on its [seminal drop's] strength or weakness, a person's days will be long or short. The intrinsic moisture and natural warmth are like a wick attached to a candle since vitality depends on them. As long as they [the moisture and warmth] are plentiful, life is healthy. Just as long as there is oil, the burning candle will continue to light, but when it [the oil] runs out, the candle will extinguish into complete darkness, as Solomon declared: 'The fire will go out with no trees.'[6] Thus, even if these various schools of thought disagree on the active cause—either one's star or constellation, one's nature or matter—they all acknowledge that from the outset it is decreed whether man's life is lengthened or shortened. In death, everything of his life is taken away[7] and he is called 'one who died in his time.' The [proper] time

[1] Psalm 90:10.

[2] Cf. Leviticus 22:18.

[3] Ibn Ezra on Exodus 2:2. Yagel also quotes Hermes as an authority on astrological prognostication in the discourse on the Siamese twins below. His source, an anonymous pamphlet on the twins (see the introduction above), also quoted Hermes and might have been the source for this reference as well. On Yagel's interest in Hermetic sources and "Ancient Theology," see Ruderman, *Kabbalah, Magic, and Science,* chap. 9.

[4] Psalm 103:14.

[5] Nahmanides, *Iggeret ha-Kodesh,* Chavel ed., 2:377, commenting on B. T. Berakhot 5b. On the false attribution of this kabbalistic moral work to Nachmanides, see J. Dan in *EJ,* 8: 1237–8.

[6] Proverbs 26:20.

[7] Cf. Psalm 49:18.

apportioned and decreed him is the same whether he dies at a tender or a old and hoary age. Therefore, what do you mean, my master, when you state that man dies before his time? Give me understanding so that I shall live."[1]

[24] He responded: "Listen attentively and I will teach you wisdom[2] regarding what constitutes the essence of truth. Know that man's fate is decreed in heaven during the time of his conception and birth. His days are numbered, either few or many, according to the power of the growing and dominating constellation.[3] The strength or weakness of his physical matter and constitution will depend on how these stars turn. Thus the rabbis declared in *Midrash Tanḥuma:* '[The biblical verse] "If you walk in my statutes" is related to the verse "His days are determined."[4] In other words, in the time that the Holy One, blessed be He, created the world, He determined the days of everyone, etc.' Thus the rabbis alluded to what we said. From the time God created the world and ordered nature in all its manifestations, He determined and apportioned the days of each person, as it is written: 'I will fulfill the number of your days.'[5] There is then a determined number [of days]; the angel of death passing by cannot overcome a person who gains a full life until [God] wishes [it be so], just as the worker is hired for the day.

"The rabbis alluded [to the same idea] in the Jerusalem Talmud *Berakhot*[6]: 'When R. Abin bar Ḥiyyah was dead, R. Zeirah entered and spoke of him [quoting the following verse]: "A worker's sleep is sweet, whether he has much or little to eat."[7] This is like a king who hired workers, and among the workers was one who hired himself out more than the others. Similarly, R, Abin bar Ḥiyyah toiled more in twenty-eight years than an earnest scholar would have toiled in a hundred.' Thus the rabbis alluded to the fact that sometimes a man dies at his [right time] when he is still young, reaching the end of his life as if he had lived one thousand years. Although R. Abin bar Ḥiyyah died at the age of twenty-eight, his days and years were not cut off, for this was his time decreed to him by his constellation. In this [alloted] time, he acquired perfection coming 'to the grave in ripe old age as shocks of grain are taken away in their season.'[8]

[1]Cf. Psalm 119:144.
[2]Cf. Job 33:33.
[3]The next word is unclear. "In the eighth," perhaps eighth heaven or sphere.
[4]*Midrash Tanḥuma,* Beḥukotai, 1, on Leviticus 26:3 and Job 14:5.
[5]Exodus 23:26.
[6]J. T. Berakhot, 2 (5c).
[7]Ecclesiastes 5:11.
[8]Cf. Job 5:26.

[25] "Both the astronomers and naturalists agree that the stars of a person's soul determine his nature and constitution with respect to the despicable qualities, such as murder, theft, haughtiness, and the like. In this way, they [the stars] affect his material constitution [so as to be influenced] by one of the four qualities: heat, dryness, coldness, and wetness. For example, when Mars affects a person's constitution, [causing him] to murder or to become irritable or haughty, it is because this star imparts the quality of heat and dryness to his matter. For this reason, the person possesses these qualities. The rest of the stars exert their influence in like manner.

"However, when a [natural philosopher] examines a person with these qualities, he will simply declare that his matter is thus disposed to be hot or dry, causing him to become irritable. He will not look to the heavens to observe Mars's force or to the rest of the stars, since it is not his discipline. The subjects the natural philosopher writes about are the material world and nature; only to them will he direct his words and investigations. Accordingly, he only will investigate this man from the perspective of his material being and his nature. On the other hand, since the astronomer's subject matter is the heavens and their firmaments, he directs his words and investigations to the latter. He will thus make his horoscopes and will ignore the writings of the naturalist who is concerned with the matter of nature alone, since it [astrology] is the subject of the astrologer. Therefore, what is decreed—whether longevity, good life, wealth, or wisdom—will be [according to each man's perspective].[1]

"The *Tosafot* [the school of medieval Jewish commentators in France and Germany who wrote glosses on the Babylonian Talmud] similarly explained in the chapter *Kol ha-Yad*[2] that [everything] in the life of a man— his qualities, illnesses, punishments, and evil decrees—is ordained for him and he cannot protect himself [from them]. So it is written in *Ḥullin:*[3] 'No one bruises his finger unless it was so decreed in heaven.' The rabbis likewise declared in the same chapter of *Kol ha-Yad:*[4] 'The name of the angel in charge of conception is "night." He takes a drop and places it in the presence of the Holy One, blessed be He, and says: "Master of the universe!

---

[1]We should note that the stark contrast between the naturalist and the astrologer that Yagel draws here bears little relationship to the reality of Yagel's practice as an astrological physician. His "eclectic therapy" clearly fused Galenic medicine with astrological (and kabbalistic) diagnosis. For a discussion of Yagel's medical approach, see Ruderman, *Kabbalah, Magic, and Science,* chap. 2.

[2]B. T. Niddah 16b.

[3]B. T. Ḥullin 7b.

[4]B. T. Niddah 16b.

What shall be the fate of this drop? Shall it produce a strong or weak person, a wise or stupid one, a wealthy or poor one?" He does not mention whether [it will produce] a righteous or evil one, etc.'

"Therefore, the head of the poets, our master David declared: 'The Rock of Israel said concerning me: "He who rules men justly, he who rules in awe of God [is like the light of morning etc.]" '[1] For in this area [i.e., moral conduct], the constellation has no power to determine [one's fate] but only to influence it. God gave men a choice to do good or evil, as it is written: 'I have set before you life and death. . . . Therefore, choose life.'[2] A person can change his fate with his good deeds, as the Bible wrote regarding Abraham: 'Look toward heaven.'[3] The rabbis also stated: 'What is your calculation? Because Jupiter stands in the west? I will turn it back and place it in the east, etc.'[4] Thus with prayer and good deeds, man's life and years are lengthened. This was the case of Hezekiah, king of Judah, who prayed to God, as it is written: 'I hereby add fifteen years to your life.'[5] The rabbis also declared that twenty-two years were added to the life of Benjamin, the righteous one.[6] Conversely, man changes his good fate to bad with evil deeds. Even if all the heavenly conjunctions decreed a judgment of seventy good years for him, it [the judgment] would be torn up and the blessing would be overturned, etc.[7] So we observed that in the case of the kings of Israel and Judah, when they defied God through their evil actions, they immediately were given over to the hand of the foreign nations.

[26] "Yet we should know, (and with this [knowledge], those who weary themselves with the question of the suffering of the righteous and the happiness of the wicked may rest), that in order to change an individual's judgment from bad to good, his actions must be exceedingly good and superior. He must cling to God as Abraham, our father, and the other righteous and pious ones [did]. Their merit enabled them to transform the evil decree and the wicked constellation to good. Likewise, to change the good decree of a man to evil, one must commit many evil acts as Ahitofel, Gehazi, Menasseh, and others like them [did].[8] Average acts are not potent enough to transform to good or evil what had been decreed for a person.

[1]2 Samuel 23:3.
[2]Deuteronomy 30:19.
[3]Genesis 15:5.
[4]B. T. Shabbat 156a, indicating that man has the capacity to overturn his astral fate with God's help.
[5]Isaiah 38:5.
[6]B. T. Babba Batra 11a.
[7]Cf. B. T. Berakhot 31b.
[8]Cf. 2 Samuel 15–17; 2 Kings 4–5; 2 Kings 21.

Instead, God's general justice will reward him for his deeds in the next world. 'Behold, He who formed the mountains and created the wind and has told man what is [said in] his conversation,'[1] even a light conversation between a man and his wife, will bestow a [just] decree in the next world. The rabbis similarly state: 'One who prepares on Sabbath eve will eat on the Sabbath in the world of eternal rest which is all a Sabbath.'[2] Only in this world are one's ways and actions under the force of his constellation and fate, as we have said. The truth is that, with his intelligence and free choice, man can save himself from many accidental and harmful occurrences.

[27] "Similarly, even if a person is protected from his constellation, he should also protect his life from exposure to such dangers as [exist in] a place of plague, war, or pestilence, and the like, since in these situations permission is given to 'Satan' to hurt and the general decree weakens the potency of the individual decree and overcomes it. Thus the rabbis wrote in *Bereshit Rabbah:*[3] '[What is meant by the verse:] "But there is that which is swept away without judgment"?[4] It means [one is] without judgment in his own town, which is like what happened to a man from Sepphoris who went to Tiberias etc.'[5]

"So a man should protect himself from accidents, bodily illness, and harm, as the rabbis warned in chapter *Elu Na'arot:*[6] 'Everything is in heaven's hands except a bitter cold.' They similarly warned in many places [in rabbinic literature] not to misuse the force of the constellation lest one not be protected. For if a person does not take care when it is in his power to protect and save his life, then he is liable for his own life. This is the meaning of 'one who died before his time,' that there exists a nature whose damages are fixed. This is the reason for many deficiencies that alter one's fate either positively or negatively through the force of the constellation. The rabbis thus stated at the end of *Ḥullin:*[7] 'It was taught that R. Jacob said: "The revival of the dead depends on any commandment in the Torah with a ready reward. . . ." And didn't R. Eliezer declare that those who perform commandments are not harmed, either in their goings [and com-

---

[1]Cf. Amos 4:13.

[2]Cf. B. T. Avodah Zarah 3a.

[3]*Bereshit Rabbah* 49:8.

[4]Proverbs 13:23.

[5]The incident involved a citizen of Sepphoris who was seized for not paying a fine while in Tiberias. While Sepphoris later granted remission from payment, this still was obliged to pay according to the law of Tiberias. Thus the general decree "weakened" the potency of his individual decree.

[6]B. T. Ketubbot 30a.

[7]B. T. Ḥullin 142a.

ings]. This is a shaky ladder [i.e., formulation], for it is different in a place of fixed damage, as it is written: "How can I go? If Saul hears of it, he will kill me." '[1] Thus you can see that even the person who is protected from the constellation but puts himself in danger, if he is caught in a snare, bears the responsibility for his own life and thus dies before his time. These people are called 'generation' in the language of the rabbis, as in the biblical verse: 'One generation goes and another comes.'[2]

[28] "What we have said is illustrated in the first chapter of *Ḥagigah:*[3] 'Is there anyone who passes away before one's [allotted] time? Yes, as in the story [heard] by R. Bibi b. Abaye, who was frequently visited by the angel of death. [Once] the latter said to his messenger: "Go bring me Miriam, the women's hairdresser." He [the messenger] went and brought him Miriam, the children's nurse. He [the angel] said: "I told you Miriam, the hairdresser." He [the messenger] said: "If so, I will take this one back." Said he [the angel] to him: "Since you have brought her, let her be added [to the dead]. But how were you able to get her [since it was not yet her time to die]?" [Said the messenger]: "She was holding a shovel in her hand and was heating and raking the oven. She took it and put it on her foot and burnt herself; thus her constellation was impaired and I brought her." Said R. Bibi b. Abaye to him [the angel]: "Do you have permission to act this way?" He answered him: "Is it not written: 'But there is that which is swept away for lack of judgment'?"[4] He [R. Bibi b. Abaye] countered: "But, in fact, it is written: 'One generation passes away and another comes, and the world stands forever.'"[5] He [the angel] replied: "I have charge of them until they have completed the generation. Then I hand them over to Dumah [the angel in charge of the dead]."'

"Thus you see that this woman died before her time because she was burnt and her constellation was impaired. [However,] she was not handed over to Dumah, the guardian of the dead [immediately], but wandered instead in the world until her time came. Then she went to Dumah when the angel of death handed her over. This also happened to these unruly souls [that are] coming toward us. Thus the wise men invented medicine to protect people from such a death and from other harm unrelated to the constellation, as the rabbis wrote [regarding the verse] 'And shall cause him

---

[1] 1 Samuel 16:2. Samuel's response to God on being asked to find a new king among the sons of Jesse.
[2] Ecclesiastes 1:4.
[3] B. T. Ḥagigah 4b.
[4] Proverbs 13:23.
[5] Ecclesiastes 1:4.

to be thoroughly healed.'[1] From this we derive that God gave permission to the doctor to heal. Men similarly make a shield and a breastplate to protect themselves from a bow bent in battle.

"However, one might still ask if God fully knows what the actions and ways of man will be before he is born. If He knows that a person will be righteous, why would He allow him to be born under a certain constellation or evil conjunction, as in the case of R. Eleazar ben Pedat and Hananiah who subsisted on scanty food from Sabbath to Sabbath,[2] along with other such examples? Similarly, why doesn't He allow a baby who emerges from the womb of evil speakers and doers to be born under a good constellation? However, before responding to this question, (from the secret of wise and intelligent men, the blessed rabbis of sacred memory, who fathomed the divine mysteries, comprehending all subjects, knowing what God will do on heaven and on earth), let us come and hear what these two souls are screaming and yelling about.[3] Their measure was filled before their days and they died before their time, wandering without finding tranquility until the time came for them to die. The light and darkness of their days already has passed, but this day is still young. Let us approach them and bow down from afar before getting close to them in order to say: 'May God have compassion on you. Please do us no harm and do not become agitated on the way,[4] my brothers. Please tell us why you are crying.'"

When they heard our words, they raised their voices and cried aloud, but then restrained themselves.

## The Story of a Man Who Summoned Satan and Visited Gehenna

Then the first [soul] opened his mouth and said: [29] "I was a rhetorician. From the time of my youth, I chose to speak in subtle words[5] and I contemplated those books and that craft, or what is called 'wisdom.' It came to pass that one day a tyrannical king saw me, took me, and placed me under his charge, and I was well liked by him. Everything he owned he placed in my hand, and by my command, all his people were directed.[6] Yet

---

[1]B. T. Babba Kamma 85a on Exodus 21:19. The integration of proper medical care with Jewish theology is most characteristic of Yagel's writings in general.

[2]Cf. B. T. Ta'anit 10a.

[3]Literally, the sound of yelling. Cf. Exodus 32:18.

[4]Cf. Genesis 45:24.

[5]Cf. Job 15:5.

[6]Cf. Genesis 39:6, 41:40. Yagel probably hints at the parallel between the man's story and that of Joseph.

he knew nothing of me except for the food that he ate [for which I was responsible]. This king was doglike, born in the constellation of Sirius, cruel, and uncompassionate. He required his people and servants to perform despised and terrible work rigorously, work which he himself would not do. Moreover, he made his yoke fall equally on young and old, men and women. But he liked me and I became his executor and provider,[1] and after I spoke they [the members of his household] had nothing to say.[2]

"But one day I unintentionally killed a small dog of which he was especially fond.[3] He was angry at me and commanded that I be put in a pit and held captive in tresses and chains.[4] They put my feet in stocks and my body was laid in iron.[5] The pit was not empty but filled with water. Frogs had settled in it and all kinds of owls and birds of prey were hovering over it. They fed me barley bread[6] and offered me vinegar filled with worms to quench my thirst. I was on the verge of dying and in distress, so I loudly called to Satan[7] and said to him: 'Please take my soul and remove me from this jail; remember me and take me with you either in fire or in water,[8] wherever you desire. Answer me, answer me[9] this time.'

"When I opened my mouth wide,[10] Satan, whose only concern is for Cain and his associates,[11] answered me and appeared to me in a harsh prophecy.[12] He took me and brought me to his home, showing me his treasure house at the bottom of the earth. There were infinite treasures of fire, brimstone, salt, and aridity; also mud and clay, snow and hail. I saw many of my acquaintances and allies dwelling there.

"Then I came to a threshing floor [made of] of thorns and found there kings and noblemen. Among them was a man wearing red clothes whom I recognized since he had been a general and an associate of the king who had imprisoned me. I bowed down before him and inquired about his well-being. The officer answered: 'I have no peace because of my sins.' He asked

[1]Cf. 2 Samuel 5:2; 1 Chronicles 11:2.
[2]Cf. Job 29:22.
[3]Note the connection between the king's doglike disposition and the crime of killing a dog.
[4]Cf. Song of Songs 7:6.
[5]Cf. Job 13:27; 33:11; Psalm 105:18.
[6]Cf. Judges 7:13+.
[7]Cf. Psalm 118:5.
[8]Cf. Psalm 66:12.
[9]Cf. 1 Kings 18:37.
[10]Cf. Isaiah 5:14.
[11]Cf. *Bereshit Rabbah*, 20:16.
[12]Cf. Isaiah 21:2.

me about the king, whether his hand was still outstretched to direct his chariots fiercely and with a high hand, with intense brutality and with anger. Then he showed me a large chair of fire in the lowest baths of hell prepared for him [the king] unless he repented and gave up his evil way. Afterward, he said to me: 'Tell the king, her highness, and the nobles what you saw when you return to the world full of vanities.'

"When I still was awake in body and spirit during that vision, the prison guard came to offer me food to eat at mealtime, as was his custom. But when he looked, no one was to be found, even though the jail gates were locked with no apparent break [in the wall]. The man was very puzzled, so he looked at the bottom of the pit. But he found the ropes of my affliction as they had been, bound and sealed with his stamp. He was even more astonished since there were no traces of me.[1]

"He ran off to the king's court shouting: 'Spare me, my master, the king, for this is precisely what happened. I am innocent of any sin; my hands did no wrong nor did my eyes see anything [they were not supposed to see]. I stood on guard day and night with my associates, but we heard or saw nothing. Perhaps a spirit carried him or a wind swept him away,[2] and he went out stealthily,[3] for we have no idea of his whereabouts.' The king restrained himself and was quiet since he recognized that he [the guard] had told him all he knew and had no deceit in him. He then sent his slaves to inquire in every city—from house to house, from place to place, and from one corner to the next—but he found and heard nothing.

"Then, on the third day, the prison guard heard a loud and bitter scream from the pit. I cried as a ghost out of the ground, as a woman in labor.[4] He opened [the gate] and saw me in my place; my hands and my feet were bound by the ropes of my affliction as in the beginning. I asked for food to sustain [me]. The aura of my countenance had been transformed and my skin was shriveled on my bones.[5] A yellow color had spread over me and my bleary eyes had sunk in their place. The hair on my head also stood erect. So marred was my visage [that I was like one] having no form.[6] He [the guard] then asked me what this was, how did it come about, and what happened to me.

[1]The Hebrew *merkevotai* (my chariots) is probably a mistake and should be *ikvotai* (my traces). Cf. Psalm 77:20.

[2]Cf. 2 Kings 2:16; Ruth 3:7.

[3]Cf. Ruth 3:7.

[4]Cf. Isaiah 29:4; Isaiah 42:14.

[5]Cf. Lamentations 4:8.

[6]Cf. Isaiah 53:2.

"I then responded to him: 'Go and bring me quickly to the king for I have a secret message to tell him.'

"They rushed me from the pit and I came before the king and said: 'Know my master that in my illness, I was on the verge of dying, so I called to Satan and he answered me. He was attentive to my voice and brought me to a parched place lacking vines, dates, and pomegranates. I looked at the earth and it was desolate,[1] and at the heaven, and it had no light. I looked at the mountains and they were quaking and all the hills were rocking.[2] It was a dark place without light, all gloom and disarray,[3] and a place ordained for punishment. "Alas, the Lord has shamed," since there are places where the word for "guilty" [*ḥayeva*] is pronounced *ayeba* [from *ya'iv*—shamed]. [Thus, the latter may mean guilty.][4] Who in fire and who in boiling water?[5] All the slain of my poor people[6] are covered with sackcloth, darkness, fire, and smoke. There I also saw the fallen sons of the giants[7] who terrified humanity, and among them the general of the king[8] who was wearing his red uniform as he did in this world.

"'He told me various things regarding my master [the king] and he showed me your eternal seat [in hell]. He told me that your origin is from a fetid drop and your work is a thing of nought,[9] [deriving] from a hundred shrieks of a panting woman at the moment she is ready to give birth.[10] But you applauded it [this immoral behavior] and continued doing evil in God's eyes. You also went where He did not desire you to go. Now know that you surely will die a spiritual death; a fire fanned by no man will consume you.[11] The king will be brought to this place long ready [for him].[12] This will be a sign for you that he actually spoke these things to me. In order that you will believe my words, he told me your highly guarded secret regarding a certain battle and place hidden from anyone else in the world, known only to the two of you.'

[1]Cf. Genesis 6:12.

[2]Cf. Jeremiah 4:23–24.

[3]Cf. Job 10:21–22.

[4]The line in Aramaic, seemingly intrusive in the text, is from *Ekhah Rabbah*, 2:2, commenting on Lamentations 2:1. Yagel apparently uses it to emphasize the relation between the desolation of hell and the guilt of the sinners there.

[5]Based on the High Holy Day liturgy for the additional morning service.

[6]Cf. Jeremiah 8:23.

[7]Cf. Numbers 13:33.

[8]As in the Cincinnati manuscript; Mani's version is unintelligible.

[9]Cf. Isaiah 41:24.

[10]Cf. *Vayikrah Rabbah*, 27:7. The idea is that she is closer at that moment to death than to life.

[11]Cf. Job 20:26.

[12]Cf. Isaiah 30:33.

"I told him the secret and declared: 'I, in my sin, desired to approach him, to touch his clothing, but instead, a consuming fire[1] appeared with many lights—green, white, red, and brown. When one looked at a color, it disappeared, changed like clay under the seal, and stood up by itself as a garment.[2] It consecrated me but burned the hand which almost touched him.'[3] I showed it [the hand] to the king and it was scorched by fire.

"The king believed me because of the hidden secret I conveyed to him and the evidence of the mighty hand which touched me. He and his nobles were most fearful for their lives. They cried to the Lord, wept and tore their hearts and clothing, and wore sackcloth. The king then commanded that I should be taken to my house. But the men and the women of my household considered me a stranger whom they did not recognize. I was alien to them and my visage was unlike that of other men.

"After ten days had passed, I was stricken by heart failure and fever, pined away, and died, for I had been stricken in seeing Satan and my constellation turned bad. So now I wander throughout the earth until my time comes to be handed over to Dumah, the guardian of the dead. Look! Is there pain greater than mine? I later heard it said of me that since I gave my soul to Satan and called for him, no one would listen to me in heaven in order that I may be joined to God's inheritance, until seventy weeks and a time and times had passed,[4] because of the crime and sin I committed."

## A Story of Murder and a Wife's Revenge

[30] The second soul then responded: "I was born of a distinguished family. My ancestors were noblemen, well-known and wise lords, chiefs of the lords of my city and country, and men of understanding whose opinion was sought by every state. Moreover, they continued to grow in stature, wealth, and dignity. With this honor, I was born during a full moon.[5] I was the favorite son of my father, playing in his presence every day and at every opportunity. He never caused me grief by questioning me about my actions. He even accompanied me to school. But after going to observe [the school] for [only] two weeks, I claimed that my studies were completed. And when I was told to go to the house of God, [I complained] that my

[1]Cf. Deuteronomy 4:24 and elsewhere.
[2]Cf. Job 38:14.
[3]Cf. Exodus 29:37; Leviticus 6:20+.
[4]Cf. Daniel 9:24, 7:25; i.e., until the messianic era.
[5]A further indication of his good fortune.

head ached. Even though I was brought up in wisdom and morality, I still could not distinguish 'Haman's curse' from 'Mordecai's blessing.'[1] Moreover, I detested all wisdom, scholars, books, and authors, and if I had been permitted, I would have burned them all. I also would have held a sword at the entrance to the house of study, piercing anyone who might enter and striking down anyone interested in any book.

"Instead I chased women, since young girls liked me. I especially was attracted to one beautiful maiden of noble stock and I asked her to be my wife. But her parents refused to give her to me because of the wickedness of my actions and [they] offered her to my friend who was more righteous than I. He too came from a well-to-do family of good qualities and manners. He also was versed in intellectual and divine manners, was well liked by others, and had a pleasant appearance. He loved his wife as much as himself, and she also was attracted to him, so that both of them were of one flesh.[2] That which one loved, the other did not despise, and that which crossed one's lips, [the other] willingly performed.[3]

"Nevertheless, the spark of love which incited my desire toward her when she was still a virgin was never extinguished. Just as before, when laying in bed, I had lustful thoughts of enticing and seducing her due to the obstinacy of my evil heart. Yet when I spoke to her each day, she was never attentive to me either regarding trivial or important matters; nor would she ever speak to me in intimate surroundings.[4]

"Then one day her husband was ambushed by enemies who intended to kill him. I ran to save him from destruction and from those who sought to harm him. When this man realized what I had done for him in saving him from his enemies, he adored me. He became so attached to me that he pondered each day how he might do me a good turn. He would go wherever I went. He would go wherever I was and [conversely] he could not be found where I was not. I would frequent his home day and night as [if I were] one of his brothers or close associates, and no one would ask me what I was doing there. Even his modest wife would honor me upon realizing her husband's affection toward me and the good deed I had done him. But in her good wisdom, she always would act in a manner that preserved her full modesty and dignity.

"When I saw this woman, her conversation with and her deep affection for her husband, I asked myself: 'How can I amount to anything? It is just

[1]Cf. B. T. Megillah 7b; in other words, he lacked moral sensitivity.
[2]Cf. Genesis 2:24.
[3]Cf. Deuteronomy 23:24.
[4]Literally, "from behind the curtain." Cf. B. T. Ḥagigah 15a.

foolishness and vain aspiration to think badly of her.' I should have re-moved these lecherous thoughts from my heart because of her love for her husband and because of his honor, since the honor of my friend should be as dear to me as my own.[1] But I did not drop the matter. Even though I estranged myself [from her] out of respect, the great love in my heart continued to burn like fire, deeply ingrained in me as before. I searched for a way to remove her husband so that when she became a widow, it would be decreed [in heaven] that the dead be forgotten.[2] I would then inquire about her at the end of her mourning period and ask her to be my wife. I tried to devise a strategy to murder this righteous and fine person who trusted me, but to conceal my act so that no one would know my secret.

"One day we were riding together in a forest where we were ac-customed to roam to hunt prey two or three times a week. Suddenly, a wild boar, enormous in appearance and unlike any we had ever seen, emerged from an opening in the forest and headed toward us. We were terrified by this large animal which approached the horse my friend rode to trample it. He drew his sword from his sheath and wounded the beast on its head. When I saw my friend struggling with the boar, I said to myself: 'It is time to laugh.'[3] I approached him from his rear, looking around to see that no one would observe anything. I then struck my friend on the head, wound-ing him only slightly. He fell to the ground, stretched out to his full height, but I changed the position of the body so that he couldn't raise his head and left him for prey to the animal. The wild boar then gnawed at his head, producing large bruises and [eventually] killing him. I subsequently pur-sued the beast, struck it between its forehead and its ears until it fell to the ground. I dismounted the horse I was riding, decapitated the animal, cut off its shanks and hooves, and turned toward the city.

"When I came to the city, I screamed with a bitter and mournful voice, ripped up my own clothing, and brought the corpse to his [my friend's] house. Everyone [in the city] was terrified when they saw him, and they mourned the loss of a pious man who had been devoured as prey by a wicked animal. They all took it to heart. His wife appeared, fell on his body, hugged and kissed him, and refused to be comforted. I then showed her the head and feet of the beast and I cried with her. I also showed her how my clothes were soiled by the blood of the animal. But from that moment, the woman would not accept the fact that the beast had actually murdered her husband. The dead man's relatives and friends soon buried him while I

[1]Cf. Avot 2:10.
[2]Cf. B. T. Pesaḥim 54b.
[3]Cf. Ecclesiastes 3:4.

stood at the head of them all. All the inhabitants of the city paid him great honor. However, after the period of mourning had passed, I went to ask the woman to be my wife, but she continued to embitter herself in sobbing. She told me she would descend [to be with] her husband, her master, to wear away in the nether world, while all along, she cried for him.

[31] "Since it is decreed in heaven that everything is heard in the end, (as *Targum Yerushalmi* translates: 'Everything that happens in the world is decreed to be made public for all humanity, etc.'[1]), it so happened that when I murdered this man in the forest, someone else, who also had hidden himself in order to hunt, had observed me. He saw the act as it actually [had] occurred and how my own hands [had] shed that blood. After a month had passed, he came to the city and informed the [dead man's] wife on the very day that I had asked her [to be my wife] and she had refused me. She finally deduced that because of my love [for her], I had shed the blood of her husband; the proof being in that fact that I had asked her while his body was still warm in the grave. Day and night, she plotted how to take revenge on his behalf but she revealed her intention to no one.

"When I spoke with her a second time, she responded: 'Know, my master, that I always have loved you and I desire to be your lovemate and wife. Since my first husband is now dead, for what else can I hope? Is it not better for two to dwell together than [for me] to remain a widow?[2] To whom, other than you, my master, would I desire to be honored by marriage? I certainly have known that you have loved me with eternal love. I am fit for you as Bathsheba was fit for David ever since the [first] six days of creation.[3] But you certainly are aware of what the rabbis, of blessed memory, have counseled, that a woman should wait at least three months after the death of her first husband before remarrying.[4] Thus one can distinguish between a child she might bear, born after [a full pregnancy] of nine months, which belongs to her first husband, or a premature baby born in the seventh month, belonging to her second husband. Besides, there is a dispute among the *Tanna'im* [rabbis of the first and second centuries c.e.] whether a widow should wait for twelve months [before remarrying] because of mourning.[5] Although the law states that it is sufficient to wait

[1]Cf. Targum to Ecclesiastes 12:13.

[2]Cf. B. T. Kiddushin 42a.

[3]An ironic allusion to the parallel story of David, who had Uriah the Hittite murdered in order to have Bathsheba. Cf. 2 Samuel 11–12.

[4]See Mishnah Yebamot 4:10; B. T. Yebamot 42b; Maimonides, *Mishneh Torah, Nashim,* Hilkhot Gerushin 11:18; *Shulḥan Arukh, Eben ha-Ezer,* 8:1, 4.

[5]Yagel's reference to a dispute about a waiting period of twelve months is unclear to me, as it was to Mani, p. 15a.

for ninety-one days, nevertheless, women of noble stock are accustomed to remarry only after twelve months have elapsed, out of respect for the living and the dead. Therefore, I need to wait twelve months because of my honor. Please wait for me and the days will pass by us, and then you shall marry me. But since I have been aware of the flame of your great and powerful passion implanted in your heart, come to me to satisfy it at a certain night and at a certain place at midnight, by way of the garden upon which the window of my house looks out. Then we shall speak and get relief and delight in love.'[1]

"When I heard her words, I was exceedingly overjoyed. I did as she requested, coming to her on the appointed evening as quickly as a bird returns to its nest. But I did not find her there in the bedroom. Instead, I found an old woman of the household in her place who spoke to me: 'Wait a little longer for she makes coverlets for herself.[2] In the meantime, since I realize that you are very weary, eat a little of this sponge cake[3] and drink, and you shall feel good.' I did as she asked. I ate and I drank and I was happy about my deferred expectation.[4] I did not realize that in that aged wine, someone had placed a drug which induces sleep so that one is unable to feel any of his limbs, as if he were dead. And, in fact, this happened. I fell into a deep slumber and slept.

"Finally, the widow arrived and addressed [me]: 'Are you the man who shed the blood of my husband? I will now take my revenge on you, but [I] will not kill you with a sword lest you leave the world without experiencing the bitterness of death. Rather, I will torture you with afflictions worse than death, for blindness is reckoned as death.'[5] She then took a long needle without a hole which she had in her possession, and she thrust it into my two eyes three or four times until she saw that both of them had become like a sieve. She then turned in the direction of a sword which was there and said: 'Since I have avenged the blood of my master, my husband, why need I live any longer? I now shall die upon seeing my enemy stricken with pangs worse than death.' So she fell on the sword and died.

"On the morrow, her relatives learned of what had transpired and they discovered me stretched out on the ground, tottering between life and death, due to the incredible pain from my eyes and the drug which I had drunk in her bedroom. They took me to the authorities. The old woman

[1]Cf. Job 32:20.
[2]Cf. Proverbs 31:22.
[3]Following the correction of Mani, p. 15a, *sofganin* instead of *sangavim*.
[4]Cf. Proverbs 13:12.
[5]Cf. B. T. Nedarim 64b, *Pirke de R. Eliezer*, 32.

gave a full account of what had happened. The man who had witnessed my killing of the righteous victim also came and testified against me. They [the authorities] subsequently placed me in the lowest cell of the watchtower until I awoke and made my own admission, for an admission in court is worth one hundred witnesses.[1] In the meantime, the woman was buried with great honor next to her husband.

"When three days had passed and the wine wore off and I [fully] awoke, I was unaware of anything that had happened to me except that I felt the enormous pain in my eyes and the general weakness in all my limbs. I then cried loudly; the prison guards came and told me everything that had occurred. My heart expired within me[2] and my sorrow was greatly magnified over what I heard and because of the pain in my eyes, until I fell on my face. My soul left me and I died suddenly.

"All who saw me, ridiculed me, declaring: 'God is righteous.' They then took my corpse and buried it among the common people, since I was unworthy of burial in the place of my ancestors. Moreover, all the members of my family rose up together and declared: 'This impure one shall not come among us and his secret [story] is beneath our dignity.' It was also said of me: 'Moreover, he was not accorded a burial.'[3] Thus I was not buried in the family burial plot, and certainly the aborted fetus is better off than me. The officer of the city later sent for all my belongings, since the law stipulated that they should be confiscated for every murderer. The law could do no more violence to my body,[4] since my soul [had] left me. Please take notice and understand how, in one moment, that wealth was lost due to an evil matter, and how my honor and soul departed me.

[32] "Thus you surely should know that God is righteous and that I disobeyed his word. As the wise man said when he saw a skull floating on the surface of the water: 'Because you drowned others, they have drowned you.'[5] Just as conception leads [inevitably] to birth, labor and pain cannot be withheld from a evil person who plants it [through his own evil actions]. Filth always accompanies an evil person and evil, by its very nature, damages itself, as Eliphaz the Temanite stated: 'He will not be trusted; He will be misled by falsehood. . . . He will wither before his time, his boughs never having flourished.'[6] This I observed and I will report it; I was a

[1]Cf. B. T. Gittin 40b; Kiddushin 65b; Babba Meẓiah 3b.
[2]Cf. Jeremiah 23:9.
[3]Cf. Ecclesiastes 6:3.
[4]Cf. Jeremiah 22:17.
[5]Avot 2:7.
[6]Job 15:31–32.

symbol for all humanity. Now this is my fate to wander all day until my days and years are completed. Because of the constellation and nature, I am fated to wander without finding rest or comfort, to perform a satanic act, and then to encounter a multitude of hosts, a bundle of troubles, evil decrees, horrible afflictions, dispatch to hell, the place of suffering, the nethermost pit, Sheol and destruction, the pit of desolation, all gloom and disarray,[1] and the lowest earth which is the worst of all,[2] unless God has mercy on me and saves me from some or most of them [these fates]. After everything, I still do not know if I am included among the sinners and evildoers of Israel who commit corporeal [sins], whose bodies perish and whose souls burn.[3] Perhaps my death will atone for some of my iniquities and there still is hope for my soul; 'if it is cut down, it will renew itself; its shouts will not cease.'[4]"

My father then said to him: "You have your verdict which you determined yourself.[5] You brought the evil on yourself. How shall one answer the messengers of the nations regarding you[6] other than [to state] that your sins brought this on you? Who can I take as witness or liken to you to console you?[7] God knows that in all your trouble, He is troubled.[8] Because of His compassion, He will deal with you mercifully, save your soul from destruction, and declare that your suffering is sufficient."

## On the Moral Lessons of the Two Stories

[33] We then passed by them [the two souls] and my father turned to me: "Know and believe, my son Abraham, that it is proper for a man to punish his sons and the members of his household, to reprove them, and to direct them in the good and straight path, as Solomon, of blessed memory, said: 'Discipline your son and he will give you peace, he will give delight to your soul.'[9] The rabbis enlarged upon this idea in *Devarim Rabbah*[10] in reference to the verse: 'His father had never scolded him' about this. If his forefathers

[1]Cf. Job 10:22.
[2]Cf. B. T. Eruvin 19a.
[3]Cf. B. T. Rosh Ha-Shanah 17a.
[4]Job 14:7.
[5]Cf. 1 Kings 20:40.
[6]Cf. Isaiah 14:32.
[7]Cf. Lamentations 2:13.
[8]Cf. Isaiah 63:9.
[9]Proverbs 29:17.
[10]The quote (interpreting 1 Kings 1:6) is not found there but in *Shemot Rabbah*, 1:1; *Kohelet Rabbah*, 7:3.

had reproven him about this, his end would not have been like one of the vile people. If one educates a young person according to his [the parent's] way, he will not turn from the path in which he was directed when still a youth, even if he becomes old. If this had been the case, he would not have repudiated wise and ethical men, nor would he have been inclined to commit evil and deceitful acts such as these. For habit leads to control; the naturalists call this second nature.[1]

[34] "Thus this is the habit of anyone who breaks the yoke of heaven: If he becomes accustomed to committing small sins today,[2] one sin leads to another, until he is driven, in the end, from this world and the next. It is similar to the rabbinic saying that one who breaks his vessels [i.e., his merchandise] out of anger is like an idolator.[3] His heated passion urges him on until he finally is encouraged to go and worship idols. They also stated in *Yom ha-Kippurim*[4] '[regarding the verse]: "As it [red wine] gives its color in the cup, as it glides down smoothly."[5] R. Ammi and R. Ashi [disagreed on the meaning of the verse]. One said: "To anyone who drinks too much, the world seems like a plain [i.e., there are no impediments in his way] to him." The other said: "To anyone who drinks too much, all lewdness appears like a plain to him."' They also said there:[6] 'If a person commits a sin and repeats it, it becomes permissible. Permissible! Is that what you think? Rather, it [only] appears to the person as though it is permissible.'

"When a person breaks the yoke of fearing [God] and the yoke of the Torah, to act without restraint, and to leave the community in a high-handed manner; [when he] follows his heart's desire and proclaims with his tongue and talks excessively with his lips and [questions] in his heart: 'Who is my Lord?'; then many many factors lend him assistance in being brought down to the nethermost pit. He performs intentional sins as easily as unintentional ones, as in the case of this unfortunate man whose initial unintentioned neglect of his studies was the cause of breaking his neck. For this reason, the Torah contains the commandment regarding the stubborn and rebellious son,[7] so that the same thing will not happen to any other individual. If his beginning is indicative of his end, it is better that he

---

[1]For both phrases, see J. Klatskin, *Oẓar ha-Munaḥim* (Berlin, 1928), vol. 2, p. 211.
[2]Cf. Avot 2:1.
[3]Cf. B. T. Shabbat 105b, but also compare Maimonides, *Sefer ha-Maddah,* Hilkhot De'ot, 2:3, which is similarly formulated.
[4]B. T. Yoma 74b–75a, where the order of the statements is reversed.
[5]Proverbs 23:31.
[6]B. T. Yoma 86b.
[7]Cf. Deuteronomy 21:18–21.

should die while still innocent rather than guilty, as R. Jose the Galilean taught:[1] 'Did the Torah decree that the rebellious son should be brought before the court and stoned merely for eating a *triens* [a weight] of meat or for drinking a log of Italian wine? The Torah foresaw the ultimate destiny of the stubborn and rebellious son. In the end, after expending his father's wealth, he would [still] seek to satisfy his accustomed wants. Being unable to do so, he would go to the crossroads [where merchants pass frequently] to steal from others. Therefore the Torah stated that it is better that he die innocent rather than guilty; for the death of the wicked both benefits themselves and the world, etc.'

"The world benefits from the death of the wicked since they no longer are able to teach others their evil and crooked ways, nor do they tip the scales of divine justice toward a stern decree with their sins. Thus we discover that the wise men were careful in warning people never to reach this [wicked] attribute by loosening the bonds of the Torah and the commandment and changing one's shoe strap.[2] In a time of persecution, it is better for one to be killed rather than [to] break a commandment[3] in order not to begin to unfasten the rope that ties us all together and establishes peace between the household of heaven and the one on earth.

[35] "I remember that I heard from an old man who had been among the Spanish exiles about [the following incident]. The Spanish scholars wished to enact a law for the reform of the state by eliminating the inspection of the lungs [of slaughtered animals].[4] [They claimed] that we should not presume that there is any problem regarding them [the lungs].[5] On the contrary, an animal, when slaughtered, is presumed to be suitable

---

[1]B. T. Sanhedrin 72a.

[2]Cf. B. T. Sanhedrin 74b.

[3]This is a position debated within rabbinic thought and usually restricted to the extreme cases of murder, idolatry, and incest. In B. T. Sanhedrin 74a, for example, Rabbi Ishmael maintains that when faced with the alternative of death or practicing idolatry, one should chose the latter course if practiced privately, but the former course when practiced publicly. Cf. also B. T. Avodah Zarah 27b. While Maimonides regarded the preference of death over conversion as the highest form of religious devotion, he still advocated forced conversion in the case of the Almohadan persecution. See *Sefer ha-Maddah*, Hilkhot Yesodei ha-Torah 5:2–3; *Iggeret ha-Shemad* (Koenigsberg, 1856) p. 11b. For a good summary of the variety of rabbinic attitudes on the question, against the background of Jewish life in fifteenth-century Spain, see B. Netanyahu, *The Marranos of Spain* (New York, 1966), pp. 6–22.

[4]For a summary of the subject in halakhic sources, see *Enziklopediyah Talmudit*, 2 (Tel Aviv, 1949), pp. 356–60, especially Rashi on B. T. Hullin 12a; Maimonides, *Mishneh Torah*, Hilkhot Shehitah, 2:3–7; *Tur-Shulhan Arukh,* Yoreh De'ah, 39:1; B. Z. Katz, *Mizekanim Etbonan* (Warsaw, 1894).

[5]For the expression, see B. T. Hullin 56b.

for consumption [according to Jewish law] unless we are aware of a prohibition that forbids it. By law, we need not search thoroughly to seek
grounds to prohibit the food. Only if such grounds become apparent to us
do we follow the regulations of Jewish law. Since such grounds were
lacking and the animal was presumed to be suitable, these scholars almost
decided to annul the custom of inspecting the lung because of the reform
[measures undertaken by] the state. [Their decision was meant] to please
certain nobles and bishops who did not wish to permit the Jews to slaughter in the city streets except in this manner.

"When a certain pious and wise man, respected by the entire community, saw what the scholars were planning to do, he arose from the congregation with coral hooks in his hands. Each [hook] had a hole [that
enabled it] to be connected to the others by a string. At the end of the string
was a knot that prevented the coral from coming off. He arose and opened
the knot; all the hooks then fell to the ground. He then declared: 'Know
and observe, my masters, that it is the same with respect to the matter in
which we now are involved. If you loosen the bonds of a custom or law, the
silver cord which sustains us will come undone precipitously, and the
golden bowl which is with our God will crash.[1] And in a short time, we will
not be called any longer by the name of Israel. Today they will tell us to do
this, while tomorrow they will write on the bull's horn[2] that we have no
place or inheritance with God.'[3]

"All the people were frightened by the voice of this man of God. They
all wept, thanked him for his words and annulled their [previous] thoughts
in favor of his clear and pure opinion.[4] Moreover, this specific incident has

[1]Cf. Ecclesiastes 12:6.

[2]For the phrase, see *Bereshit Rabbah,* 44:17; 2:4, and elsewhere.

[3]The story bears a striking resemblance to a violent controversy that broke out in Spain
some years before the expulsion. It concerned the use of the fat from beneath an animal's loins
and involved the antagonists. R. Isaac de Leon and R. Isaac Zayet. De Leon had the backing of
Don Alfonso de la Cavalleria, the distinguished jurist and vice-chancellor of the kingdom of
Aragon. Zayet was backed by Luis Sanchez, the royal bailiff. According to Joseph Karo, whose
source was R. Joseph Taitazak, "This fat was permitted [to be used] by the people of Aragon
until the great rabbi, the late R. Isaac de Leon took a contrary view and forbade them to use it"
(*Beit Yosef* on *Yoreh De'ah,* Hilkhot Terefut, 64:11). Zayet and de Leon had argued over other
legal matters and were known as adversaries. Could Yagel have been referring to Isaac de Leon
as the rabbi who preached the dramatic homily on the coral hooks? On the de Leon-Zayet
controversy, see Y. Baer, *A History of the Jews of Christian Spain* (Philadelphia, 1966), vol. 2,
pp. 373–75; A. Marx, *Studies in Jewish History and Booklore* (New York, 1944), pp. 90–91; *Shevah
Einayim* (Leghorn, 1745), pp. 55–63. My thanks to Professor Joseph Hacker for directing me to
this controversy.

[4]For the phrase, compare Avot 2:4.

general significance regarding an individual's relations with God in permitting him [to break a law] whether small or large. 'As a dog returns to his vomit, so a fool repeats his folly.'[1] One almost is handed over to Satan's spoil and to that of the evil impulse. For if he [Satan] tells you today that such and such is permitted you [which is truly permitted], he will then tell you that such and such is permitted [when it is not], as the ancient serpent said to Eve following the rabbinic interpretation in *Bereshit Rabbah*.[2] Finally he [Satan's victim] will break completely the yoke of the Torah from around his neck and will shame himself publicly.

"The best advice[3] if a man sins (for there is not a righteous person on the earth who does good and does not sin[4]) is that he should recognize and know immediately the sin he committed, be contrite, conclude never to repeat his folly, and ask for pardon and forgiveness. Thus he will find an opening [in heaven] to be received in repentance; like a father to his son, God will desire him. This is the best repentance which reaches the throne of glory; it is the repentance of King David who immediately said: 'I sinned.' It was also said [there]: 'The Lord has remitted your sin, you shall not die.'[5] Thus his sin will not cause him to commit another iniquity, as the rabbis stated: 'The reward of a commandment is the commandment, and the reward of a sin is a sin.'[6] So he [David] corrected his perversity with the commandment of repentance; malicious deeds were then reckoned for him as meritorious. If this poor and miserable man had walked on this path [of David], he would not have experienced what he did experience."

[36] I then asked: "What was the sin of the first man who was visited by all this calamity in being put in prison and dying in the middle of his life?"

He responded: "Is the Holy One, blessed be He, suspect in your eyes that he would issue a verdict without cause? Who knew the ways of that man? Not for nothing did the starling follow the raven but because it is of its kind.[7] Thus he [the first man] associated with an evil person to do evil things, as it is written in Scripture: 'A ruler who listens to lies, all his ministers will be wicked.'[8] Even if one says that his own iniquities did not cause all the trouble, that he was just and righteous, and that his bad fortune

[1]Proverbs 26:11.
[2]*Bereshit Rabbah*, 19:3–4.
[3]Cf. Isaiah 14:26.
[4]Cf. Ecclesiastes 7:20.
[5]2 Samuel 12:13.
[6]Avot 4:2.
[7]Cf. B. T. Babba Kamma 92b.
[8]Proverbs 29:12.

brought about his condition, he still should not have gone to serve kings and noblemen in the first place.

[37] "All who go to her [to a strange woman, i.e., to the courts of kings] cannot attain the paths of life.[1] Moreover, as the popular expression goes, one who lives in the courts of the king will die on rubbish. Note how much Samuel complained when Israel requested a king of him,[2] since all Israel are the sons of kings,[3] and God rules over them and calls them his sons. So it is written: 'You are my children.'[4] By Him actions are measured[5] to bestow on them a judge to judge them [the children of Israel], to be the head of the community to go out and come before them, and to provide them a plan for their battles, as Moses, Joshua, and the rest of the judges did. But he [this leader] will not be called by the title of king, but only the head of the community or the prince of God. How is it possible for a man to worship his Creator, to observe His commandments related to a specific time [of observance], while at the same time to be obliged to serve an [earthly] king who requires that a person always direct his heart and mind to understand how to please him? How is he capable of understanding his studies and involving himself in the Torah with the yoke of God's kingdom on his neck, when the [earthly] king is especially evil and tyrannical like the king of this man?

[38] "Second, the man had no right to hand over his soul to Satan when he was put in prison. Many people have been imprisoned and have been afflicted by having their feet bound while they remained there for many days, but did not give up hope that God would release them from jail; they received God's punishment with love. Go out and learn from [the case] of the righteous Joseph who remained in jail for thirteen years.[6] In any case, he always blessed bad things as well as good.[7] We discover that because he said: 'But think of me [to the chief cupbearer],'[8] he was punished [by God] and remained imprisoned for another two years.[9]

"Daniel, a precious man,[10] never gave up hope in his God when he was

---

[1]Proverbs 2:19.

[2]Cf. 1 Samuel 12.

[3]Cf. B. T. Babba Meẓiah 113b and elsewhere.

[4]Deuteronomy 14:1.

[5]Cf. 1 Samuel 2:3.

[6]On the difficulty of calculating the number of years of Joseph's imprisonment, see Mani's note, p. 17b.

[7]Cf. Mishnah Berakhot 9:5.

[8]Genesis 40:14; Joseph asked the cupbearer to mention him to Pharaoh.

[9]As Genesis 41:1 indicates, Joseph had to wait two more years before the cupbearer mentioned him to Pharaoh, and only then did he gain his freedom.

[10]For the expression, see Daniel 10:11.

thrown into the lion's den. This man should have done the same thing, first by praying, to pour out his complaint to God, as it is written: 'Some lived in deepest darkness bound in cruel irons,'[1] and [similarly] 'In their adversity, they cried out to the Lord.'[2] For He [God] is compassionate and heard their cries; 'He brought them out of deepest darkness, broke their bonds asunder.'[3] After his prayer, he should have spoken eloquently before the king, extolling his righteousness, until he [the king] felt compassion for him so that he might declare: 'Redeem him from descending to the pit, for I have obtained his ransom.'[4] [This situation also recalls] the statement of King Solomon: 'The king's wrath is a messenger of death, but a wise man can appease it,'[5] and not be handed over to Satan. Would you really take this sin lightly? We even find that the rabbis tried to drive out Samson, the son of Manoah, from heaven because he declared: 'Let me die with the Philistines.'[6] All the more so in the case of a grandson of a *kal va-ḥomer* [an inference a minori ad maius] as with this man and what he said.[7] Furthermore, his sin or his ill fate may have caused his constellation to turn bad and to bring him calamity. A twisted thing cannot be made straight,[8] and when the stone is thrown from the hand, who will return it to him?[9] But why complain of damage in the case of ignoramuses who become crooked and whose foolishness perverts their way, since they were responsible themselves, as I told you.

[39] "A man should prepare his heart[10] to be careful of accidents, to fight against fate, to flee from its arrows with his effort, especially by prayer and good deeds; [all this] will be beneficial and save him to cool its [fate's] fire. In order to transform a bad constellation into a good one, as Abraham our father and the other righteous ones did, one must actually be empowered with the special merit of a great person to contend with his Creator, as I have said to you. In order that you may understand the matter fully, here is an example: If the constellation of a man indicates that he will

---

[1]Psalm 107:10.

[2]Psalm 107:6, 28.

[3]Psalm 107:14.

[4]Cf. Job 33:24.

[5]Proverbs 16:14.

[6]Judges 16:30.

[7]A grandson of a *kal va-ḥomer* is also a *kal va-ḥomer*. If a is greater than b, it is certainly greater than c as well. In this case, the man's sin is obvious if Samson and others greater than he were also guilty of it.

[8]Cf. Ecclesiastes 1:15.

[9]For the source of this saying, see Mani's note, p. 17b, who quotes J. L. Margaliot, *Tal Orot* (Pressburg, 1843), p. 65b.

[10]Cf. Proverbs 16:1.

be poor all his life, he [nevertheless] may be able to secure food for himself and earn a respectable living through prayer and good deeds. If he lives a sorrowful life, he can do as other righteous persons did, like R. Eleazar ben Pedat.[1] However, one can still reverse [the influence of] an astral conjunction so that if it points to poverty, it may instead point to affluence. But this is only possible through the merit of a master like Abraham, our father, for whom the Holy One, blessed be He, placed the constellation Jupiter beside him, returning it to the east from the west.[2] [God similarly acted for] Hezekiah[3] and others like him who benefited by their own merit.

[40] "Now I will hold forth to you; listen to me[4] regarding what the wise say. Why does the Holy One, blessed be He, allow man, whose ways and actions He sees, to be born under the influence of evil stars and constellations? The question is similar to that asked by Moses, the man of God, when he saw R. Akiva and his great wisdom, as the rabbis describe in the third chapter of *Menaḥot*.[5] After he [Moses] saw his Torah, he then saw them weighing his flesh in a slaughterhouse. He then asked: 'Master of the universe, is this the Torah and is this its reward?' The Holy One, blessed be He, answered him: 'Be quiet! Thus I have decreed.' Therefore, you should know that justice goes before Him[6] and that He only thinks of truth, modesty, and justice. For shall not the judge of all the earth do justly?[7] God forbid that He would issue a verdict without cause! As Bildad said to Job: 'Will God pervert the right? Will the Almighty pervert justice?'[8] It is a truthful assumption which should not be doubted that God, blessed and exalted, orders and establishes the world on pillars of righteousness and justice. Only righteousness will emerge from His just court. But know that not every one who considers himself pious [enough][9] to examine these matters should come and do so. We really are not capable of penetrating the depths of these discussions without the *kabbalah* [tradition],[10] for our

[1]On Eleazar (d. 279 C.E.), see *EJ*, 6:596–98. On his successful means of coping with his poverty, see especially B. T. Ta'anit 25a; Megillah 28a; J. T. Babba Meẓiah, 2:3; B. T. Succah 49b.
[2]Cf. *Bereshit Rabbah*, 42:3; B. T. Shabbat 156b, 196b. Yagel also emphasized Abraham's role as a super magician in *Beit Ya'ar ha-Levanon*, end of part 2.
[3]On God's lengthening Hezekiah's life span, see above.
[4]Cf. Job 15:17.
[5]B. T. Menaḥot 29b.
[6]Cf. Psalm 85:14.
[7]Cf. Genesis 18:25.
[8]Job 8:3.
[9]Cf. Mishnah Berakhot 2:8; B. T. Berakhot 16b.
[10]It is not clear here whether Yagel is referring to the Jewish mystical tradition, the kabbalah, or simply to Jewish tradition; from the context, he appears to have meant the latter.

knowledge is modest and our lives are short. Thus we are obliged to accept those responses of our ancestors, just as Bildad also said to Job: 'Ask the generation past . . . for we are of yesterday . . . surely they will teach you and tell you.'[1]

## On the Belief in Metempsychosis

[41] "Therefore, for this [reason], you must establish in your heart the belief in the transmigration of souls, that it is a truthful tradition as is revealed and known to anyone who calls himself by the name of Israel.[2] Only a root that bears gall and wormwood[3] would deviate from this belief. A person who drinks the words of the philosophers as water and desires to harmonize the words of Torah together[4] with philosophical speculations, so that miracles are understood as natural processes and similarly confused beliefs, will never understand that our holy Torah, its words, investigations, and miracles, and all the events [it describes], are superior to nature and [physical] reality.[5]

[42] "It [the Torah], in its greatness and majesty, preceded the world's creation by some two thousand years, as the rabbis declared.[6] This is also similar to the verse: 'Now Hebron was founded seven years before Zoan of Egypt.'[7] The rabbis likewise wrote that the Holy One, blessed be He, created the world while studying the Torah.[8] All of these statements thus indicate to us that the splendid majesty[9] of the Torah ascends on high to heaven. Man can never know its value[10] [in relation] to nature and human investigation since all flesh is silent before her [the Torah].[11]

[1]Cf. Job 8:8–10.

[2]This is a central theme for Yagel in this work and in all his writings. Cf. D. Ruderman, "On Divine Justice, Metempsychosis, and Purgatory: The Ruminations of a Sixteenth Century Jew," *Jewish History*, 1 (1986): 9–30; idem, *Kabbalah, Magic, and Science*, chap. 8; and see the introduction above. Note how the discussion on divine justice and dying before one's time led eventually to the subject of metempsychosis.

[3]Cf. Deuteronomy 29:17.

[4]Cf. Proverbs 22:18.

[5]This is also a common theme for Yagel. His objection is not to mixing naturalistic learning with that of Torah; it is to subordinating the latter to the former.

[6]*Bereshit Rabbah*, 8:2.

[7]Numbers 13:22. Rashi indicates that this phrase points to the superiority of the land of Israel. It is thus analogous to the superiority of the Torah over the creation of the world.

[8]A paraphrase of *Bereshit Rabbah*, 1:2, thus indicating as well the priority of the Torah over Creation.

[9]Cf. Esther 1:4.

[10]Cf. Job 28:13.

[11]Cf. Zachariah 2:7.

"Many great philosophers also believed in the transmigration of souls such as the sect of the Pythagoreans and the Platonists.[1] Many philosophers among our people have even offered philosophical proof to substantiate this idea, such as the author [Isaac Arama] of *Akedat Yizḥak*, commenting on the scroll of Ruth, and the scholar [Isaac] Abravanel in his commentary on the portion *Ki Tezeh* in his *Mirkevet ha-Mishnah*.[2] The latter brought proofs there to annul the opinion of anyone who denies this belief. But in any case, we do not need to authenticate [this view] since the correct tradition is already in our possession through our holy rabbis, members of the great assembly, who received this truth from Moses at Sinai. For Scripture cries out: 'Truly, God does all these things, two or three times to a man,' as Nahmanides interpreted there.[3] Bildad, Job's associate, also remarked in his response: 'Such is his happy lot; and from the earth others will grow,' that is, God is his [a person's] happy lot for removing sin from the earth, because righteousness is before him. However, those souls will grow from another earth[4] and God will be freely compassionate to them. They actually will overcome their deficiency a second or third time as they potentially had [been able to do], for 'he that is banished is not an outcast from Him.'[5] The commandment of levirate marriage also proves this [idea].[6] Proofs from the Torah that hint at this [idea] and substantiate it are greater in number than the hair on your head.[7] Thus when we accept graciously this holy and true belief, all doubts regarding the good and righteous who suffer are removed.

"God will reprove on another occasion whoever He loves for the sins that person committed while he was in this world, since he remains guilty before his master. 'If his master will give him a wife,'[8] that is, this corporeality for a second or third time, he will then pay up his debts and give birth to children out of repentance and good deeds. 'The wife and children shall belong to the master' and 'he shall leave alone,' free of all his debts. And because of this, the righteous, like R. Akiva and his associates, were afflicted with punishment in Israel for the sale of Joseph. Thus the law is a

[1]The views of these groups and their similarity to Yagel's understanding are discussed in Ruderman's "On Divine Justice" and *Kabbalah, Magic, and Science*.

[2]Cf. Isaac Arama, *Perush la-Megillot* (Pressburg, 1809), p. 145a, where he presents the kabbalistic view with reservations; and Abravanel's commentary on Deuteronomy 25:5.

[3]Cf. Nachmanides' commentary on Job 33:29.

[4]Yagel interprets "other" in Job 8:19 to refer to "earth" and not to those who grow.

[5]Cf. 2 Samuel 14:14.

[6]Cf. Deuteronomy 25:5 and especially Abravanel's commentary on the verse.

[7]Cf. Psalm 40:13.

[8]Cf. Exodus 21:4. The verse is interpreted to indicate that it refers to the doctrine of metempsychosis.

law of truth, as it is written: 'He who kidnaps a man—whether he has sold him or is still holding him—shall be put to death.'[1]

[43] "Observe the wonderful words of the sage [Menahem] Recanati [in his commentary] on the Torah portion *Va-Yeshev,* who calculated the numerical value of the names of the tribes to equal the numerical value of the ten martyrs.[2] The Holy One, blessed be He, positively influences the wicked by ordering a good astral conjunction for them at the time of their birth. [He thus] rewards them for any good service they performed in this world, since it is not worthwhile for them to inherit the next world. For the Holy One, blessed be He, does not withhold reward from any creature.[3]

[44] "The rabbis declared in *Pe'ah* of the Jerusalem Talmud:[4] 'One whose merits are many and whose sins are few is punished in this world in order to pay his reward in the next. One whose sins are many and whose merits are few receives his reward in this world for the lesser commandments he performed so that he will be punished in the next.' The rabbis also stated in *Midrash Kohelet:*[5] 'R. Josiah said, "God prolongs the life of the wicked for three reasons: perhaps they will repent; or they have performed commandments for which the Holy One, blessed be He, is rewarding them in this world; or perhaps they will produce righteous children. We thus find that Ahaz's life was prolonged because he produced Hezekiah, etc."' This is also what Zophar the Naamathite said to Job: 'Would you discover the mystery of God? Would you discover the limit of the Almighty?'[6]

"Pay attention and listen to the divine words of R. Simeon bar Yohai in the *Sefer Tikkunim,* tikkun 69:[7] 'A person is meritorious who sustains his life and does not force his fortune, as it is written: "Whoever forces his [good] fortune, will be dogged by [ill] fortune."[8] R. Pedat was dogged by [ill] fortune, so the Holy One, blessed be He, said to him: "Do you want a world to be destroyed[9] since it is possible that you have fallen at the appointed time?" The Holy Candle [R. Pedat] responded: "Is this indeed so?" He [bar Yohai] explained: "This is a great secret. Thus I have heard of a

---

[1]Exodus 21:16.

[2]Menahem Recanati, *Perush al ha-Torah al Derekh ha-Emet* (Venice, 1523), beginning of parshat Va-Yeshev Ya'akov (no pagination).

[3]Cf. B. T. Babba Kamma 38b, Nazir 23b, and elsewhere.

[4]J. T. Pe'ah 1:1(5a).

[5]*Midrash Kohelet,* 7:15.

[6]Job 11:7.

[7]*Sefer Tikkunim,* tikkun 69, 101a, the high point and culmination of this long discourse on divine justice.

[8]B. T. Berakhot 64a, literally: "Whoever pushes his hour will be pushed by it."

[9]The assumption being that every sage is a world unto himself.

man who was reincarnated but was liable to his Master before coming into this world.[1] Even though he performed meritorious deeds [in his second life], he was not sustained by his merits but by his constellation, which was the determining factor. Regarding what He [God] asked: 'Do you want a world to be destroyed since it is possible that you have fallen at the appointed time?,' I [bar Yoḥai] certainly have heard that every saintly person possesses a world unto himself.[2] Indeed, man is called a microcosm. God therefore asked: 'Do you want a world to be destroyed?' He thus transported him [the rabbi] into another body, and [therefore] 'it is possible that you have fallen at the appointed time.' "'

"He [bar Yoḥai further] explained: 'Is it not written: "If he marries another, he must not withhold from this one her food, her clothing, or her conjugal rights, etc." and "Truly, God does all these things, etc." and "If he fails her in these three ways, then she shall be freed without payment"?[3] This superior secret has surely been revealed, as the masters of the Mishnah have declared: "One's wife is like one's own body."[4] That she is his [whole] life is suggested by [the meaning of] the verses: "Enjoy happiness with a woman you love" and "She is a tree of life for those who grasp her."[5] She can also be his source of livelihood, as it is written: "A land you can eat food without stint,"[6] for from her [one receives] children, life, and sustenance.[7] Accompanying these transmigrations are change of place, change of name, and change of deeds. Change of place is analogous to the case of the Holy One, praise be He, about whom it is written: "The Lord shall go forth from His place."[8] When He goes forth, a change occurs from [divine] justice to [divine] mercy and from mercy to justice, as the masters of the Mishnah have declared: "My name [literally, 'I'] is not pronounced as it is written."[9]'

[1] He was guilty of sins performed in a previous life.

[2] Cf. *Shemot Rabbah,* 52:3; *Vayikrah Rabbah,* 27:1, and elsewhere.

[3] Exodus 21:10; Job 33:29, and Exodus 21:11, respectively. All of these passages are interpreted to refer to metempsychosis.

[4] B. T. Bekhorot 35b, *Sefer ha-Zohar,* 2:117b. The assumption here is that the author of the *Zohar* was "a master of the Mishnah." These "masters" were the ones to interpret these passages about the wife to refer to the multiple lives of a person.

[5] Ecclesiastes 9:9; Proverbs 3:18.

[6] Deuteronomy 8:9.

[7] Cf. B. T. Moed Katan 28a, *Sefer ha-Zohar,* 2:6a.

[8] Isaiah 26:21.

[9] B. T. Pesaḥim 50a, *Sefer ha-Zohar,* 3:230a. The four letters of the divine name are thus pronounced "Adonai" and not as they are written. This suggests the dynamic quality of the divine which is analogous to the dynamic quality of human life engendered by the process of metempsychosis. Thus this rather obscure passage from the *Tikkunim* reinforces for Yagel the primacy of the belief in the transmigration of souls within the scheme of divine justice.

"Thus I [Abraham's father] have informed you of some of the secrets of your Creator. I have guided you in straight courses, in order to survey the path you shall take, for God will call you to account for all things.[1] Every person will be judged even with respect to a light conversation between a man and his wife.[2] Therefore, be careful, my son, lest sinners entice you[3] to believe any one of those evil beliefs which were not singled out for honor in the counsel of our sages, of blessed memory, as I already warned you in the beginning of my talk to you. But it is now time to return to [telling me] your affairs, for half the night already has passed and the shadows of evening are growing long[4] in the lower region."

I responded: "My master, you have revived me with your words and now I observe with an intelligent eye that your declarations were correct, that God is upright, and that His judgments are righteous."

## The Continuation of the Son's Life Story

[45] "Having summarized for his honor [you] the major conditions of the agreement between the woman [Rina] and me, I will now inform you that she also said to me explicitly and not indirectly that she no longer wished to involve herself in this business with me, [that] I should find another partner or another person to replace her in the course of a year. Nevertheless, it subsequently was apparent from her ways and actions that she kept one foot in and one foot out. Continually hopeful, we still remained without a decision on her part. The truth of the matter is that all her actions and involvements were based on weakness, as the rabbis declared: 'Cain stood as a standard to the nations in weakness until the flood came and drowned him.'[5] Similarly, all her thoughts were indecisive until some impure incident occurred and flooded them, or a wind blew them, or a storm swept them away.

"As the end of the first year approached, and I saw that the days were drawing near regarding [the outcome] of the woman's action and [her] conversation [with me], I approached her and asked if she still wished to continue [in] this venture, or did she want the documents to be confirmed so that I could find a designated person[6] to take her place. She responded

---

[1]The line is constructed from Proverbs 4:11, 4:26, and Ecclesiastes 11:9, respectively.
[2]Cf. *Vayikra Rabbah,* 26:7.
[3]Cf. Proverbs 1:10.
[4]Cf. Jeremiah 5:4.
[5]Cf. *Bereshit Rabbah,* 22:12.
[6]Cf. Leviticus 16:21.

that she desired that I search [for another person]. I thus searched and found someone. I entered into negotiations with the late Samuel Almagiati, may his memory be blessed, and we almost reached a compromise [regarding the partnership].[1] However, the manner in which she [Rina] insisted that her [initial] investment be returned remained an obstacle for us: she wanted it paid in full in legal tender. She did not want to receive any fair installment[2] at suitable and appropriate intervals. Rather she stood in an open place[3] with her eyes focused in anticipation of receiving one complete payment, as mentioned. She did this deceitfully in order that she would not remove herself [completely] from the arrangement or allow me [the opportunity] to renew the documents in a manner that would be more advantageous to me and provide them a valid basis. Thus her feet stood on both sides of the decision.[4] She would pretend piety[5] in saying that she did not want to deal with anyone else. Even the late Almagiati was willing to offer her half the money in hand,[6] without penalty. He wanted to give the second half in the form of a pawn acquired from two banks in Guastalla and Luzzara. Nevertheless, she refused the deal, until her own husband, Jacob de Lacairo, became angry with her since he desired the agreement [be concluded]. Since she kept changing her mind about the deal, once consenting to it and then reversing herself by denying that any such promises had ever been made, it ultimately reached the point that he [Almagiati] departed in anger and the entire arrangement collapsed.

"I returned to my home empty-handed, while my expenses continued to increase. What was broken down exceeded what remained standing.[7] Besides this, we [Rina and I] had purchased a certain amount of produce at the beginning of our partnership. But when we had written the papers, she had not wished to include this produce in the body of the agreement, seeing that its value had decreased. What we had purchased for one shekel was

---

[1]On the Almagiati family and their banking operations in the Mantovano, see Simon-sohn, pp. 224, 228, 252–53. On p. 224, Simonsohn records that on 11 May 1577, Lazzaro (Eliezer) and his brother, the sons of Samuel Almagiati, received a license to open a bank in Luzzara. The struggle for control of the bank between Yagel and this family obviously took place in the years immediately preceding the issuance of this license. The latter sealed the outcome of the miserable events described below and forced Yagel out of the banking business.

[2]*Partita.*

[3]Cf. Genesis 38:14; that is, she announced her wishes publicly and firmly.

[4]*Ḥaruẓ* should read *ḥariẓ*, literally, she "stood on both sides of the ditch."

[5]Literally, "she would show the cloven foot" like a swine, as if saying: "I am clean!" Cf. *Vayikrah Rabbah,* 13:5.

[6]Cf. Proverbs 16:5.

[7]Cf. Mishnah Kilayim 4:4.

now worth only a half shekel and [thus] this amounted to another loss over and above the standing costs known to anyone who deals in this trade.

"Time passed until Almagiati, with whom I had dealt, died, and I returned to persuade this woman. I even brought many friends to request her to sit with me and to consider what I could offer her. I entrusted my spirit into her hand[1] so that she would decree and I would fulfill [her every wish].[2] But all my devices were for naught. I could not extract anything [else] from her. I was [merely] expected to find a person to agree on one leg[3] to hand over all her money, good and perfumed,[4] prior to entering [the partnership].

"After the death of their father, the sons of Almagiati subsequently reopened the discussions I had conducted with him. They claimed [that it was their] responsibility to maintain the [good] name of the deceased so that it [his memory] would not be erased from the place [i.e., the transaction]. But the difficulty we had encountered with the dead man remained with them. They continued to try to persuade the woman, but she maintained her initial position. Finally, I returned, as before, to my home in Luzzara, bitter and angry, and disillusioned with the [entire] affair, and I pondered what would be the final outcome and purpose. I also knew that no good end could come out of it, for the struggle had originated in heaven. A constellation was determining [it], and if I was not worthy, my constellation was worthy.[5]

"Subsequently, the Lord struck the people,[6] for the plague began in the land.[7] Everyone tried to save his own life and ignored all other extraneous concerns. Thus, skin for skin,[8] a person will do anything to rescue himself. So all the matters of the bank came to a standstill. Then, one day, a refugee appeared [to me] with a letter written and signed in the name of the aforementioned woman [Rina]. Since everyone was fleeing Mantua, escap-

---

[1]Cf. Psalm 31:6.

[2]Cf. Job 22:28.

[3]Cf. B. T. Shabbat 31a.

[4]That is, up front and paid in full.

[5]Cf. B. T. Megillah 3a, Sanhedrin 94a.

[6]Cf. Numbers 11:33.

[7]On the impact of the plague of 1575–76 on the general and Jewish communities, see Simonsohn, p. 30; Leon Modena, *Zikne Yehudah,* ed. S. Simonsohn (Jerusalem, 1956), no. 78; M. Benayahu and G. Laras, "The Appointment of Health Inspectors in Cremona in 1575" (in Hebrew), *Michael,* 1 (1973): 78–143; P. Preto, *Peste e societa à Venezia, 1576* (Vicenza, 1978). Yagel composed his own plague tract some years later, which perhaps evolved from his own personal experience with the horrendous disease in Luzzara.

[8]Cf. Job 2:4.

ing wherever they could find refuge, she desired to take up residence with her household in this place [Luzzara] until the danger had passed. For God said to the angel: 'Enough! Stay your hand!'[1]

"I was happy that she was coming; [I] found her living quarters and sent word to her to finish her business quickly and to come promptly, for the roads would soon be closed. I noticed that the local populace had set up guards; a herald called out with a loud voice: 'Watch out for the Mantuan citizens and their possessions!' As every hour passed, the guards increased in order to keep watch and save themselves. The woman [Rina] and her family waited to come after the time I had told her. A proclamation from the health authorities finally appeared, forbidding any household from harboring any man or woman from Mantua, with the threat of bodily or financial penalty. I sent word to her that when she arrived in this place [Luzzara], she should first let me know before entering the vicinity of the city, so that I would come outside the [city] border to inspect her party with a notary of the city, a health authority, and a physician. Second, [I instructed her] to bring certification from the Mantuan health authorities that no contagious disease had come near her house for a period of forty days.[2] Meanwhile, I remained in negotiations with the authorities. I had approached the authorities with my request prior to the time that the entire community had assembled in a certain place [in Luzzara] to enact special legislation concerning the plague. These people approved the request with considerable difficulty and with the hard and fast condition that she would take these precautions.

"However, she and her family completely rejected my advice and came confidently to the city at midday, in broad daylight and in public view. When I saw the carriage in which she was riding, I felt sharp pangs and was petrified lest the health authorities and the community become angry with me. I took her security papers and presented them to the authorities, but they refused to accept them, saying that I had abused and ridiculed them. I imposed myself on all my friends and associates that day. But I observed how agitated the entire community had become because of these people's arrival and by my allowing them to stay overnight in my house.

"A large crowd soon gathered in the city, joined by villagers of the

[1]Cf. 2 Samuel 24:16.
[2]For the general context of these measures to control the plague, see C. M. Cipolla, *Fighting the Plague in Seventeenth Century Italy* (Madison, Wis., 1981); R. J. Palmer, "The Control of Plague in Venice and Northern Italy," University of Kent, unpublished doctoral diss., 1978.

surrounding area as rumor spread that some wounded and sick Jews had come to contaminate and to infect them [literally, "us"] with the evil [disease]. [They proclaimed:] 'Let us take counsel together and devise a way to tear them to pieces. Moreover, the man who gave them shelter, along with the members of his household, also shall not escape from our hands.' There were those who advised such a course [solely] in order to gain spoil and to plunder. The outcome of all this was that a crowd of people suddenly gathered while I was speaking and entreating the city's authorities. They took the drum,[1] sounded it, and shouted: 'Hurry up your activity and get out of that place lest its evil go up like fire and we kill you!' I begged the authorities to let these people stay in my house for one more night and that by morning they would be on their way; for where would they turn like bats[2] [flying around] the dead in the desert? The woman and children would be plundered by thieves of the night.

"I turned to one of my friends and begged him to find armed mercenaries.[3] He immediately sent me twelve men, all armed and knowledgeable in warfare; each one of them was capable of challenging ten men. They came and surrounded my house and wall. When the crowd saw these men, they feared for their lives [and] went out from the center of the city to its main square, where they deliberated and devised a plan based on their evil thought. In the meantime, their numbers swelled with other villagers who joined their ranks.

"My only salvation was from either of two pillars—the podesta[4] of the city or the priest who dwelt in the city—to whom I spoke. They went out to speak to the crowd and to allay their anger. But the crowd turned on them and drew hollow spears that shoot out rocks with a loud noise and with blazing fire. They [the people in the crowd] said to them: 'Don't interfere with us lest these desperate people fall upon you so that your lives will be like those of the Jews who came among us to infect us with the illness of Mantua.' With sweet talk, the podesta and the priest hastened to escape this unruly mob and returned to the city, shutting the city gates after them.

"When the citizens of the city noticed that the gates were closed, some of them considered breaking them down. But others cautioned: 'Do not do

---

[1] *Tamburo.* But Yagel then indicates that they "blew," using the verb appropriate to a horned instrument rather than a drum.

[2] But compare Isaiah 59:10.

[3] Hebrew: *paldarim.* Mani, p. 20b, suggests that the word is related to the *parhedroi* or *paredrin,* assessors or counselors. Cf. B. T. Yoma 2a. Yet the context here suggests my translation.

[4] I have designated the imprecise titles of *moshel* as podesta, and *kohen* as priest.

wrongly, our brothers, lest we increase the king's [i.e., the duke's] wrath and our mischief recoil around our own head.[1] Do this [instead]: Wait until tonight, and if they and their possessions have departed by morning, and not a trace remains in this place, we shall leave them alone to go wherever they find [refuge], and our hands will not touch them. If not, let us then gather a second time and give them [their punishment] when the dew hits the ground. We shall drag them to the valley[2] against their will and not one of them will remain.' They listened to the advice of this person and went home.

"Nevertheless, I did not rest that entire night but remained on guard with my men around the city, inquiring as to what would happen and how [we might] find rest and refuge for the woman and her family. I then told them [her and her family] to do the following: 'Either return to the city from whence you came in the morning or flee to a certain estate of the podesta. But know well that he will expect rent for it, which I will provide, and he will demand a higher price from you.'[3]

"The woman refused to return to the [her] city but decided to go to the estate. On the morrow, she and her family left in a chariot of horses owned by the podesta accompanied by two of his servants. The armed guards who had been with us in the house also accompanied the woman to this [new] location. The citizens of the [other] town were also upset in seeing them approach since the citizenry of Luzzara had expelled them [the family] and considered them deceitful, as they were [considered to be] stricken and afflicted by disease. I knew about this situation and arranged for the podesta to write to the head of the regiment there and to send one of the nobles as well as the twelve men who had [previously] accompanied her until the commotion had abated. But despite this, people remained upset with me. They complained to the podesta and the health authorities about me and locked me and my family in my house for eight days.

"These things which I have told you are surely not to be believed. However, believe me, my father, by the life of God who created my soul. Not one word has been omitted from this account. May my witness be in heaven who probes the mind and conscience,[4] that I tried with all my strength, with a full heart and with great compassion, and I risked my life and that of my family. I did not rest nor was I quiet[5] in trying to win friends

[1] Cf. Psalm 7:17.
[2] Cf. 2 Samuel 17:13.
[3] Cf. Genesis 34:12.
[4] Literally, heart and kidneys. Cf. Psalm 7:10.
[5] Cf. Job 3:26.

and allies [on her behalf] until I saw that she and her household were secure and the voices ceased. My God, remember these things[1] for my own welfare and that of my household."

## The Appearance of the Siamese Twins

[46] While I was relating these things to my father, two souls flew toward us who were attached to each other.[2] The head of the first was between the feet of the second. They spoke together secretly and quietly; their speech sounded like a ghost's from the ground so that I could only hear the chirping of their words.[3] One declared: "There will be a war or famine in the land or one of the other calamities that threaten to come to the world.[4] The best advice[5] is to flee to one of the places [of refuge] lest you be swept away because of the iniquity of the city.[6] Even from there, one should seek God and beg Him to protect and save his life from these horrible afflictions, as in the case of Elisha. [The latter] had spoken to the woman whose son he had restored to life saying: 'Leave immediately with your family and go sojourn wherever you may sojourn, for the Lord has decreed a seven-year famine upon the land.'[7] We see that she heeded his warning, as it is written: 'The woman has done as the man of God had spoken, etc.'[8] But the rabbis declared: 'If there is a plague in the city, remain where you are.'[9]"

[47] When I heard these words, I inquired of my father whether they were human souls who died, or spirits who were thus created, or demons. [I also asked] why they were attached to each other and whether they were one creature or two.

My father responded: "These are the souls of children who were born in Venice three years ago."[10]

I remarked: "I would have thought that these children were like a

[1]Cf. Nehemiah 5:19 and elsewhere.
[2]On these Siamese twins, see the introduction above.
[3]Cf. Isaiah 29:4.
[4]Cf. Mishnah Avot 5:11; B. T. Babba Kamma 80b; Ta'anit 14a.
[5]Cf. Isaiah 14:26.
[6]Cf. Genesis 19:15.
[7]2 Kings 8:1.
[8]2 Kings 8:2.
[9]Cf. B. T. Babba Kamma 60b.
[10]Yagel refers to the Siamese twins born to the daughter of Gabriel Zarfati (the wife of a Jew named Petaḥiah) on 26 May 1575 in the ghetto of Venice. The event is described in various Hebrew responsa as well as in Italian pamphlets composed soon after the event. See the introduction above.

buried stillbirth, like babies who never saw the light.[1] Just as their bodies perished together, so too did their souls and spirits, which also returned to the earth and to dust. As one died, so did the other, since they did not merit [the opportunity] of observing even one commandment from which they would have earned a remnant of the estates of God in the land of the living [paradise]. Please inform me, your honor, by what merit their souls were saved from the pit [hell] to live in the hereafter."[2]

## A Digression on the Soul and the Noahide Commandments

[48] He answered: 'You surely should know that our [Jewish] form is not like theirs [of other peoples], nor our souls like that of the rest of the nations. The soul placed in us is pure from its inception and perfect before entering the body. It is derived from a great treasure which is called 'body.' There all the souls destined to come into the world are placed, as the rabbis declared in the chapter *Kol ha-Yad:*[3] 'The son of David will not come until all the souls in "the body" will be used up.' Rashi interprets [there] 'body' as a proper noun for the chamber where future souls are born.

"However, what is the essence of the soul and its purpose; what does it come to do in this world? The subject is too long to speak about this evening for there will still be another revelation [on this matter].[4] It is sufficient for you to know that it [the soul] possesses a life prior to conception. It is perfect and gives perfection to the body, as the rabbis stated in chapter *Ḥelek:*[5] 'Antoninus asked Rabbi: "When is the soul placed in man? As soon as it [the embryo] is conceived or when it is fully formed?" He answered: "From the time of its formation." He [Antoninus] objected: "Is it possible for a piece of unsalted meat to stand three days without becoming putrid?[6] It must be from [the time of] conception." He [Rabbi] responded: "Yes, from the time of conception." Rabbi added: "Antoninus taught me this idea and a biblical verse supports him, as it is written: 'Your providence watched over my spirit.' "[7]

[1]Cf. Job 3:16.
[2]Literally, "the world in which all is well-balanced." Cf. B. T. Kiddushin 39b.
[3]B. T. Niddah 13b.
[4]Cf. Habbakuk 2:3.
[5]B. T. Sanhedrin 91b.
[6]Similarly, the embryo could not stand so long without receiving its soul.
[7]Job 10:12, apparently implying from the moment of conception, i.e., during the entire span of one's life.

"Thus you can see that from the time the angel conceives a droplet and presents it before God and relates what will become of this drop, a soul is cast into it. Its essence is spiritual, very fine, and very perfect, with a perfection described by the rabbis in chapter *Ha-Shoal:*[1] 'The rabbis taught [regarding the verse]: "And the spirit shall return to God who gave it."[2] Just as He gave you what He gave you in purity, so should you return it in purity. This may be compared to a mortal king who distributed his royal clothes to his crafty servants. They folded them and layed them out in a chest, etc.'

"It [the soul] comes to this world to gain actual perfection, for it already possesses it potentially from its [the soul's] conception. For everything is for a higher purpose. It [the soul] acquires perfection through commandments, good deeds, and Torah study, which is equal to everything else.[3]

"In order to explain these things which I have related to you in a few words, much more time than [even] another night is required. At such a time [when it becomes available], I [Abraham's father] shall discuss this matter and bring proofs to you from the words of the sages, may their memory be blessed, in order to understand these things. It is enough for now that you know that, prior to the time the body emerges into the air of the world, while [still] in the stomach and the womb, it [the soul] is perfect in members of the Israelite nation, since they are able to understand the words of these aforementioned quotations. For the Lord of Hosts has planned [it] and who then can foil it? And he who is banished shall not be an outcast from Him.[4] When they stood on Mount Sinai, all the souls destined to be created acquired perfection. This is what the rabbis meant when they declared: 'When Israel stood on Mount Sinai, their filth ceased.'[5]

[49] "This is the difference between Jewish souls and those of the gentiles, for the latter cannot acquire any perfection since they did not say: 'We shall do and obey,'[6] as our souls proclaimed at that mount [Sinai]. In order to reach this point, however, they require much validation through concepts that will draw them near to seeing the light that shines through the cracks.[7] [These are] that the Holy One, blessed be He, lives and is one;

---

[1] B. T. Shabbat 152b.
[2] Ecclesiastes 12:7.
[3] Mishnah Pe'ah 1:1.
[4] Cf. Isaiah 14:27; 2 Samuel 14:14.
[5] B. T. Shabbat 146a.
[6] Exodus 24:7.
[7] Cf. Song of Songs 2:9.

His providence extends over all creatures; and He grants a reward to those who do good and punishment to evildoers. By this knowledge acquired through rational investigation, a person also comes to perceive the divinely revealed Torah and the perfection of a human being over the beast, for this is natural law. Therefore, one should not do anything to another person which he does not want done to himself, as it is written: 'You shall love your neighbor as yourself.'[1] The rabbis declared: 'This is an all-encompassing rule in the Torah. What is hateful to you, do not do to your neighbor.'[2] With this knowledge, each person will ascend the ladder, step by step, until his eyes are illumined and he sees eye to eye the true faith and the greatness of the divine Torah. Thus the rabbis declared: 'This ladder is Sinai. The numerical value of one equals the numerical value of the other.'[3] [50] In such a way, Aquila the convert and Onkelos,[4] Shemayah, Abtalion, and the other converts acquired perfection. They are now considered as residing among us and their worthiness is very great. They dwell with the other righteous who enjoy the splendor of God's countenance [in heaven].

[51] "Thus know that the rabbis called converts who accept the seven Noahide commandments the sons of Noah, righteous converts.[5] These commandments are just and right; if they had not been written, they should have been written, for reason contradicts none of them. However, those who converted and joined the community of Israel should be called sojourning proselytes since they live among us and are also sojourners like all our ancestors. They acquired the [aforementioned] concepts and came to know the truth after making their inquiries, step by step. After their investigations informed them that divine providence is capable of bestowing on human beings the Torah and commandments; and when they saw that no revelation in the world is like that of Israel, whose statutes and

[1] Leviticus 19:18.

[2] Two passages are fused together here. The first is from *Bereshit Rabbah*, 24:8; J. T. Nedarim 9:4; the second is from B. T. Shabbat 91a.

[3] *Bereshit Rabbah*, 68:12. Both the *gematriah* of *sulam* [ladder] and Sinai equal 130.

[4] Yagel's conscious differentiation between the two translators strongly suggests that he had read Azariah de' Rossi's discussion of the two in *Me'or Einayim* (Imrei Binah, chapter 45), a book Yagel had consulted on other occasions. On the earlier confusion in rabbinic literature which treated them as one, see A. Silverstone, *Aquila and Onkelos* (Manchester, 1931). Cf. Mani's note on p. 22a.

[5] The seven Noahide commandments are found in B. T. Sanhedrin 56a. They prohibit idolatry, murder, theft, blasphemy, incest, eating the flesh of a live animal, and they demand the promotion of justice. They were practiced by partial sojourning proselytes who did not adopt Judaism in its entirety. Righteous proselytes, on the other hand, embraced all of the commandments of Judaism and were considered Jews and not merely the sons of Noah. Mani, pp. 22a–b, already noted Yagel's confusing formulation which is repeated below.

laws, both the general and specific, are established together;[1] and even though they might have found some righteous laws about which their intellect and evil inclination could have questioned, [nevertheless], they accepted them with a pure mind saying: 'If only the knowledge of their purpose was within our capacity!'[2] They believed them [the laws] in perfect faith as our ancestors did, and they spoke about them as the rabbi did: 'I made this law; I decreed this decree. You are not permitted to question them.'[3]"

[52] I then inquired: "My master, how did you explain that reason would accept and not contradict the seven Noahide commandments? Isn't it true that they include the prohibition of eating flesh torn from a living body, which is similar to the commandment of ritual slaughter, a law that might be questioned by the gentiles and by the evil inclination? Why does the Holy One, blessed be He, care if one slaughters [an animal] from the front [i.e., throat] of the neck or the back? What is the difference between one who slaughters only half of the esophagus of a fowl, or the esophagus and half the trachea in a cow, thereby prohibiting its consumption, and one who slaughters the majority of these organs, thereby making the animal fit? The evil inclination might also raise the question: Why should the Holy One, blessed be He, care if one eats a limb torn from an animal who is dead or [eats it] prior [to the time] that her soul has departed?"

He answered: "One is not equivalent to the other. Eating flesh torn from a living animal is like the tearing and eating of wild animals. With such behavior, one cannot conceptualize the preeminence of man over the beast,[4] as we already said. Man will thus learn to hunt man [in order] to eat him as it [wine] lends its color to the cup.[5] All the world will become a [hunting] plain to him; he will prey and eat as a lion preys and eats. The fundamental issue is that all the welfare necessary to society and the state will be negated by him, like the beasts upon a thousand mountains[6] where the mighty rule,[7] or like the fish of the sea, where the bigger fish swallows

[1]Cf. Proverbs 22:18.

[2]In other words, only God understands fully the reasons for all the commandments; nevertheless, we accept them all as righteous laws.

[3]*Bamidbar Rabbah,* 19:1. We might note the irony of the above discussion encouraging converts to Judaism, written in Counter-Reformation Italy during one of the most aggressive campaigns to encourage Jews to approach the baptismal font.

[4]Cf. Ecclesiastes 3:19.

[5]Cf. Proverbs 23:31. The act of eating man will become natural to him as the color of wine in a cup.

[6]Cf. Psalm 50:10.

[7]Cf. B. T. Gittim 60b, Babba Batra 34b.

the smaller one. On the other hand, what do we actually understand regarding the ritual slaughter of animals that will appeal to reason? Why does the Holy One, blessed be He, care if one slaughters at the front or the back of the neck? Therefore, you surely will call this a law which we are commanded to observe as given. It is a decree of the king and we are not permitted to question it.

## The Speeches of the Siamese Twins

[53] "Now come and hear what these children have to say and why they are attached to each other. Let us get closer[1] and I shall ask them the reason for their being attached."

The first [twin] answered by addressing me: "Who gave you the credentials[2] to investigate such concealed and esoteric matters? Even the ancient philosophers were incapable of penetrating these truths with the profundity of their investigations. You rather should go and ask the Creator who made me. Your question is similar to one of a certain fool who thought of himself as wise.[3] On one occasion he discovered Wisdom while in a field of watermelons. The fool asked her [Wisdom]: 'Why has nature created this large fruit, the watermelon, which grows in an area as small as a man's finger upon which it cannot lean? It would have been more appropriate for this large fruit to be on a tree with large and strong branches capable of supporting it.' He later observed a nut tree. He looked up and saw how large the tree and its branches were and how small its fruit. He said: 'It surely would have been more appropriate for nature to have grown large fruit on this large tree rather than small ones like the nut. How nice it would have been for the watermelons to be on this tree and nuts of the tree in the place of the watermelons!' Wisdom laughed at the retort of the fool and did not answer him lest he think of himself as wise. Rather she departed and hid herself from him, leaving him alone with his own foolishness and confused thoughts on the subject.

"The fool went and lay down and fell asleep under the same nut tree. When Wisdom saw that the fool was sleeping on the ground, she climbed the tree and knocked off a nut [which landed] on his nose. The fool was aroused by the pain of being struck and declared: 'If this tree would have

[1]Cf. Exodus 3:5 and elsewhere.
[2]Cf. Exodus 2:14.
[3]Cf. Proverbs 26:5 and elsewhere.

held watermelons, as I initially had conceived to be good and fine, it would have broken my head. May God now be praised who created everything in the most perfect way possible! According to the specification of the material, he provided the most perfect form possible.' Thus you are like this fool and you are not supposed to know. For if we had not been attached to each other, wouldn't we be separated? And why are you [dealing] with the secrets of God?"[1]

[54] The second [twin] responded: "Why, my brother, do you hasten to give this man so flimsy a response? What right do you have to provide him such an answer which [merely] pacifies and tranquilizes his mind? If he had asked me, I would have answered him in a manner to satisfy his intelligence, although the essential reason is hidden to the eyes of all [who are] living[2] and man truly is incapable of knowing it. Nevertheless, it is fitting that we should search for it, [at least] as far that our arms reach.[3] As the philosopher wrote in his introduction to the *Metaphysics*,[4] every person by his very nature has the desire to know and understand everything; the little that we do understand of divine matters is good, etc. Now permit me to speak so it will not be considered a sin on my part to interrupt your speech."

He [the first boy] said: "Speak!"

He [the second boy] then turned to me and said: "You surely know that the three worlds—intellectual, celestial, and material—are all connected to each other and are influenced by each other.[5] Anything created on earth possesses a root above which brings it into existence.[6] Thus when we investigate anything, we are required to know its agent and cause and hence we easily will learn its effect. At the beginning of his inquiry the philosopher investigates general principles which lead him to particulars. As our investigation ascends from the lowest to the highest general cause in the intellectual world, we shall not dismiss any other cause because in like

[1]Cf. B. T. Berakhot 10a. The source for this story is a contemporary Italian novella. See the introduction above, pp. 33–34, n. 96.

[2]Cf. Job 28:21.

[3]This summarizes, as well as any other line in *Gei Ḥizzayon,* the purpose of the work and the nature of Yagel's quest to understand the world.

[4]Aristotle, *Metaphysics,* I, 1–2.

[5]As indicated above, the interconnectedness of the three worlds is the major theme of Yagel's writing, with broad implications for him as a physician, astrologer, and kabbalist. See the introduction above, and Part II of this work.

[6]D. Cohen-Aloro, in "The *Zohar*'s View of Magic as a Consequence of the Original Sin" (in Hebrew), *Da'at,* 19 (1987): 32, n. 5, brings forward a number of medieval Hebrew sources to illustrate this concept.

manner [i.e., in ascending order], God conceived it [the entire structure of the universe].

"Just as we are incapable of knowing Him, we are incapable of knowing His ways, as Scripture states: 'For as the heavens are higher than the earth, so are My ways higher than your ways.'[1] And since it is a basic principle for us that He is just and righteous regarding everything of which He is the sole cause, we shall declare that all His words are just and that none of them are perverse or crooked.[2]

[55] "If He brings about evil, let us search and examine our ways and turn back to the Lord,[3] as our master King David, of blessed memory, did when there was a famine in this land [which lasted] for three years. The rabbis explain in chapter *Ha-Arel:*[4] 'In the first year, he [David] asked if there were idolators among them, for it is written: "And they worshipped other Gods, etc."[5] They searched but did not find any [idolators]. In the second year he said: "Perhaps there are sinners among you, for it is written: 'And when showers were withheld and the late rains did not come, etc.?' "[6] They searched but did not find anything. In the third year he asked them: "Perhaps there might be those among you who announce specified sums for charity but do not give them, as it is written: 'Like clouds, wind, but no rain, is one who boasts of gifts not given?' "[7] They looked but found nothing. He immediately said: "The matter entirely depends on me [as it is written:] 'David immediately inquired of the Lord etc.' "[8] Thus you see how King David, of blessed memory, followed the full force of his investigation as far as his hands could reach. He also requested the *Urim* and *Tummim,* as Resh Lakish declared there, until he learned of the bloodguilt of Saul and [his] house.[9]

"Thus when anything [bad] happens to us, we must search our ways and our actions. We will discover that the evil came upon us because of our own faults. It is taught that no evil descends from above except that which our sins caused and that from which our iniquities prevented the good.[10] If

[1]Isaiah 55:9.
[2]Cf. Proverbs 8:8.
[3]Cf. Lamentations 3:40.
[4]B. T. Yebamot 78b.
[5]Deuteronomy 11:16.
[6]Jeremiah 3:3.
[7]Proverbs 25:14.
[8]Cf. 2 Samuel 21:1.
[9]Cf. B. T. Yebamot 78b on 2 Samuel 21:1. The *Urim* and *Tummim* were the mysterious objects on the breastplate of the high priest which were said to possess magical powers. Cf. Exodus 28:30.
[10]On the history of the expression and its place in sixteenth-century Jewish thought, see M. Ḥalamish, "A Gnomic Collection" (in Hebrew), *Sinai* 80 (1977): 278; J. Dan, "No Evil

what happened in the state is a miracle that transcends the boundaries of nature and accepted practice, it is proper that we attribute it to a general cause. This was [certainly] the case regarding our birth which, by our estimation, had not occurred in Venice, nor in any states adjacent to it, for a thousand years. Moreover, everyone took notice and wondered about us. Thus we came to all the city's inhabitants to inform them that this incident which came from God has general as well as specific implications. Good things are brought about through the agency of good people [and vice versa].[1]

[56] "We learned this idea from the lesson regarding the heifer that was to be beheaded by the elders of the town nearest the corpse [which had been discovered lying in the open].[2] Furthermore, 'your elders and officials' were supposed to come.[3] The rabbis explained[4] that this refers to the most general category of judges and officials [whose jurisdiction extends] over all the towns, namely, those of the high court of Jerusalem. The Torah commanded the elders of that town to be stirred to action regarding the terrible incident of a discovered corpse. The elders of the high court, the priests, and the elders of that town washed their hands and called heaven and earth as their witness [in declaring] that this incident was not caused by their own negligence [in tending] to the general needs of the state.[5] The rabbis similarly stated:[6] 'Could it have crossed our mind that the elders of the court were shedders of blood? No, for [they indicate] that he [the victim] did not come into our hands. We did not send him away without food nor did we observe him [traveling] and leave him with none to accompany him.'[7] Afterward, the priests would say: 'Absolve, O Lord, your people Israel, etc.'[8]

"With this context in mind, [we can state that] the incident [of the twins] was caused by God to teach us the path to follow regarding anything that happens to [all of] us. Just as individuals are responsible for [promoting] individual righteousness, so are the rulers and the heads of an individ-

---

Descends from Heaven: Sixteenth-Century Jewish Concepts of Evil," in *Jewish Thought in the Sixteenth Century,* ed. B. Cooperman (Cambridge, Mass., 1983), pp. 89–105. Compare especially Moses Cordovero's similar view, as presented by Dan, with that of Yagel.

[1]Cf. B. T. Shabbat 32a and elsewhere.

[2]Cf. Deuteronomy 21:1–9.

[3]Cf. Deuteronomy 21:2.

[4]Cf. B. T. Sotah 44b.

[5]Cf. Deuteronomy 21:6–7.

[6]Mishnah Sotah 9:6.

[7]Note the language of the declaration in Deuteronomy 21:7: "Our hands did not shed this blood, nor did our eyes see it done."

[8]Deuteronomy 21:8.

ual state responsible for [promoting] more general righteousness. More-over, the king and high court, whose jurisdiction extends over all states, are responsible for [promoting] the most general righteousness, as was the case for the high court in Jerusalem. If the person who commits this crime [i.e., murder] in Israel is not discovered, the elders of that town must bear the responsibility. Accordingly, the elders of the high court came to that place [where the corpse was discovered] not to see if the elders of the city were guilty of shedding the blood of the murdered victim, God forbid, for this did not cross their minds, as the rabbis stated; [they came only to ascertain] whether they [the town elders] were negligent in providing for the needs of the state and its administration. Thus they [the town elders] would testify before them [the elders of the Jerusalem high court] that they were not responsible for the evil.[1] In this manner, they removed any suspicion regarding their general and specific responsibility [for promoting] righteousness. Only the person who consciously committed the act, raised his hand, and smote his brother, remains guilty and bears individual respon-sibility for the specific part of the injustice [he committed]. The priests subsequently came to pray for the sake of the general justice, [acknowledg-ing] that they did not commit any sin related to their [public] administra-tion, as it is stated: 'They go out innocent before God and Israel.'[2] But they did not pray to God to forgive the murderer for his sin, since he cannot be atoned except by having his own blood spilled.[3]

"Thus we learn that just as there were three different parties who were affected by their involvement with the murdered corpse, so there are also [three parties] in our own situation today. In place of the slain corpse is our father's house; in place of the town court is the entire city of Venice; and in place of the high court, we stand guilty before our Father in heaven. We are deserving of this [fate] because of the verdict which came to us from His court of justice, which created [us] in this manner. But because anyone who [publicly] proclaims his sin is considered impudent,[4] as Scripture states: 'Happy is he whose transgression is forgiven, whose sin is covered up,'[5] I will not tell you of the sins that caused our fate. It is sufficient for you to know that everything that happened to us was just. If our father's house-

---

[1]This appears to contradict the statement in Mishnah Sotah 9:5, that the Jerusalem elders previously departed from the place. See Mani's note, p. 24a.
[2]Cf. Numbers 32:22.
[3]Cf. Genesis 9:6.
[4]Cf. B. T. Berakhot 34b.
[5]Psalm 32:1.

hold likewise was guilty of committing that sin, the ramifications [of the sin] need not serve as a warning to everyone.[1] Yet how horrible that person must have been for whom the order of creation was changed so that the nature of his children was distorted in such a manner![2] The city in which we were born is also culpable for her sins which [likewise] caused nature to pervert its ways and actions. The days arrived when the divine justice sought to exact from her [the appropriate punishment] for her sins, through some blow [meted out] from its [repository of] blows and afflictions. So it happened that the Lord's hand was upon her. Many in her midst later died from plague and from the bitter illnesses that accompanied it which were not disclosed to any specialist.[3] No one was able to identify how their ways and deeds were perverted secretly in the innermost chambers.[4] God also distorted the way of nature for them [the victimized citizens of Venice]; they were like dry grass that falls before it rises. If out of the mouths of babes and sucklings[5] they would have learned to return to the Lord, as the people of Ninevah did,[6] and give up the iniquity on their hands, who knows if God might have turned and relented? He may have turned back from His wrath toward them.[7] For God is merciful and forgiving and does not desire the death of the wicked, but that the wicked turn from his [evil] ways and live.[8]

[57] "In this miracle of our strange birth, they [the citizens of Venice] should have learned a moral lesson and returned to God. They should have realized that this [event] came from God to instruct all the inhabitants of the land about the evil [amongst them]. If you investigate the chronicles of kings and states, you will find that a strange creature like these [Siamese twins] was born in the midst of a state prior to any crisis. [Such was the case] in the region of England, where a set of twins were born attached to each other as we are. A short time later, a group of people rose up against

[1]The nature of their sin, like that of the twins, need not be divulged.

[2]Yagel probably hints at the parents' role in handing the twins over to the local *gemilut hasadim* society, who preserved the corpses and publicly exhibited them for profit. On the whole incident, see the introduction above.

[3]Yagel refers to the Venetian plague of 1575–77, which struck the Mantovano, as we have seen, with similar intensity. On the plague, see especially Preto, *Peste e societa à Venezia, 1576*, and G. B. Gallicciolli, *Delle memorie venete antiche profane ed ecclesiastiche* (Venice, 1795), II, p. 214. Both authors mention the appearance of the twins in relation to the plague.

[4]Cf. B. T. Hagigah 5b.

[5]Cf. Psalm 8:3.

[6]Cf. Jonah 3:5–8.

[7]Cf. Jonah 3:9.

[8]Cf. Ezekiel 33:11.

the king, conspired against him, and killed him.[1] Also afterward, a cruel blow struck the people in the year 5312 [1552]. Moreover, in the year 5332 [1572], in the region of France, twins were born whose form was similar to ours. In those very same days, there was a conspiracy of the Ammiraglio and the war of the sectarians. Only a short time later King Charles IX died.[2] There is also a reference in the history of the Romans that during the great war between Philip, the king of Greece and Macedonia, and between the Romans, a strange creature was born in Rome.[3]

"The sage Aben Ragel, the astronomer, wrote that in his days the queen gave birth to a boy with a strange appearance. When the boy emerged into the air of the world, he opened his mouth with hands outstretched to heaven and said: 'I came to this world to tell you that the kingdom is lost and that the king will be defeated by a great people from Almanazi.'[4] Similarly, Zenophon wrote that the son of King Cyrus, named Ati, spoke to his father on the day of his birth about a great misfortune destined to happen to the king and his ministers.[5] The scholars also know that when a woman gives birth to a creature who looks like a pig, it is a sign that a plague will break out among the people, for this happened many times in various ancient kingdoms and lands. [You might] investigate books and read of incidents regarding the birth of strange creatures more numerous than the hair on your head; they always represent evil and not

[1]This information about monstrous births, as well as the information below, is all taken from an anonymous Italian pamphlet, printed in Venice in 1575, titled *Discorso sopra gli accidenti del parto mostruoso nato di una Hebrea in Venetia nell'anno 1575 a di xxvi di Maggio*. I have used the second edition of the work, which was printed in Bologna in the following year and is located in the library of the Hebrew Union College in Cincinnati, Ohio. Cf. A. Sapadin, "On a Monstrous Birth Occurring in the Ghetto of Venice," *Studies in Bibliography and Booklore*, 6 (1964): 153–58. The reference is taken from p. 12 (my pagination).

[2]*Discorso*, p. 12: "Nel 1572, . . . fu preparata la conguiura contra l'Ammiraglio e Ugonnoti, et segui popo dopo la morte del Re Carlo IX."

[3]*Discorso*, p. 12.

[4]*Discorso*, p. 10: "Di tal sorte si riferisce essere stato quel parto, che raccorda Hali, che nacque al Re della sua regione, perche inalzo le mani, e si levo a sedere, e poi disse: In son nato infortunato, e son nato a demonstare la perdita del Regno d'Az dessit et la destruttion della gente d'Almanaz." On Aben Ragel and Yagel's use of this same quotation in another work, see D. Ruderman, "Three Contemporary Perceptions of a Polish Wunderkind of the Seventeenth Century," *Association for Jewish Studies Review*, 4 (1979): 157. See also G. Busi, "Sulla *Ge Ḥizzayon* (La valle de vision) di Abraham Yagel," *Annali della Faculta' di lingue e letterature straniere di Ca'Foscari*, 23 (1984): 25, who identifies the precise quotation from Aben Ragel. See also introduction above, p. 44.

[5]*Discorso*, p. 10: "Ati figliuol di Ciro dimonstro se non con parti mostruose, col parlar ne' primi mesi al padre la ruina che gli soprastava." Cf. Ruderman, "Three Contemporary Perceptions," p. 157, n.48.

good portents. The people of the city should have learned a moral lesson from this and returned to God with great fortitude.[1] This [explanation] should be sufficient for you regarding the cause that emanated from the upper intellectual world.[2]

[58] "However, the more proximate cause is engendered by the heavenly world which turns and is activated by the upper [intellectual] world.[3] The astronomers call this the specific message of our birth. However, if we were to provide a general explanation of this, it would prolong the account, since every strange creature born on the earth has a heavenly constellation from which it was formed and created. Therefore, we will not speak of them [i.e., the constellations]. Anyone who desires to know should consult the works of Ptolemy, Democritus, and Aben Ragel, along with other astronomical texts.[4] Accordingly, we will speak [only] about ourselves, since your question was about us.

"I will say that it is clear from what Hermes, the great philosopher and astronomer, wrote that all that happens to the fetus in the mother's womb is determined by the ascendant constellation at conception and the other stars of one's soul.[5] In another place, he wrote that we are able to determine the ascendant constellation and the position of the moon at the time of impregnation from the ascendant constellation and the position of the moon at birth.[6] With this determination, made with little effort, anyone who has learned a little about astronomical horoscopes will be able to draw up a horoscope directly, without error. Notice a great man who testified on this, the great Rabbi [Abraham] ibn Ezra, in his commentary on Exodus, where he claimed: 'I also tried it five times.'[7]

"Since our birth was on Wednesday, the twenty-sixth of May 5335 [1575], sixteen hours and fifty-three minutes after noon, the time of the

[1]Cf. Jonah 3:8.

[2]The *Discorso* follows the same threefold explanation that Yagel adopts. On this and Yagel's general fascination with monstrous births, see the introduction above, as well as Ruderman, *Kabbalah, Magic, and Science,* chap. 5.

[3]This discussion primarily relies upon chapter 2 of the *Discorso,* titled "Della causa agente remota seconda l'opinione de gli astrologi."

[4]This is Yagel's way of abbreviating the *Discorso*'s longer discussion. Yagel also shortens the discussion by describing the astrological circumstances of the birth day alone and not the day of impregnation. Both days are discussed with the aid of charts in the *Discorso.*

[5]For the probable reference to Hermes' astrological work, see M. Steinschneider, *Die Hebraeischen Ubersetzungen des Mittelalters und Die Juden Als Dolmetscher* (Berlin, 1893), p. 515.

[6]Cf. *Discorso,* p. 10. Yagel quoted Hermes on other occasions, most notably a prayer from the *Pimander.* For Yagel's general interest in the ancient theologians, see Ruderman, *Kabbalah, Magic, and Science,* chap. 9, and see above.

[7]See ibn Ezra on Exodus 2:2.

impregnation would be, according to what we wrote, 7 September 1574 at 2:48 P.M.[1] The constellations of the sky were situated in this way: The ascendant rested ten degrees from the constellation of Capricorn; the moon was twenty degrees from Gemini; and the head of Drago was also ten degrees from Gemini. Jupiter was seven degrees from Cancer. Venus was fourteen degrees from Leo. The sun was twenty-four degrees from Virgo. Mercury was fourteen degrees from Libra. The zenith rested nine degrees from Scorpio. Saturn was three degrees from the constellation of Sagittarius; Mars was twenty-one degrees from it, and the tail of Drago was also nine degrees from it. Thus, according to Ptolemy's directions, the twins were caused because most of the planets were in the constellations of two bodies or in general constellations.[2] Since Mars and Saturn dominated the ascendant in a general constellation of two bodies, the birth was determined by Gemini.

"The falling lights indicate [the birth's] strangeness. The sun fell from the line of the ninth house and the moon fell from the top of the eastern horizon. If the sun had not approached the ascendant so that it appeared in the third watch and in a constellation benevolent to the moon, and if the sun and the ascendant had not received a successful spark from the constellation of Jupiter, we would have been born in the form of an animal. But since Mercury dominated the two lights and the head of Drago, and since it was in the ninth house, this indicated that our soul was taken from on high.[3] Since the sun was in the fourth watch with the moon, this indicates that our soul was taken from the dens of lions and a certain evil spirit dressed up with skin, flesh, and sinews.[4] You surely should see that these two things are not in conflict with one another and that both of them are valid. You should consult the book of *Alkabito*,[5] which indicates the number of degrees [from the ascendant sign] to the moon at the time of impregnation required to determine whether the creature born will be monstrous. But this is enough for you to know of the secondary cause according to the words of the astronomers.

---

[1]Cf. *Discorso*, p. 4. The details that follow are taken from a chart on the reverse side of that page.

[2]*Discorso*, p. 4v: "che la maggior parte de' planet sia in segna di dui corpi o comuni."

[3]The *Discorso*, p. 4, expresses it this way: "Ma Mercurio signor di tutti dui li luminari e del capo del dragone, essendo in nona, dimostra qualque diabolica operatione."

[4]Again Yagel slightly altered his source, which reads (p. 4): "Et il Sol che fa il quadrato con la Luna mi da a credere che sia qualque malignita di spirito."

[5]Probably Al-Kabi'si, known as Alchabitus or Alkibitus, the tenth-century Arabic astrologer. On him, see Steinschneider, *Die Hebraeischen Ubersetzungen*, pp. 561–62.

[59] "However, [let us turn] to explain the most proximate natural cause of the twins' birth and their attachment, for which we call them a strange creature, or by the term of the natural philosophers, a monster, that is, a perversion of nature.[1] Just as a wise craftsman can make a mistake in his work for whatever external or internal reason, and the mistake is counter to his intention, so wise nature, in creating a strange creature, can be forced against its will, out of external or internal reasons, into perverting its ways with this creation. For it [nature] always desires to preserve the order of creation in the most perfect way possible. As in the art of casting called *gettare*, when the print is perfect, the dust that is cast is fine and proper in a perfect manner. Also the material with which one works is proper without any dirt in it. Likewise, at the time of casting the craftsman does not move his hands, either to the right or to the left, within the space he imprints a form facing another. Thus the form looks proper and perfect. In like manner, wise nature [operates], as long as the 'print' is perfect, which [is equivalent to] to the essence of the female's womb, and as long as the dust is proper, which [is equivalent to] to the placenta,[2] that is, the fine and flaky[3] skin around the body. The material used, that is, the male sperm and the female's blood, should not be too great or small in quantity or quality; [it should be] at a median between cold and heat; it also should be clean of all filth and dirt, about which Scripture writes: '[O Lord of Hosts . . .] if You will grant Your maidservant the seed of men,'[4] that is to say, semen with which to create human beings with a perfect human [form] and not beastly or strange form. The craftsman also cannot move his hands during casting [which corresponds to the action of] the man and woman during the precise time of intercourse. [They] should not move to the right or to the left because of excessive animal appetite, nor should they act in any abnormal way. The rabbis warned against this [behavior] concerning 'the overturner of his table' [i.e., one who has abnormal intercourse] or one who acts [otherwise] abnormally with his wife; he has not done well and his teaching is not that of the pious.[5]

[1]On the significance of monsters for the sixteenth and seventeenth centuries, see J. Céard, *La nature et les prodiges: L'insolite au XVIe siècle en France* (Geneva, 1977); K. Parke and L. J. Daston, "Unnatural Conceptions: The Study of Monsters in Sixteenth and Seventeenth Century France and England," *Past and Present*, 92 (1981): 20–54; and see above.

[2]Cf. Mishnah Niddah 3:4, B. T. Niddah 26a.

[3]Cf. Exodus 16:14.

[4]1 Samuel 1:11.

[5]Cf. B. T. Nedarim 20a. Yagel's analogy between the craftsman's act of creation and that of human life in nature is reminiscent of similar analogies among early modern enthusiasts of science. By such an analogy, the medieval distinction between human art and divine nature

[60] "Instead, the rabbis warned man to treat her in a holy and pure manner, as they stated:[1] 'Anyone who sanctifies himself at the time of intercourse will have male progeny, as it is written: "Sanctify yourself and be holy"; and it is later written: "If a woman conceives and bears a male child."[2]' Maimonides, of blessed memory, wrote in the twenty-first chapter of *Hilkhot Issurei Bi'ah:*[3] 'Anything a man wants to do, he may do. . . . However [one who possesses] the quality of pietism should not be light-headed but should sanctify himself at the time of intercourse. He should not stray from the normal way since this act is only for the purpose of procreation.'

"The rabbis also stated in the second chapter of *Nedarim*[4] that R. Yohanan b. Dehavai said: 'People are born lame because they overturned their tables [i.e., practiced abnormal intercourse]; dumb, because they kiss in "that place"; deaf, because they speak at the time of intercourse; blind, because they look at "that place," etc.' Even though the law does not follow R. Yohanan but rather allows a man to do what he desires with his wife[5] (The one exception is [the requirement] to discharge semen only in 'that place,' outside of which a man is called a discharger of semen for naught. R. Yohanan even proclaimed that anyone who discharges semen for naught is liable to be killed;[6] for this crime, Er and Onan were punished and killed.),[7] in any case, it is a quality of pietism to treat one's wife normally as Maimonides wrote from the wise counsel of the glorious sages. Then the progeny of a man will be proper persons with complete limbs and not be strange [creatures].

"The fact that they [the rabbis] permitted a person to do as he pleases with his wife was done to counter the evil inclination. Thus the Torah permitted an attractive woman to have her first intercourse during a time of war;[8] and similarly [permitted the easing of the laws prohibiting the eating]

---

was abandoned. Compare Decartes' statement, for example: "There is no difference at all between the machines that the artificers make, and the bodies nature makes on her own account." Cf. R. Hooykass, *Religion and the Rise of Modern Science* (Edinburgh and London, 1972), pp. 61–67; the quotation is on p. 66. Elsewhere, Yagel drew a similar analogy between the creation of the universe by God and that of a clock in his advocacy of the human role in creation. Cf. Ruderman, *Kabbalah, Magic, and Science,* chap. 7.

[1]B. T. Shevu'ot 18b.
[2]Leviticus 11:44; 12:2.
[3]*Mishneh Torah,* Hilkhot Issurei Bi'ah, 21:9.
[4]B. T. Nedarim 20a.
[5]B. T. Nedarim 20b.
[6]B. T. Niddah 13a.
[7]Cf. Genesis 38:7–10.
[8]Cf. Deuteronomy 21:10–14.

of bacon.[1] If these were not permitted, people would do them even though they were forbidden. However, a person who protects his own life and that of his children will distance himself from these [abnormal] acts. When he [a man] thinks of this act only for the purpose of procreation, as Maimonides wrote, he will be following the Torah as the rabbis instructed. His natural faculties will function normally so that his progeny will be proper and he will protect himself.

[61] "Let us return to our [original] intention regarding the cause of [the birth of] the twins. Many have said that there are many sacs in the womb of the mother [and that they] total seven: three are on the right side, three on the left side, and one is in the middle. Spermatozoa that enter those [sacs that are] on the right side produce male progeny; on the left side, female progeny, and in the middle, an androgyny, a unique creature with both male and female signs.[2] Hippocrates wrote that any man or woman can create twins in any sac; both of them can be born on the same day and at the same hour.[3] Perhaps this is what the rabbis meant in *Shemot Rabbah*[4] '[regarding the verse]: "[The Israelites] were fertile and prolific."[5] Every woman bore six [children] in one belly, as it is said: "The Israelites were fertile and prolific." Another [rabbi] said: "twelve," etc.' They [the rabbis] meant that the person who said six thought that a woman could bear one child in each sac; the person who said twelve thought, like Hippocrates, that twins could be formed in each sac.

"They did not mention the seventh sac since the Holy One, blessed be He, did not wish to bring a strange creature of the adrogynous strain into the world among the Israelite nation. [This was so] because it is a strange creature, neither man nor woman with respect to the observance of the commandments, even though it is required to observe all the commandments stated in the Torah that apply to men.[6] In any case, it is not equal to either of them [either men or women] with respect to many things, as the

[1]Cf. B. T. Ḥullin 17a. Bacon was permitted to be eaten during the time of the Israelite conquest.

[2]This explanation, along with the previous excurses on the craftsman-printer and abnormal intercourse, are not found in the *Discorso* and represent Yagel's own contributions to the subject. On the seven sacs and their place in Jewish folklore, see J. Trachtenberg, *Jewish Magic and Superstition* (New York, 1970), p. 188, 303, n. 13, and Mani's note, p. 26b.

[3]The *Discorso*, p. 4, quotes Hippocrates regarding Siamese twins; the author claims they are formed when the spermatozoa enter two sacs instead of one.

[4]*Shemot Rabbah*, 1:8.

[5]Exodus 1:7.

[6]Elsewhere in his writing, Yagel quoted Galen's *Ars Parva* on androgynous creatures and attempted to discover an analogy between them and demons. See Ruderman, *Kabbalah, Magic, and Science*, chap. 3.

rabbis taught in the chapter on androgynous creatures.[1] For that reason, [the women] gave birth to six [children] in one belly[2] and not seven.

"Since man's spermatozoa is bountiful and part of it can leak into two sacs [simultaneously], a woman may become pregnant with two fetuses and give birth to twins. If the sperm is increased further but cannot fill the third adjacent sac or cannot enter its opening and remains by the curtain, then this sperm will join with another which does enter the sac. This is like an animal whose head is within the sac while his tail hangs out. This is also analogous to the art of casting, as we have mentioned. If there is too much material, it [the material] passes over the first form and clings to the second form that is imprinted next to it.[3] This is the case [regarding procreation] and also is the reason for our being attached.[4] But let us leave this subject now since it was not our intention to inform you [about] what happens when the material [i.e., the sperm] is scarce, in which case the created fetus lacks one of its limbs. Similarly, when the material is filthy and incapable of producing a human form, the form [that] emerges depends on the quality of the material.[5]

"Wise nature always watches over this process, providing form to matter according to its [particular] character, just as we see that even from decayed matter, mosquitoes and worms are born. [62] At times, scholars have even found mice dwelling in people's stomachs. They dwelt there because the matter was appropriate for them, as Levino Lemnio, physician of Zerezio, testified in his book on the secrets of nature.[6] Therefore, those creatures who are born from such ugly matter have strange animal forms.

[63] "The imagination of a man or woman at the time of intercourse can also play a great role [in determining the fetus's form]. The rabbis report the case of a black woman in *Bereshit Rabbah*.[7] She married a black man and gave birth to a white child. The rabbis did not consider the boy a

[1]Printed as chapter 4 of Bikkurim in most Mishnah editions.

[2]As stated above in *Shemot Rabbah*.

[3]This is a good illustration of Yagel's penchant for finding analogies in nature. For its importance in his thought, see Ruderman, *Kabbalah, Magic, and Science,* chap. 4.

[4]Curiously, Yagel devotes almost the entire section to a discussion of the origin of twins, not Siamese twins, with the exception of this last afterthought. In so doing, he ignores the more complex discussion of the *Discorso.* The few sentences that follow attempt to summarily pass over the latter discussion.

[5]Both these points were fully developed in the *Discorso.*

[6]Yagel refers to the Dutch physician, Levinus Lemnius, whose *Occulta naturae miracula* was published in Antwerp in 1559. Yagel clearly was familiar with this work and its themes; it may even have served as a model for his own scientific encyclopedias, the *Beit Ya'ar ha-Levanon* and the *Be'er Sheva.* See Ruderman, *Kabbalah, Magic, and Science,* chap. 4.

[7]*Bereshit Rabbah,* 73:10.

bastard because of the pictures of white [persons] the black father had in his house.[1]

"What we have said is enough to answer your question. But this I say to you: The truth of the matter is hidden from every living person and from the [natural] philosopher who follows one explanation or another. When Aristotle, the head of the philosophers, and Albertus Magnus realized that this matter was so concealed, after having offered many naturalistic explanations of it, they ultimately decided that the essential cause of strange creatures born on the earth is heavenly conjunctions which influence lower beings, as we have stated previously."[2]

[64] When the second boy had finished speaking, he bowed down and said: "Pray to God on our behalf so that He will restore us to our resting place. Let the joy of salvation and a vigorous spirit sustain us.[3] We also have been chastised for all our sins and the writ of our debts is already ripped up. But once your brother is degraded in your eyes,[4] he can no longer be called wicked, for he is like your brother.[5] In any case, we require compassion from God. May He be gracious to us and bless us and cause His face to shine upon us, selah.[6] Anyone who returns to God, after having concluded his prayer with sackcloth, fasting, and the tearing of the heart and clothes, is guaranteed by law and by universal justice that his writ of indebtedness will be torn up. Whatever happens, a person should pray to God, who will bestow on him a clear vision to gaze on the beauty of the Lord,[7] to return to his Creator as in former days. So we find in the case of King David, may peace be with him, that he prayed to God and said: 'Restore me the joy of Your salvation.'[8]

[65] "For this reason the Torah includes the guilt and sin sacrifices to connect the cords[9] of the upper world with the lower, to influence the latter with an abundance of blessing and adoration, and to reconcile a slave with

[1]On the idea that the imagination plays a role at the time of intercourse, see Trachtenberg, p. 187. Yagel also devoted an entire chapter of his *Beit Ya'ar ha-Levanon*, 4:75, fols. 173b–174b, to the force of suggestion and the imagination in healing.

[2]For a summary of their views on the cause of monsters, see Céard, *La nature et les prodiges,* pp. 3–6, 31–59, esp. 36.

[3]Cf. Psalm 51:14.

[4]Cf. Deuteronomy 25:3.

[5]That is, his suffering evokes sympathy in the beholder so he is like a brother. Cf. Mishnah Makkot 3:15; B. T. Makkot 23a and elsewhere. The original passage in Makkot, unlike this version, is a play on words where the reversal is easier to understand.

[6]Cf. Psalm 62:2.

[7]Cf. Psalm 27:4.

[8]Psalm 51:14.

[9]Cf. Job 38:31.

his master. Now, when the sacrifice and the priest have disappeared from us, may it be His will that the words of our mouths be as a pleasing odor before Him,[1] as it is written: 'Instead of bulls we will pay [the offering of] our lips.'[2]"

[66] We said to them: "May the Lord our God comfort you and hear the sound of your cries."

The two of them bowed and prostrated themselves, and left us with a more cheerful countenance than that which they had before we had spoken to them. God had given them cause for joy[3] by our discussion with them, as Scripture states: "Anxiety in a man's heart depresses it,"[4] and the rabbis declared: "He will depress others."[5] Thus the sage remarked: "Either friendship or death."[6] This is so even in that world of pleasures [enjoyed] by the souls who sit together and speak with each other.

The rabbis also wrote in chapter *Sho'el:*[7] "Every righteous person receives a habitation befitting his honor." By this they meant that each one's delight will be distinguishable from that of his neighbor depending on the individual's own attainment. Similarly they declared:[8] "Everyone is afflicted because of [his envy of the superior] canopy of his friend." This is because of the [different] level of [each of them in heaven]. However, there is no doubt that they [the righteous souls] will take sweet counsel together[9] and will rejoice in the heavenly academy, as we see from what the rabbis wrote in the chapter *Mi she-Metu*[10] regarding what happened to Samuel, who went up to the heavenly academy and saw Levi sitting outside. Therefore, there must be a heavenly academy where souls enter together to enjoy and listen to the lessons. They see their teachers and learn Torah from Him [God], which He expounds anew for them each day.

[67] I asked my father: "Why did the face of the first child appear so hostile toward me? Why was he so agitated with me? And why was he so

[1]Cf. Exodus 29:25 and elsewhere.
[2]Hosea 14:3.
[3]Cf. Ezra 6:22.
[4]Proverbs 12:25.
[5]B. T. Sanhedrin 100b.
[6]B. T. Ta'anit 23a. A troubled person cannot live without good companions.
[7]B. T. Shabbat 152a.
[8]B. T. Babba Batra 75a, referring to how God rewards each righteous person with a canopy (*ḥuppah*) at Mount Zion, as described in Isaiah 4:5–6. This statement is in response to the question, Why did God create a flaming fire on the mount?
[9]Cf. Psalm 55:15.
[10]B. T. Berakhot 18b. Levi was denied entrance into the heavenly academy because he had refused to enter R. Efes's academy and instead studied outside it. When Samuel came, Samuel asked that Levi be forgiven and he subsequently entered the heavenly academy.

disconsolate when I spoke to him and asked him about the reason for his being attached?"

He [my father] answered: "He recognized that you were still among the living and he feared lest you ridicule the dead.[1] He said to himself: 'This man will soon come to us; for now, he shames, mocks, and ridicules us because of his sins that caused us all these [troubles].' You also were guilty of an impropriety in not asking him gently, for a gentle response allays wrath.[2]

[68] "Surely when you ask anything of a person, your words should be most sweet to him. We find this to be the case with King David, of blessed memory, who said: 'Who can discern errors? Clear me of unperceived guilt.'[3] Afterward, he said: 'and from willful sins, etc.'[4] The rabbis in chapter *Ḥelek*[5] compared him to a gentile merchant [who presents his wares one at a time]. David said to the Holy One, blessed be He: 'Master of the universe! Who can avoid errors?' God answered him: 'I leave it to you [i.e., you are forgiven].' [Said David:] 'Clear me of unperceived guilt.' [God answered:] 'I leave it to you.' [David again inquired:] 'And presumptuous sins which will not be discussed in the house of the sages.' [God answered:] 'I leave it to you.' Similarly, they [the rabbis] learned a lesson, in chapter *Hayah Koreh*,[6] in declaring a favorite saying of Abaye: 'One should always be astute in fear[ful situations], answering softly in responding to anger, making peace with one's associates, with one's relatives, and with everyone, even with the gentile in the market; thus such a person will be loved above and cherished below and accepted by all humanity.' Anyone who is pleasing to humanity is pleasing to God. 'It was said of R. Yohanan b. Zakkai that no one ever greeted him first, even the gentile in the market.'[7]

[69] "You also should know that there are good and bad creatures among all those created on high and below. This secret always eluded Aristotle and his school, as [Abraham] ibn Ezra hinted in commenting on the verse: 'You shall be as God, knowing good and evil.'[8] The author of the *Pardes* [*Rimmonim*] explained his words in the following manner: 'This sage ibn Ezra thinks that there are those who know good and evil among

[1]Cf. B. T. Berakhot 18a on Proverbs 17:5.
[2]Proverbs 15:1.
[3]Psalm 19:13.
[4]Psalm 19:14.
[5]B. T. Sanhedrin 107a but abbreviated here.
[6]B. T. Berakhot 17a.
[7]B. T. Berakhot 17a.
[8]Genesis 3:5.

the heavenly host. The word "riders" hints at this for him since these are the angels associated with good and evil, etc.'[1] Even among the spirits, there are good [spirits] and bad ones [spirits], as we see from the words of the rabbis in *Midrash Rabbah*.[2] [They relate] the incident of a spirit dwelling in a spring. It came time for it [the spirit] to depart and another spirit more evil than the first was to go there [to the spring]. In order that people would not be hurt by it [the latter spirit], he [the first spirit] revealed the matter to the rabbis and instructed them to say: 'God is with us; God is with us,' while ringing bells until the [second] spirit fled. Thus, as we said, all creatures are either bad or good. Similarly, between the two souls who just left us, one is better than the other. The second hinted at this when he said that 'a glance' from heaven looks down upon them, indicating that there is evil opposite their faces, while another constellation indicates that their soul is taken from on high. Now speak your words before the light of day is upon us or before other souls meet us and interrupt us."

## Resumption of the Son's Life Story

[70] I answered: "While the woman [Madame Rina] was living on the podesta's property, I sent someone to speak with her about the business of the bank, to [inquire] whether she now wished to assume responsibility for it. For time had passed and these [recent] developments had caused her to settle in this area. At the same time that the woman had come down to Luzzara—she and her family as we have said—several of the Almagiati brothers also had come down, fleeing from the hostile region [of Mantua].

[1]Neither Mani, p. 27b, nor I could find such a quote either in Moses Cordovero's *Pardes Rimmonim* or in ibn Ezra. Cordovero does express a similar idea regarding good and bad angels (without referring to ibn Ezra) in *Or Yakar* (Jerusalem, 1963), 2, sha'ar 6, siman 37, p. 194. My thanks to Professor Bracha Sack for the reference. On the other hand, Yagel could have referred not to Moses Cordovero but to Shem Tov ben Jacob ibn Shaprut, the author of a work also titled *Pardes Rimmonim*, published in Sabbioneta in 1554 (reprint, Jerusalem, 1968). In this work, ibn Shaprut quotes ibn Ezra often but not with this precise reference. He does quote from ibn Ezra's *Sefer ha-Ibbur*, which is also quoted by Yagel elsewhere (see below, Part II, pp. 232–33). I also could not find the above reference to Genesis 3:5 in ibn Shaprut's super-commentary to ibn Ezra's Bible commentary, titled *Zafenat Pa'ane'ah* (MS. London 200; Jerusalem microfilm 5059). Both ibn Ezra and ibn Shaprut refer to the cherubim in Genesis 3:23 as angels. Perhaps Yagel meant *keruvim* (cherubim) instead of *rokhvim* (riders), but the printed text and both manuscripts read *rokhvim*.

[2]*Vayikrah Rabbah*, 24:3. Yagel's accepting and unfearful attitude toward demons was shaped in part by such rabbinic materials. Cf. Ruderman, *Kabbalah, Magic, and Science*, chap. 3.

They had gone to Guastella but were driven out by the local citizens and they then came to live in Luzzara. This happened prior to the outbreak of the controversy between the populace of Luzzara and the woman. However, on the same night that they had wished to drive out the woman, the local citizens were also ready to drive them out [the Almagiati brothers], since the woman had defamed them as well. May God remember on my behalf what I did for them until the community's anger had passed and the populace had locked them in their houses for a few days.

"While they [the Almagiati brothers] were dwelling in the area, they spoke with me several times about my willingness to conclude a deal on the same terms proposed when their father was still living. Thus the partnership would not be dissolved, as is the case when one of the partners dies.[1] Before concluding the arrangement with them, I sent someone to convince the woman [as to the terms of her payment], but in the end, she responded to me as she had done previously. I saw that I could not expect anything from the woman. I thus turned to them [the brothers] and we remained in negotiations with each other. Then we went [together] to persuade the woman until she finally agreed to satisfy them and me and to accept her payment in four [equal] installments. We did an accounting of the bank and the men prepared a payment of one fourth of the money as they had promised the woman. But the woman refused to take it, claiming that before she could accept the money, she wanted the advice of wise experts in Jewish and general law in order to arrange her affairs legally.

"But they [the Almagiati] had been grievously corrupt,[2] as only a short time passed before the money flew away as a raven from the hands of the brother, spent for an unsavory purpose. The behavior of the eldest of the brothers [Lazzaro, or "Eliezer"] was like that of Jehu, the king of Israel, whose mother crowned him with three crowns when he was born, the same crowns [worn] on the heads of the vulgar who presume to instruct [Torah when they are not scholars]. This man tried to win friends and associates and gain popularity with jest and lightheadedness until they [the brothers] lost all their money and were left with nothing. By the time the woman wanted them [to conclude the agreement], they no longer wanted her. Not much time passed before they became disheartened of the area and its inhabitants. Their attitude had been totally different when they initially had been involved in the negotiations. But either because they were unable or because they were discouraged by it [the negotiation], [they withdrew] and

[1]Cf. *Shulḥan Arukh,* Ḥoshen Mishpat 176:19, and the literature cited there.
[2]Cf. Hosea 9:9.

I was left entirely alone. [All of this happened despite the fact] that the woman even pressured me to conclude the arrangement and I likewise exerted pressure on the men.

"When the woman [Rina] and her family eventually returned to Luzzara, since the local inhabitants [now] wanted her [to stay in the community], the important old lady [of the family][1] was stricken by the plague and died at a good ripe age, full of days and good deeds.[2] When she died, the glory of the woman's [Rina's] family departed,[3] for with her [the old lady's] protection, she [Rina] had lived among the gentiles. Seven times she fell[4] and she was saved from her despoilers. However, when this merit disappeared, the creditor discovered the opportunity to recover his debt and permitted destruction to reign. Serious calamities now confronted her. First, she was bedridden with the illness that afflicted her and her entire family, including every single male.[5] Also in that time, the hand of the Lord was upon her,[6] taking from her the betrothed of her eldest son. Both her outer and inner grief became so great that she no longer could concern herself with the bank, so no one spoke a word to her [about business].[7] Yet we all tried to pity and comfort her and act compassionately toward her; for I truly felt sorry for her.[8] As God lives, in all her troubles, I was troubled.[9] I did not restrain myself from crying and mourning for her. May the Prober of hearts and the Knower of secrets have compassion for me as I had for her, and remember me [on account of] these [things] in every place; for in distress, I will call Him.[10]

"Many days passed and subsequently God's angel began to destroy the people in this area. The plague thus began and everyone tried to escape; anyone would offer all he owned to save his life. Nor would anyone withhold any expense in order to stay clean and not contract anything of the evil [disease].

"The Almagiati brothers left the city and returned to Mantua. While I

[1]Yagel does not identify the woman; perhaps she was Rina's mother.
[2]Cf. Genesis 25:8.
[3]Cf. *Bereshit Rabbah*, 68:7.
[4]Cf. Proverbs 24:16.
[5]Cf. 1 Samuel 25:22 and elsewhere.
[6]Cf. Exodus 9:3.
[7]Cf. Job 2:13.
[8]Cf. Song of Songs 5:4.
[9]Cf. Isaiah 63:9.
[10]Cf. Psalm 118:5. The syntax of the last part of the sentence is awkward. I have disconnected it from the next sentence where it would have made little sense, even though it appears to be connected.

rebuked them daily, they would mislead me with words which gave me continued hope. They did not appreciate the affliction of my heart and the emptiness of my pocketbook, [whose emptiness] increased daily. All the funding agencies of the community[1] inundated me [with requests] to support the poor,[2] those who could not support themselves, and those who could not overcome the deficit. The claim that 'if he doesn't have [any wealth], etc.,'[3] which is increasingly useful in any place, did not help me. I also could not collect from my debtors since the courthouse was closed and everyone did as he pleased.[4] Many times, I became so dejected[5] about my work that I disdained my life. My only comfort was that I had made up the documents with those brothers. But because of the welfare of the state, I was required to locate money wherever I could find it by borrowing it on interest or by selling a *seah* [an ancient measure] of wheat for a [mere] *shekel* [an ancient coin] in order to find a source for money. On many occasions, the podesta and community testified against me that I withheld money necessary for helping[6] the needy poor.

"Days passed and the serious afflictions of the woman's household almost disappeared. She continued to complain to me, so I went to Mantua on three separate occasions to finalize some contractual agreement with the aforementioned brothers—either to confirm the wording of the documents or for each party to go its own way. After some days [had passed], we took arbitrators and we each parted, after so much labor and effort and after having remained in Mantua for the third time for [a period of] around a month.

"I returned home and told the woman what had happened and how the separation had transpired. I imagined that she would be pleased and satisfied by the [arrangement], since she had murmured many times against them [the brothers], had been incensed, and had complained about this [entire] affair. But instead, she reversed her earlier opinion before the separation [i.e., that she had wanted no part in any dealings with the Almagiati]. I gave her plausible, good, and correct arguments, saying: 'To whom is the place more fitting than for you? It will serve you as a vindica-

[1]Literally, "the entire community of the fiscal locality [*me-ha-makom ha-mamoni*]."
[2]Cf. 2 Kings 24:14.
[3]Perhaps, "then he doesn't have to give." Alternatively, cf. B. T. Yoma 18a: "Whence do we know that if he doesn't have [any wealth], his brethren the priests endow him?" (referring to the high priest).
[4]Cf. Judges 17:6; 21:25.
[5]Cf. Job 21:4.
[6]Cf. Psalm 107:9.

tion[1] to bestow on one of your sons as an inheritance; it will be a way of earning a living for you. The land is large enough for you.[2] You will be able to become great and augment your business as you desire. Conclude [the deal] and do it, for the business will be good for you. Thus Abraham [Yagel] will benefit because of you[3] and he will survive on your account. Ask of him and he will do anything you say. The paper is white before you so write on it as you wish. It will be signed, sealed, and carried out. If you want to lease or rent out the bank, do as you wish. The building also is available to you for anything you may request; so is the man you wish to be on guard, who will hand over its receipts to you each evening as a trustee faithful to you. But if you do not desire such an employee, that's all right too. But, in any case, don't retreat [from this agreement] since nothing prevents God[4] from saving [the bank] other than for the effort of these negotiations.'

"I testified before faithful witnesses that I had said these things to her by myself, and also through those intermediaries whose names I shall mention, for the living will not deny [the words] of the living. They are the most distinguished Azariah Finzi,[5] the honorable Barukh Senigo,[6] the honorable R. Reuben of Perugia,[7] R. Uziel of Camerino,[8] and the late R. Barukh Finzi.[9] I pleaded with her many times: 'Please don't desert me; rather, take this place [in the partnership]. By so doing, all your complaints about your money will disappear. Then you will know the location of your bank so that nothing will be unaccounted for. I will even sell the hair on my head so that you receive everything.'

[1]Cf. Genesis 20:16.

[2]Cf. Genesis 34:21.

[3]Cf. Genesis 12:16.

[4]Cf. 1 Samuel 14:6.

[5]On Azariah (Bonaiuto) b. Solomon Finzi, see Simonsohn, pp. 226–28, 236. Azariah was the brother and banking partner of Yagel's closest friend, Hananiah Finzi. They opened banks together in San Martino and Gazzuolo. Yagel copied the correspondence between Azariah and two rabbis, Ishmael Hananiah of Vallemonte and Hillel Modena of Viadana, regarding the murder of Azariah's daughter in 1577 in their home in Ferrara. Azariah's son was the murderer, who claimed his sister was a whore. See MS. Moscow Günzburg 127, n. 27, and see Ruderman, *Kabbalah, Magic, and Science,* chap. 1 on Hananiah.

[6]On Barukh b. Joseph Senigo, see Simonsohn, p. 30. He was one of the three community health supervisors for the Mantuan Jewish community during the plague of 1576.

[7]He was also known as Reuben Yare, who served as a teacher in the home of Solomon Segal Ostiglia of Mantua and reported to Yagel about the supposed appearance of demons in Solomon's house. Cf. Simonsohn, p. 716.

[8]On this family in Mantua, see Simonsohn, index.

[9]On Barukh (Benedetto) b. Abraham Finzi, see Simonsohn, pp. 348–50, 407. Finzi was a banker in Gazzuolo who was granted the patent to run the inn of the Jewish community, which consisted of a tavern, restaurant, and hostelry serving visitors and the poor.

"These discussions continued for many days since I believed that there is no crooked and hard heart that is not softened by tears, nor is there a stone cut of flint rock that is not pierced by a steady, continual dripping. My talk with her was like a hammer splitting rock, but it did not benefit me in the least. Rather, she remained stiff-necked and her words were like the [immutable] laws of the Persians and the Medes.[1] What they [her words] have decreed, no one can break. And while she would not change them [her views], she continually pressured me with her demands.

"When I saw this I got up and returned to Mantua with the absolute conviction that I would give the place to the first person with whom I spoke about it, no matter who he was, even a *natin* [Temple servant] or a bastard.[2] With this [act], I would rid myself of the woman's complaints. I remained there a long time but could not find a supporter[3] since Mantua and its borders were completely closed off. No one went in or out because of the frightening rumors of the plagues and pestilences that God had inflicted upon her."[4]

## The Appearance of Job

[71] While I was speaking these words, I looked up and saw opposite me a well-dressed old man of eminence. He was wearing a robe [signifying] fame and glory and a great light enveloped him. I asked my father [about him] and he [my father] said that he was Job. He had been sent on a mission for his Creator as an angel of God. I was astonished for a moment about the sight and said: 'Blessed are you, O God, who has rewarded me [by allowing me] to see this divine man!' For I had wrongly concurred with that rabbi who, sitting before R. Samuel bar Naḥmani, had said: 'Job never existed nor was he ever created but was only a parable.'[5] When I had witnessed all the other sages of Israel disagreeing as to whether or not Job really lived,[6] I had concluded even more certainly that the law accorded with the view that he was only a parable. I also found support [for this position] in the view of 'the great eagle,' Maimonides, of blessed memory, who, in his honorable

[1]Cf. Esther 1:19.

[2]Two groups excluded from the ancient Israelite community with regard to intermarriages. See Mishnah Yebamot 8:3.

[3]Cf. Numbers 11:12.

[4]Cf. Deuteronomy 29:21.

[5]See B. T. Babba Batra 15a.

[6]See especially B. T. Babba Batra 14b–15a. For other references, see L. Ginzberg, *Legends of the Jews* (Philadelphia, 1968), vol. 2, pp. 225–42; vol. 5, pp. 381–90.

book, *Moreh Nevukhim,* explained the matter.[1] [He interpreted] the name 'Uz' in the verse: 'There was a man in the land of Uz'[2] as an equivocal term [referring also] to the name of a man as in the verse: 'Uz, his first born.'[3] The word is the imperative form of the verb *ezah,* meaning advice and counsel, as in the verse: *uzu ezah,* take counsel together[4] and pay attention to the things written in this book on the diverse opinions regarding providence. Thus they [these opinions] must have been related by an innocent and righteous man rather than by a sage. If it had been a sage, he never would have doubted these matters. So how can you declare, my master, that this man coming toward us is actually Job?"

[72] My father responded: "Yet, you still should have known that Job lived and that he was created. For R. Yohanan declared in *Bereshit Rabbah:*[5] 'Every man of whom it is said [in Scripture], "he was," remained unchanged from beginning to end.' [This is the meaning of the verse], 'There was a man in the land of Uz'[6] who was chastised with afflictions, etc. So too, in *Tanḥuma*[7] [it says concerning the verse], 'After these things':[8] 'Abraham was frightened by the afflictions. The Holy One, blessed be He, said to him: You don't have to [be afraid]. A man already has been born who will receive them [these afflictions].' Moreover, in *Bamidbar Rabbah*[9] [it is written]: 'And Uz was Job as it is written: "A man was in the land of Uz and Job was his name, etc."[10]'

"That man [Job] is related to us; he is one of our redeeming kinsmen,[11] He was born in the land of Aram Naharayim, in the city of Nahor, and he went to live in the land of Uz, which is [known today as] Constantinople, the largest city in the Turkish kingdom, which formally was called Uz. Thus R. Joseph[12] translates the verse in the scroll of Lamentations: 'Rejoice and

[1]*Moreh Nevukhim,* 3:22.

[2]Job 1:1.

[3]Genesis 22:21.

[4]Isaiah 8:10.

[5]*Bereshit Rabbah,* 30:8.

[6]Job 1:1.

[7]I could not find the reference in *Tanḥuma;* see, however, *Bamidbar Rabbah* 17:2, where the same thought is expressed in relation to the verse in Genesis. On the comparison of Job to Abraham in rabbinic literature, see N. N. Glatzer, "The God of Job and the God of Abraham: Some Talmudic-Midrashic Interpretations of the Book of Job," *Bulletin of the [London] Institute of Jewish Studies,* 2 (1974): 41–58.

[8]Genesis 22:1.

[9]*Bamidbar Rabbah,* 17:2.

[10]Job 1:1. The midrash also claims that Job received those afflictions meant for Abraham by linking the name of "Uz" in the Abraham story (Genesis 22:21) with "Uz" in the Job story.

[11]Cf. Ruth 2:20.

[12]The Aramaic translation of the Hagiographa traditionally was attributed to R. Joseph b. Ḥama, the Babylonian rabbi.

be glad, O daughter of Edom who dwells in the land of Uẓ'[1] as 'Rejoice and be glad . . . in the city of Constantinople, etc.'[2] And when the verse speaks of him [Job] being 'in the land,' this means in that land into which the afflictions came. However, he was not born there but in Aram Naharayim. From there he went to live in the land of Uẓ in a town called Kirianos, as the rabbis related in the Midrash:[3] 'See how the Holy One, blessed be He, pressed his punishment upon Job when he came to the town of Kirianos for three years, etc.' [There] he enlarged his property primarily 'in the land' until he became wealthy and honored and in [his possession of] a very large household, just as the verse testifies.[4] In the same town he was afflicted, and it was to the same place that his three associates came from Aram Naharayim to pity and comfort him, as the rabbis related in chapter *Ha-Shutafim*.[5] We find that the distance from Constantinople to Aram Naharayim is three hundred parasangs.

"And how did they [his friends] know of Job's grief from so distant a land? Some say that each friend had a crown of three faces and one man's name was engraved on one face. When one of them was afflicted, his face changed.[6] Know as well that even today in the city of Constantinople there exists a monument at the grave of Job. The place is greatly revered; people treat it as a house of God. It is decorated with lit candles and with a hospice for travelers in the blessed memory of a righteous man.[7] Moses, our teacher, also wrote his own book [i.e., the Pentateuch], the section of Balaam, and the book of Job, etc.[8]

[73] "What was meant by the man who sat before R. Samuel bar Naḥmani and said that this [the story of Job] was a parable is this: Even if it were merely a parable, it still would have been worthy of being written

[1]Lamentations 4:21.

[2]The text in A. Sperber, *The Bible in Aramaic* (Leiden, 1968), vol. 4a, p. 148, closely approximates our text in mentioning Constantinople.

[3]See *Vayikrah Rabbah*, 17:4, ed. M. Margaliot (Jerusalem, 1953), p. 379, including his note there.

[4]See Job 1:3.

[5]B. T. Babba Batra 16b. It states there that each friend lived in a different place, located three hundred miles away from one other.

[6]B. T. Babba Batra 16b. Job and each of his friends had the pictures of the others (besides himself) set in his crown, and whenever one of them experienced adversity, it was revealed in his picture.

[7]Yagel is referring here to the traditional belief that the monument of the Arabic general Ayyub in Constantinople was that of Job. On this belief, see Ginzberg, *Legends*, 5, p. 382, and the sources he cites. The medieval monastery in Hauran, Syria, was also thought to house Job's tomb. Cf. L. Besserman, *The Legend of Job in the Middle Ages* (Cambridge, Mass. and London, 1979), p. 65.

[8]See B. T. Babba Batra 14b. On the line and its parallel in a passage from Josephus, see Ginzberg, *Legends*, 6, p. 134.

down as a book because of the important matters in it. We can still declare that this famous man actually existed, just as the prophetic statement indicates: 'And Noah, Daniel, and Job, etc.,'[1] and as the rabbis also said:[2] 'Each of them saw a world destroyed and then built up, etc.' Even so, Job's story was used by Moses, our master, as a parable through which he composed that book and recorded the discussions about providence among people with dissenting views. Job, who suffered and experienced afflictions, came with three friends to testify by experience on the subject of the suffering of the righteous and the flourishing of the wicked."

After [my father had spoken] these words, we came closer, bowed down to him [Job] and said: "Do not be angry[3] [at us] if we ask where you are going."

## Job's Story

[74] Job replied: "I heard the cry of a maiden from the land of Egypt, a young woman of good family, an innocent virgin. She was captured beyond the Nile river by pirates who brought her to the land of Ethiopia.[4] There they sold [her] to a wealthy nobleman, one of the brothers of Nabal the Carmelite,[5] who had been born, like him, under the sign of Canis. As soon as this man saw the girl's good taste, beauty, and fine intelligence, he purchased her in order to mistreat her and take her virginity. At first, he spoke to her in a pleasant and comforting way: 'Don't be afraid. You will be like a daughter to me.' The girl prostrated herself before the man and worked for him as a maidservant with great diligence so that she was equal if not superior to anyone who made light of her.

"The nobleman fell in love with the woman. One day, he found her alone in the house and revealed his innermost feelings to her. He promised her that if she submitted to him, he would give her a dowry, liberate her, and marry her to one of his servants. The girl refused. She wept and begged him not to do so shameful a thing as to take her virginity. Besides, this

---

[1] Ezekiel 14:20.

[2] See David Kimḥi on Ezekiel 14:20.

[3] Cf. Genesis 18:30, 18:32.

[4] For the possible sources of this story, see the introduction above, pp. 34–36.

[5] See 1 Samuel 25. Nabal came from the town of Maon and owned much livestock near the neighboring town of Carmel, southeast of Hebron. Although David extended protection to Nabal's flocks, Nabal refused to reciprocate by offering him a gift. In rabbinic literature, Nabal referred to himself as a descendant of Caleb (cf. 1 Samuel 25:3) in order to compare his more noble ancestry with that of David, who was descended from Ruth. On Nabal's unfavorable image, see Ginzberg, *Legends*, 6, p. 235.

would make her a rival to his wife, who is like his own body and who only would be jealous of another [woman].[1] The young girl acted wisely. She left him so, and the wicked man did not carry out his intentions. Every day, however, he continued to implore her but she did not submit to his request to sleep with him, even without intercourse. She became only more modest. When she saw what he did every day, she finally said to herself: 'Eventually I will be unable to escape from him. He is my master and his desire is intense. Vast floods will not quench the love.[2] He will chain me by my legs. Who knows if I will be able to escape from the snare and from the pit? Now is the time for me to seek advice in order to flee from under his net so that the slothful man shall not hunt his prey.'[3]

"Accordingly, the girl went to her mistress and wept bitterly, secretly revealing to her exactly what had happened. Her mistress saw that she was about to cry, and she recognized the truth, for the truth follows its own course.[4] She then said [to the girl]: 'Be silent. Do as I command you.' The girl answered: 'I will do whatever you command. I am your maidservant and I place my soul and my virginity in your hands.[5] I hope you will rescue me.'

"Her mistress gave her the following instructions: 'Listen, daughter, and observe your master when he speaks to you again, tempting you as is his regular custom. Tell him that you wish to fulfill his desire and that you will sleep with him this very night, before the middle of the second watch [1:30 A.M.], a time when no one is heard and the streets are deserted. But [at that hour] you will go and hide yourself in a certain place and remain there, while I shall go in your place and satisfy your promise.' The maiden bowed down and prostrated herself, and did everything her mistress had commanded her.

"Only a short time passed before she spoke with her master. When the man heard that the girl would respond to his request around midnight, he was astonished and silent in anticipation of the appointed day and time. Overjoyed that she was about to fulfill his desire, he stopped thinking about his wealth or property. At midnight, the man rose in the dark, closed the door behind him, and went to take his fill of love at the appointed place[6]

[1]Cf. B. T. Megillah 13a; literally, "who is only jealous of the thigh of another."
[2]Cf. Song of Songs 8:7.
[3]Cf. Proverbs 12:27.
[4]A Maimonidean phrase used frequently by Yagel. See Maimonides, *Shemoneh Perakim*, end of chap. 4.
[5]Cf. Psalm 31:6.
[6]Cf. Proverbs 7:18.

and to delight in lovemaking until the morning. When he arrived there, he was so overwhelmed with passion that he trusted the words of the woman [he found there]. The place was so dark that he did not recognize his wife. He drank from his cup while thinking it was another.[1]

"In the early morning, the man wished to depart before he might be recognized, lest someone say he had fornicated with a woman the previous night. But his wife asked him: 'Where are you going so early in the morning? Where do you think you were sleeping all night? I am your wife, the woman of your youth, but you thought badly of me[2] and turned your heart to arrogance,[3] to Egypt, to the people that has ceased to be.[4] Did you think that you did right in acquiring a name and glory for yourself in your old age, now that you have lost your virility? If this ever becomes public knowledge, how will you carry your shame and disgrace before all the old men with whom you take counsel? But do this and this matter will be known only between us. No one shall hear our voice outside. Speak no longer with the maidservant, neither for good nor for bad,[5] for this does not suit your honor. What has happened is done; for the sake of our previous love, I shall be quiet and restrain myself. I will be to you as before, obedient to your words and attentive to your voice. For you are my master; I shall bow down to you. However, if you do not follow these instructions and if you, the king, do not desire my beauty,[6] and turn your heart to this maidservant in our house, God will permit me to reveal your shame publicly; for your own sake you will be disgraced. No longer will I be your wife. I will leave your house and go to my father's and brother's. And this evil will be greater than anything you have experienced from the time of your youth until now.'

"When the man heard his wife's words, he became as stone, stunned as a man seized by delirium.[7] He had no idea whether he sat among the living in this world or in the next. He greatly feared for his life and honor, and was terrified by the words of his wife, a courageous woman, a daughter of nobility and stature, and a scion of an important family. So he changed his mind, spoke kindly to her and laughed. 'Who would have thought,'[8] he

[1]Cf. B. T. Nedarim 20b.
[2]Cf. Genesis 50:20.
[3]Cf. Psalm 40:5.
[4]Cf. Isaiah 23:13.
[5]Cf. Genesis 31:24.
[6]Cf. Psalm 45:12.
[7]For the expression, see Mishnah Gittin 7:1.
[8]Cf. Genesis 21:7.

said, 'that an important person like me would be caught in a game of whores like a worthless person? What should I do? Passion corrupts the rules of conduct and there is no protection against unchastity.[1] Do not fear! I will not continue to act as I have done. My fantasy was satisfied by spending the night with you and my mind continues to focus on it. The passion that was in my heart has receded and my soul cleaves still to you.'

"The woman graciously accepted his words. The two got up, and no one other than [she and] her husband knew of the matter. From that day on, he no longer spoke to her [the maidservant]. His courageous wife also did not leave the girl for even an hour. Yet the man harbored a grudge in his heart against the young woman because of the affair. The powerful love that had been implanted in his heart now changed to intense hatred. This loathing grew stronger than the love he had felt.[2] He devised ways of afflicting the girl, he struck her with horrible blows, and he piled hard work upon her. She, in turn, cried to God out of her great labor and He heard her cry and sent me to be a guardian for her and a refuge, a shield and breastplate, to show her a chord of divine grace,[3] and to make her beauty known to the son of the Ethiopian king so [that] he will seek and take her to be his wife. Tomorrow this sign shall come to pass.[4]

"All this happened because of the girl's great modesty and because she withstood the test. I swear that I have not found a woman like her since the time Ephraim departed from Judah.[5] She is fit to be a queen; furthermore, she comes from a family [of people] who are friends of Elihu, the son of Barachel the Buzite.[6]

## The Lessons of Job's Story

[75] "You should know that the Holy One, blessed be He, bestows greatness on a person only if there is something good in him or if he possesses a certain merit. This was [even true in] the case of Nebuchadnezzar whom Heaven made great by virtue of the four steps he ran to honor God, as it is described in chapter *Ḥelek;*[7] or it may be because of one's good quality, like

[1]Cf. B. T. Sanhedrin 105b, Ketubbot 13b, and *Bereshit Rabbah,* 55:7.
[2]Cf. 2 Samuel 13:15.
[3]For the expression, see B. T. Ḥagigah 21b and elsewhere.
[4]Cf. Exodus 8:19.
[5]Cf. Isaiah 7:17.
[6]Cf. Job 32:2.
[7]B. T. Sanhedrin 96a. The rabbis embellish here an incident described in Isaiah 39. In the

Moses' compassion, as the rabbis declared in *Midrash Rabbah Shemot;*[1] or like David's [kindness], as it is written: 'He brought him from minding the nursing ewes [to tend His people Jacob, Israel, His very own].'[2] [God also makes a person great] if that person encounters sin but is saved from it, as we find in the case of Joseph and others who rose from horrible oblivion to incredible heights among the Jewish people or among the other nations. These men were selected by Heaven to lead their people because they possessed merit, or a good quality, or moral virtue or wisdom, and this enabled them to achieve greatness and honor. Search thoroughly in every book and read them all. None will lack a reference [to this fact]. So do not be surprised that in a single day this young maiden rose from being a lowly maidservant to becoming the wife of the Ethiopian king's son. For there is nothing new under the sun."[3]

I then inquired: "May your servant say something to my master?"[4]

He answered: "Speak!"

[76] I spoke: "My master has said that anyone who achieves greatness possesses a good quality, like wisdom, or moral virtue, or some other merit, as in the case of Nebuchadnezzar, whom my master cited, or of Hiram, king of Tyre, who was Hirah the Adullamite,[5] or of Og, the king of Bashan, who was the fugitive who told Abraham that the son of his brother had been captured, etc.[6] This was also the case with the other officers of kings and sultans. And yet, we have seen that Haman, the son of Hammedatha the Agagite, rose to greatness even though it is nowhere mentioned that he possessed a good quality. On the contrary, he wished utterly to uproot the remnant of Israel, which stood as an ensign to the nations. Solely because God was with us was Haman's effort countered. Analogous examples exist among the gentiles: for example, Emperor Nero, whose worship was alien, and other individuals who, in a short time, rose to greatness and were

---

biblical story, Merodach-Baladan, son of Baladan, the king of Babylon, sent a messenger to bring greetings of peace to Hezekiah, the king of Judah, in Jerusalem. In the rabbinic account, Nebuchadnezzar, then the Babylonian king's scribe, tried to intercept the messenger in order to rewrite the message, since it had been composed improperly in his absence. However, the angel Gabriel stopped him after he had taken only four steps. Had he not been stopped, his reward might have been so great as to enable him to destroy Israel completely.

[1] *Shemot Rabbah*, 2:1.

[2] Psalm 78:71.

[3] Ecclesiastes 1:9.

[4] Cf. Genesis 44:18.

[5] See *Bereshit Rabbah*, 85:4, where King Hiram, who assisted Solomon in the building of the Temple, is identified with Hirah, the friend of Judah (Genesis 38:11).

[6] See *Bereshit Rabbah*, 42:8, where Og is identified as the fugitive mentioned in Genesis 14:13.

catapulted from the dunghill to great majesty. Enable me to understand this, my master, since I am your servant."

[77] He [Job] responded: "There is no difficulty. Neither I nor you, is familiar with the [intimate] lives of these people, with their goodness, their wisdom, and deeds. Consider this! Haman was also a barber in the same town where I lived for three years prior to my afflictions, as the rabbis mention in *Megillah*,[1] where Mordecai told Haman that he was a wicked person, and [asked] whether he was not once a barber from the town of Kirianos, etc. Even so, I do not know of any special goodness in his actions that would enable me to specify the quality that allowed him to achieve greatness, for I went to him only when I needed a haircut and I curtailed my talk with him, since I knew that he was from the accursed seed of Amalek. A good cub does not become a bad lion.[2] Still, I saw that he had a courageous heart, the heart of a lion, and eventually he came to despise that work [of a barber]. He joined the ranks of the army, and became great, acquiring wealth and honor. His one good quality was the courageous heart he possessed. Likewise, Nero, the emperor, had acquired the perfect skill of musical knowledge and that mollified his cruelty.

"Aside from these things, one should not look for positive attributes in these persons. The Holy One, blessed be He, created them solely in order to destroy and pour out his anger on humanity when it [humanity] rebels and sins against Him. Accordingly, we should attend to the general principle we stated that God uses all things as His messengers, even a snake or frog.[3] He created them all to serve as a hammer in His hand. In addition, there is a principle in which we believe that anyone who hurts Israel is made a 'head' in his time, as the rabbis indicate in *Ekhah Rabbah* regarding the verse: 'Her adversaries have become the head.'[4]"

[78] I asked: "Tell me, master, why is it that everyone who hurts Israel becomes a 'head'? If [the children of] Israel are God's children, then, by justice, anyone who harms them should become a 'tail,' not a 'head'?"

[79] Job answered: "When one knows something, he also knows its contrary. For the wise man, the knowledge of opposites constitutes [knowledge] of the same object.[5] When [the children of] Israel are at the 'head' and

---

[1] See B. T. Megillah 16a.

[2] Cf. Rashi on B. T. Megillah 11b, *Vayikrah Rabbah*, 19:6, and elsewhere for a similar but not identical phrase.

[3] See *Bamidbar Rabbah*, 18:22; *Vayikrah Rabbah*, 22:4.

[4] Lamentations 1:5; *Ekhah Rabbah*, 1:31. R. Hillel b. Berekiah explains in this passage that whoever harms Israel becomes a "head." Since Israel is so exalted, she only could be overcome by a general of eminence. When Jerusalem was destroyed, other cities rose in stature.

[5] Cf. Aristotle, *Categories*, 10 (11b25). Yagel had previously referred to this statement above.

not at the 'tail,'[1] and if someone touches them, it is as though he had touched the pupil of God's eye, so to speak, since they are His children, as the verse says: 'You are my children, etc.'[2] Their [Israel's] constellation rises as the constellation opposite them falls. However, when they fall because of their evil deeds, their constellation is low and it descends. At that time, their oppressor is protected by the constellation opposite Israel's, and as his constellation rises, he rises. For God has decided and who shall reverse it?[3] The Torah also testifies about this when it declares: 'The stranger who is among you shall mount up above you.'[4]

"Thus, if we examine carefully all the comings and goings of a man who becomes great, we will discover in him some possitive attribute of wisdom or morality, just as we have said, and as the rabbis stated:[5] 'God bestows wisdom solely on the person prepared to receive it, as the verse states: "He gives wisdom unto the wise."[6]' They also stated: 'Prophecy is also found in a wise, courageous, and rich person.'[7] As is known, a courageous person is one who controls his passion, as the rabbis state:[8] 'Who is courageous? One who controls his passion; and [who is] rich? He who is happy with his lot.' He is a person who is satisfied with what the Creator has given him, either much or little."

[80] I responded: "Therefore, according to what you have said, Israel has a constellation. Yet I have learned in chapter *Mi she-Hiḥshikh*[9] that Israel has no constellation. Even though it was said in the name of R. Hanina [b. Hama] that Israel has a constellation, we do not hold this view. But R. Yohanan claimed that Israel has no constellation and his view is shared by Rav and Samuel, R. Akiva, R. Nahman bar Isaac, and all those who think likewise and who substantiate their opinion with biblical verses.[10] So how can you claim, my master, that Israel has a constellation? I request that you please explain to me the truth. And if they do have a constellation, which one is it?"

He answered: "Know well that Israel has a constellation even though

[1]Cf. Deuteronomy 28:13.
[2]Deuteronomy 14:1.
[3]Cf. Isaiah 14:27.
[4]Deuteronomy 28:43.
[5]B. T. Berakhot 55a.
[6]Daniel 2:21.
[7]B. T. Nedarim 38a.
[8]Avot 4:1.
[9]B. T. Shabbat 156a.
[10]See the statement of Rav on B. T. Shabbat 156a and the others on 156b; see also Sukkah 29a.

it was said in the name of R. Yohanan that Israel doesn't have a constellation, and [even though] all those *Amoraim* [rabbis of the third–fifth centuries C.E.] agreed with him. [81] We hold that any such form [of expression] is an [individual] opinion, and the law does not follow an [individual] opinion.[1] Rather, it was the manner of the sages to be brief. Since we see that they specify who holds this opinion [that Israel has no constellation], even indicating their names, we know that they are in the minority. The majority holds the opposite view, and thus the law does not follow anyone of them [in the minority]. [On the contrary,] the law follows what was said in the name of R. Hanina, namely that Israel does have a constellation.[2]

"You also should know that Capricorn and Aquarius are the constellations of Israel;[3] their planet is Saturn, since these constellations are its [Saturn's] houses, as [Abraham] ibn Ezra explains in *Sefer ha-Azamim*,[4] and R. Abraham b. David in his commentary to the *Sefer Yezirah*.[5] Because of these constellations, they [the Jews] are liable to plunder and destruction, to toil and to burdens, like those of our ancestors in Egypt. None of the heavenly hosts are as devastating as these two in summoning evil and suffering to this world. Accordingly, the astrologers assigned as its [Saturn's] lot the black plague, illnesses, slaves, graves, the prison, and a place of corpses.

[82] "Astrologers also know that one finds the form of a flying eagle nineteen degrees from the constellation Capricorn which affects sick people, particularly those with irritable skin and eczema. Astrologers predict that a person who is born during the time it [Capricorn] is ascending in the east while the sailorless ship [another heavenly formation opposite it at the end of the constellation of Aries] is about to sink in the sea, will be afflicted

[1] Cf. B. T. Babba Meẓiah 69a.

[2] Of course, the issue is not a matter of law, as Mani points out, p. 32b.

[3] Note that Yagel's strong interest and expertise in astrology thoroughly inform his discussion of the issue of Israel's constellation. He noticeably ignores the kabbalistic exegesis of this subject. Cf. *Tikkunei Zohar, tikkun* 100.

[4] The work was wrongly attributed to ibn Ezra. It was a primary source for magical and astrological knowledge for both Yohanan Alemanno and Yagel and is quoted several times by the latter. Cf. M. Idel, "The Study Program of Yohanan Alemanno" (in Hebrew), *Tarbiz*, 48 (1979): 312, n. 76. See *Sefer ha-Azamim* (London, 1902), pp. 18, 21. On Saturn as the planet of the Jews, see E. Zafran, "Saturn and the Jews," *Journal of the Warburg and Courtauld Institutes*, 42 (1979): 16–27.

[5] This is the fourteenth-century commentary of Joseph b. Shalom Ashkenazi, written in Spain, and wrongly attributed to R. Abraham ibn David in printed editions. See G. Scholem in *Kiryat Sefer*, 4 (1928): 286–30. See [pseudo] Abraham ben David on *Sefer Yezirah* (Jerusalem, 1962), pp. 102–3, which explicitly mentions the *sefirah binah* and Saturn and their special relationships to Israel. Cf. below, Part II, p. 303.

by the aforementioned diseases and will have his life curtailed and filled with trouble.[1] Most Jews suffer from these illnesses, which derive from the general constellation to which they are all subject. Even though each person has his own constellation in the heavens that determines his life, he also is subject to the influence of the regnant constellation of all the members of his community. This is hinted at by the answer of my friend, Bildad the Shuhite: 'You who tear yourself to pieces in anger, will the earth be abandoned for your sake? Will rocks be dislodged from their place?'[2] He meant by these [words]: 'Do you consider it appropriate that you be immune from evils arranged in the general order? [Is it proper that] God would destroy the disposition of stars and dislodge the rocks from their place [merely on your behalf]?'

[83] "Just as an individual is capable of changing his fate from good to evil and from evil to good by repentence and good deeds, as Abraham, our father did, as described by the rabbis in chapter *Mi she-Hiḥshikh*,[3] similarly, if Israel is attentive to God's commandments and [if they] will all repent, almighty God will not be contemptuous[4] of their prayer and will hear the cries of the many. They will be able to overturn their fate and transform evil into good, as the prophet declared: 'While they are courting among the nations, now I will gather them up, etc.'[5] Thus they will be able to hasten the redemption, as Elijah said to R. Joshua b. Levi: 'Oh, if you would but heed his charge this day.'[6] The rabbis also said there in [chapter] *Helek*:[7] 'If they merit [the redemption], I will hasten it; if not, it will come in its time.' No doubt a 'time of mischance'[8] will come, due to the nature of these constellations [Capricorn and Aquarius]. Yet they [these constellations] can also ascend to [become] the cornerstone and influence their nation favorably. And opposite them, the constellation of Aries will sink into the depths of the sea, as the verse states: 'Then the moon shall be ashamed and the sun shall be abashed, for the Lord of Hosts will reign, etc.'[9] The verse speaks of the moon and the sun because the houses of these stars are Cancer and Aries, which are opposite Capricorn and Aquarius.

"The astrologers know that [when] any lower star that forms a con-

[1]Cf. Job 14:1.
[2]Job 18:4.
[3]B. T. Shabbat 156b.
[4]Cf. Job 36:5.
[5]Hosea 8:10.
[6]Psalm 95:7, B. T. Sanhedrin 98a.
[7]B. T. Sanhedrin 98a.
[8]Cf. Ecclesiastes 9:11; i.e., death.
[9]Isaiah 24:23.

junction with a higher one or 'aspects'[1] with it, the lower [star] will give the higher power and and serve it, depending on the natural disposition of the higher [star] with the lower. Thus the moon will bestow its strength on the six 'servants' [the six other planets]; all of them will give strength to Saturn, although the latter will not give its strength to any of them. Accordingly, the Indian sages declared: 'Since Saturn signifies the Jews, all the gentiles will acknowledge their Torah and bow down to them while they [the Jews] will not acknowledge them [the gentiles], as the prophet [Zephaniah] stated: "For then I will make the peoples a pure speech so that they all will invoke the Lord by name."[2]'

"The philosopher [Aristotle] acknowledged this fact and was not ashamed [to declare] that everyone will accept Israel's Torah in the future. This is recorded in his name by R. Joseph Albo in the third chapter of his third book:[3] 'There must come a time when all men will pursue the truth and endeavor to know God as far as it is possible for man . . . otherwise, the existence of the human species will be in vain.' It is a known fact that there is no Torah like that of Israel and thus everyone will believe in it, as the philosopher stated.

"Know well that *binah* [intelligence], the supernal mother, nourishes these constellations and their planets.[4] She is called in the language of the rabbis 'the constellation of Israel' and also 'repentance,' by which all repent. [She also is called] 'jubilee,' and through [her power] the slaves were liberated and Israel went out from Egypt, as the verse states: 'In distress I called on the Lord; the Lord answered me with great enlargement.'[5] Since

---

[1] That is, is affected by the special qualities or signs of the higher star. For the term and the general context of Yagel's astrological discussions, see A. Chapman, "Astrological Medicine," in *Health, Medicine, and Mortality in the Sixteenth Century,* ed. C. Webster (Cambridge and New York, 1979), pp. 288–89.

[2] Zephaniah 3:9. The reference to the Indian sages is probably taken from the astrological writings of Abraham ibn Ezra, who often quotes them. I could not locate this specific reference.

[3] Joseph Albo, *Sefer ha-Ikkarim,* ed. I. Husik (Philadelphia, 1946), 3, pp. 33–34. Yagel clearly stretches the meaning of the quotation as Albo gives it. Note that Husik calls this line "a pseudo-Aristotelian citation" whose source he cannot identify. It should be considered together with Yagel's previous discourse on the conversion of the gentiles to Judaism. See above, p. 138. Note that the second phrase is actually Albo's interpretation of the previous quotation and not part of the quotation.

[4] The third of the ten *sefirot* of the theosophic structure of the kabbalists. The *Sefer ha-Temunah,* written around 1300, already emphasizes that the *sefirot* and not the stars determine the course of the world. The seven *sefirot* apprehendable to man emanated from the *sefirah binah.*

[5] Psalm 118:5. In the scheme of the cosmic cycles (*shemittot*) described in the *Sefer Temunah,* at the end of 50,000 years a "great jubilee" takes place, at which time all the lower

*binah* is common to every intellect, emanation, and the six ends [the seven bottom *sefirot,* excluding *tiferet*], it thus contains two types of actions. When it [binah] clings to the uppermost heavens, there is destruction below; when it clings to the six ends, there is an abundance of goodness and blessing which renews itself.

"Thus Israel's ascent depends only on commandments that pull toward them the power of *binah.* Therefore, it [Israel] is victorious without a sword, spear, or armaments for God will save without a sword or spear.[1] When they [the people of Israel] depart from the commandments, the abundance of *binah* immediately departs from them and they descend to the uttermost end. This is the secret of the verse: 'If you will follow my commandments,'[2] and the secret of all the [divine] admonitions.[3] The prophet spoke of this saying: 'No, the Lord's arm is not too short to save, nor His ear too dull to hear'[4] the pressure which they exert upon us in order [for Him] to hasten redemption. 'But our iniquities have been a barrier between us and our God; our sins have made Him turn His face away'[5] from hearing our prayer. However, when a person acknowledges that [God] will come like a hemmed-in stream which the spirit of the Lord drives on,[6] and that His own hand will win Him triumph and don victory like a coat of armor,[7] then He will speed it [redemption] in good time[8] through the nature of the lower and higher constellations, as we [have] said.

"That is the secret of the statement of the rabbis:[9] 'R. Alexandrai said: R. Joshua ben Levi juxtaposed two [biblical] verses, for it is written: "One like the son of man came with the clouds of heaven,"[10] while [elsewhere] it is written: "Behold your king comes to you . . . humble, riding on an ass."[11]' How can this be? If they [the Jewish people] are meritorious, [he,

---

worlds and the seven supporting *sefirot* are reabsorbed into *binah.* Cf. G. Scholem, *Kabbalah* (Jerusalem, 1974), pp. 120–21; idem, *Ha-Kabbalah shel Sefer Temunah* (Jerusalem, 1965); and idem, *Origins of the Kabbalah,* ed. R. J. Z. Werblowsky, trans. A. Arkush (Princeton, N.J., 1987), pp. 460–75. [Pseudo] Abraham ben David, in his commentary on the *Sefer ha-Yezirah,* pp. 102–3, also discusses the *sefirah binah.*

[1]Cf. 1 Samuel 17:47.
[2]Leviticus 26:3.
[3]The entire passage beginning "Since *binah*" until this point is copied from [pseudo] Abraham ben David's commentary, p. 103.
[4]Isaiah 59:1.
[5]Cf. Isaiah 59:2.
[6]Cf. Isaiah 59:19.
[7]Cf. Isaiah 59:16–17.
[8]Cf. Isaiah 60:22.
[9]B. T. Sanhedrin 98a.
[10]Daniel 7:13.
[11]Zachariah 9:9.

the messiah, will come] with the clouds of heaven; if not, [he will come] humble, riding on an ass, etc. This means that if they [the Jewish people] are worthy, their good quality will influence their redemption not to come in its time [i.e., to come earlier], but on account of their merit and 'like the son of man, one came with the clouds of heaven.' If they are unworthy, it will come only in its time; the blessing will not spring forth because of its nature, [but] as we said, rather 'humble, riding on an ass.' Rather, the Holy One, blessed be He, will cause it [redemption] to come 'like a hemmed-in stream [at a slower pace].'

"The rabbis likewise wrote:[1] 'If you see a generation whose sorrows overtake them, wait for him [the messiah].' Thus they will call to God 'from out of the straits'[2] and He will answer them. By the merit of the repentance which they make, He will order the quality of repentance to bring repentance and have compassion upon them. 'He shall come as redeemer to Zion to those . . . who turn back from sin.'[3] As the rabbis stated:[4] 'Israel is only redeemed through repentance.' Through repentance, they went out from the servitude of Egypt; so too, repentance will liberate them from this formidable exile and God will hasten deliverance speedily in our days. Amen. Let it be His will.

"But now the time of the nightingale has arrived.[5] I must leave you and go on my mission to save the young woman from the hand of the hard master who rules her, and help her to gain power over him."

He thus blessed us with peace, left us, and went on [his way]. When this divine man had departed from us, my father asked me to complete my [previous] discussion. So I continued:

## Continuation of the Son's Life Story

[84] "After remaining in Mantua for a long time and seeing that no one [of the parties in dispute] engaged me in any discussions, either for good or for bad,[6] I lost hope of finding any appropriate person [to take on the partnership][7] there because of the treacherous time in those regions.[8] The

---

[1] B. T. Sanhedrin 98a.
[2] Cf. Psalm 118:5.
[3] Isaiah 59:20.
[4] B. T. Sanhedrin 97b.
[5] Cf. Song of Songs 2:12.
[6] Cf. Genesis 31:24.
[7] Cf. Leviticus 16:21.
[8] Apparently, Yagel still referred to the time of the plague, when no one was in the mood to worry about such matters.

intermediaries[1] spoke with me about restoring the partnership with the Almagiati brothers for a second time. The elder brother had pressed the matter, but he said yes and no and remained indecisive[2] like the vapors rising from the stomach to his brain [either] shut up or freed.[3]

"One morning, one of the intermediaries pressured us [the parties in dispute] to establish the partnership for a second time, but in a way different from the first. He arranged the *partito*[4] to be carried out completely by the honorable Maẓliaḥ [Prospero] residing in Guastalla.[5] He would have full decision-making power with the business to do as he pleased and no one would tell him otherwise. The manager residing [there] to assist him could also take what he liked. In addition to these [conditions], they were to give me forty scudi[6] as my yearly salary and as rent on the house where the bank was located. I also would sell him the right of possession [of the bank, enabling him] to pay her [Madame Rina] annually for five consecutive years. They were to do this is such a way that Madame Rina would concur and remove all her grievances against me.

"We [all three parties] came to Luzzara. The brothers and the woman reached a compromise over the purchase of the right of possession of the partnership and also to possess the bank in partnership. We then went to the borders of Revere, for there was our exalted majesty, our lord.[7] I presented him with the [new] names on the *decreto*[8] instead of my one [name] and the [new] terms.[9] I waited for their signatures so that this entire matter would come to an end since the citizenry [of Luzzara] and some of Mantua pressured me to help finance the urban poor. No one had any capital and nothing remained for them except their land and produce as [plentiful as the] sand in the sea. And I would give good things to everyone,

---

[1] Apparently those individuals named above in section 70.

[2] Cf. B. T. Kiddushin 65a, literally, "it was undecided in his hand."

[3] Cf. Deuteronomy 32:36 and elsewhere. Note the medical analogies Yagel naturally employs. Like the vapors that are either shut in or freed, he remained undecided.

[4] Agreement, resolution. Note the frequent use of Italian words in the autobiographical sections.

[5] I could not identify this person. There was an active Jewish presence in this town south of Luzzara. See Simonsohn, index.

[6] On the relative value of the Mantuan scudo in this time period and other information on exchange rates in this area, see Simonsohn, pp. 742–44.

[7] The duke Guglielmo of Mantua. In 1577, the duke had signed similar contracts with eight Jewish bankers in the capital and twenty more in the Mantovano. See Simonsohn, pp. 221–22.

[8] Decree.

[9] In the terms of the contracts signed in 1577, a Jewish banker was allowed to transfer his business to another Jew on condition that he inform the duke. See Simonsohn, p. 222.

shielding and saving, protecting and rescuing,[1] with the expectation that we might strike [a deal] with a hammer to conclude this matter in one or two weeks. But my hope was dashed because his exalted majesty, the duke, became ill and [he] also had no desire to conclude any terms with the Jews.[2] Furthermore, the plague was beginning to wane in the land and he had to establish order and give thought to uprooting 'a stock sprouting poison weed and wormwood,'[3] [that is,] the [remaining impact of the] contagious disease.

"I would complain all the time about the wrath of the oppressor: 'Who will give us money for daily wage; who will give us [money] for daily wage?' When necessary, I sent to Madame Rina pawns from the bank with which to lend to the poor of the land in a limited way. The woman so lent, and we continued with this procedure for some months until it became known that the pawns of silver and gold handed over to her from the bank had run out, since the cash box had [also] been sent to her. Many important people in the area were also angry with me me since I no longer fulfilled their requests [for loans] on the pawns they held. Many protested loudly; some even acted perversely toward me and the woman since she [only] had loaned money to them with pawns on silver or gold. But to anyone who did not have these [pawns], he awoke to find himself empty[-handed].[4]

"They spoke with the head of 'the satyrs who danced in this place'[5] and the man who was wise in the ways of wrongdoing and crafty as the original serpent. He slandered the woman regarding matters of interest, took the cash box from her house, and placed me in jail for questioning and tried to punish the woman and me to the extent that he could. I sent for my supporters, spoke with them, and arranged for a trial before the podesta. I made countercharges against that big 'satyr' until I fortunately was released. The woman also was unscathed; she incurred no expense, not even a penny.

"I explained to her at this time that everything had happened because of [my] lack of money. [85] You certainly must know that money answers every need.[6] If a person has wealth, everyone responds to him and he has many friends, as King Solomon wrote: 'A rich man has many friends.'[7] If a

---

[1] Cf. Isaiah 31:5.

[2] This obviously happened before his agreements with the Jewish bankers in 1577.

[3] For the expression, see Deuteronomy 29:17.

[4] Cf. Isaiah 29:8.

[5] Cf. Isaiah 13:21. Apparently, Yagel is referring to Eliezer Almagiati or to one of his associates.

[6] Cf. Ecclesiastes 10:19.

[7] Proverbs 14:20.

person lacks money, he is afflicted, for 'all the brothers of a poor man despise him.'[1] [I said to her:] 'But now it is time to act to remove any crooked and twisted thing.[2] So do this: Each of us should contribute fifty gold pieces which together will total one hundred [pieces]. Since you trusted me in the past for a sum larger than this, you surely can trust me for this smaller sum until this entire affair is over. With this [sum], I will supply the citizens of the city.'

"The woman wrote to the Almagiati from Mantua about my imprisonment and [about] what had happened to me. After seven days had passed, the elder Almagiati brother [Eliezer] and Barukh Senigo[3] arrived. I spoke to them in the woman's house and in her presence about the delivery of the aforementioned money, as I had spoken to her earlier. They responded to me in the woman's company: 'Your words are sincere but it is appropriate that you deliver the money which you borrowed to a designated [third] person[4] whom we trust, and he will offer a solution as required.' I wondered about the matter[5] and said: 'You were familiar with our initial agreement whereby I would not be harmed by the *partito* arranged between the Almagiati and the honorable Maẓliaḥ of Guastalla. What is this that you revoke your sacred promise? I do not delight in these [things].'[6]

"At the same time, I was told secretly by some people that [Eliezer] Almagiati plotted maliciously against me. Since he had written and sealed all the terms completely, he no longer desired my association. On the contrary, he made false accusations that I had seen fit to take five hundred gold pieces into my possession. He was unwilling to accept from me any old business, or any good or bad credit [of mine], and certainly any completed transaction, since I was unable to locate immediately the aforementioned sum [I required]. [Having ruined my reputation], he then expected to enter my house and dispossess me of the title [of the bank] and of everything he laid his eyes upon. In addition to everything else, his words would constantly distress me. With his loud voice in the markets and the streets, he would slander me, saying that I had reached the end of the line. He thus caused me to lose even the *credito* [credit] I still had.

"I heard of this libel and was most displeased by it. Instead of assuming that I could be vindicated this time [without acting], I instead erased the

[1]Cf. Proverbs 19:7.
[2]Cf. Deuteronomy 32:11.
[3]On him, see above, p. 160.
[4]Cf. Leviticus 16:21.
[5]Cf. Ecclesiastes 5:7.
[6]Cf. Jeremiah 9:23.

thought and went to Mantua. There I spoke to Jacob de Lacairo and told him what I knew, and what the manager [of the bank] had said, and what was going on between us [the parties in dispute]. He responded: 'If you take my advice, you will silence all the complaints and charges. Since the Almagiati don't think well of you, perhaps they might want to deal better with your friends than with you directly. Satisfy their desire by ignoring your [desires] for theirs.[1] So do this: place the matter in the charge of people who are liked by all the parties and let them [these intermediaries] now conclude [the affair] to secure for you what you are able to claim for the time spent in the partnership. You clearly are unable to do anything else and [this] will not cause you loss either in that place [Luzzara] or another. Thus you will go out innocent before God and Israel.'[2]

"I answered him: 'My master, let it be as you describe. I am willing and ready to hand the matter over to my master's charge because you have liked me, because you are also respected by the Almagiati, and [because you are] the husband of the woman [Rina]; all of them [the three parties] favor you.' Jacob responded: 'I am unable alone to involve myself in your affairs. Do this. Speak with Gershon Porto, for I know he is a friend and associate through your son.[3] Disclose your view to him but don't expect too much![4] We shall take sweet counsel together.[5] We shall speak with the Almagiati and we will consider and reach a compromise over the difficult affair of the split between you so that each party can go on its way in peace.'

"Abraham [I] rushed[6] to do as he requested for I knew this man to be one who walks on an upright[7] and straight path and [who] would not tolerate any malice. I spoke with the honorable R. Gershon Porto and said to him: 'If these people will pledge to give me the price of the title [of the bank], to be paid in five installments from this day, along with eighty scudi, which constitute my wages for the duration of the partnership, I will be willing to hand over to them all that they are entitled to receive from me, the best parts,[8] to the last penny. Even if I am required to sell the hair on my

[1]Cf. Mishnah Avot 2:4.

[2]Cf. Numbers 32:22.

[3]On Gershon [Grassino] b. Abraham Porto, see Simonsohn, pp. 221–22, 423–24, 511. In 1577, he was a banker in Mantua. This is the first mention of Yagel's son in the narrative. Yagel had been married some years earlier to Dina, the daughter of Bathsheva Fano and Hosea [Salvatore] da Colonia. His son could not have been more than ten years old during the dispute over the bank. It is unclear why he is mentioned in relation to Porto.

[4]Literally, "don't ascend to the heights of the top of palm trees."

[5]Cf. Psalm 55:15.

[6]Cf. Genesis 18:6.

[7]Cf. Jeremiah 18:15.

[8]Cf. B. T. Pesaḥim 3b.

head to pay them, I will do so, so that with this [action], I will be free of the bank.'

"R. Gershon was pleased by my response and said: 'I certainly expect that we can reach a compromise together between you [the three parties] regarding this affair. Even if you must subtract a little from the aforementioned eighty scudi, do so in order to get out of this mess. Then your wish will be fulfilled, for I know you have been troubled [by this][1] for a long time.' I answered him: 'I will do everything you tell me to do.'

"The man went and spoke with Jacob de Lacairo and both of them together spoke with [Eliezer] Almagiati. But when he [Eliezer Almagiati] heard my request, he remarked: 'Does Abraham Yagel think that I will even give him a penny for his exit from the affair? Truly more than the calf wants to suck, the cow wants to suckle.[2] If I desire his exit, he wants it more than I do. So I conclude that if he wants to satisfy his desire, I should be paid by him. How else can he fulfill the terms between us and locate five hundred good and measured scudi with no loss?'

"He repeated these demands a second and a third time for the duration of the period they spoke with him, even though I had instructed these men [de Lacairo and Porto] to try and effectuate a compromise between us in order to proceed mercifully and end all disputes. In the end, I told the honorable R. Gershon Porto that I would not be a spoiler any longer if they would just give me the money for the right of possession [of the bank] and forget the eighty scudi. He went and spoke [to them] and did everything in his power, but was unsuccessful. Moreover, when I realized his [Almagiati's] evil intentions, I warned him through the aforementioned men not to devise harm against me:[3] 'Not only does he think [such] thoughts but so do I, and we shall see which one comes to pass. Don't allow me to be handed over to *disperazione* [desperation] lest evil befall us. Peace certainly cannot emerge out of a dispute.' He would respond to all of this with disparaging and bitter words as wormwood[4] and [with words] inducing anger.

"I then returned home to Luzzara and 'the trumpets remained within the sacks' as the popular expression goes.[5] By my being here [in Luzzara], I also heard daily the sound[6] of the snare [of Almagiati to trap Yagel] in my

[1]Cf. Jeremiah 45:3.
[2]Cf. B. T. Pesaḥim 112a.
[3]Cf. Proverbs 3:29.
[4]Cf. Proverbs 5:4.
[5]"Andarsene con le trombe nel sacco," disillusioned without gaining anything.
[6]Cf. Exodus 32:18.

ears which they had prepared for me. My master, you know that disgrace clings to the soul so that even the dead are careful [not to allow] anyone to mock them. For this reason, the rabbis forbade anyone from wandering in the cemetery with *tefillin* [phylacteries] on his head or with [ritual] fringes showing on his garment. Thus no one could later say that this man who had come to us now mocks the poor.[1] How much more difficult it is for a living person [like myself to be humiliated] who naturally feels that 'I also was formed from clay'![2]

"Aside from all of this, when the dispute broke out and when my opponent made his view public, complaints against me abounded from within and without. Furthermore, an internal dispute is always more difficult than an external one; just as with bodily illness, the struggle of the elements closer to us is the most difficult. The Scripture states: 'You should love your neighbor as yourself,'[3] for this is the last fence and boundary [regarding one's bodily health]. Thus my heart was pierced within me[4] and the fear of death hovered over me. I waited with great anticipation for a long time that a miracle would somehow transpire from any place, even from Ben Temalyon.[5] In addition [to these problems],[6] the elder Almagiati brother [Eliezer] spread the rumor, either intentionally or unintentionally, that I had leased property from a nobleman, an illegal act for Jews living in those regions.[7] He made his charge public and the *fiscalo* [public prosecutor] investigated the matter and tried to harm me. I greatly feared for my life for this and for other reasons, lest I be imprisoned.

"When I realized there was no other way for me to escape, I chose to wander to a distant place and to go where I could find [refuge], like a bear robbed of her cubs. Perhaps in this way, the men and women would be kind[8] and give solace to my soul and all the slander would disappear. Since all things overcome their opposite condition, there can only be existence

[1]Cf. Proverbs 17:5. *Shulḥan Arukh*, Yoreh De'ah 367:2–4. By wearing these ritual objects, one might shame the dead who are no longer able to perform these commandments.

[2]Cf. Job 33:6, i.e., I, as a living human being, am entitled to be treated with dignity.

[3]Leviticus 19:18. That is, you should love your neighbor as "your body" and avoid struggles with him as you avoid the internal struggles of your bodily elements. Cf. Mani, p. 35a.

[4]Cf. Psalm 109:22.

[5]Cf. B. T. Me'ilah 17b. The name of a demon who supposedly accompanied R. Simeon b. Yoḥai on his journey to Rome and entered into the daughter of the Roman emperor.

[6]The rest of the paragraph appears on the margin of the page of the Cincinnati manuscript.

[7]Perhaps Yagel alluded to Duke Guglielmo's proclamation of March 1576, which forbade Jews from purchasing property. See Simonsohn, p. 113, 773: "Che non acquistino beni stabili sotto pena della confiscatione de essi beni."

[8]Cf. Jonah 1:6.

[when it is] preceded by nonexistence or peace [when it is] preceded by war. David expressed a thought similar to this when he said: 'We lie prostrate in the dust; our belly clings to the ground.'[1] But then God's deliverance comes like the blinking of an eye, as the verse states: 'Arise and help us, etc.'[2] Thus I told myself that by departing and wandering far off [I would encourage] these people to seek a compromise and hasten the [resolution] of the matter with those at home. Furthermore, I had the thought that God-fearing people would arise to make peace between the camps. In order to stay and see if God would grant me success, I did not distance myself [far] from my wagons [i.e., the place of my affairs]. I stayed in an appointed place where I would listen [for the news] every morning.[3] I also told my exalted uncle[4] that these people would [eventually] reach an agreement and do something worthy in the eyes of God and man so that I would [eventually] come in song [return]."[5]

My father remarked, however: "You really were foolish in this trip of yours for you actually removed the covering of shame from these men's faces, released the muzzle from their mouths [to allow them] to speak slanderously against you, and [you] showed them your backside.[6] It would have been much better to be tough and stay in your house, standing at the breach before them. If they had seen you, they would not have dared to tell lies. There is a God in Israel,[7] and your forefathers left you a way to distinguish yourself.[8] Furthermore, you should not have taken the slanderer so seriously since both of us know how a person can feed and rest[9] his action with such talk. Man's face should be like that of a lion[10] to stand at the breach and to increase his friends and advocates.[11] But bribery blinds the clear-sighted.[12] So men should never flee, because all theologians and lawyers state that anyone who flees makes himself appear guilty, and the beginning of [one's] fall is [with his] escape."[13]

[1]Psalm 44:26.

[2]Psalm 44:27.

[3]Cf. Job 7:18 and elsewhere.

[4]This is the first time Yagel mentions this relative. See below.

[5]Cf. Isaiah 35:10 and elsewhere.

[6]Cf. Exodus 33:23.

[7]Cf. 1 Samuel 17:46.

[8]Cf. B. T. Ḥullin 7a. The rest of the paragraph is written in the margin of the manuscript page.

[9]Cf. Song of Songs 1:7. Both of us know how a person makes so little impression on others with such talk.

[10]Cf. Ezekiel 1:10.

[11]Cf. Job 16:20.

[12]Cf. Exodus 23:8.

[13]Cf. B. T. Sotah 44b. Rashi on Judges 20:9.

I answered: "I know this, my master. I certainly know [this], but I was prompted to do this because I heard that they wanted and tried mightily to pervert justice in my case through men close to the authorities. [They sought] to put me in jail and to get at me in an indirect way even though this was not justice. Nevertheless, God does not [necessarily] notice a person who acts perversely in argument. Evil does not emerge from God's mouth[1] and He is long-suffering. Substance is swept away for lack of righteousness,[2] as you told me this night, my master. This fear prompted me[3] to flee.

"I also placed God before my eyes in declaring that if these men reach a compromise, how good it will be; if not, it will be adequate if they [merely] submit to Jewish law, for from the latter, I will never flee. Let my witness be in heaven and He who can testify for me be on high[4] that I did this neither in rebellion nor in treachery.[5] My intention was exactly as I told you. Blessed be He who knows and examines hearts and minds [literally, kidneys]. God will know if I am guilty and see my innocence, which shall be proven. If I perhaps had anticipated the future, I would not have done it [entered into the partnership] even if they would have tortured my flesh with a comb and sold it in the meat market. However, I am not a prophet.[6] I rather thought that I would be judged by people who place God before them and do not break the limit of the Torah, nor that of the Mosaic and Jewish religion. However, the opposite was the case, as you shall hear, since wanton men rose up against me.[7] You should say to yourself: 'Happy is the generation which is like this, for the feet of the messiah [are upon it], and everything has turned a pure white.'[8]"

## The Story of Two Women

[86] I lifted my eyes and saw two woman coming toward us, one from the east and one from the west. The first woman looked like a matron, a lady of valor and of high standing. A touch of grace[9] was upon her face and all her

---

[1]Cf. *Tanḥuma,* Re'eh, 3.
[2]Cf. Proverbs 13:23.
[3]Literally, "girded my loins."
[4]Cf. Job 16:19.
[5]Cf. Joshua 22:22.
[6]Cf. Amos 7:14.
[7]Cf. Psalm 86:14.
[8]Cf. Leviticus 13:13. The intent of this line would parallel that of Mishnah Sotah 9:15: "With the footprints of the messiah, presumption will increase."
[9]Cf. B. T. Ḥagigah 12b; Megillah 13a; literally, "a cord of grace."

words were [filled] with wisdom. Even as she walked, she surveyed her course[1] so that all who saw her would bow down, since she was [one] of the faithful of Israel. The other woman coming toward us looked like a widow who was unable to lift her eyelids to see the face of any person because of her great anguish and distress.[2] Moreover, she refused to be comforted in her grief.[3]

I asked my father about these women and he replied: "Wait a little while[4] and we shall question them [about their lives]."

When they were close to us, we questioned the first [woman] who came toward us. When she first saw us, she bowed down from afar before coming closer, and she greeted us with a shining countenance.

She answered: "I will tell you of my walking and reclining[5] from the day I was born until I became old and until I appreciated the goodness [of life] and departed from this world with joy. Blessed be the Lord, for I now journey to seek repose upon my bed since I deserve it. How bountiful is the good stored for me! I saw it and it made me glad. I have been one of those who ate the fruits of this world; a capital of redemption and inheritance is laid aside for me in that eternal world[6] [so that I can] take pleasure in the lands of the living [of the next world]."

My father asked her: "Tell us about the great things you have done, your good deeds, your behavior toward your husband and your household. Also what was your occupation; where were you born; and what did you leave behind in this world—boys or girls, riches or honor?"

[87] She answered: "I was born to a poor man, the son of good people. [Actually, he had been] a rich man who had become poor, and I was his only daughter. My father would go to work in the field. On the day of her delivery, my mother was seized with labor pains[7] and died; my father became my only guardian, since I had no mother. Since the poor are unable to hire a woman to suckle, he bought a lamb to suckle me with her milk.[8] He would go to work every day and leave me in the company of the lamb, who was like a mother to me. Upon returning from the field, my father

---

[1]Cf. Proverbs 5:21, that is, she scrutinized her ways.

[2]Cf. 1 Samuel 1:16.

[3]Cf. Jeremiah 31:15 and elsewhere; literally, "the tears on her cheeks refused to be comforted."

[4]Cf. Job 36:2.

[5]Cf. Psalm 139:3.

[6]Cf. Mishnah Pe'ah 1:1.

[7]Cf. 1 Samuel 4:19.

[8]On the possible source of this motif, see the introduction above, p. 34.

would bathe me, wash my blood and excrement, and cover me with oil and hot water.[1] The oil with which my father covered me in my youth stood me in good stead in my old age,[2] until I grew up and took care of my father.

"But when I attained my womanhood, my breasts became firm, and my hair sprouted,[3] my father summoned me and said: 'My daughter, you know that our sins caused this poverty. Come, therefore, and accept God's affliction out of love.[4] Live with honor in your home, do your work, and spin wool while I go to the field each day. I won't be able to stay home with you for you know our need is great. Since you know that much [sin] is wrought by poverty, and much by childishness and bad neighbors,[5] if sins and frivolous company seduce you, guard your soul and do [so] for the sake of the great and awesome name of God, who earnestly desires that the girls of Israel be modest. Although we are now of lowly station, our family, nevertheless, is from noble and distinguished stock.[6] Thus be careful not to tarnish your soul, for who knows? Perhaps God will be responsive[7] to the sound of your prayer and send His compassion and awe from heaven so that he will lift up the needy from the refuse heap.[8] Therefore, my daughter, listen and notice that your father is speaking to you; distance yourself from ugliness and anything similar to it. Know what is inappropriate to do for the sake of appearance; even in [the privacy] of one's rooms, it is forbidden, since eyes always see and ears always hear and all your conversations and deeds are written in a book.[9] In sum, when all is said and done,[10] that which one does secretly is bound to become public in daylight.'

"I replied: 'Don't take your daughter for a worthless woman[11] and don't worry about me, for I will do as you say.' When he would go out to the field early in the morning each day, as was his custom, I would shut the

[1]Cf. Ezekiel 16:9.
[2]Cf. B. T. Ḥullin 24b.
[3]Cf. Ezekiel 16:7.
[4]Cf. B. T. Berakhot 5a.
[5]Cf. Mishnah Sotah 1:4.
[6]Note Yagel's emphasis on the importance of noble lineage. The family he describes had once been rich and respectable; the family preserved its values even as it lost its wealth. This emphasis should be understood in the context of Yagel's constant contacts and dependence on well-to-do Jewish families. Yagel's portrait of the ideal Jewish woman here is similar to that in his small book, *Eshet Ḥayil*, a short commentary on Proverbs 31, dedicated to Rachel, the wife of Hezekiah b. Isaac Foa, the wealthy banker, and published in 1605.
[7]Cf. Jonah 1:6.
[8]Cf. Psalm 113:7.
[9]Cf. Mishnah Avot 2:1.
[10]Cf. Ecclesiastes 12:13.
[11]Cf. 1 Samuel 1:16.

door after me, not going out but turning to my work. I would not be idle for even an hour, for I was happy with my work. Even the women neighbors had no idea whether I remained in the house or whether I had gone out to the field with my father; [they did not know] what I was like and what my work was. When my father returned from the field in the evening, he would find a lit candle, a set table, and a made bed. He also would see that my work was satisfactory and that everything I did in the house was proper and clean of all filth and impurity, for I swept everything with 'the broom of extermination.'[1] When he saw everything in order, he would bless me, and [he] was happy with me. My father also taught me to bless [God] regarding everything that happened to me, for the bad as well as the good, [and] to declare like Nahum Ish Gamzu that 'this is also for the good.'[2]

"One day, a young man came to the house accompanied by my father. He was the son of a widow, a metal craftsman, trained to work with copper and iron, who also was very wealthy. He took note of me as well as the order of the house and attic. He came to love me and desire me and asked my father if I would be his wife. When he [my father] heard this, his heart melted because he did not believe him, [knowing] that a poor man has nothing to offer that would be proper for me to bring [as a dowry] from the woman's household. He answered: 'Don't deceive your servant.' But the [young] man consented to speak on my behalf [in asking for my hand in marriage] because he greatly desired me. He said: 'If you give me this young woman as a wife, you will be like a father in my house. By your command,[3] all my affairs at home and in the field will be directed, that which goes out and comes in, and you will supervise all the male and female servants of my household.'

"When my father understood that he was sincere and was not making fun of the poor, he hurried to remove his shoe from his foot to fulfill the custom in Israel that one removes his shoe and gives it to his neighbor [to finalize the arrangement].[4] He also advanced the positive formulation of the condition before the negative one, as the sons of Gad and Reuben did, so that the man would not go back on his word.[5]

[1]Cf. Isaiah 14:23.
[2]Cf. B. T. Berakhot 48b, Ta'anit 21a.
[3]Cf. Genesis 41:40.
[4]Cf. Ruth 4:6–8; B. T. Babba Meẓiah 47a; J. T. Kiddushin 1:5.
[5]Cf. Numbers 32:20–22: "If you shall do this thing . . . then this land shall be unto you a possession; and if you shall not do so . . . behold, you have sinned, etc." Cf. Mishnah Kiddushin 3:4; B. T. Kiddushin 61a, Gittin 75a.

"The man went home and gathered clothes and utensils. He then came to me, clothed me with embroidered garments, and gave me sandals of sealskin to wear.[1] He also put bracelets on my arms and a chain around my neck.[2] He then brought me to his house with great happiness and honor, and I became his wife. He also gave my father clothing to wear, brought him to his house, placed authority on his shoulders,[3] and put in his hands all the possessions of my lord and husband so that no one would lift a hand or foot without his approval.

"Despite all this, I did not become haughty, nor did I pursue more great and wonderful things than I initially had possessed while in my father's home. Rather, I carefully carried out his [my husband's] word as I had promised him. I directed the male and female servants and all the other members of the household with such pleasant words that everyone liked me. My mother-in-law initially was not in favor of my marriage to her son but I was so much like a servant to her, doing her work, that she changed her opinion [about me] and loved me. She used to say daily how blessed was the day that I entered her house.

"I was accustomed to do my husband's work quickly and diligently and in the light of his shining countenance. I always considered his words and instructions in order to satisfy his will. He never had to call me twice, for my awe of him was like the fear of heaven. What he liked, I did not dislike and what he hated, I did not like. I never asked to know his secrets and I always extolled his virtues, background, and family. Whatever he gave me, whether great or small, I accepted with great love. I also would enjoy [the same] food and nourishment [he liked] and whatever else he liked or desired. Whenever I adorned myself in order to be beautiful before him, I did so modestly. I always would appear before him with a cheerful countenance [and I was] never angry [as I] oversaw the activities of my household.[4] I would bless the Lord for everything that happened to me, as my father had taught me. And God blessed my husband's house wherever I turned [5][and] enlarged and enhanced all that he had in the house and in the field. He also opened for me His good treasure[6] and rewarded me with sons and daughters, and I raised and nursed them forever.

[88] "I would criticize women who gave their infants to others to nurse

[1]Cf. Ezekiel 16:10.
[2]Cf. Ezekiel 16:11.
[3]Cf. Isaiah 9:5.
[4]Cf. Proverbs 31:27.
[5]Cf. Genesis 30:30.
[6]Cf. Deuteronomy 28:12; Jeremiah 50:25.

in order to keep their breasts firm,[1] for these breasts were created for only this purpose [of nursing]. In my mind, they [these women] are inferior to the beasts of the field and the animals of the forest, for even the jackel offers the breast and suckles [its] young.[2] The rabbis stated:[3] '[Even] a crow wants [and cares for its] children.' We also find that Sarah, our mother, nursed children, as Scripture declares: 'Sarah would suckle children.'[4] In this manner, I would love my children and teach them my ways and actions.[5] The natural philosophers understand that a person's nature is determined by the food he eats. Similarly, the nature of the woman suckling an infant determines his [the child's] nature. Thus they declared that an animal that produced bile had been eating mustard.

"I also observed the goodness of their [my children's] actions and relationships with other human beings, and I also was rewarded by seeing them have their own sons and daughters, each of them dwelling in his own house in honor. I never forgot that God gave me all this wealth and lifted me up from the great deep to all this honor. So I acted charitably and compassionately with the poor who came to the door of my house every day and I clothed those who were naked. I also acted in such a way that my husband similarly gave charity from his pocket, was thoughtful of the wretched,[6] and lent them money, either a small or large amount. I went out to perform charitable acts [and] to comfort the bereaved and afflicted of the land with good words, but always with my husband's approval regarding that commandment. Wherever he wanted me to go, I went without deviating from his command, either to the right or to the left. I also would comfort the poor who came to my house with good words, telling them to trust in God. His compassion would not cease[7] and they should cast their burden on Him.[8] Their feet will not slip;[9] they surely will not remain alone, as it is written: 'So the Lord your God may bless you in all the enterprises you undertake.'[10] Finally, I grew old and gray[11] and was gathered to my kin[12]

[1]Cf. Ezekiel 16:7.
[2]Cf. Lamentations 4:3.
[3]B. T. Ketubbot 49b.
[4]Genesis 21:7.
[5]Cf. Ezekiel 20:43 and elsewhere.
[6]Cf. Psalm 41:2.
[7]Cf. Lamentations 3:22.
[8]Cf. Psalm 55:23.
[9]Cf. 2 Samuel 22:37; Psalm 18:37.
[10]Deuteronomy 14:29.
[11]Cf. 1 Samuel 12:2.
[12]Cf. Numbers 27:13.

in dignity. Now I go to my ancestors [in the next world], enjoy God's beneficence, and frequent His sanctuary."[1]

[89] We then inquired of the second woman and she answered: "I am a hard-spirited woman who never saw goodness in her lifetime. Even after my death, it was decreed from heaven that I would enter a mad dog's body. Furthermore, the prayer I offered to save my precious life from the clutches of a dog[2] did me no good since the judgment had already been issued and sealed with the seal of blood,[3] and my fate could not be reversed.

"Now let me respond to your question and inform you of my walking and reclining[4] since I am an example and a byword[5] for everyone. Know accordingly that the Almighty has made my lot very bitter,[6] and I have been a worthless treasure to my father. When I was born, he was wealthy and ruled the citizens of his city, but after I emerged from my mother's womb, great evils surrounded him. His merchandise was lost at sea and what remained of his possessions at home was confiscated by the government because certain merchants informed against him[7] at the king's court. In that same ship [that carried his merchandise], there were armaments, spears, and swords to be delivered to another king, the enemy of the king of our state who wished to harm our king. Furthermore, they [the merchants] had falsely accused him [my father] and he was helpless to do anything [to defend himself]. Everything he possessed was taken from him and he was left completely naked and barefooted,[8] with nothing in his hand. His brothers and members of his household came to him and consoled and comforted him for all the misfortune.[9] Each gave him one jewel and one gold ring,[10] and with them he bought more merchandise so that he and his household subsisted.

"When I became a young woman, I desired one of the merchant sons who sailed each year in floating vessels[11] to the kingdoms of the sea for trade. This man returned my love, and the many floods could not quench

[1] Cf. Psalm 27:4.
[2] Cf. Psalm 22:21.
[3] Cf. *Esther Rabbah*, 3:4.
[4] Cf. Psalm 139:3. For the possible sources and the context of the following story, see the introduction above, pp. 32–33.
[5] Cf. Deuteronomy 28:37 and elsewhere.
[6] Cf. Ruth 1:20.
[7] For the expression, see Targum Isaiah 58:1; Proverbs 11:13, and elsewhere.
[8] Cf. Isaiah 20:2–4.
[9] Cf. Job 42:11.
[10] Cf. Job 42:12.
[11] Cf. Isaiah 33:21.

the love between us.[1] He spoke for me [asked my father] to take me as his wife. However, my father refused him because the father of this young man had been one of the same merchants who had slandered him and caused him to lose his wealth. When I realized that my father refused to allow me to become his [the young man's] wife, I devised a plan with the young man, arose in the night, and went to him. He took me to his house, came upon me, and I became his wife.

"Then one day, my husband set out for a port city with his merchandise, as was his custom from time to time. But God cast a mighty wind upon the sea, and the ship was in danger of breaking up.[2] They [the sailors] flung the ship's cargo overboard to make the ship lighter for them.[3] My husband and his companions[4] fled in a small boat that was attached to the larger vessel in order to save their lives. They followed a route on which they were swept by the wind. They remained [in the boat] for seven mad days without knowing where they were. On the seventh day, pirates met them at sea, captured them, brought them to Egypt, and sold them as slaves to a certain merchant.

"The large vessel eventually returned to its original port of departure and all the people of the land went out in alarm to meet it.[5] The captain explained to them [the people] what had happened. I listened and then fell on my face. Afterward, I began to speak and cursed the day of my birth.[6] But I, in my iniquities, never sought God, who would [have] answered me in distress[7] and harken to my voice. Rather, I would curse everything that happened to me; I would also turn my back, not my face to all the people who came to console me. My tears never stopped flowing from my eyes. I was like a great owl in the wilderness,[8] and like a bear bereaved of her whelps.[9] I poured out my heart like water in the night, at the beginning of the watches.[10]

"After three years had passed while I had remained in living widowhood,[11] still not knowing if my husband was alive in the stomach of the

[1]Cf. Song of Songs 8:7.
[2]Cf. Jonah 1:4.
[3]Cf. Jonah 1:5.
[4]Cf. Targum Onkelos on Genesis 26:26, which is the same as my translation.
[5]Cf. 1 Samuel 16:4.
[6]Cf. Job 3:1.
[7]Cf. Psalm 118:5.
[8]Cf. Psalm 102:7.
[9]Cf. 2 Samuel 17:8; Hosea 13:8.
[10]Cf. Lamentations 2:19.
[11]Cf. 1 Samuel 20:3.

fish, or in that of the Leviathan or the poisonous serpant,[1] certain merchants came and told me that my husband was still alive in Egypt. He and his companions were slaves in the house of a certain merchant who liked them and showed them mercy by giving them light work. The man had also told them that if someone would offer him the price he had paid for them, he would set them free. I inquired of my informer about the amount of money the merchant had paid for these men and he responded that it had been two hundred gold pieces for each man. I hastened [my husband's] redemption by selling everything I possessed at home and I put my money in my bag.[2] I then set out with another man, a brother of one of my husband's companions [in captivity] who also had money to purchase him [his brother].

"Upon arriving in Egypt on a merchant vessel, we made inquiries and found the men enslaved to their master. We told them we had come to redeem them from slavery and we spoke with their master, who was responsive to us. My companion delivered him the money he had brought to redeem his brother and he [his brother] was liberated. I subsequently went to take the money I had left on the ship in my bag, but I saw that it had disappeared. Then I realized that a merchant[3] who had been on the ship with us had stolen the money and had sailed on a small vessel to Jaffa to hasten his voyage [to that place]. When I saw what had happened, I tried to kill myself with a knife that was in my possession, but I was restrained from shedding blood. I then considered selling myself [into slavery] as a maidservant and [then] redeeming my husband with the money from the sale, and if I were to perish, I would perish.[4] But despite all this, I never sought God, nor did I pray to Him. Instead, I did this [sold myself into slavery], took the money of the sale, and handed it over to my companion, who went and freed my husband.

"When he [my husband] heard what had happened, his soul left him because of the terrible grief which suddenly struck his heart; he fell on the ground and died. So I remained a maidservant, and despite this [action], I did not [succeed in] freeing my husband but rather caused his death. I ripped my coat, strew dust on myself,[5] and wept.

"When the merchant who had purchased me heard what had happened, he was displeased; [he] came to me and comforted me. He then

[1] Cf. Isaiah 27:1.
[2] Cf. Genesis 42:28.
[3] Or Canaanite.
[4] Cf. Esther 4:16.
[5] Cf. Jeremiah 6:26 and elsewhere.

noticed my beauty, which pleased him, so he then tried to seduce me. I listened to him but refused many times, acting in such a manner to save myself from sinning. When he realized that I had no desire for such an affair, he even told me that he would take me as his wife. Yet I did not want[1] to be with him. He then plotted to come upon me with guile; he took spiced wine that contained a drug that induced deep sleep, and he had me drink it unwittingly. When I fell asleep, he removed everyone from my presence,[2] took me and carried me to his bed, and slept with me all night long, abusing me as he pleased.[3] That very evening I was like Lot who slept with his eldest daughter without knowing when she lay down and when she arose.[4] The rabbis maintained that the letter 'vav' [in *uvekuma*, "when she arose"] was punctuated to indicate that he [Lot] did not know that she had slept with him but did know when she arose.[5]

"So in the morning I [found myself] [in this predicament] when the [effect of] the wine wore off. I saw the man with me and knew what he had done to me. I wept bitterly to him and pleaded with him to please marry me as he had offered in the beginning, since I had fallen in the net he had spread at my legs.[6] But the man went back on his promise to me and said: 'You have made a mistake by not listening to my pleading and not paying me attention. You would have gained honor, been freed, and become your master's wife. But now, since I have satisfied my craving for you, I do not want a maidservant for my wife. I will treat you harshly instead. If you fail to obey me, to perform willingly what you did when you were drunk, and to satisfy my every whim and wish, I will reveal publicly what you have done secretly. I will also write a report to your land and people as I see fit.' He did all of this to frighten me so that I would sin to satisfy his heart's desires. I remained a lover and adulteress in this manner for twelve long months.

"Members of my family subsequently arrived, redeemed me, and brought me back to my homeland. But they did not know that I had been made impure by this Egyptian man and they married me to another man. Only two years later, this last man died and I again became a widow. My most recent pain was even greater than the earlier one. I asked to die and prayed to God to take my soul, for I would rather die than live.[7] When I

[1]The Hebrew text, "I heard," is apparently corrupted.
[2]Cf. Genesis 45:1.
[3]Cf. Judges 19:25.
[4]Cf. Genesis 19:33.
[5]Cf. B. T. Nazir 23a.
[6]Cf. Lamentations 1:13.
[7]Jonah 4:3, 8.

saw that my prayer was not heeded, I put a deadly poison in my food and swallowed it. My stomach swelled and the members of my household recognized what had happened and called the doctors, who gave me an antidote to counter the poison. He [one of the doctors] performed a miracle and I did not die suddenly, as I had expected, but was stricken instead with a serious illness worse than death and [I] languished for a long time. My soul finally left me after that same [bodily] death. Now I am going to enter a mad dog's body and dwell there for the duration of my time that I was supposed to have lived on the earth.

"You should write about this incident in a history book as testimony for anyone who disobeys the words of God. Despite all the troubles that might befall him, he [such a person] will never seek God nor will he ever be judged righteously [in Gods's eyes].[1] Neither will he pray to Him [asking] to be rescued from them [God's judgments]. Rather, he will desire a curse, like I do today, just as I have cursed my day and night every day. Even when I sat peacefully, I would still turn to heaven for every little thing that happened to me and [I would] curse myself. Evil and suffering came to me to such an extent, as you have heard, that the ears of all hearers should be protected from hearing [about this]." She then raised her voice and wept loudly.

We consoled her: "May God listen to the sound of your cry, have compassion upon you, and treat you with the beneficence of His great mercy, going beyond the letter of His strict justice. May He rip up your verdict." She left us and went on her way.

## The Lessons of the Women's Stories

[90] My father exclaimed: "How many great things and useful lessons have we learned from these two women who have passed before us! First, a righteous person is never abandoned, as the prince of the world [King David] declared: 'I have been young and am now old [but I have never seen a righteous person abandoned].'[2] If God has punished a man with a human affliction, as long as he [that man] never gives up hope in Him, God will return to him with goodness and send him a blessing. This is what happened to the poor man, the father of the woman of high standing, whose wife died and had no means to nurse his daughter. God subsequently sent him a lamb to suckle her. This man's miracle was even greater than the one

[1] Cf. B. T. Ta'anit 8a.
[2] Psalm 37:25.

related by the rabbis in the chapter *Bemah Behamah:*[1] 'There was an incident regarding a man whose wife died and left him an infant to nurse. He had no wage [to pay] a wet nurse, so a miracle happened to him. His breasts were opened like those of a woman and he nursed his son. R. Joseph said: "Come and observe how great this man is who had a miracle like this happen to him!" Abaye said to him: "On the contrary, how terrible this man is, since the order of creation was changed on his account, etc."' I would place [the case of] this poor man between [the views] of Abaye and R. Joseph. He is a very great man since the order of creation was not changed on his account, although a miracle happened and food was provided him.[2]

"Second, even though a man may have a modest and proper daughter or wife, he should not be reluctant to supervise her and keep an eye on her, reminding her of the correct path and being strict with her, just as the rabbis taught a lesson at the end of *Gittin.*[3] What is the straight and middle path? One should act with words which put the mind to rest, without anger or provocation, lest one's solution become one's harm. This happened to many men whose foolishness caused their proper wives to turn away from their good conduct, to go after vanity so as to anger their husbands. The rabbis warned of this in the first chapter of *Gittin:*[4] 'A man should never terrorize his household, etc.' Maimonides also wrote:[5] 'The children of Israel are commanded by the sages to be jealous of their wives, as it is written: "And he be jealous of his wife."[6] Anyone jealous of his wife has a pure spirit within him. But one should not be jealous of her out of frivolity or lightheadedness, nor out of contentiousness, nor to instill fear in her, etc. Rather, the relationship between man and woman [should be based] on satisfaction, on a course of purity and admonition, so [the man] will lead her on the straight path and steer her away from stumbling blocks. Anyone who does not watch over his wife and children, warning them, and always supervising their ways until he sees they are perfect and [free of] all sin, is called a sinner, as it is written: "When you visit [i.e., supervise] your wife [literally 'home'], you will never fail."'[7] We also find that Abraham, our father, may he rest in peace, similarly followed this course, as it is written:

[1]B. T. Shabbat 53b.
[2]Paraphrasing the text of B. T. Shabbat 53b.
[3]Cf. B. T. Gittin 90a, which discusses the various ways men treat their wives.
[4]B. T. Gittin 6b.
[5]Maimonides, *Mishneh Torah,* Nashim, Hilkhot Sotah, 4:18–19.
[6]Numbers 5:14.
[7]Job 5:24.

'For I have singled him out, that he may instruct his children and his posterity to keep the way of the Lord, etc.'[1]

"Third, it is fitting for women to receive moral instruction. Even if they are proper, it is still fitting for them to receive it with a cheerful countenance, as this woman of high standing did with her father. Thus the biblical verse states: 'Reprove a wise person, and he will love you.'[2]

"Fourth, a person should be proper and pure in his house and should remove all ugliness, filth, and impurity from it. By doing this, the Divine Presence will dwell in that place, and the hosts of angels will be in headlong flight,[3] while the prince of poverty will distance himself from the same place. He [the prince of poverty] will have no authority over it since his name will be disgraced and he will be called 'disgraced'; furthermore, he only can dwell in a place of filth, as the rabbis stated in the chapter *Kol ha-Basar*.[4] Accordingly, this was the woman's verdict and she succeeded.

"Fifth, one should be accustomed to saying about any occurrence that whatever happens, God does it for good reason,[5] as it is written: 'I came upon trouble and sorrow and I invoked the name of the Lord.'[6] In such a manner, this poor man commanded his daughter to say 'this is also for the good' regarding all that happened to her. Subsequently, a person will not become excited or confused. If a greater effort needs to be expended, he shall do what he can while God will do what is good in His eyes. After such effort, he need not feel guilty. This is not the case for a person harried with sorrow and lament as the second woman behaved, whose heart sank in utter dismay.[7] What is she capable of doing in her grief when God turns away from her? The Divine Presence is only present in happiness.[8] [If one asks:] 'What does happiness accomplish?' [one might retort:] 'What harm does it do?' On the contrary, when someone is excited and is consumed with grief, his vital strength is weakened and the bearer [of this grief] is harmed, as it is written: 'If you faint in the day of adversity, your strength is small indeed.'[9] [Similarly, it is written] 'Leave the drunkard alone; he will fall by himself.'[10]

[1]Genesis 18:19.
[2]Proverbs 9:8.
[3]Cf. Psalm 68:13 where "kings" has been changed to "angels."
[4]The reference is to B. T. Pesaḥim 111b rather than the chapter in Ḥullin.
[5]Cf. B. T. Berakhot 60b.
[6]Psalm 116:3–4.
[7]Cf. Joshua 7:5; literally, "melted and turned to water."
[8]Cf. B. T. Shabbat 30b.
[9]Proverbs 24:10.
[10]B. T. Shabbat 32a.

Ben Sira likewise declared: 'Suffer not grief to enter the heart, for grief kills the strongest men.'[1]

"Sixth, a man who chooses a woman in marriage should choose one worthy of him, as the rabbis declared in chapter *Asarah Yuḥasin*.[2] She should be the daughter of good parents and [should be] modest, as the rabbis also stated in chapter *Yesh Noḥalim*.[3] She should be diligent in all her duties and should not lust after money, since wealth held by its owner sometimes can be harmful to him. Nor should she be preoccupied with beauty 'for grace is deceitful and beauty is vain.'[4] Rather, he should marry her for the sake of heaven, for great is his reward, as the rabbis declared in the first chapter of *Sotah*:[5] 'Anyone who marries a woman for the sake of heaven, Scripture accounts it to his credit as if he begot her, for "a woman who fears the Lord shall be praised."'[6]

"Seventh, we have learned about the judgment of a woman who acts prudently with her husband and [with] all the members of her household. She should expend her full energy so that everyone will adopt her energy and love her as they loved that woman of high standing.

"Eighth, when one has been brought up from the dunghill of poverty, he should not be haughty in declaring that he accomplished what he did by his own ability. Rather, he should attribute everything to God, praise Him and thank Him, and always contemplate Him, since God always has the power to return him to his lowly state. 'Your beneficence is like the high mountains; Your justice like the great deep,'[7] as the rabbis interpreted in *Midrash Rabbah*.[8]

"Ninth, a person should give charity to the poor and lend to them, as it is written: 'Happy is he who is thoughtful of the wretched.'[9] Regarding the woman who possesses a loaf of bread and clothing at home, [it is said]: 'She gives generously to the poor, her hands are stretched out to the needy.'[10] It is also fitting to comfort the poor with good words and to speak kindly to them.

[1]B. T. Sanhedrin 100b. Yagel (in *Beit Ya'ar ha-Levanon*, 4:34, fols. 79a–81a) discusses extensively the suitability of reading Ben Sira as well as the other works of the Apocrypha.
[2]B. T. Kiddushin 70a.
[3]B. T. Babba Batra 109b.
[4]Cf. Proverbs 31:30.
[5]B. T. Sotah 12a.
[6]Cf. Proverbs 31:30.
[7]Cf. Psalm 36:7.
[8]Cf. *Bereshit Rabbah*, 23:1; *Vayikrah Rabbah*, 27:1.
[9]Psalm 41:2.
[10]Proverbs 31:20.

"Tenth, siblings and relatives should help one another, as we find in the case of Job, and as the relatives of the merchant did for him, for it is written: 'You shall uphold him [your brother].'[1] Don't allow him to fall. Thus Aristotle wrote in the *Ethics:*[2] 'A friend should help his friend with finances in his hour of need; he should even restore him to a good situation when he strays from the [right] path.'

"Eleventh, one should not prevent his daughters or sons, out of hatred, from marrying whomever they desire, especially at the time they have fallen in love. Certainly, if they are not granted permission, they will act without it, since love is as fierce as death.[3] In a similar vein, the rabbis wrote that Jacob, our father, was punished for forbidding Dinah, his daughter, from marrying Esau, his brother. Because of this, she was violated by Schechem, the son of Hamor the Canaanite.[4]

"Twelfth, everyone should pray to God when he is in trouble. For this reason, Asa, the king of Judah, was punished for not seeking God during his illness, but only physicians.[5] The second woman was similarly punished for not seeking and praying to God to save her husband in the time of her adversity, as was fitting for her to do.

"Thirteenth, even if a woman is a woman of valor who knows well the ways of the world, she should never involve herself in them alone, without the assistance and advice of men. We have never found them successful in their activities since their light-headedness denies them honor.[6] If only the second woman had entrusted the money for redeeming her husband with those aforementioned men in her company, all that had happened to her would not have occurred. This is because the man who held the bundle of money on deposit knew that money is never safe at home but only in the ground, covered with a handbreadth of dirt.[7] When traveling, money is only safe when stored next to the heart or held in the hand, as Scripture states: 'You shall bind up the money in your hand.'[8] Out of fear that he

[1]Leviticus 25:35.

[2]Yagel probably referred to the *Nicomachean Ethics,* bk. 8, 1155a. Cf. Maimonides, *Moreh Nevukhim,* 3:49.

[3]Cf. Song of Songs 8:6.

[4]Cf. *Bereshit Rabbah,* 80:4; 73:9 (discussing Genesis 34:2, which reads "Hamor the Hivite").

[5]Cf. 2 Chronicles 16:12.

[6]Although Yagel praises women in his *Eshit Ḥayil,* he still idealizes the obedient, subservient female. His view here is therefore not out of character. Cf. the introduction above, p. 64.

[7]Cf. B. T. Babba Meẓiah 42a; Pesaḥim 31a.

[8]Deuteronomy 14:25.

might lose the money, he [the man] would have been responsible and not left it in bags on the ship. Rather, he would have taken it with him and freed the wretched man with it. Accordingly, the man [her husband] would not have died from his sorrow and the woman would not have been sold as a maidservant nor sexually violated, as it happened. All women should be reproved for wearing pants like men do and for transgressing the prohibition forbidding a man from wearing women's attire. [The latter] includes the prohibition of women wearing men's clothing although the biblical text [only] mentions explicitly the present [i.e., usual] custom [of men wearing female clothing and not the reverse].[1] Women should do nothing, either great or small, without men's advice, for they [women] will never succeed [on their own]. They also might encounter a disaster or an impure accident, just as the second woman, who lost her husband and money and was sold as a maidservant. In the end, she also sold [herself] and lost her dignity. Happy is the person who can learn from the mistakes of others.

"Fourteenth, in a place of trouble, a person should choose the least amount of evil. When he is at the hand of an enemy more powerful than he is, he should try to pacify him and do what pleases him [the enemy]. His honor will remain intact[2] and he will not be in danger. Who can contend with someone who is stronger than he?[3] The popular saying goes: 'One should kiss the hands of those who want to consign him to the fire, for the sake of the welfare of society.' Thus, it would have been better for that woman to marry that merchant in dignity, rather than refuse him, when she realized that he loved her and owned her and that she had no right to escape. Instead, he was forced to approach her deceitfully and sinfully.

"Fifteenth, every person should be careful of wine, since wine is a scoffer and he who is muddled by it will not grow wise.[4] With wine in him, he [a person] will reveal secrets,[5] and even more so [in the case of] women, who are light-headed. We find that even demons are careful of wine, as we see from the incident of Ashmedai, the king of the demons, and King Solomon in *Gittin,* in the chapter *Mi she'aḥazo Kordiakos.*[6] We also find that there was a custom in the kingdom of the Kittim not to allow their women

[1]As Mani points out in his note, p. 40a, Yagel is confused here. Deuteronomy 22:5 reads explicitly: "A woman must not put on man's apparel, nor shall a man wear woman's clothing; for whoever does these things is abhorrent to the Lord your God."

[2]Cf. B. T. Bekhorot 30b.

[3]Cf. Ecclesiastes 6:10.

[4]Cf. Proverbs 20:1.

[5]Cf. B. T. Eruvin 65a.

[6]B. T. Gittin 68a. The story relates how Solomon outsmarted the demon by getting him to drink wine.

to drink wine.[1] The rabbis likewise stated:[2] 'One glass is fine for a woman; two is an obscenity for her, etc.' If only the second woman had guarded herself from wine, she would not have been sexually violated. She would not have been initially forced against her will, nor, in the end, would she have submitted freely.[3]

"Sixteenth, no person should curse himself, for ultimately the curse he desired will be fulfilled, as in the case of this evil woman. She is like the person to whom Abaye referred in chapter *Ha-Ba al-Yevimto:*[4] 'She has a tray [his meal] ready for him with a mouth ready for him [to curse him].' Rashi interpreted 'mouth' [there] to mean 'to curse and to abuse, for example, an evil wife.' We also find that R. Simeon bar Yoḥai wrote in the *Sefer ha-Zohar*[5] that the fate of a person who curses himself is to strengthen the successful activity of Satan, who always stands by his right side. In the time of danger that follows, he will receive retribution and the curse will be accounted to him. So, sharpen the knife when the ox is fallen.[6] He [bar Yoḥai] likewise interpreted the biblical verse: 'I would keep my mouth muzzled while the wicked man was in my presence.'[7]

"Seventeenth, one should remember that while all punishments [in a Jewish court] have been abolished, [divine] retribution has not been abolished, as the rabbis taught in the first chapter of *Sotah:*[8] 'With what measure a man metes it shall be measured to him again,' as it is said: 'In full measure, when You send her away, You will contend with her, etc.'[9] Just as this evil woman was mad in her actions and turned to heaven to curse herself concerning anything that happened to her, in like manner, she received retribution from heaven to enter a mad dog until she paid for all her sins."

## On Metempsychosis into Animal Bodies

[91] I then asked: "How can a human soul enter the body of an animal by metempsychosis?[10] Doesn't the biblical verse state: 'Truly, God does all

[1]The Kittim were a nation mentioned in the Bible and whose origin was obscure. They were associated with the Romans in later rabbinic literature. I could not find the source of Yagel's statement here.

[2]B. T. Ketubbot 65a.

[3]B. T. Ketubbot 51b.

[4]B. T. Yebamot 63b.

[5]*Sefer ha-Zohar,* Pekudai, 2:266a.

[6]Cf. B. T. Shabbat 32a, and see Rashi's comment there; that is, take advantage of the opportunity and keep quiet, lest the ox get up again and your luck change.

[7]*Sefer ha-Zohar,* Pinḥas, 3:246b, interpreting Psalm 39:2.

[8]B. T. Sotah 8b; Mishnah Sotah 1:7.

[9]Isaiah 27:8.

[10]As we have seen earlier, this is a major concern for Yagel, one to which he returns on

these things, two or three times to a man,'[1] thus implying [metempsychosis] with a human being and not with an animal? Please explain to me, my master, if the rabbis said something about this matter. If they have a tradition, we shall accept it and not ponder it. But if it is [merely their] inference, then there exists a counter-argument [which can be brought against it]."[2]

My father answered: "Know that the later kabbalists hold the view that was brought by R. Menahem Recanati in his commentary on the laws of unchastity [Leviticus 18] that sometimes the human soul is transmigrated into an animal, beast or fowl, depending on the sin which a person committed.[3] However, this view is not considered correct by all the kabbalists and some do not accept it [at all].[4] However, be aware that the Pythagorean sect believed in it, and [they] used to say that the soul of a murderer will enter a dog.[5] Perhaps for this reason King David, of blessed memory, prayed when he declared: 'Save my soul from the sword.' In other words, I will not kill so that 'my only one [will be saved] from [entering] the clutches of a dog';[6] that is, the soul, which is called 'my only one' because it is unique in the body.

[92] "I also heard [of an incident] from an elder from the land of Israel who related it in the name of R. Lappidot, a great sage and kabbalist who predicted the future.[7] There was once a man in his day who owned an ass who brayed all the night. Once it brayed more than usual. Moreover, in the

---

several occasions. For a full treatment of the subject and its significance in Yagel's thought, see Ruderman, *Kabbalah, Magic, and Science*, chap. 8.

[1] Job 33:29; a standard verse for deriving the principle of transmigration of souls among Jewish writers. See above, p. 128.

[2] The same question was raised in a heated exchange between Yagel and the rabbi of Modena, Barukh Abraham da Spoleto, in 1585. Spoleto had delivered a sermon on the subject of metempsychosis in which he argued that there was a tradition that sinful human souls migrate into the bodies of animals. Yagel disagreed and sought to clarify what the tradition actually meant. See Ruderman, *Kabbalah, Magic, and Science*, chap. 8.

[3] See Menahem Recanati, *Perush ha-Torah al Derekh Ha-Emet* (Venice, 1523), parshat Shemini; compare also parshat No'ah. Cf. also Meir ibn Gabbai, *Avodat ha-Kodesh* (Venice, 1566), helek ha-avodah, chaps. 33, 34; Isaac Abravanel, *Perush al ha-Torah* (Jerusalem, 1964) on Deuteronomy 25:5.

[4] For a summary of the debate and other sources, see G. Scholem's essay on *gilgul* in *Pirkei Yesod be-Havanat ha-Kabbalah u-Semaleha* (Jerusalem, 1977), pp. 305–57.

[5] For a summary of the Pythagorean view, see H. S. Long, *A Study of the Doctrine of Metempsychosis in Greece from Pythagoras to Plato* (Princeton, 1948); W. Burkert, *Lore and Sciences in Ancient Pythagoreanism*, trans. by E. L. Minar, Jr. (Cambridge, Mass., 1972), pp. 120–24. Yagel's original text reads "murdered" rather than "murderer" and is emended according to Mani's suggestion, p. 41a.

[6] Psalm 22:21.

[7] Moshe Idel has recently identified this man as R. Lappidot Ashkenazi, a figure with occult powers who lived in Safed and who maintained relations with R. Moses Cordovero and

morning, it would not carry the load on its back to which it was accustomed. The owner of the mule treated it harshly, hit it, and wounded it in order to restore it to its original state of doing his work. One day, however, the ass opened its mouth because of the pain of the beating and said to the man hitting it: 'Have I been in the habit of treating you like this?'[1] And he [the owner] said: 'No.' [The mule continued,] 'Know now that it [your beating] is in vain since I am the soul of your father, your begetter, who was decreed by heaven to dwell in the body of this unclean animal because of his sins, until a specified time has passed. So now be kind to me. Don't make this mule work and carry until the aforementioned time has passed when I will leave it [this body].'[2]

"The man was astonished, so he went to the wise R. Lappidot and told him of the incident. The sage responded to him: 'Do this, then, my son, to extricate yourself[3] from any speck of sin. Don't work him [the mule] as he commanded you because it is possible that this evil man's iniquities trapped him. Since he committed an animalistic act, it was decreed that he should enter an animal. Even if it is not so, and he is not your father who bore you, perhaps it is an evil spirit that is capable of harming you if [you] violate his command. You cannot know what his name is, or that of his family or legion to adjure him [by incantation] so that he will go out from there.'[4] The man obeyed the wise man. When the time which the soul had mentioned as the time he would leave the mule came, the mule suddenly died. The sage ordered it to be buried in the field and not to throw its carcass to the dogs.

"These are the words that this elder told me. If they are true, accept the truth from whoever tells it, and if they are false, let the truth follow its course.[5] But now, my son, blessed be God, return to your story, since three-

---

R. Ḥayyim Vital. He also offers a number of parallel versions of the following story, especially that of R. Judah Ḥallewa, the kabbalist from Fez, Morocco. See M. Idel, "R. Judah Ḥallewa and his *Ẓafenat Pa'ane'aḥ*" (in Hebrew), *Shalem*, 4 (1984): 126–27; 146–48.

[1]Cf. Numbers 22:30.

[2]The story bears a clear resemblance to the sarcastic reference of Xenophanes regarding Pythagoras. The latter similarly forbade the beating of a dog because he recognized in its howls the voice of a friend. Cf. Diogenes Laertius, *Lives of Eminent Philosophers,* trans. by R. D. Hicks (Cambridge, Mass. and London, 1958), VIII, 36, pp. 352–53.

[3]Cf. Proverbs 6:3.

[4]Yagel relates elsewhere a number of cases of spirit possession among contemporary Jews, especially a case of a Jewish woman in Ferrara initially reported by Gedaliah ibn Yaḥya. On Yagel's interest in his phenomenon, see Ruderman, *Kabbalah, Magic, and Science,* chap. 3.

[5]Two favorite expressions of Yagel, which he used earlier. They were used by Maimonides, among other medieval writers, in his introduction to the commentary on *Avot* and in his *Shemoneh Perakim,* chap. 4.

quarters of the third watch [of the night] have passed, and the time for a man to return to his tent before morning approaches, as I told you."

## Resumption of the Son's Life Story

[93] I replied: 'When people learned that I had left the place [Luzzara], the elder Almagiati brother appeared armed, calling loudly in the markets and streets wherever shopkeepers are found and [claiming] that I really had despoiled and robbed him. [He also declared] that I had left [Luzzara] because I had stolen and deceived and [that I had] placed [the stolen goods] in my possession like a usurping occupant[1] from the time of the battle [of the Romans] in Judah, and, further, like a person who stands on the crossroads robbing anyone. Thus this man made me out to be worse than him. Even the thief takes his life in his hands[2] when he plunders, but this man acted deceitfully and stole my heart[3] [without any risk to himself].

"With such words, he would address anyone he found, instantly dishonoring me wherever he went. He did not act as he should have acted, [which was to call] for peace and placing the matter in the custody of Jewish arbitrators who spurn ill-gotten gains.[4] Rather, this man went most obstinately to do evil. And his arm was still outstretched[5] as he used to speak in the city streets: 'Don't think that the money I gave him [Abraham Yagel] was for the purpose of lending on interest. I did not do as others did among my people, such as Madame Rina and Mr. Gershon Porto, who devoured and crushed him[6] with interest which they took from him. I, [on the contrary,] did not give him my money on interest.'

"Thus he would enhance his own reputation before many people, making his case seem just and appearing to be the primary righteous party in his argument. He spoke similarly before the podesta and the *presidente*,[7] and the satyrs would dance in that place.[8] He also increased his recriminations and did evil in the sight of God and men. When the noble R. Isaac

---

[1] *Sicaricon,* one who had seized the property of those absent or killed or taken captive in war during the period of Roman rule of Judea. Cf. Mishnah Gittin 5:6.

[2] Cf. 1 Samuel 19:5.

[3] Cf. Genesis 31:26.

[4] Cf. Proverbs 28:16.

[5] Cf. Isaiah 5:25 and elsewhere.

[6] Cf. Jeremiah 51:34.

[7] The text adds "and the first" (*ve-ha-rishon*), which makes no sense and has been emended to "rosh" as in "yoshev rosh," or the head, perhaps *presidente,* as appears below.

[8] Cf. Isaiah 13:21.

Porto, may his memory be blessed,[1] R. Azariah Finzi,[2] and R. Judah Ya'aleh of Colonia[3] came to quiet the dispute and to engender a compromise, this man arose to slander them at the podesta's house. The noble R. Isaac Porto and R. Azariah were incarcerated in the prison compound together with a group of other Jews, although they had done no injustice.[4] However, the foresighted[5] R. Judah of Colonia narrowly escaped from prison.[6] He [Almagiati] warned those men in jail: 'You will not get out of there until the two [of you] hand over every last penny—good, measured, and fragrant [money].'

"At the same time, he [Eliezer Almagiati] and Madame Rina de Lacairo further increased their recriminations by approaching the *auditore*,[7] the exalted and enlightened judge of the Jews for all of the Mantovano, requesting him to write to the podesta of Luzzara to influence the judgment on their behalf. He [the *auditore*] was to inscribe, with his signature and with the [distinguishing] 'mark' of Luzzara, the sum of the principal and profit that they were to receive for the bank. Subsequently, they testified regarding the profit they wished to receive from that money.

"Come and see, my master, the blindness of those who lend on interest! If one calls his associate an evil person [claiming], 'you lent money on interest,' he lies to him and torments him to death. Moreover, these people brought witnesses, a scribe, a quill and ink; they dictated and sealed [the document] in court, charging that so and so and so and so lent their money on interest. Moreover, Almagiati did not merely insinuate but pronounced explicitly that R. Gershon Porto had taken interest from him. He testified that he [Porto] had brought me documents a year earlier and a ledger [*lista*] on which there was an account of interest and profits. In the end, the podesta and the *presidente* agreed on the matter and summoned R. Gershon and Madame Rina by official decree to be put in prison and to accept the

---

[1]On Isaac b. David Cohen Porto, see Simonsohn, pp. 30, 218, 253, 415, 622, 727; D. Kaufmann, "Meir b. Ephraim of Padua: Scroll-Writer and Printer in Mantua," *Jewish Quarterly Review*, o.s. 11 (1899): 218. Isaac had served as an arbitrator in other communal disputes.

[2]He was already mentioned above, p. 160.

[3]Simonsohn, p. 226, identifies him with Judah Sinai of Colonia, but perhaps he was the banker Judah b. Solomon (Simonsohn, p. 224) mentioned in transactions with the family of Yagel's father-in-law. This Judah also interceded on behalf of Yagel's friend Azariah Finzi regarding the tragic murder of his daughter by his son, mentioned above.

[4]Cf. Isaiah 53:9.

[5]Cf. Ecclesiastes 2:14.

[6]Literally, "There was about one step between R. Judah of Colonia and the jail."

[7]The duke's appointed commissioner and judge of the Jews. See the many references to this officer in Simonsohn, index.

judgment. The exalted duke learned of the matter and he[1] acted in his usual manner, sustaining the land with justice, detesting robbery and crime.[2] Upon reading the letter brought to him, he fulfilled the request.

"The accused Jews requested a judge within the jurisdiction of the podesta of Luzzara. [They asked] that he be certified and that his *doctoro* [law degree or license] be recognized [by those who practice law under the jurisdiction] of the podesta of Luzzara. He should hold court and make an honest judgment, and let there be justice, whatever the outcome.[3]

"Almagiati continued to make other accusations. He came with the head of the 'satyrs,'[4] [entered] my house and walls, and searched through all my records for papers, documents, and letters in my files, in order to find evidence to clarify and to substantiate the slanderous charges. They looked wherever they wanted and took whatever they wanted. Whatever they did not examine, they sealed in a small room with the seal of the podesta. Afterward, they sealed off all the rooms and attics and did not leave any open space except for two rooms where the women and children lived.

"He [Almagiati] had dug a pit and deepened it and would fall into the ditch he had made[5] on account of his brothers' [his fellow citizens'] fall. He would be caught in the trap which he prepared for them since the files for which the authorities searched contained documents, memoranda, and ledgers that recorded his dealings with me regarding loans on interest. When the *presidente,* who was a very cunning fellow,[6] saw them, he hid them from his face [of Almagiati] and placed them in his keeping. He was silent until he [i.e., the plaintiff] had completed all his accusations and testified against the righteous man whom he had libeled.

"However, when he [Almagiati] had finished and had received what he wanted, his mischief recoiled around his head.[7] With the measure he meted out to others, they measured out to him.[8] He also did not escape because the *presidente* accused him about the interest loans. He put him in a jail where the prisoners of the king [i.e., duke] are held and [there] he remained in solitary confinement away from the cells of the other prisoners.

"But the slander continually grew and this poison spread throughout

[1]Literally, "the king."
[2]Cf. Proverbs 29:4, Isaiah 61:8, or "robbery with a burnt offering," according to the new Jewish Publication Society translation.
[3]Literally, "let the law cut through the mountain." Cf. B. T. Sanhedrin 6b.
[4]It is unclear whether he is the same person called "the head" (*presidente*) elsewhere.
[5]Cf. Psalm 7:16.
[6]Cf. 1 Samuel 23:22.
[7]Cf. Psalm 7:17.
[8]Cf. Mishnah Sotah 1:7 and above.

the entire region of Mantua. This man gave a hand to the criminals of Mantua and like Jeroboam, he sinned and caused others to sin.[1] Certain members of the community then arose and vilified their Jewish brethren for good reason,[2] not merely for interest dealings, but regarding other matters for which one is punished bodily and financially. Yet because of God, who was with us and with all the community, the most exalted duke was favorably disposed toward them [the Jews][3] and did not wish to destroy [them]. He was merciful to them[4] and didn't want to do [them] harm as their actions warranted. He ordered those in charge of his household to inform them [the Jews] that he would be pacified by an appropriate sum. [It would constitute] a general recompense for all the Jews residing in the state of the Mantovano [in payment] for all the sins and iniquities that they had committed until this time. However, since the Jews did not recognize their miracle and the great benevolence the most exalted duke extended to them, they failed to accept his offer. Consequently, he was incensed with them. He increased his dominion over these people but still remained merciful to them.[5] He turned to them and was compassionate with them, 'saying to the prisoners; "Go free," and to those in the darkness of iniquities and crimes, "show yourselves."[6]' Finally, he issued documents and a *decreto*[7] regarding the matter, and the land became peaceful.[8]

"When the area had quieted down, I returned to my previous home in Luzzara. But even during my stay at the place to which I had fled, Almagiati pursued me, attempting to imprison me in fetters. The 'satyrs' had been sent there at great expense, but God nullified their plan since I had foreknowledge of their intention some two hours earlier. I arose at midnight and went to another [safe] place which I had located nearby, a village under the jurisdiction of the Mantovano.

"On the morrow, the refugee, who originally had been sent by the two *rettori*[9] as an emissary to the place where I had [previously] been, came to [see] me.[10] I decided to come home at the request of the exalted duke and

---

[1] Some of Jeroboam's sins are mentioned, for example, in B. T. Sanhedrin 101b.
[2] Cf. B. T. Kiddushin 44b.
[3] Cf. Genesis 39:21.
[4] Cf. Genesis 43:30 and elsewhere.
[5] Cf. Lamentations 3:22.
[6] Cf. Isaiah 49:9.
[7] An edict, or decree.
[8] Cf. Joshua 11:23; 14:15.
[9] *Moshlanim* or *moshlim,* principals or rectors; presumably the two aforementioned political leaders.
[10] It is unclear who the "refugee" was.

with [a promise] of security delivered by the emissary from one of the *retttori*. [I did this so that] I would not sin, since it was written [in the emissary's message] that if I failed to come, they would publicly declare me [a criminal] and the exalted duke would shun me all the days of my life. At the same time that I had been reading this epistle, another messenger came and informed me that my blessed mother-in-law was bedridden and was dangerously ill.[1] I observed, reckoned, and contemplated all these factors. However, I noticed that all regions that surrounded our area had prohibited anyone from entering them for fear of the plague while Mantua and its borders were still closed tight.

"Nevertheless, I decided to return to Luzzara and to prepare my response to the investigations and inquiries to which the authorities would subject me regarding everything that was known to them. The proof would then emerge from the documents or from documents based on them so that one would not need to invent anything. I also asked a Jew named R. Judah Basola of Viadana,[2] in whose house I had lived, to inquire of a Christian scholar as to how I should act, how not to wrong anyone, and how not to antagonize the authorities. The man returned with the response of the scholar upon his lips. I did all that he said and also continued to do good to the extent that God enabled me. I informed many sound people of my affairs and of the refuge to which they could flee for help.[3] Let my witness be in heaven along with the following persons in those regions [who were my human witnesses]: R. Mordecai Trabotto,[4] who came here [to Luzzara] with Madame Rina; R. Uziel Camerino,[5] who knew what I had done at her request; and R. Judah Basola, who also knew about the same matter. Among the elders of the town[6] it was well known that I was ready to prove my innocence with argument and evidence from Jews and Christians alike regarding all the slander and of all those evil things that had happened to the Jews of this region.

"On the contrary, I was ready to prove that I had endangered my life[7]

---

[1]Yagel's mother-in-law was Batsheva Fano, the wife of the already deceased Hosea [Salvatore] da Colonia. Yagel had married their daughter Dina soon after his arrival in Luzzara in the late 1560s or early 1570s. For more details regarding Yagel's family, see the introduction above.

[2]On other members of this family residing in the Mantovano, see Simonsohn, index.

[3]This sentence is also unclear. Did Yagel mean to say that the many sound people informed him of the refuge to which he could flee for help rather than vice versa?

[4]On his family in Mantua, see Simonsohn, index, "Trabotto."

[5]He already was mentioned above.

[6]Cf. Ruth 3:11.

[7]Cf. 1 Samuel 19:5.

to quiet them, even with respect to the accusations made against the Almagiati, either at the time [they had been made] or at the time I was brought to this prison. I would prove that it [the libel directed at Almagiati] was not at my instigation. I had proofs and testimonies as numerous as the hair on my head to respond to what he or anyone else had said to cause them to suspect me, and to show them the truth. If there are persons who prematurely[1] raise their voices to speak falsely against me about these matters, let them come to me so I may inform them of my ways. Please do not say things about me unless they are stated in my presence so that the truth will follow its course. For He [God], whose seal is truth and whose ways are all righteous, will clarify the truth and reward me with kindness and truth. Anyone who rejects truth, does not wish to know the truth, and suspects me for no reason, will also receive the truth as a bitter curse, because anyone who suspects the innocent is stricken in his body.[2]

"After all this truth and all this recrimination, the land became quiet, and I returned to my home as [I] have mentioned. I sent for righteous, God-fearing people and those who spurn ill-gotten gains,[3] namely R. Azariah Finzi and R. Judah Ya'aleh of Colonia, since the honorable Isaac Porto, who had initially come, was called to his resting place in heaven; may the memory of this righteous one be a blessing. I demanded of them to complete the commandment that they had begun[4] by going to Mantua and by requesting that Madame Rina and Almagiati submit to arbitrators between us. [This would be done] according to the law of our Holy Torah by way of each party choosing its own arbitrators. Following their [the arbitrators'] instructions, we would act and succeed [in achieving] both justice and a compromise.

"The men went out, carrying a writ of authorization and acted prudently by handing over all of the affairs and the provisions of all three parties to the three arbitrators: R. Judah Ya'aleh, representing our part; Samuel Grasseto,[5] arbitrator and agent for Madame Rina; and Isaac Almagiati,[6] arbitrator and agent for the Almagiati brothers. A document of compromise [compromesso] would be drawn up conforming to that which is done in the Jewish community as established by rabbinic law. These three

[1]Literally, "with fat and blood in their ears," i.e., wet behind the ears. Cf. Ezekiel 44:7, 15.

[2]Cf. B. T. Shabbat 97a.
[3]Cf. Proverbs 28:16.
[4]Cf. Tanḥuma, Ekev, 6; J. T. Pesaḥim 10:5.
[5]On him, see Simonsohn, p. 713.
[6]On him, see Simonsohn, p. 228.

men could do as they please, following either [the principles of strict] law or [the principles] of compromise as they saw fit regarding all the provisions intertwined among the parties. (I had always testified, [for my part] that I wished to pay them only in a proper manner, in the way that law and truth are dispensed, and in the way the arbitrators or other judges who sit in judgment will decree in reaching a determination among the parties, adjudicating and resolving all the claims and the many issues between us.)[1]

"They [the arbitrators] came afterward to Luzzara, where I showed them faithfully and honestly everything that was in my house and within my walls. There wasn't a thing I failed to show them. I stated in their presence that I was prepared to take a divine oath, as stipulated in the Torah,[2] to the effect that no small or great thing was hidden, and that I had said nothing deceitfully, saying one thing with my mouth, while intending something else in my heart. . . .[3] They also would be permitted to apply a general ban[4] and to do all they desired to remove any speck, tinge, or connection [of wrongdoing] from us with their rod[5] as they perceived.

"When the men [Yagel's adversaries] saw what was happening, they made illegal demands[6] of our arbitrator, R. Judah Ya'aleh, requesting that he change the place of the pawns by placing them on deposit with Madame Rina until a judgment was made and until they would know what to do with them. He answered that he was unwilling to accept their request. They became angry and broke the compromise [*compromesso*] law, again sealing everything that was with us in the house.

"The penitential season was approaching, for it was already the month of *Elul* [September–October], but they [Yagel's adversaries] paid no attention to this fact. They also requested to close and seal the synagogue that was in the house so that we could not go there[7] to pray on the Days of Awe. But they were unsuccessful since I contacted the *console* [consul] of the city

[1]The line in parentheses is found in the margin of the Cincinnati manuscript.

[2]Rabbinic law classified judicial oaths chronologically, with the earliest one—namely, the Pentateuchal oath (*shevu'at ha-Torah*)—being the most severe. Cf. A. Gulak, *Yesodei ha-Mishpat ha-Ivri* (Tel Aviv, 1967), vol. 4, p. 130.

[3]Cf. B. T. Pesahim 113b and elsewhere. The ellipsis points indicate an area of the Cincinnati manuscript that is illegible. See Mani's note, p. 43a.

[4]*Ḥerem setam*, an unconditional or unqualified ban used by the Jewish court to extract evidence from a person without subjecting him to the more severe consequences associated with the oath. Cf. Gulak, 4, pp. 132–33. On the status of the *ḥerem* in Italy, see Bonfil, *Ha-Rabbanut be-Italia bi-Tekufat ha-Renesans*, pp. 44–51; for other references, see p. 45, n. 130.

[5]Cf. Job 9:34.

[6]Cf. Deuteronomy 22:14, 17.

[7]On this synagogue in Yagel's house, see the interesting document of 1640, cited by A. Balletti, *Gli Ebrei e gli Estensi* (Emilia, 1930; reprint, Bologna, 1969), p. 100, which points out that the synagogue had been used continuously for seventy years, from the time Yagel first

in order to ascertain all the necessary legalities [regarding the house] and including the synagogue; so it was left open. I also complained bitterly to them [his opponents], but it was to no avail. They afterward traveled to Mantua and returned the following week.

"But I [still] desired to reach some conclusion regarding this matter, for I asked: 'Must the sword devour forever?'[1] I asked them to reach an agreement with me that went beyond the letter of the law. I did this by sending for Samuel Grasseto and Isaac Almagiati [and asking] them to appear in the house of the city's notary and to declare in his presence that while I remained in negotiation over the matter, [I was prepared] to hand over the pawns of the bank as a deposit to Madame Rina as they had requested. The ledger of credit would remain sealed up in its present location until the time of judgment. In the meantime, the pawns and credit would remain in this manner for a month. If the three arbitrators would reach a compromise during this time, how good it would be, and if not, we would take two others to decide. Moreover, in order to avoid a controversy over the selection of these [new] men, we chose unanimously the distinguished erudite scholar R. Judah Moscato[2] and R. Gershon Katz Porto.[3] They would have the authority to judge, reach a compromise, and decide. By their word, all the provisions would be resolved among the aforementioned parties to the arbitration. Since a [Jewish] court must never have an even number of members,[4] we would give them [Moscato and Porto] authority to take anyone they desired as the third [arbitrator] and to decide among themselves. We reached this agreement in the presence of the aforementioned notary in his office and we agreed to send a message to Viadana to contact R. Judah Ya'aleh [who was residing there]. In the following week, on the day after Yom Kippur [the Day of Atonement] (the day Moses ascended Mount Sinai a second time),[5] [we agreed] to give form to the matter and begin the venture.

---

acquired his property in Luzzara. In a series of letters, written in 1623 from San Martino dall'Argine in the Mantovano, Yagel also mentioned the synagogue in the context of his financial dispute with Hananiah Rieti and his son, Elhanan of Luzzara. See the introduction above.

[1]Cf. 2 Samuel 2:26.

[2]Moscato was the famous preacher and rabbi, one of the most illustrious Jewish figures of his generation. See Simonsohn, pp. 721–22.

[3]Simonsohn, p. 253, identifies him as someone other than Gershon b. Abraham Porto, already mentioned by Yagel above.

[4]Cf. B. T. Sanhedrin 3b.

[5]This is clearly a mistake, for Moses descended the mount with the second set of tablets on that day, as Mani points out, p. 43a.

"The men went their way and the first of the week arrived which, I thought, would bring an end to the matter still in mediation, as I have said. The elder Almagiati brother and Samuel Grasseto appeared and sent for me to come outside [the city]. They set up an ambush outside the city with three 'satyrs' who had accompanied them from Mantua. These men captured me cunningly, speaking peacefully with me but with deceit and malice in their hearts. They kept me in the dark[1] with pleasant words while they were actually plotting their ambush, intending to take me to Mantua as a prisoner in iron fetters. Had it not been for God, who was with me, [I would not have been saved] since they had captured me without the podesta's permission and illegally. The podesta inquired about the matter, unwilling to allow them to transport me to Mantua until he had ascertained if the arrest was good or bad, that is, if they could arrest me legally or not. But because some differences about this affair developed in the region between this podesta and the *auditore* of the Jews, the matter remained unresolved [until the time when] the Tishbite [i.e., Elijah] will solve all the difficulties and problems.[2]

"To make matters worse,[3] the elder Almagiati slandered me by claiming they had caught me possessing a small knife called a *pugnale* [a dagger]. The exalted duke had recently decreed that no man could arm himself without the permission of the ruler specified[4] in writing, except for those who had resided on the land for a minimum of ten years or those permitted[5] by his highness. Since I had not lived in this land for ten years, he thought badly of me because he did not know that I had the *decreto* [i.e., the permission] for holding the dagger. He [Almagiati] slandered me but it proved to be my deliverance[6]; for this reason, I was prevented from going down to Mantua to be held captive in the tresses.[7] Nevertheless, it was considered a criminal matter,[8] so I was put in prison, as your eyes beheld me this night, my master.

"My father, surely notice how they snared me like a bird and they plotted maliciously against me. From the beginning to the end of the affair, see how they tried to destroy me for no good reason[9] and [how they tried]

---

[1]Literally, "stole my mind"; cf. Genesis 31:26.

[2]For a complete discussion of this last phrase, see M. Friedmann [Ish-Shalom], ed., *Tanna de-Vei Eliyahu* (Vienna, 1904), introduction, pp. 20–24.

[3]Literally, "he added the moist to the dry." Cf. Deuteronomy 29:15.

[4]*Neodro.*

[5]*Decretiti.*

[6]Cf. Exodus 15:2 and elsewhere.

[7]Cf. Song of Songs 7:6.

[8]*Criminalo.*

[9]Cf. Job 2:3.

to return evil for the good I did them and for which I endangered my life, as you have heard. All the elders of my town know,[1] God also knows and bears witness,[2] and Israel too shall know[3] that it isn't enough that these men harmed me and instigated all that happened to me. They also never followed the ways of Israel in all their actions but surrounded me like bees.[4] Nor did they wish to follow the ways of the gentiles. According to the mores of any nation or people, one is forbidden to initiate anything during the time of the mediation [*compromesso*]. When someone comes to pay his creditor from what he possesses or from what he has deposited as a pawn against his wife's marriage contract, you take it but have compassion upon him and don't mash his blood [i.e., don't humiliate him], as those men did who acted like wild animals, just as a lion tears and eats [and has no shame], etc.[5] Moreover, our holy Torah establishes a rule and ordinance not to imprison anyone if he has no more money or, all the more so, if he accepts the law.[6]

"So I have complaints about these men and especially about the woman standing next to me in this place, who sold me to an Ashkenazic[7] people and to a stranger who did not know me. A peel of garlic is just as important to him as quenching his thirst. He cannot distinguish whether a person means well or acts with bad intention.[8] And she [Rina] did not recall what I had done on her behalf either before this affair or after, when Almagiati began his libel, as I have said. Nor was she attentive to the fact that my great sorrow was on her account and that she indirectly harmed me, as I must prove in a place where I will be heard [in court].

"If babes weened from milk would know of all these developments from beginning to end—as little as I have told you, since it is impossible to relate everything—they would cry on my account for the great wrong done me. If the stones in the wall only knew how to speak, they would cry out on

---

[1]Cf. Ruth 3:11.

[2]Cf. Jeremiah 29:23.

[3]Cf. Joshua 22:22.

[4]Cf. Deuteronomy 1:44.

[5]Cf. B. T. Pesahim 49b.

[6]This is the position of Maimonides, for example, regarding the debtor. Cf. *Mishneh Torah,* Hilkhot Malveh ve-Loveh, 2:1. The issue was extensively discussed and debated by later medieval rabbis. See M. Elon, *Herut ha-Perat be-Darkhei Geviyyat Hov* (Jerusalem, 1964).

[7]A sarcastic reference to the Almagiati family whose name is written in Hebrew as "ha-Almeya" and sounds like Alemania or Germany, the land of Ashkenaz.

[8]A reference to Eliezer Almagiati. Literally, it means that he doesn't know whether it is done for *akal* (cutting branches to make a basket, a legitimate act in a sabbatical year) or for *akalkalot* (perverseness, mere cutting of branches, which is prohibited). Cf. B. T. Sanhedrin 26a.

my behalf while the wooden rafters would answer them. May God now see and judge that this not be considered a complaint [in the heavenly court] against the one who happened to be caught first.[1] Since there is nowhere I can flee, no one cares about me.[2] Were not the Lord my help, I should soon dwell in silence.[3]

"How pleasant are the words of Resh Lakish, in the Jerusalem Talmud *Berakhot,* chapter *Ha-Ro'ah,*[4] who said: 'If a human being has a relative who is rich, he acknowledges him; if he is poor, he doesn't acknowledge him. But the Holy One, blessed be He, is not like that. Even when Israel is at its lowest decline, He calls them brothers and friends, as it is written: "For the sake of my brothers and friends, etc."' Similarly, the rabbis wrote in chapter *Beme Madlikim:*[5] 'Rav Papa said: "At the gate of the shops, there are many brothers and friends, but at the gate of prison, there are neither brothers nor friends."'

"I am like the verse that states: 'You make my companions shun me; You make me abhorrent to them; I am shut in and do not go out.'[6] Therefore, take my prayer[7] before Him so that He will not be far from me, for [my] trouble is great and there is none to help.[8] I have dwelt among the tents of Kedar[9] and the Ishmaelites, who were cruel to me [and] sought to castrate me so that I would have no root or branch.[10] Thus my progeny will be able to say: 'These are the men who destroyed us and silenced us.' These men had said to themselves: 'Hew down the tree and cut off its branches and pluck its fruit.'[11]

"However, the harm which comes to the victim and the oppressor daily is not equal.[12] The lion cubs open wide their mouths for they [his oppressors] have sons and daughters [who cry] 'give, give,' but they are not satisfied and they never say 'enough.'[13] Beyond the door and doorpost is an eye that mocks them and disdains their actions.[14] They will surely say: 'You

[1]Cf. B. T. Rosh Ha-Shanah 16b.
[2]Cf. Psalm 142:5.
[3]Cf. Psalm 94:17.
[4]J. T. Berakhot 9:1.
[5]B. T. Shabbat 32a.
[6]Psalm 88:9.
[7]Cf. Psalm 141:2.
[8]Cf. Psalm 22:12.
[9]Cf. Psalm 120:5.
[10]Cf. Malachi 3:19.
[11]Cf. Daniel 4:11.
[12]The oppressor's punishment is ultimately greater than that of the victim. The following lines, cast in prophetic language, predict the future doom of Yagel's adversaries.
[13]Cf. Proverbs 30:15.
[14]Cf. Proverbs 30:17.

have seen this people who continually quarrel with each other.[1] We shall certainly look forward to relief.' But there is no mine for silver for [the use of] hired archers handling the bow,[2] except in time of war.

"As for me, I will hope always[3] and my eyes are ever toward the Lord, for He will loose my feet from the net[4] and have pity on me.[5] He will gather up my soul from among sinners whose hands are full of bribes.[6] I shall walk without blame and say tasteful things. May God have mercy upon me from heaven, [may He] free me and pardon me because of His compassion, so that I may lift up my standard in the assemblies and bless God."[7]

## The Appearance of Angels and the Disclosure of Heavenly Secrets

[94] After this conversation, a caravan of angels came toward us, singing songs and praises [relating] that it [the night] already had expired and that it had been good. [God] had begun to light up the entire east as far as Hebron.[8] It [the caravan] continued to stand up and recite a song. I inquired about them from my father. He answered that they belonged to the third watch[9] which already had departed and sung their song. It was already time for the divine angels to wake up and sing together for the morning stars.

I then asked my father: "If they have departed and [already] have sung their song, what do they still sing?"

He responded: "Know that the heavenly angels never allow them [the angels of the third watch] to be silent. They are now singing 'Hallelujah, Praise God in His sanctuary,'[10] which is the choicest of the psalms. They always conclude their singing with it since it contains hints of all the effects of the worlds joined together in the secret of tens.[11] It [the entire structure

[1]Cf. B. T. Kiddushin 71b.

[2]Cf. Job 28:1 and Psalm 78:9, whose language is borrowed and transformed into Yagel's own phrasing. The apparent meaning: contentious people can never be at peace; they only succeed at war.

[3]Cf. Psalm 71:14.

[4]Cf. Psalm 25:15.

[5]Cf. 2 Samuel 12:22.

[6]Cf. Psalm 26:9–10.

[7]Based on Psalm 26:11–12.

[8]Cf. Mishnah Yoma 3:1; B. T. Tamid 30a.

[9]The night was divided into three watches. These angels performed their duty of singing psalms during the last of the night hours and were soon to be relieved by those "on watch" for the morning hours. Cf. B. T. Berakhot 3b.

[10]Psalm 150.

[11]The psalm is divided into ten parts beginning "Praise Him" and corresponding to the primary ten life processes, the *sefirot;* each of the four worlds contains its set of *sefirot.*

of the linked four worlds] flows and gives abundantly until it ends up with the Creator of everything, so that every soul will praise Him, as the verse goes: 'Let all that breathes praise the Lord, Hallelujah.'[1] Know that the name of God [i.e., *Yah*, from the two letters "yud" and "he"] is mentioned in this psalm since the Holy One, praised be He, created the two worlds with it [this name]—this one [world] and the one to come—as it is written: 'For in *Yah* the Lord you have an everlasting rock.'[2] The rabbis interpreted [the verse], 'As they were created,'[3] [to read], 'with a "he" He created them'; that is, this world was created with [the letter] 'he' and the next world with [the letter] 'yud.' "[4]

[95] I then asked: "If this is so, [then] there are two worlds. Yet the philosophers conceived and presented definitive proofs, [based] on their investigations, that there is only one world, since it is commonly accepted that no vacuum can exist.[5] This world contained by the diurnal sphere [*primum mobile*] is spherical. All of these assumptions can be proven. If another [world] could be found to meet this world, there would be, by necessity, a vacuum in this world. For this reason and for other proven arguments, they [the philosophers] decided that there can only be one world, unlike the view of the Mutakallimun sect who established the atoms as the first of God's works[6] and derived from them [the atoms] the creation of a plurality of worlds.[7] But they [the atoms] are all vanity; the wind will sweep these atoms away; and a whirlwind will scatter them[8] so that they will remain in the mouth of every wise-hearted person as if they never existed. Even those who believe [in the doctrine] of reward and punishment can maintain that there is only one world so long as it is stated that the

[1]Psalm 150:6.

[2]Isaiah 26:4, or a rock of worlds (this one and the next).

[3]Genesis 2:4.

[4]Cf. B. T. Menaḥot 29b; *Bereshit Rabbah,* 12:10.

[5]This is a standard Aristotelian assumption of medieval philosophy. Cf. Maimonides, *Moreh Nevukhim,* 1:72.

[6]Cf. Job 40:19.

[7]Their views are discussed by Maimonides in the *Moreh Nevukhim,* 1:73. That Yagel should mention the view of the atomists as an alternative to the Aristotelian cosmos is significant in view of the renewed interest in atomism among a number of Jewish thinkers in the late sixteenth and seventeenth centuries, who thus followed their Christian contemporaries in this regard. Cf. M. Idel, "Differing Perceptions of Kabbalah in the Early Seventeenth Century," *Jewish Thought in the Seventeenth Century,* ed. I. Twersky and B. Septimus (Cambridge, Mass., 1987), pp. 178–97. On seventeenth-century Jewish discussions of the plurality of worlds, see D. Ruderman, "The Impact of Science on Jewish Culture and Society in Venice," in *Gli Ebrei e Venezia,* ed. G. Cozzi (Milan, 1987), pp. 437–38.

[8]Cf. Isaiah 41:16.

mover of the first sphere is God, blessed be He, the first cause and the 'place of the earth.'[1] The souls who leave this material world and ascend to heaven are rewarded by enjoying the spheres, each [soul] according to his own station. Take for example the case of a person who is saved from [sinning] with a gentile woman. When he was confronted with the affair, he did the will of God, as Joseph did with the wife of his master [in refusing her invitation].[2] Such a man is worthy to observe and rejoice in the glorious light of the sphere of Venus. Similarly, for someone who is saved from spilling the blood of his friend in vain, his soul will ascend to rejoice in the light of the sphere of Mars.[3] Accordingly, this is the case with the rest of the sins; a person who does not guard himself is trapped by his sin. However, during his [soul's] ascent to heaven, he will meet the sphere of fire [empyrean], where he will be purified and his soul will be washed of its iniquity.

[96] "So we find that this sphere is dark, for if it were lit up the night would be illuminated by its light as that of the day, as Naḥmanides wrote in his commentary on Genesis.[4] Likewise, Scripture demonstrates that the place of Gehenna is darkness and gloom 'for the wicked perish in darkness.'[5] There, in this sphere of fire, a person will reap the fruit of his actions.[6] His sorrow will be augmented by additional sorrow when he departs from there and ascends to heaven to the sphere appropriate to him according to his sin, in the way I have described.

"Just as one is rewarded by the joy he receives [from his sphere], so, too, in precisely the same way, he is punished by his same sphere. The angels of death of the same sphere will approach him and make him run there [by his sphere] for ever, as the verse states: 'Their worms shall not die, nor their fire be quenched, etc.'[7] Furthermore, a person can only remain for twelve months in the sphere of fire that he met during his heavenly ascent, as the rabbis declared: 'The judgment of the wicked in Gehenna is twelve months.'[8] The rabbis call the constellation of fire *Gehenna* [*gehinnom*], to teach us that this world is like the valley of the son of Hinnom.[9] An oven is

---

[1]Cf. *Bereshit Rabbah,* 68:9.

[2]Cf. Genesis 39.

[3]These last lines are written in the Aramaic language of the *Sefer ha-Zohar.* I am unable to identify the passage; it most likely was composed by the author to imitate the *Sefer ha-Zohar*'s language.

[4]Naḥmanides on Genesis 1:1.

[5]Cf. 1 Samuel 2:9.

[6]Cf. Isaiah 3:10.

[7]Isaiah 66:24.

[8]Cf. Mishnah Eduyyot 2:10 and elsewhere.

[9]The biblical valley of Moloch worship. Cf. Joshua 15:8, 18:16, and elsewhere.

fired by a baker there,[1] as the rabbis recalled in chapter *Lulav ha-Gazul:*[2] 'There are two palms in the valley of the son of Hinnom and smoke rises between them, etc.'

"So the sphere of fire is in this world under the heavens, which is where the fire of Gehenna is located. The proof that Gehenna is identical with the sphere of fire, as I have said, is derived from what the rabbis related in that same *mishnah* in the second chapter of *Eduyyot:*[3] 'Five things endure for twelve months.' Just as four are from this material world under the sphere of the moon—the judgment of the generation of the flood,[4] [the judgment of] the Egyptians,[5] [the judgment of] Job,[6] and [the judgment of] Gog and Magog[7]—so is the judgment of the wicked in Gehenna in this world, which is the fifth thing. Many rabbinic statements can be commonly linked[8] regarding this [idea].

[97] "Moreover, the sages know that just as there are good angels who generate good influence and treat human beings well in every one of the heavenly spheres, there are also demons and bad angels who influence human beings perversely. They are the opposite of the good ones [angels] for God made one opposite the other. This subject is explained by the proof of the magicians, the masters of talismans.[9] Therefore, it is not necessary to believe in the reality of a plurality of worlds. On the contrary, a person who believes the opposite of what I stated is in fact mistaken. Thus, what did you mean, master, [when you said] that there are two worlds and that the rabbis declared that this world was created with [the letter] 'he' and the next world with [the letter] 'yud'? I thought that they meant by 'this world' the material world, and that created with [the letter] 'he' [i.e., five] meant four elements and the world soul. The next world created with [the letter] 'yud' [i.e., ten] meant namely the ten spheres. There is nothing outside of them [the ten spheres] except the Place [God], blessed be He. He is the 'place of the world' which contains it [the world] and He transcends the boundary of 'place' since He is not a circumscribed matter.

[1]Cf. Hosea 7:4.
[2]B. T. Sukkah 32b.
[3]Mishnah Eduyyot 2:10.
[4]Cf. Genesis 7:11; 8:14.
[5]This assumes a little more than a month for each of the ten plagues.
[6]The rabbinical interpretation of Job 7:3.
[7]Cf. Ezekiel 38.
[8]Cf. Proverbs 22:18.
[9]Yagel discusses angels in greater detail in his other writings, especially in his *Beit Ya'ar ha-Levanon,* pt. 2, chaps. 13 and 14. On Yagel's strong interest and commitment to magical activity as an extension of his medical activity and Jewish identity, see Ruderman, *Kabbalah, Magic, and Science,* chap. 7; on his interest in demons, see chap. 3.

"On this subject, the rabbis warned, in chapter *Ein Dorshin:*[1] 'Anyone who looks at four things does not deserve to come into the world: What is above and what is below, etc.,' since this quest reaches God and no [human] intelligence or idea can reach His perfection. Therefore, please inform me, my master, about this subject, whether it is as I conceived [it] or if you conceive of it differently. Give me understanding that I might live."[2]

[98] My father answered: "Everything you said is based upon the root and foundation of the words of the philosophers who hold that the cause of the first sphere is God. Perhaps Maimonides, Gersonides, and other philosophizers among our people are also inclined to this position since they drank like water the words of the Greek [Aristotle] in his investigation. He maintained that there is only one world, and that above the first sphere there is nothing but its causal agent, which is the blessed Creator. One who believes this view is close to falling into the pit of believing in the eternity of the world about which the Greek presented his proofs.[3]

"However, regarding what you said [about the view] that human souls only ascend to heaven and find enjoyment among the separate intelligences of the spheres, this is the opinion of the scholarly advisors of the wicked Pharaoh, the Egyptians, and the ancient astronomers.[4] The philosophers did not maintain that their souls reached heaven; rather [they reached] only to the sphere of the moon. Through their philosophizing, their souls would cling to the Active Intellect, which is the tenth level of the separate intelligences, from top to bottom. In their terminology, the latter is called 'the world soul.' According to Maimonides, in the second chapter of *Hilkhot Yesodei ha-Torah,*[5] it is called 'persona' [*ishim*], whose ascent is that of human intelligence. From there the souls of exceptional human beings ascend further, according to their view. Averroës, the philosopher, hoped for this ascent all his life, until he realized on the day of his death that his hope was unfulfilled and he complained about the matter.

"However, know and believe especially that their rock [their origin] is unlike ours. All of the schools of these wise men and philosophers speak in vain because they walk in darkness. The splendor of the Torah and the

---

[1]B. T. Ḥagigah 11b.

[2]Cf. Psalm 119:144.

[3]Gersonides especially was accused of believing in the eternity of matter, among other issues, and was attacked in Italy in the previous century by Isaac Abravanel, Judah Messer Leon, and David Messer Leon. For references, see Ruderman, *The World of a Renaissance Jew,* pp. 112–13.

[4]Note how their position agrees with that of the kabbalah and ultimately is acceptable to Yagel.

[5]Maimonides, *Mishneh Torah,* Hilkhot Yesodei ha-Torah, 2:7.

kabbalah, which faithfully teaches the reality of God's angels in addition to the casual agents of the spheres, if they have an agent, did not illuminate them. [The Torah also teaches] that the first agent is not God, blessed be He. Rather, it was called 'youth' or 'officer of the world.' Beyond it [the first agent], there are infinite legions of God, multitudes of angelic hosts, thousands upon thousands;[1] the kings and their armies are in headlong flight.[2] All of them are on ten levels, one above the other, until they reach the ten holy *sefirot,* with the secret of the four worlds, that is [the worlds of] emanation, creation, formation, and production, which no human has ever seen, O God, but You.[3] Thus shut your mouth from speaking and your mind from pondering. If your mind runs, return to the place about which it is said: 'And the living creatures ran and returned.'[4] For this reason, the covenant was made.

[99] "Furthermore, you should know that all the works of the heaven and earth from the peak of the first sphere until the center of the earth, are called 'this world,' since it is in front of us and each person can point it out to his neighbor with his finger. It is also called 'this world' to indicate that just as this reality in front of you is formed out of the clay[5] of these elements, so, too, all the heavenly matter is formed out of clay, except that the [heavenly] clay is purer and cleaner than that of the elements and has no relation or resemblance to them. Therefore the Greek [Aristotle] called it the *quinta essentia.* What is beyond the first sphere is 'the next world,' which contains no matter at all. There the souls of the righteous rest, one above the other, according to the superiority of their actions [on earth].

[100] "Then why did the rabbis declare that this world was created with [the letter] 'he' while the next world was created with [the letter] 'yud' alone?[6] This subject contains a secret known to the kabbalistic sages and

---

[1]Cf. Psalm 68:18.

[2]Cf. Psalm 68:13; *Shir ha-Shirim Rabbah,* 8:11.

[3]Cf. Isaiah 64:3. On the kabbalistic doctrine of the four worlds, essentially the three worlds of medieval philosophy—angelic, heavenly, and sublunar—with the addition of the world of the Godhead, see G. Scholem's summary in *EJ* 16: 641–43. Yagel often interchanged this concept with that of the three worlds which he employed in his medical and naturalistic writings.

This entire discussion is a good example of how Yagel aligned kabbalistic wisdom with an essentially anti-Aristotelian position regarding the cosmos. For a more extended discussion of Yagel's utilization of rabbinic and kabbalistic ideas to buttress his more empirical and anti-Aristotelian approaches to the natural world, see Ruderman, *Kabbalah, Magic, and Science.*

[4]Ezekiel 1:14.

[5]Cf. Job 33:6.

[6]Cf. B. T. Menaḥot 29b; *Bereshit Rabbah,* 12:10.

this is not the place to recall it.[1] We only can say that just as the [letter] 'yud' is five times as much as the [letter] 'he'[2] so the next world is five times more than this world. Moreover, the [letter] 'yud' is like a point which is indivisible; anything indivisible contains no matter at all. This world is created by [the letter] 'he,' that is, those five substances which include the four elements and the *quinta essentia,* out of which the heavens and the spheres are made. This is enough information for you now about these matters which are the mysteries of the world.[3] Their investigation is longer than the measure of the earth,[4] and if not for the true kabbalah, no [human] intelligence or idea would be sufficient to examine them, for how can the blind evaluate lights?

"But now I will send you forth, for the sun rises and my time has arrived to sing my song. If, on another occasion, when I will come to you and bless you, you shall desire to roam with me, let me hold forth my opinion[5] to you and your friends regarding these matters. However, I will first introduce you to matters appropriate as an introduction in order for you to understand them.[6] Everything I will show you is engraved on the tablets in gold and fine gold,[7] in the words of our splendid sages for whom no mystery baffles.[8] You should go to your place but remember that as long as time pursues you [i.e., as long as you live], your iniquities will divert you toward evil,[9] [and cause] the depravity of your heart and the lessening of your intelligence. If you return to God with all your heart, He will rejoice over you for good[10] and will transform the curse to a blessing. He will prosper your end over your beginning so you will do the straight and good [thing] before Him; for those who trust in Him will inherit the earth and possess His holy mountain.[11]

"Therefore, remember well what the rabbis explained in *Midrash Shir*

[1]Cf., for example, *Sefer ha-Zohar,* 3:215b, 298a.

[2]As Mani indicates, p. 46a, Yagel appears mistaken here since "yud" is two times "he," not five times. For the term *yaddot* used here, cf. Genesis 43:34.

[3]Cf. B. T. Ḥagigah 13a.

[4]Cf. Job 11:9.

[5]Cf. Job 36:2.

[6]This is an apparent hint to the reader that Yagel expects to describe another heavenly journey (in the second half of his book) in order to expand upon the theological issues raised during the first journey.

[7]Cf. Psalm 19:11; 119:127.

[8]Cf. Daniel 4:6.

[9]Cf. Jeremiah 5:25.

[10]Cf. Isaiah 62:5.

[11]Cf. Isaiah 57:13.

*ha-Shirim* regarding the biblical verse: 'Your name is like the finest oil':[1] 'Just as this oil is bitter in the beginning but sweet in the end, so your beginning will be in pain, but in the end, you will greatly prosper. Just as the oil is not made fine without crushing, so too Israel will not repent without suffering, etc.' With these words, the rabbis taught that suffering is the cause of man's attaining perfection since his nature requires crushing; the dough is poor since the leaven in it prevents its perfection. Therefore, we find in many places in the writings of the rabbis how they praise suffering, which is like rain on cut grass,[2] and the means for man to return to his God. Therefore, suffering should be dear to you;[3] so pray to the One who gives it to you. It will transform your darkness into light. Thus don't despise it [suffering] but tolerate it as an atonement for your sins. You should pour forth your plea before the Lord and supplicate before the Almighty.[4] You will find [Him] only if you seek Him with all your heart and with all your soul."[5]

But some time later, a wind swept me away.[6] I heard the sound of the rooster and I woke up. I was [lying] on my bed in prison at the place I had gone to lie down in the beginning of the night. Although I meditated on [various] things, I am still uncertain[7] whether most of it came to me in a dream or whether it was a vision, as I initially beheld. I stood on the lookout in the morning. If only I could return to see him [my father] again on the next evening!

[1]Cf. Song of Songs 1:3; *Shir ha-Shirim Rabbah,* 1:2.
[2]Cf. Psalm 72:6.
[3]Cf. B. T. Babba Meziah 85a and elsewhere.
[4]Cf. Psalm 102:1, Job 8:5.
[5]Cf. Deuteronomy 4:29.
[6]Cf. Ezekiel 3:12 and elsewhere.
[7]For the expression, cf. B. T. Shabbat 113a, Kiddushin 65a, and elsewhere.

# 3. *A Valley of Vision*, Part II: The Second Night

When I was in the prison compound,[1] I was accustomed to read from the Book of Psalms during the watches of the night.[2] On one night, when I reached the psalm [which begins]: "A song of ascents. In my distress [I called] to the Lord, etc.,"[3] my eyes flowed with tears[4] since I realized that the words of this psalm alluded to me. I was like a docile sheep led to the slaughter.[5] I did not realize the deceit that they had cast around my legs nor the plots they had fashioned against me. [They had proclaimed:] "Let us destroy the tree with its fruit; let us cut him off from the land of the living."[6] I prayed to God[7] with this exalted psalm, magnifying my voice by weeping, wailing, and lament. [I cried]: ["O Lord,] save me from treacherous lips. How can you profit from deceit, [you] scoundrel? What can you gain, O deceitful and unjust tongue?[8] You have whetted your tongue like a sword[9] and you have enticed me like the original serpent so that I was seduced by your words."[10]

[1] How sweet are the words of R. Yohanan in the third chapter of *Arakhin* [commenting on Psalm 120:3]:[11] "The Holy One, blessed be He, said to the tongue: 'All members of the human body are standing while you are lying. All members of the human body are outside while you are inside. Not only that, but I surrounded you with two walls, one of bone and one of flesh. So "what can you profit, what can you gain, O deceitful tongue, etc.?"'" [I would continue to interpret the psalm:] "A warrior's sharp

---

[1]Cf. Jeremiah 32:2.

[2]Cf. Psalm 90:14. The day and night were each divided into four watches. Cf. B. T. Berakhot 3a.

[3]Psalm 120.

[4]Cf. Mishnah Sotah 7:8.

[5]Cf. Jeremiah 11:19.

[6]Cf. Jeremiah 11:19. The phrase "the deceit . . . legs" is added by Yagel.

[7]Cf. Daniel 9:4.

[8]This is all adapted from Psalm 120:2–3. The word "scoundrel" (cf. 2 Samuel 20:1) obviously refers to Yagel's enemy, Eliezer Almagiati.

[9]Cf. Psalm 64:4.

[10]Adapted from Jeremiah 20:7.

[11]B. T. Arakhin 15b.

arrows,"[1] [that is], your [Eliezer Almagiati's] mouth, utters deceit and injustice like sharp arrows that emerge stealthily from the quiver of a mighty warrior [and] which murder at a distance anyone who is not careful of them. "With hot coals of broom-wood,"[2] [that is, they] appear externally as dust and ashes as they burn internally. In a similar fashion, you are the man [who is] a viperous serpent who cannot be charmed.[3] You speak to me with gestures of peace, while in your heart you set up an ambush to capture my soul like a bird wandering on my roof.

"Woe to me, that I live with Meshech"[4] and Tubal,[5] that fierce, impetuous nation,[6] [and] "that I dwell among the clans of Kedar,"[7] the Ishmaelites, Moab, and the Hagrites,[8] rather than [living with] the children of Israel, who are merciful people, the children of merciful people! "Too long have I dwelt"[9] with the evil and cruelty that he [Almagiati] has proclaimed while sickness and wounds are before me constantly.[10] This is the man "who hates peace."[11] From the day that I first saw him, "I was for peace, but when I spoke, they were for war."[12]

That man [Almagiati] spoke abundantly of easily healing my wound, claiming: "peace, peace, when there is no peace."[13] [2] As the verse states: "There is no peace, saith the Lord, for the wicked,"[14] that is, don't believe in the words of the wicked even when they utter: "peace, peace," since there is no integrity in their words and they have no peace. While they appear to you with a smiling face, their thoughts are like a sharpened razor that works treacherously[15] and unjustly. It is like the popular expression "While the joke in the mouth is ready, the razor below is prepared."

## The Appearance of Yagel's Father in the Company of Three Women

But while I was still alone, speaking these thoughts to myself, and while I was so distressed, murmuring, wailing, and mourning, as tears descended

[1]Psalm 120:4.
[2]Psalm 120:4.
[3]Cf. Jeremiah 8:17.
[4]Psalm 120:5.
[5]Cf. Ezekiel 32:2.
[6]Cf. Habbakuk 1:6.
[7]Psalm 120:5.
[8]Cf. Psalm 83:7.
[9]Psalm 120:6.
[10]Adapted from Jeremiah 6:7.
[11]Psalm 120:6.
[12]Psalm 120:7.
[13]Cf. Jeremiah 6:14.
[14]Cf. Isaiah 48:22.
[15]Cf. Psalm 52:4.

from my eyes in a running stream, I fell asleep and beheld [a vision] in a dream of three women coming toward me in the company of my father.

[3] The image of the first woman was that of a very distinguished noblewoman whose face was precious and whose eyes glowed and shined beyond human estimation.[1] But their [the eyes'] pride was trouble and sorrow.[2] The person who looked, gazed, and reflected on them was caught in the net of her love because they were so exceedingly beautiful. Indeed, certain poisonous sparks emerged and were diffused from them [the eyes] [so that] the affection of her eyes influenced the heart[3] of anyone who gazed on them and they cast gall [on him]. This woman was so old that her body was unlike that of any other person living on the face of the earth. She also was dangerous, changing, like clay under the sea,[4] into several forms before my eyes. Sometimes she appeared as large as giants who seize the globe of the sun,[5] and sometimes as small as those people who live in the land of the graveyard, as the rabbis mentioned in *Midrash Rabbah*.[6] Her clothing was spun with her own hands,[7] from fine threads which do not come apart [and] which she wove by herself, according to what I heard afterward. At the extremity of her garment was a seal with the letter "tav" engraved on the right and on the left. However, both the front and the back ends of the same garment were ripped by those treacherous men who had requested to sleep with her unnaturally in order to rape her. She carried books in her right hand and a kind of scepter overlaid with impure gold in her left.

The second woman was also comely and attractive, dressed in azure-colored clothing. On her garment were sparks of light like stars. In her right hand was a small ladder with seven steps. Each step was covered with letters and flowers that I initially could not comprehend [the reason for their being there]. Her image was overlaid on the top of the seventh step with a crown of olives on her head and a scepter of sapphire in her hand. This was how the ladder in her right hand appeared. In her left hand was a form of a

---

[1]This woman is none other than Boethius's Lady Philosophy, as described in his *Consolation of Philosophy* (Loeb edition [Cambridge, Mass., 1918] pp. 131–33), a work of great significance to Yagel, as I have described earlier. Yagel's portrait of this woman, as well as of the other two, was probably based in part on the iconographic representations of philosophy, astrology, and theology in Cesare Ripa's well-known *Iconologia* and other similar handbooks of emblems of the sixteenth and seventeenth centuries. Cf. Ripa, *Iconologia* (Padua, 1625), pp. 234–45. See the introduction above.

[2]Cf. Psalm 90:10.

[3]The expression is based on B. T. Avodah Zarah 28b.

[4]Cf. Job 38:14.

[5]Cf. *Bereshit Rabbah,* 26:7.

[6]*Bereshit Rabbah,* 37:8.

[7]Cf. Exodus 35:25.

globe, rotating by itself without beginning or end. In fact, from the middle of the circle, very fine lines emerged, forming one center; some turned to the right and some to the left. But some of the lines appeared to stray from their places and shifted to another location.[1]

The image of the third woman was that of an angel of God in light of the beauty and splendor which radiated from her. She was large since her head reached the heaven and even burst through it [i.e., her head was higher than the heavens]. Under her feet was the likeness of a pavement of sapphire, like the very sky.[2] The clothes that she wore were so white that when someone tries to gaze at them, he is unable to see, like the person who is unable to stare directly at the sun. A large gold crown was on her head and all the precious stones and pearls in the world were set in it. From the crown emerged a kind of frontlet[3] on her forehead, upon which was engraved four letters of [God's] name in Chaldean writing. In her right hand was a scepter of pure gold from the kind of gold called *parvaim*,[4] which is red like the blood of a cow and which also bears fruit.[5] This staff likewise yielded petals and buds[6] whose beauty had never been seen before and whose scent is like the scent of the field which God blessed.[7] In her left hand was a cup full of gold pieces. The more one took from the cup, [the more] it was never emptied. There was also a kind of large horn filled with flowers, roses, citrons, and pomegranates near the cup. In like manner, the more one took from the varieties of these delicacies and from the roses and flowers, [the more] the horn remained full. Indeed, it was like an overflowing fountain whose power never ceases.[8]

When I saw this great sight, I was stricken and became ill[9] and would not allow myself to gaze at these women. I stood on my guard in order to ascertain where they were going. In the meantime, my father approached me and asked: "How can you be sleeping so soundly[10] in a torpor greater than sleep? Arise [and] approach these women. Surely they will teach you and inform you, speaking out of their understanding."[11]

---

[1]The portraits of astronomy or astrology in Ripa, pp. 54–55, bear some resemblance to this description but are not identical.
[2]Cf. Exodus 24:10.
[3]Cf. Exodus 28:36.
[4]Cf. 2 Chronicles 3:6.
[5]The root of the word *parvaim* is supposedly related to *parah* (cow) and *perot* (fruit).
[6]Cf. Exodus 25:33, 37.
[7]Cf. Genesis 27:27.
[8]Cf. Avot 6:1.
[9]Cf. Daniel 8:27.
[10]Cf. Jonah 1:6.
[11]Cf. Job 8:10.

I answered my father: "I am a young boy, despised and forsaken by men.[1] How can I speak before them [either] briefly or at length lest I appear as a deceiver to them?[2] I also am distraught[3] and remain in dread of all my suffering.[4] May you teach me what I cannot see and let a vigorous spirit sustain me."[5]

My father responded: "How long will you speak these things[6] and not forget about your complaint[7] and your misery? Please gird your loins like a man and come with us and let us go out to the field[8] in the company of these noblewomen, as is our custom. They have strength and understanding[9] to fathom what God does in heaven and on earth, and nothing they propose is impossible to them.[10] If they reprove you with an open rebuke,[11] [you should know] that even a fool who keeps silent is deemed wise.[12] Just as there is hope for a tree, that if it is cut down, it will renew itself,[13] so it is for a person who keeps silent and listens and drinks with thirst the words of the wise[14] and their secrets. At the scent of water it [the tree] will bud and produce branches like a sapling."[15]

I answered: "How would you help someone who is without strength; how would you counsel someone without wisdom; [and] how would you save the arm that has no power?[16] The rope for him lies hidden in the darkened earth[17] where the sun and the stars never shine. There[18] the lilith reposes [and] the owl and ostriches find rest.[19] I have followed in His [God's] tracks.[20] I have followed their ways and paths and I have not strayed to the right or to the left. Today my complaint is again bitter; my hand is heavy on account of my groaning[21] and my misery. But you, my

[1]Cf. Isaiah 53:3.
[2]Cf. Genesis 27:12.
[3]Cf. Job 9:21.
[4]Cf. Job 9:28.
[5]Cf. Job 34:32; Psalm 51:14.
[6]Cf. Job 8:9.
[7]Cf. Psalm 142:3.
[8]Cf. 1 Samuel 20:11; Song of Songs 7:12.
[9]Cf. Job 12:16.
[10]Cf. Job 42:2. Instead of *yebazer*, Yagel has *ya'azor*.
[11]Cf. Proverbs 27:5.
[12]Cf. Proverbs 17:28.
[13]Cf. Job 14:7.
[14]Cf. Avot 1:4.
[15]Cf. Job 14:9.
[16]Cf. Job 26:2–3.
[17]Based on Job 18:10.
[18]The manuscript reads "however," which I have amended to "there."
[19]Based on Isaiah 34:14, 11, 13.
[20]Cf. Job 23:11.
[21]Cf. Job 23:2.

master, have known what has happened to me. You would sink appallingly[1] to save me and to remove my sackcloth from upon me, to steady[2] my feet in stocks[3] so that they would not slip. Therefore, why should I be afraid of your presence[4] and from this great vision? I will think good [thoughts] about the fine appearance of the women and their garments [and] I will reflect on their fate.[5] [4] It is like what R. Abba bar Kahana said in *Bamidbar (Sinai) Rabbah:* '[on the verse] "A heart that has backslided [i.e., an unprincipled man] is satisfied by the fruit of its [his] ways."[6] That same heart, filled with impurities from its ways [behavior], is bound to satisfy itself.' So now I am ready to approach these noble women. I will act according to your command and I will not lose heart,[7] for you will be a tower of strength to me and a provider of [my] sustenance."

Thus I arose as I had done on the first night and went with my father to the field where these serene and successful ladies were sitting. I bowed down from afar before approaching them. I then asked my father about these women and he replied: "Know that one father bore them all, although [only] the third is from his own wife while the other two [were born] from his concubine. Furthermore, the two will sometimes continue to offend[8] the important daughter of the wife, but, in the end, both of them will bend the knee and bow down before her. They will be frightened and silenced by her words since the words of the third woman are like fine flour sifted in thirteen sieves. All flours are flour, but the flour of Kimḥit [like the words of the third woman] is fine flour,[9] like invaluable pearls."

## The First Woman's Speech

[5] We came closer and the first woman spoke: "Who gave man a mouth and who permitted him to preach flawed homilies as you do this day, interpreting the Psalms and the words of the prophets to apply to your suffering and

---

[1]Cf. Lamentations 1:9.
[2]Cf. Psalm 40:3.
[3]Cf. Job 13:27; 33:11.
[4]Cf. Job 23:15.
[5]Cf. Psalm 73:17.
[6]Cf. *Bamidbar Rabbah,* 14:2, on Proverbs 14:14.
[7]Cf. Isaiah 7:4 and elsewhere.
[8]Cf. Isaiah 1:5.
[9]Cf. J. T. Yoma, 1 (38d). Kimḥit was the modest mother of seven sons who each became high priests in succession.

pain? Aren't these the words of the living God which refer to higher concepts that are revealed in allusions? It is like what the divine sage, the beloved member of my sister's household, said:[1] [6] 'Woe to the person who regards the Torah as [a book] of mere tales and ordinary matters! If this were so, we might even write a Torah today dealing in such matters, etc.' [7] Another great man stated in chapter *Ḥelek:*[2] 'Whenever anyone intones a verse of the *Song of Songs* as an [ordinary] song, the Torah dons sackcloth [in mourning].'

"Thus you have acted foolishly[3] in doing two evil things: first, what I already have said to you, [8] and second, that you should not have become excited. A person should not cry nor mourn about anything that happens to him, as women and children do and like any light-headed person [does even more] than the two [i.e., women and children]. Similarly, [one should not] compose poems about his miseries or recite a poem set to music which arouses sighing. These [methods] not only fail to comfort; they [even] augment his sighs and all[4] his sorrow. He will then forsake his intelligence, since the light of his eyes will be darkened. The true light will depart for a place of darkness and the shadow of death to a land of thick darkness, as darkness itself.[5]

[9] "Perhaps for this reason our blessed sages forbade anyone from reading the Hagiographa on the Sabbath during the time [that they studied] in the house of study, as it is written in the chapter *Kol Kitve:*[6] 'For they are drawn to it [the books of the Hagiographa] and therefore refrain from going to the house of study,' as Rav states there. Samuel's opinion was to prohibit the common people from reading it even at times other than in the house of study because of the reason I stated to you. This is because the common folk understand the simple meaning of the verses and are attracted by the flowery language. If a person experiences a hardship or tragedy affecting his children or friends or something else, he might expound [the psalm] in a faulty manner for himself as if the poet only wrote this particular

---

[1]*Sefer ha-Zohar,* 3:152a. The entire passage is translated into Hebrew by I. Tishby, *Mishnat ha-Zohar* (Jerusalem, 1961), vol. 2, p. 402, and into English in G. Scholem, *On the Kabbalah and Its Symbolism* (New York, 1965), pp. 63–64. Note how Yagel makes the author of the *Sefer ha-Zohar,* assumed to be Simeon bar Yoḥai, into a relative of the third sister who, as we shall see, personifies the truths of the highest world.

[2]B. T. Sanhedrin 101a.

[3]Cf. Genesis 31:28.

[4]Literally, "the moist and dry alike." Cf. Deuteronomy 29:18.

[5]Cf. Job 10:21–22.

[6]B. T. Shabbat 116b.

psalm for this specific matter. Consequently, he might not direct his attention to understand intelligently what is actually hinted there.

[10] "Look and take note of how many common folk think in such a manner. [For example,] many consider Psalm 109: 'O God of my praise, do not keep silent,' to be instituted by King David so that a man may curse his brother or friend when a quarrel or argument arises between them. But God forbid that the annointed one of the God of Jacob [i.e., King David] would place a sword in the hand of human beings [in order for them] to murder and to curse, as the rabbi, the author [Isaac Arama] of the *Akedat Yizḥak,* wrote in gate six.[1]

[11] "Therefore, I shall give you counsel and God be with you![2] When anything happens to you, stand before God and know faithfully that God gives intelligence to men to be master over all their acts of choice. The person who guards his soul will distance himself from all harmful things. He who considers it unimportant to be master of his own spirit will fall into the trap and pit[3] in attributing, God forbid, the divine actions to vanity. This is like what Eliphaz said to Job: 'Or darkness, so you cannot see, a flood of water covers you,'[4] that is, since you will not see, why should He show the thick darkness which arises from the many clouds in the air of the heavenly firmament? Accordingly, you will not sense [the need] to escape for your life [and] then a flood of water will cover you, as the prophet stated: 'When the ram's horn is sounded in a town, do the people not take alarm?'[5]"

## The Second Woman's Speech

[12] The second woman responded: "My son, you should have taken instruction from the higher entities, the heavenly bodies, which are of such exalted material, although they are, nevertheless, subject to change either by movement or by variations of [their] aspect. This is well known in the case of the moon, which sometimes diminishes its light and sometimes augments its light and vitality the more it approaches or distances itself from the sun. When it is in opposition [to the sun], its circumference is all filled out. It then begins to diminish until [it reaches] the time of its

[1] Isaac Arama, *Akedat Yizḥak* (Pressburg, 1849), vol. 1, p. 54a.
[2] Cf. Exodus 18:19.
[3] Cf. Isaiah 24:17.
[4] Job 22:11.
[5] Amos 3:6.

meeting the sun. At that point, it has no light but immediately afterward, the light reappears. If this is the case for the higher entities, is it not more so for the lower [earthly] entities, for they must be subject to change, either for good or for bad?

"A student among the students of my older sister,[1] whose name was R. Simeon ben Pazzi alluded to this fact in chapter *Elu Terefot:*[2] [13] 'R. Simeon ben Pazzi pointed out a contradiction [in the biblical verse] which states: "God made the two great lights," and [immediately] the verse continues: "The great light to dominate the day and the lesser light to dominate the night."[3] The moon said before the Holy One, blessed be He: "Sovereign of the universe! Is it possible for two kings to wear one crown?" So the Holy One, blessed be He, said to her: "Go and diminish yourself!" She [the moon] spoke before Him: "Because I suggested that which is proper, must I diminish myself?" He [God] answered her: "[Go] and rule by day and by night." She replied: "What use is a lamp [i.e., the mere light of the moon] at midday [in broad daylight]?" He responded to her: "Israel will reckon the days and the years [of the calendar] by you." [She replied]: "But aren't the days also under her [the sun's jurisdiction], as it is written: 'They shall serve as signs, etc.?'[4]" He replied: "Go, the righteous will be named after you, [as we find] Jacob the small, Samuel the small, David the small." She would not be consoled, so the Holy One, blessed be He, said: "Bring an atonement for Me for making the moon smaller." '

"The basic meaning of this passage is to demonstrate that the moon is an example to the righteous, as He [God] said: 'The righteous will be named after you.' Just as the moon's movement is most rapid, so it is proper for the righteous to run to do the will of the Creator, as Judah b. Tema said in tractate *Avot:*[5] 'Be as fleet as the gazelle to do the will of your Father in heaven.' Thus in their fulfilling this judgment, they [the righteous] will run and not tire but will renew their strength as eagles, as it is written: 'For they who trust in the Lord will renew their strength.'[6]

"If, in their movements, they encounter any resistance which might darken their splendor a little, as it happens to the moon when it meets the sun, their stride will not be broken;[7] nor will the Holy One, blessed be He,

---

[1]The third sister, who is clearly linked again with the knowledge of the rabbis and the kabbalists.

[2]B. T. Ḥullin 60b.

[3]Genesis 1:16.

[4]Genesis 1:14.

[5]Avot 5:20.

[6]Isaiah 40:31.

[7]Cf. Proverbs 4:12.

leave them in that confusion, except for a short time, as our rabbis stated in *Bereshit Rabbah:*[1] [14] 'The Holy One, blessed be He, does not allow the righteous to suffer for more than three days, as it is written: "In two days He will make us whole again; on the third day He will raise us up."[2]' This is analogous to the fact that there is only a momentary diminution of light from the time of the meeting [of the moon with the sun] to the [time] when [the moon] begins to receive light [again]. This is why He [God] said to her [the moon]: 'Go and diminish yourself,' that is to say, don't feel that since the time of mischance[3] is increased, that God will cause this nadir to diminish your flesh and body. Although the righteous are diminished in this world (which is the dominion of the sun) more than the other nations, they do rule during the day and the night in this world and the next, [something] which He [God] doesn't do for any [other] nation. Just as no man is worthy of two tables,[4] so the sun never functions at night like the moon, which functions [both] in the day and at night, as it is written: 'to dominate the day and the night.'[5]

"She [the moon] said to Him: 'What use is a lamp at midday?,' that is, of what value is the little the righteous enjoy in this world since their nature is unknown because of the great light of the wicked that darkens their splendor? The great light darkens the small one, so what use is a lamp at midday?

"Thus He responded to her: 'What value does a person gain from the delights of this world and its vanities? What does the success of its [i.e., wealth's] owners amount to, who eat their fill and clothe themselves elegantly, other than feasting their eyes?[6] It is natural that anyone who flees from power, power flees from him,[7] just as the more the moon pursues the sun, the more it darkens its light. [On the other hand,] when it distances itself from it [the sun], which is after the new moon, its light increases. This then is a metaphor for the person dismissed from power; power [still] pursues him. In like manner, the more people seek to enjoy the delicacies of kings, [the more they are bound] to count their days and years in the dwelling of the sun, that is, as the lights do [i.e., the moon's light is diminished by the sun]. Even [for those who are willing] to count [their

---

[1] *Bereshit Rabbah,* 91:7.
[2] Hosea 6:2.
[3] Cf. Ecclesiastes 9:11, a euphemism for death.
[4] That is, to have more than one reward. Cf. B. T. Berakhot 5b and elsewhere.
[5] Genesis 1:18.
[6] Based on Ecclesiastes 5:10; Isaiah 23:18.
[7] Cf. *Tanḥuma,* Vayikra, 3 (Buber ed., 4).

days] as those who are called by the name of Israel do, who are satisfied with what is essential [to them], their perfection is [still] diminished and the candles darken for a long time.'

"Afterward, He [God] said to her [the moon]: 'The righteous will be named after you,' that is, you will be an example to the righteous who will look to you and to your light. Just as the more you approach the sun, your light is diminished, so in the case of the righteous; as long as they seek to dwell in security, their perfection is diminished, as we said. [15] Therefore, this is a general sign to all the inhabitants of the world; the light of their intelligence should not be darkened by the devices of excessive wealth and its accessories. Moreover, it is a general divine good that God placed [the moon and sun] to serve as signs in the heavenly firmament to inform humanity and to receive moral instruction [from them]. They should not sink in the mire of money and in the dust of greatness and the vanities of the world.

"Afterward, 'she would not be consoled,' that is, even though the truth is thus the essence,[1] nevertheless, the flesh is still between their teeth and they are also nipped of clay.[2] As that wise man said: 'It is poor dough [the baker pronounces sour].'[3] The Holy One, blessed be He, said to her [the moon]: 'Bring an atonement for Me,' that is, before Me, 'because I made the moon smaller and this is what R. Simeon ben Lakish said, etc.'[4] The meaning is that you should not be concerned, beloved of God,[5] by the trials you will receive in loving Me in this world;[6] they are an atonement before Me for the entire generation that protects it. Thus the rabbis stated: 'We learn that the death of the righteous is atonement for the entire generation.'[7] The Holy One, blessed be He, remembers them monthly with the [sacrificial] goat of the new month and is filled with compassion for the entire generation because of the grief of the righteous. He grants atonement for all their sins, as the great Rabbi Isaac Alfasi explained in the first chapter of tractate *Shevu'ot:*[8] 'The Holy One, blessed be He, said to her [the

[1]Or bone, in contrast to the following phrase, i.e., the flesh.

[2]The last two phrases are based on Numbers 11:33 and Job 33:6. The apparent meaning is that despite knowing the truth, the moon (and the righteous) still require the assurance of a more tangible reward.

[3]*Bereshit Rabbah,* 34:10, where Genesis 8:21 follows, emphasizing man's material, base nature.

[4]Cf. B. T. Ḥullin 60b.

[5]Cf. Deuteronomy 33:12.

[6]Cf. Proverbs 3:12; B. T. Berakhot 5a.

[7]Cf. B. T. Moed Katan 28a.

[8]Isaac Alfasi, *Sefer ha-Halakhot,* Shevu'ot (Lemberg, 1865), chap. 1, fol. 2b.

moon]: "Behold I bring you honor which will settle your mind since I diminished you. [The honor consists of] Israel sacrificing a goat sin-offering before Me each month to atone for their sins, etc."'

[16] "This is what the editors of the liturgy had in mind in establishing the [following] prayer: 'The beginning of each month You assigned to Your people as a time of atonement for all their generations. When they bring [free-will offerings] and goats for sin-offerings to atone for themselves, it will be a testimony to them all etc.'[1] In other words, He assigned the beginning of each month for the sake of His name in order that they [His people] would gather together in their houses of prayer and sanctuaries; for this is a favorable moment[2] and a time of atonement for all their generations. The goats for a sin-offering represent the atonement of which I spoke, hinted at by the goat of the beginning of the month, that is, the suffering of the righteous that I mentioned. May it be remembered as a sweet fragrance before Him who is blessed, as an incense offering, and may it atone for the sins of the generation. It will be a salvation for their souls from the hand of the hater, that is, Satan, and the evil inclination and the angel of death clinging to the heel to seduce and to incite. The merit of this goat of sin-offering will atone for everyone and save our souls from the hand of this hater.

[17] "The sage [Abraham] ibn Ezra wrote that the matter of the moon's accusation against the sun is based on the known fact that the light between two stars in half a sphere, which is 180 degrees, is [at the point of] opposition.[3] At that time, the accusation of that star [takes place]. Since no [other] star reduces its light due to the sun as the moon does, which is known by experience, the moon thus accuses the sun when she stands opposite her. It is a time of opposition for, immediately, it diminishes her light, etc.[4]

"Everything revolves around one issue and [is related] to the intention that I have stated, which is to pay attention to the reduction of the moon's light and its ways, as I have mentioned. From it [this subject] earthly beings will learn a lesson not to become excited, not to run after power, and to take heed that if the heavenly entities are subject to change and mutation in their

---

[1] From the liturgy of the *Mussaf* service for the new moon.

[2] Cf. Psalm 69:14.

[3] *Mabat nokhah.* For the meaning of the term, see J. Klatskin, *Ozar ha-Munahim ha-Pilosophi'm* (Berlin, 1928), vol. 2, p. 136.

[4] The passage is based on Abraham ibn Ezra, *Sefer ha-Ibbur* (Lyck, 1874), p. 5b. It was also quoted by Shem Tov ibn Shaprut in his *Pardes Rimmonim* (Jerusalem, 1968), pp. 47b–48a, which may have been Yagel's source.

movements, according to them, earthly beings will, by necessity, also be subject to change and mutation. Therefore, for what reason should a living person complain[1] about his life history and actions? Ibn Ezra also hinted at this fact in commenting on the rabbinic statement: 'Bring an atonement for Me for making the moon smaller, etc.,'[2] that is, God commanded [the sacrifice] of a goat as a sin-offering on His account because He is the first cause of the deficiency of the [moon's] light.[3] It is thus necessary that earthly beings likewise be subject to many changes and never remain in one stable position.

[18] "The rabbis also alluded in chapter *Ha-Shutafim*[4] that because of this fact, the wheel [i.e., sphere] always comes full circle. A person standing on [the top of] this circle will descend in a moment, while one who is sitting at the bottom of the descent will instantaneously grow as high as the sky, his head reaching the clouds.[5] You see it [the sphere][6] but afterward, like that man [standing on it], it descends even to the netherworld, while the first [man standing on the bottom] returns and rises. Thus [neither of them] will ever stand in one stable situation. Similarly all human affairs by necessity can never remain in a fixed situation. [19] King Solomon alluded to this in his Proverbs: 'Pride goes before ruin;[7] humility precedes honor,'[8] that is, prior to the ruin [brought about] by the descent, there is an ascent, which is pride, dwelling like a king among his troops at the top of the sphere.[9] Then immediately, the sphere turns and begins to descend, which is ruin. Similarly, prior to honor, that is, prior to rising, [a state] of humility and lowliness [is required for the person] sitting on the bottom of the circle.

"In order to illustrate this wonderful idea, [20] the ancient philosophers among the [other] nations drew a woman whom they called Fortuna, that is, heavenly providence.[10] They called Fortuna everything that the stars

[1]Cf. Lamentations 3:39.
[2]B. T. Ḥullin 60b; see above.
[3]Ibn Ezra, *Sefer ha-Ibbur*, p. 5b.
[4]Cf. B. T. Babba Batra 16b; Shabbat 151b.
[5]Cf. Job 20:6.
[6]Cf. Proverbs 23:5.
[7]Proverbs 16:18.
[8]Proverbs 15:33; 18:12.
[9]Cf. Job 29:25.
[10]Note how Jean Baudouin, the French translator and editor of Cesare Ripa's *Iconologie* (Paris, 1644; reprint, New York and London, 1976), part 2, p. 63, is more careful to distinguish fortune from divine providence than is Yagel (in speaking about Fortuna): "Mais après tout, il faut aduoüer, contre l'opinion de ces Payens, qui est suivie encore aujuord'huy du vulgaire ignorant, que la Divine Providence, comme nous l'enseigne S. Thomas, regle & gouverne elle seule toutes les choses du monde."

pour out and emanate on to the earthly bodies, according to the change in their [the stars'] movements and configurations, whether for good or bad. If the emanation one received was good, they would say that he is loved by Fortuna and vice versa. To allude to this idea, the ancients portrayed her in several forms in order to instill fear among the common folk. But [they always placed] a sphere in her hands to indicate: 'Look and take notice that the wheel always comes full circle.'[1] When that entire generation died, the common folk forgot that allusion and conceived instead that Fortuna was a separate divine essence who had the power in her hands to appear [as] evil or good. They would bow down and worship her, make sacrifices, and erect buildings and palaces in order to bring down [upon themselves] the good [heavenly forces] and not the evil. Moreover, the sage Macrobius wrote that the moon is called by the name Fortuna since this star is closer to us than all the others. The moon's movement is also felt more by earthly bodies than that of all the other stars. Thus they called her Fortuna, and the idol worshippers would sacrifice to her."[2]

The first woman then responded to the second one: "I surely should tell you, my sister, what the sages called [natural] philosophers opined about this Fortuna who you mentioned. They said that she was neither a spiritual entity nor an earthly one. The foolish people falsely claimed that she has legs; one who cuts them off will drink [i.e., incur] damage.[3] The first person to invent the name Fortuna wished to allude to chance occurrences, whether good or bad, which regularly happen to people and whose causes are hidden from them. They also call such incidents accidental and fortuitous [literally, based on fortune].

"For example, when a man digs a pit[4] or a well at the end of his field in order to find water from which human beings and animals can drink, and [he] accidently discovers a hidden object in his excavation, one attributes it to the activities of good fortune.[5] If he arises and walks about outside,

---

[1]Baudouin, 2, p. 63: "Il faut adjouster icy qu'au lieu de la Roüe, quelques-uns luy mettent en main un Globe celeste, par où il est demonstré que comme le Globe est dans un continuel mouvement, la Fortune de mesme n'a iamais de repos, mais changeant de face à toute heure, tantost elle abaisse les uns, tantost elle prend plaisir à eslever les autres." See also Ripa, *Iconologia* (Padua, 1625), pp. 256–57; Boethius, *Consolation*, trans. by R. Green, pp. 22–23.

[2]See Macrobius, *The Saturalia*, trans. by P. V. Davies (New York and London, 1969), chap. 19, p. 136.

[3]Cf. Proverbs 26:6.

[4]Cf. Exodus 21:33.

[5]Good fortune is one of the four categories discussed by Ripa under the general heading of "fortune." The three others are "bad fortune," "fortune of love," and "fortune of gold." See Baudouin, II, p. 62.

leaving this hole deserted, but an ox or donkey or man falls into it[1] in the darkness of midnight, one attributes it to the activities of bad fortune. In each case, the reason for the accident is hidden from the person responsible [for the action]; initially, he had not intended that these occurrences would happen. The man who had opened his hole had not intended to look for the treasure which he [subsequently] discovered. Afterward, in searching for water, he unexpectedly found the treasure without intending [to do so]. Of course, there exists a prior cause [to explain] the matter of the hidden treasure; without another person who had earlier hidden it, it would not have been discovered by this man. Nevertheless, he acquired it [the treasure] by accident and with good fortune, since he dug his well in the darkness in that very place where there are treasures concealed in darkness.[2] If this had happened near it [the treasure], either in front or in back, he would not have found it. Good luck and good fortune were his bounty since he dug in the right place. One should similarly understand bad fortune and bad luck."

The second woman responded to her [the first woman]: "Your remarks surely are correct, my sister, regarding the effects that are a consequence of her [Fortuna], but you haven't spoken correctly or plausibly regarding her essence. Therefore, accept the truth from whoever declares it, which is what I first told you. [Her essence] is the effluvia and the heavenly emanation and their domain over human beings; or, in the words of the sage Macrobius, the effluvia and control of the particular star, the moon, which is nearer to us than all the rest and is called Fortuna. [21] Know that Marcrobius did not disagree with the view of the person who claimed that Fortuna is the effluvia of all the stars [and not just that of the moon]. The scholars understand that the moon receives all the effluvia of the spheres, as the sage, the author of *The Secret Philosophy*, wrote in part 1, chapter 7.[3] [This is like] a cow who has birth pangs, gives birth, and empties herself afterward onto the earth and all its inhabitants. For this reason, many thought that its [the moon's] nature is that of the element of water because of all the higher waters, that is, that which the higher beings empty upon her. However, one should not think in such a way but should place [instead] the element earth in her domain.

[1]Also the language of Exodus 21:33, excluding the reference to a man.

[2]For the last phrase, cf. Isaiah 45:3.

[3]This is the sixteenth-century occultist Henry Cornelius Agrippa's important compendium of magic, *De occulta philosophia,* a work well known to Yagel and quoted extensively by him. See Ruderman, *Kabbalah, Magic, and Science,* especially chaps. 7 and 9. Yagel actually refers here to chap. 8 and not 7.

"Therefore, Macrobius, who considered Fortuna to be the moon, did not disagree with the first view [that she is the effluvia of all the stars], since the influence of all the heavenly hosts is within her domain, as I have said. The judicial astrologers, the masters of talismans, assigned her a special place among their images of their twelve houses [of the sky]. Actually, they did not place Fortuna's dominion over all human affairs but only over those that were hidden, namely, whether a person will be rich or poor, or from which profession he will become rich or impoverished. [This is so] since there is no profession which does not entail poverty or affluence according to the merit of that Fortuna or the good and bad influence on that person.[1]

"But let us return to our original intention, which was [to speak about] every human being who has the holy divine spirit within him[2] and whose soul and spirit has not sunk in the heart of the sea or in the vanity of vanities of this world. Anyone who involves himself in the latter is like a person who relies on a broken reed. If a whip[3] comes into his possession, he should protest against these things with it. [In any case,] anyone who endeavors [to accomplish anything] in this world, does so in vain.[4]

[22] "[It is like] the statement of the great man among the pupils of my [older] sister, an important man named R. Simeon bar Yoḥai, concerning the verse: "The people will roam about and gather it [the manna], grind it, etc.'[5] ['Roam about'] indicates the stupidity they committed which they allowed [to enter into them].[6] Also observe what the shield-bearers,[7] the sages of the Mishnah declared [23] at the end of tractate *Kiddushin*.[8] 'There is no craft that does not contain [the potentialities] of poverty and wealth . . . but all depends on one's merit.' Therefore R. Meir stated there: 'One should always teach his son a clean and easy craft and ask compassion[9] from Him to whom [all] wealth and property belong.'

[1] Yagel apparently attributed his own lack of success in the banking profession to his bad fortune, as he indicates throughout his work.

[2] Cf. Daniel 4:6.

[3] The manuscript appears to read *malgev* or the like, which is unintelligible. I have read *maglev*, whip or lash.

[4] The language of this passage is clearly imitative of the Aramaic of the *Sefer ha-Zohar*, but apparently the passage is not found in the latter work. My thanks to Professors Moshe Idel and Yehudah Liebes for examining the passage and for offering me their judgments about its origin.

[5] Numbers 11:8.

[6] Cf. *Sefer ha-Zohar*, 2:62b.

[7] Cf. B. T. Bekhorot 36a.

[8] Mishnah Kiddushin 4:14, which is also found in B. T. Kiddushin 82a.

[9] The wording in the standard text of the Mishnah is "pray."

"Isn't the lower world surely subject to [finite] existence and loss, to change, either total or partial, depending on the effluvia of the stars? Therefore, on what basis should a person who lives in a world that does not belong to him sigh or complain? Why should he labor to get rich when little will help [him] to enjoy his labors[1] without the outpouring of the stars? Indeed, he builds his house like a moth and it is like the gourd of Jonah which appeared overnight and perished overnight.[2] If you would only be attentive to the goings and comings of this world, you would not be astonished. 'Only that will happen which has [already] happened . . . for there is nothing new under the sun.'[3] Therefore, sigh in silence[4] and see the many heavens; behold the skies, which are higher than you, for they too are subject to change![5] When you shall understand this [lesson], you shall become another person.[6] So only raise your spirit in praise of the One who creates all of the hosts above and below and who discerns all their actions[7] and may His name be forever blessed."

### The Third Woman's Speech

The third woman then remarked: "I have often heard such things like your words; you [the first and second woman] are all mischievous comforters.[8] Although you spoke comfortingly to him so that he would not become agitated, cry, or mourn about every evil thing that happens to man, nevertheless, [your answer was offered] on the basis of your [limited] wisdom and actions. It was a [response] based on your belief that everything that happens to man occurs either because of darkness which you cannot see or understand, and therefore, a flood of waters covers you,[9] that is, misfortune; or because of the dominion of the stars which puts a person's feet in stocks[10] [and] casts a net over him, so that, like a bird wandering from its nest,[11] he falls there, destroyed.[12] However, I am [among] the faithful of

[1]Cf. Psalm 128:2.
[2]Cf. Jonah 4:10.
[3]Cf. Ecclesiastes 1:9.
[4]Cf. Ezekiel 24:17.
[5]Based on Job 35:5. Yagel incorrectly writes *zur* instead of *shur*.
[6]Cf. 1 Samuel 10:6.
[7]Cf. Psalm 33:15.
[8]Cf. Job 16:2.
[9]Adapted from Job 22:11.
[10]Cf. Job 13:27; 33:11.
[11]Cf. Proverbs 27:8.
[12]Cf. Judges 5:27.

Israel and [among] the entire holy people who [stand at] the feet of those people and their children who believe in divine providence over all human affairs from steers' horns to lice eggs.[1] [We believe] that no evil descends from heaven [24] unless there is a reason for it.[2] The agitation from below arouses the upper [world]. It is his [man's] iniquities that caused him [to suffer] and his sins that withheld the bounty from him.[3] He should cry, and mourn, and ask forgiveness for his iniquities. He should pray to his Maker to remove his sins from him, and he should repent and save himself.[4]

"Go out and learn about what is reported there [in the Bible] regarding Jacob, [who was] a mild man.[5] When he heard that his son had been attacked by a wild beast that had devoured him, 'all his sons and daughters sought to comfort him [25] but he refused to be comforted, etc.'[6] Because of the great fear of God [which shown] upon his face, he did not accept the condolences extended to him since he assumed that he [Joseph] had died because of his [Jacob's] sins.[7] If he had restrained himself [from feeling] his pain and had removed it [the pain] from his heart, it would have been necessary [according to Jewish law] to add a heavy punishment for this [act] in the same way one is punished for disobedience.[8] [The latter punishment] cannot be removed, unlike those who are punished but then recover [from their punishment]; rather [it remains] until one's soul departs. This is why the verse stated: 'But he refused to be comforted, saying, "No, I will go down mourning to my son in Sheol," '[9] that is, the reason for his refusal to be comforted was because he desired to go down mourning for his son, which is [to descend to] Sheol. He thus did not need to initiate for himself another [kind of] mourning before he died. This is not a complaint about [God's] injustice[10] [26] but a good and desirable intention; it represents the quality of saintliness and is important. One who does the opposite of this is like one who pays his bill [of debt] but does not rip it up.[11]

[1] Cf. B. T. Avodah Zarah 3b.

[2] Yagel had stated this belief earlier in Part I. See above, p. 142, and the accompanying note.

[3] Adapted from Jeremiah 5:25.

[4] Cf. Isaiah 6:10.

[5] Cf. Genesis 25:27.

[6] Genesis 37:35.

[7] Compare the rabbinic accounts of Jacob's grief summarized in L. Ginzberg, *The Legends of the Jews* (Philadelphia, 1969), II: 26–27.

[8] *Makkat mardut;* a punishment left to the discretion of the rabbinic court, in contradistinction to the biblical punishment *malkut.* Cf. Mishnah Nazir 4:3; B. T. Nazir 23a; Shabbat 40b; Ḥullin 141b and elsewhere.

[9] Genesis 38:35.

[10] Cf. J. T. Berakhot 5 (9c); Megillah 4 (75c) and elsewhere.

[11] Thus he remains in a state of indebtedness, like the person who still requires a heavy punishment.

"Job thus declared: 'If I say, "I will forget my complaint; put off my sad countenance, and be diverted," I remain in dread of all my suffering; I know that You will not acquit me.'[1] This is also similar to the interpretation of the author [Isaac Arama] of *Akedat Yizhak* on the Torah portion *Va-Yeshev*.[2] You will also find that this is the case for all saintly people and all men of action in every generation. When someone arose to harass them or [when] a tragedy befell them, they would mourn and cry about that punishment which they experienced so that God might show them pity and compassion again, rip up their bill of indebtedness, and save them from Sheol itself.

"This is similar to what happened to King David regarding the incident of Absalom, where it was stated: 'David meanwhile went up the slope of the [Mount of] Olives, weeping as he went; his head was covered and he walked barefoot, etc.'[3] There is no doubt that he did this so that this absolution for his son would be an atonement for that iniquity.[4] Thus he walked barefooted and covered his head, as he explained his intention to Abishai when the latter desired to remove the head of the man abusing [David]: 'If my son, my own issue [seeks to kill me, how much more the Benjaminite!]. Let him go on hurling abuse, for the Lord has told him to [do so]. Perhaps the Lord will look on my punishment [literally, eye] and recompense me, etc.'[5] The meaning [of this line] is the following: Let me [be subject to God's] strict justice, which will collect its bill of indebtedness [from me] because my iniquities caused [this to happen] to me. Perhaps the Lord will look upon my iniquities and [regard the fact] that I bore all my sins so that He will return goodness to me, as it was before the sin.

"Related to this [27] is his [David's] psalm [that was written] when he fled from his son Absalom: 'O Lord, my foes are so many!'[6] and so are my enemies who slander me. Once I was quiet in my house and tranquil in my castle. After the sin 'many say of my soul that there is no deliverance'[7] in the next world. It is similar to what the rabbis pointed out [in chapter] *Helek*:[8] 'Why is it written: "But when I stumble, they gleefully gather."[9] [28] David

[1]Job 9:27–28.
[2]Isaac Arama, *Akedat Yizhak* (Pressburg, 1849), vol. I, sha'ar 28, p. 224a, upon which the entire previous section is based.
[3]2 Samuel 15:30.
[4]By absolving his son, he would atone for his own previous sin regarding Bathsheba (2 Samuel 11–12).
[5]2 Samuel 16: 11–12, regarding David's abuser, Shimei, the son of Gera.
[6]Psalm 3:2.
[7]Psalm 3:3. Yagel adds the redundancy "regarding my soul" after "soul."
[8]B. T. Sanhedrin 107a.
[9]Psalm 35:15.

said before the Holy One, blessed be He: "Sovereign of the universe! You know full well that had they torn my flesh, my blood would not have flowed."[1] Furthermore, when they [his tormentors] are engaged in studying *Oholot* and *Nega'im*,[2] they interrupt their studies and say to me: "David, what is the death penalty for he who seduces a married woman [referring to Bathsheba]?" I reply to them: "He who commits adultery with a married woman [is executed] by strangulation but he has a portion in the next world. But one who publicly embarrasses his neighbor has no portion in the next world."'

"'But You, O Lord,'[3] have compassion for me and send my punishment in this world; for the punishment meted out to me is 'my glory and holds my head high'[4] in the next world since my iniquity departs from me. Moreover, [it also departs] naturally in this world as it is explained to the sages. [29] Boethius expands upon this in the fourth book of his *Consolation of Philosophy:*[5] 'A sinning person is more successful when he receives his punishment by death or by suffering on account of his iniquities than a person who is absolved by a court for all his sins.' It is similar to what the rabbis say about [the verse]: 'Your brother be degraded before your eyes.' Because he [a man] is degraded, he indeed is [like] your brother,[6] [whose status] is denied [only] by his sin. The poet [David] similarly wrote the verse: 'But You, O Lord, are a shield about me, etc.' and afterward [30] said: 'I will cry aloud to the Lord and He will answer me.'[7] The explanation is that I will have no fear[8] although I was accompanied by afflictions and exile. Because of my iniquity, God did not hear my prayer but, from now on, 'I will cry aloud to the Lord and He will answer me.'

"The past tense [can be used] in place of the future tense [here], for it is the style of the prophecies to use the future tense occasionally instead of the past and vice versa; for all the times—past, future, and present—are all equal before Him, may He be blessed. Therefore, all is foreseen, but freedom of choice is given[9] to a person to do as he chooses. So in this place [i.e., Psalm 3], it teaches the certainty that the Lord will answer him from

---

[1]That is, because of the shame to which he had been subjected, his face would still have remained white.

[2]"Tents" and "Leprosy-signs," two tractates of the order *Tohorot* of the Talmud. In the standard version of the Talmud, the line reads instead: "studying the four deaths inflicted by the [rabbinic] court."

[3]Yagel continues to interpret Psalm 3; this is from the fourth verse.

[4]Psalm 3:4.

[5]*Consolation of Philosophy*, IV, 4, p. 343 of the Loeb edition.

[6]Cf. B. T. Makkot 23a on Deuteronomy 25:3. For the same expression, see above, p. 153.

[7]Psalm 3:4–5.

[8]Psalm 3:7.

[9]Cf. Avot 3:16.

His holy mountain, selah,[1] and indeed it is as if He answered him. If he lay down[2] in his iniquity and God turned from him, he will now wake again[3] since he received the afflictions and the Lord will sustain him.[4] Accordingly, one who comes to purify himself is sustained.[5] 'I have no fear of the myriad forces arrayed against me'[6] which inform David that he has no place in the next world since he already was pardoned for that iniquity [and he can exclaim]: 'Behold I am as if I did not sin.' 'Rise, O Lord! Deliver me, O my God,'[7] from this sorrow and confusion in which I find myself. Dwell in me and show me Your habitation and Your honor. Restore to me the happiness of Your deliverance and sustain me with Your holy spirit.[8]

"Accordingly, with these afflictions that I received, You slapped all my enemies in the face[9] so that they no longer will move their tongue to declare that God left him [me]. The eyes of the wicked are their reward[10] for Ahithophel [David's counselor who joined Absalom's conspiracy], their courageous one, the crown on their head, [the one] who formerly stood at the head of the nations,[11] and [the one] who declared that he would pursue him [David],[12] died.[13] There is no deliverer for 'deliverance is the Lord's'[14] to bring afflictions. Rather a person [can only deliver himself] through his own goodness, by which he will save his soul and provide a place for it in the world in which all is well balanced [i.e., the next world].[15] We shall pass from the afflictions [to] this 'Your blessing upon Your people, selah'[16] in order to save their souls from the pit [to bask in] the light, the light of life.[17] See how King David was happy in his afflictions and offered a thanks offering and a prayer of thanks on their account.[18] If he cried and mourned

[1]Cf. Psalm 3:5.
[2]Cf. Psalm 3:6.
[3]Cf. Psalm 3:6.
[4]Cf. Psalm 3:6.
[5]A variation of the phrase: "If a man comes to purify himself, he is helped." Cf. B. T. Yoma 38b, Shabbat 104a and elsewhere.
[6]Psalm 3:7.
[7]Psalm 3:8.
[8]Cf. Psalm 51:14.
[9]Cf. Psalm 3:8.
[10]Cf. Job 11:20.
[11]Cf. Joshua 11:10.
[12]Cf. 2 Samuel 17:1.
[13]Cf. 2 Samuel 17:23.
[14]Psalm 3:9.
[15]Cf. B. T. Kiddushin 39b.
[16]Psalm 3:9. In the Hebrew original, the line is broken up into parts.
[17]Cf. Job 33:30.
[18]Perhaps Yagel meant David's prayer of thanks in 2 Samuel 22, which appears with some variations as Psalm 18.

and his head was covered,[1] he did this in order to diminish his flesh and blood so that it would go up as a pleasing odor before the Lord[2] like the fat of rams and sheep.[3] Thus he atoned for his sin and every God-fearing person who turns away from evil should do likewise.

[31] "For this reason, the rabbis instituted the rules of mourning, establishing seven days for the mourning [period], which correspond to the seven days of the world and its revolutions. By establishing seven days of mourning, all the boundaries of time would pass within them, constantly rotating for seven days and returning again and again. Thus 'they would serve as signs for the set times—the days and the years.'[4] A living person should take to heart[5] the secret of this number when he sits silently [in] thoughts of death. If there is iniquity within him, he should remove it; he should not let injustice and iniquity reside in his tent.[6]

[32] "By commanding that one should not mourn the dead excessively, the sages wished to avoid a complaint about [God's] injustice.[7] Furthermore, one should not cry and scream only because of the [dead] person's absence; then one's flesh will ache for no other reason [than this], as in the case of bewailing women. However, one should intend to break [i.e., to examine] his own heart because there is no death without sin.[8] Each person is obliged to give an account and reckoning of his actions, even regarding a light conversation between a man and his wife.[9] Therefore let him sit alone and be silent[10] for the seven days of mourning and he will reward himself for the thought and the silence.

[33] "To fix this teaching in our hearts the rabbis declared in *Bereshit Rabbah*, chapter 27:[11] 'R. Joshua b. Levi said: "The Holy One, blessed be He, mourned for his world for seven days prior [to the flood] so that the flood would not come to the world." What was the reason? [It is stated]: "And His heart was saddened,"[12] and there is no sadness other than mourning. And elsewhere it states: "The king was grieving over his son, etc."[13]'

[1]Cf. 2 Samuel 15:30.
[2]Cf. Exodus 29:25.
[3]Yagel obviously meant this strange statement in the figurative sense of purifying himself to make himself more acceptable to seek atonement before God.
[4]Cf. Genesis 1:14.
[5]Cf. Ecclesiastes 7:2.
[6]Adapted from Job 11:14.
[7]Cf. B. T. Moed Katan 27b; Maimonides, *Mishneh Torah*, Hilkhot Avel 13:11.
[8]Cf. B. T. Shabbat 55a.
[9]Cf. Avot 3:1; 1:5.
[10]Cf. Lamentations 3:28.
[11]*Bereshit Rabbah*, 27:4.
[12]Genesis 6:6.
[13]2 Samuel 19:3.

"Moreover, during the time of the destruction of the Temple, the rabbis were purported to state [34] in the first chapter of *Hagigah:*[1] '[The rabbis asked regarding the verse:] "But if you shall not hear it, my soul must weep in secret because of arrogance."[2] What is the meaning of "in secret"? R. Samuel b. Inia said in the name of Rab: "The Holy One, blessed be He, has a place where He cries and its name is 'secret.'" What is the meaning of "because of arrogance"? R. Samuel bar Isaac said: "Because of the glory that has been taken from them and given to the nations of the world." R. Samuel b. Nahmani said: "Because of the glory of the kingdom of heaven which ascends." But is there any weeping in the presence of the Holy One, blessed be He? For behold R. Papa said: "There is no grief in the presence of the Lord, as it is said: 'Strength and beauty are in His sanctuary.'[3]" There is no contradiction. The first case [refers to] the inner chambers [of the kingdom of heaven]; the other case [refers to] the outer chambers. Thus there is no grief in the outer chambers. Yet indeed, it is written: "My Lord God of hosts summoned on that day to weeping and lamenting, to tonsuring and girding with sackcloth."[4] But the destruction of the Temple [described in the previous verse] is different, for even the ministering angels wept [over it] as it is said: "Hark! The Arielites cry aloud; the angels of peace weep bitterly."[5]

"'"My eye shall drop tears, and tears, and run down with tears because the flock of the Lord is taken captive."[6] R. Eleazar said: "What is the significance of these three [expressions of] tears? One is for the First Temple; one is for the Second Temple; and one for [the children of] Israel who have become exiled from their place." But others say: "One for the neglect of [the study of] the Torah." It is acceptable to follow the explanation that [one] is for [the children of] Israel who have become exiled from their place [which agrees with] what is written: "because the flock of the Lord is taken captive." But how does one explain [the text]: "because the flock of the Lord is taken captive" in light of the explanation that it was for the neglect [of the study of] the Torah? Since [the children of] Israel have become exiled from their place, you can have no greater neglect [of the study of] the Torah than this!

[35] "'The rabbis taught: "The Holy One, blessed be He, cries about three things each day: over he who is able to study Torah but does not; over

[1]B. T. Hagigah 5b.
[2]Jeremiah 13:17.
[3]Psalm 96:6.
[4]Isaiah 22:12.
[5]Isaiah 33:7.
[6]The continuation of Jeremiah 13:17.

he who is unable to study Torah but does; and over a leader who domineers over the community for no reason." Rabbi was once holding the book of Lamentations and reading in it. When he reached the verse: "[He] has cast down from heaven to earth the majesty of Israel,"[1] his book fell from his hands. He said: "It fell from a roof so high to a pit so deep!"'

"Regarding the intent of all these passages, although they hint at exalted things [of the kabbalah] whereby the author meant to deny[2] the hardship and the [pernicious] influence of stern judgment [the *sefirah din*] on all the secret things known as the three first ones [the three highest *sefirot: keter, binah,* and *ḥokhmah*] called 'concealed acts to be hidden' (as R. Simeon bar Yoḥai interpreted regarding the verse: 'Concealed acts concern the Lord our God'[3] that refer to the three first ones [the three highest *sefirot*]; 'but with overt acts, it is for us,' refer to [the *sefirot*] *tiferet* and *malkhut*), nevertheless, they actually contain words of the sages which hint at [both] the overt and the hidden. The overt hints at what we have said, which is to teach us the path we should follow. This is stated [by the expression]: 'The Torah speaks in the language of men.'[4] However, since these passages came into our possession, we should say something about them, but [first] we should introduce some prefaces.

[36] "So let me inform you that the great rabbi to the Jews, R. Moses b. Maimon [Rambam] was a student in my household.[5] He was a very wonderful man of God in his generation. Although he maintained a view regarding the science of philosophy about which many pious Jews indicted him, while much dissension was engendered in the Jewish community by his book *Moreh Nevukhim,*[6] nevertheless, all of this was provoked by the destroyers of vineyards[7] [37] who misconstrued his intention and the rela-

---

[1]Lamentations 2:1.

[2]As in the London manuscript, fol. 83a.

[3]Deuteronomy 29:28. Cf. *Sefer Zohar,* 3:159a; 245a.

[4]B. T. Babba Meẓiah 31b; Yebamot 71a. For an important discussion of the phrase, see A. Funkenstein, *Theology and the Scientific Imagination from the Middle Ages to the Seventeenth Century* (Princeton, 1986), pp. 213–21.

[5]Note that both Maimonides, the embodiment of Jewish philosophical speculation, and Simeon bar Yoḥai, the embodiment of mystical speculation, are perceived by Yagel as "sitting within one household." On the importance of this view in Yagel's thinking, see Ruderman, *Kabbalah, Magic, and Science,* chap. 9; and as a fundamental characteristic of Italian kabbalah, see M. Idel, "Major Currents in Italian Kabbalah between 1550–1650," *Italia Judaica,* 2 (Rome, 1987): 243–62.

[6]On the Maimonidean controversy, see B. Septimus, *Hispanic-Jewish Culture in Transition* (Cambridge, Mass., 1982), especially p. 147, n. 1, which cites earlier works on the subject.

[7]Cf. Song of Songs 2:15. A phrase often associated with the Maimonidean controversy. Cf. Maimonides, *Mishneh Torah,* Hilkhot Talmud Torah, 5:4.

tion of his chapters one to another, which can be seen by anyone who examines this exalted work.

[38] "This man of God fulfilled what the rabbis said in the second chapter of *Megillah:* '[regarding the verse] "May God enlarge Japheth and let him dwell in the tents of Shem."[1] [This verse means] that the words of Japheth will be in the tents of Shem. But similarly, what about the tents of Gomer and Magog?[2] What is written [in that verse] is that the special beauty of Japheth was in the tents of Shem.' Moreover, they [rabbis] referred there to the subject of the sweet tongue of the children of Japheth, that is, the Greek tongue. [The rabbis] permitted books [i.e., the Bible] to be written in Greek according to the words of R. Simeon b. Gamaliel, whom the law follows.[3]

"You should just understand the simple meaning of this passage with respect to its [true] subject. It does not refer to the skilled tongue[4] or to the clarity of the Greek language [39] but rather to the words of the sages and their riddles spoken in Greek, whose extraordinary beauty is greater than all the children of Japheth; these sayings are appropriate 'to dwell in the tents of Shem.' In [all] truth, one initially must remove from them a stock sprouting poison weed and wormwood,[5] as the great man, the judge [Maimonides] did, who came to the prince, spread his wings over him, and like an eagle who rouses his nestlings, glided down to his young[6] and took pity upon them, carried them on his head, and subdued the will of the philosophers in favor of their own.[7] He interpreted in an appropriate and reconciliatory manner so that his allegorizers would be able to say: 'You are fairer than all men; your speech is endowed with grace.'[8] Therefore, God has given you an eternal blessing[9] because, for eternity, your words will remain and be written down for a coming generation that people yet to be created may praise the Lord.[10] His mercies have not ceased[11] to provide Israel a redeemer and a teacher so that the Torah will not be forgotten in Israel.

[1]Cf. Megillah 9b on Genesis 9:27.
[2]The descendents of Japheth mentioned in Genesis 10:2.
[3]Cf. B. T. Megillah 6b.
[4]Cf. Isaiah 50:4.
[5]Cf. Deuteronomy 29:17.
[6]Cf. Deuteronomy 32:11.
[7]Based on the language of Avot 2:4.
[8]Psalm 45:3.
[9]Psalm 45:3.
[10]Cf. Psalm 102:19.
[11]Cf. Lamentations 3:22.

246 A Valley of Vision

"All his [Maimonides'] words are like circlets of gold[1] and an invaluable pearl[2] because he loved righteousness, which was found in the words of the Greek philosophers, and hated evil. Moreover, all his words were spoken truthfully, modestly, and justly.[3] I have told you all this so that you will not be surprised if I bring his words to assist [me] and to be useful in explicating the aforementioned passages in an overt manner or in quoting other matters in his name, as is required. Don't be surprised again[4] that he is called Wisdom[5] and don't wonder at the fact,[6] for happy is the student who is instructed by his teacher and the Guardian of Israel [God] is higher than the highest one [teacher].[7]

"One should state a law in the name of the person who [first] stated it, as the rabbis declared [40] in the *Pesikta:*[8] 'When Moses ascended to heaven, he heard the voice of the Holy One, blessed be He, who sat engaged in the study of the Torah portion on the [red] heifer.[9] He [God] cited a law in the name of the one who [initially] had stated it, Eliezer [ben Hyrcanus], My son, who said: "The heifer must be [not more than] one year old and the red heifer [not more than] two years old, etc."[10]'

"But let us return to our original intention and declare [41] from the words of Maimonides, in the twenty-ninth chapter of the first part of the *Moreh* [*Nevukhim*]: 'Sorrow is an equivocal term denoting three things. First it denotes pain as [in the verse]: "In sorrow, you shall bring forth children."[11] Second, it [denotes] anger as in: "And his father had not caused him to be sorry at any time,"[12] which means that he had not angered him; or "he was sorrowful for the sake of David,"[13] [meaning] he was angry for his sake. Third, it denotes obedience, [as in]: "They rebelled and caused sorrow to His holy spirit,"[14] [or]: "If there be in me any way of

---

[1]Cf. Song of Songs 1:11.

[2]Cf. J. T. Pe'ah 1 (15d).

[3]Yagel's high praise of Maimonides was a commonplace in sixteenth-century Italy despite his fifteenth-century detractors, especially Hasdai Crescas and Isaac Abravanel. For a strong defense of Maimonides in the sixteenth century, see David b. Judah Messer Leon's *Ein ha-Kore*. This work is discussed against its sixteenth-century background in Hava Tirosh-Rothchild's forthcoming book on David b. Judah Messer Leon.

[4]Cf. Job 10:16.

[5]Based on Proverbs 8:1.

[6]Cf. Ecclesiastes 5:7.

[7]Cf. Ecclesiastes 5:7.

[8]*Pesikta Rabbati,* piska 14.

[9]Cf. Numbers 19.

[10]Mishnah Parah 1:1.

[11]Genesis 3:16.

[12]1 Kings 1:6, referring to Adonijah, son of Haggith, who wanted to be king.

[13]Cf. 1 Samuel 20:34, referring to Jonathan's concern at his father's wrath toward David.

[14]Psalm 139:24.

causing sorrow,"[1] [or]: "Every day they cause sorrow [i.e., disobey] to my words."[2] In accordance with the second or third sense, it is said: "His [God's] heart was saddened."[3] However, in accordance with the second sense, the interpretation of the verse would be that God was angry with them [Adam and Eve] because of their evil actions, etc.'

[42] "He [Maimonides] further states, in the thirty-sixth chapter of part one, that, without any doubt or dissension, we arrive at a true conclusion by not attributing any corporeality, any state of the states of the body, or the capability of performing [human actions] to the blessed and exalted Creator; nor [should we] ascribe to Him, God forbid, any deficiency. One who believes this, God forbid, is more blameworthy than an idol worshipper, as he [Maimonides] describes there at greater length. If one finds in the Pentateuch or the Prophets words that indicate corporeality, they are to make [these texts] intelligible [to the reader] according to his capacity to understand, as the rabbis declare: 'The Torah speaks in the language of human beings.'[4] [43] You will already find in [the Aramaic translations of the Bible of] Onkelos and Jonathan ben Uziel, that in every place where they customarily interpret words and verses, they avoid as best as they can [attributions to God of] corporeality, [His association] with [human] actions, and deficiency. When the simple essence and ability of the Infinite, blessed be He, is compared [to us], as written in the Torah: 'His ways are higher than our ways and His actions are higher than ours,'[5] there can be no definition nor attribution of His image to any creature, even to those who [lived] before me and you.[6] Any idea or concept proves insufficient in this respect, as the prophet declared: ' "To whom can you liken Me, to whom can I be compared?" says the Holy One, etc.'[7] However, with respect to His actions which are what they are, one can conceive that they have a beginning, an end, and a middle, and thus [people] attributed to Him what they attributed.

[44] "To bring the matter closer to your reasoning, [let us take] the example of the point. The engineers use it in a way in which it exists [only] in thought. It does not have any of the three dimensions: length, width, or breadth and it is indivisible. Thus Euclid, the chief of the geometers, wrote: 'The point is that which has no part.'[8] Nevertheless, when it is compared

[1] Isaiah 63:10.
[2] Psalm 56:6.
[3] Genesis 6:6.
[4] Cf. B. T. Yebamot 71a; B. T. Babba Meziah 31b and elsewhere.
[5] Cf. Isaiah 55:9.
[6] Cf. Jeremiah 28:8.
[7] Isaiah 40:25.
[8] Euclid, *Elements* (Chicago, 1952), bk. 1, definition 1.

with the figure we might draw on the board or in a book with ink, it would then materialize and actually display the three dimensions of length, width, and breadth; it also would be infinitely divisible, like any corporeal thing. In like manner, the essence of the blessed and exalted God is incomparable to any being capable of change who might transform itself from justice to mercy in the manner of[1] human activities. However, from the perspective of the actions that derive from Him, may He be blessed, through His power described in the Torah, and through the emanations of holiness that He emanated at the beginning of Creation, He provides a limit and a purpose to His actions.[2]

"The emanation is called, in the secret language of the blessed sages, the kabbalists, *sefirot,* by which God supervises and guides His creation and by which justice and mercy and change are transformed from one to another. No one should conceive of this as constituting a change in His blessed essence. This is comparable to the point—which we have mentioned—that has no substance and is [only in the mind], as the geometers conceived that it has no part. However, when it is [visualized] as a substance, it has the three dimensions that we mentioned; when these three dimension are squared, the three becomes nine; with the space that holds them, there are ten. One finds a similar combination with respect to the Infinite [*ein sof*]. In relation to His [actual essence], there is no definition or relation which constricts Him. However, in relation to His emanation, although He has no body or corporeality, He is the root of them all, nevertheless, since the body, corporeality, and the elements derive from Him. Thus we are entitled to describe Him as we do, [namely] that He has a limit and [the three] dimensions. The power and root in Him enables Him to perform His actions in this world. Just as the example of the aforementioned point is divided into ten, similarly this emanation is divided into ten [parts], which are the ten *sefirot* about which you should close your mouth and not speak of them.[3]

[1]Literally, "on account of."
[2]The analogy of the point is found in Judah Ḥayyat's commentary on *Ma'arekhet ha-Elohut* (Mantua, 1558), pp. 9b–10a, and may be the source of Yagel's comments here.
[3]Yagel's comparison of the *ein sof* and the *sefirot* with a mathematical point that can be made to yield ten in number is related to a major controversy among kabbalists regarding the nature of the *sefirot,* whether they are part of the divine essence or are nondivine in essence. Like many of his predecessors, Yagel, here and later in this work, reinterpreted the *sefirot* in a philosophic framework, arguing that their apparent multiplicity did not signify their mode of existence but only the manner in which their diverse activities appear to human beings. On the context of this debate, especially in the late fifteenth and sixteenth centuries, see M. Idel, "Between the Concepts of the Sefirot as Essence and Instruments," (in Hebrew) *Italia,* 3

[45] "You certainly possess the true tradition which establishes that they [the *sefirot*] are ten, no less and no more. So rely upon the eternal tradition of our forefathers; surely they will teach you and tell you, speaking out of their understanding.[1] And one should not investigate this matter because it is impossible for human intelligence to grasp it; it is higher than the highest [thing],[2] and as the rabbis declared: 'Don't investigate what is beyond you or what is hidden from you; rather reflect on what you have planted, etc.'[3]

[46] "Likewise, the author [Maimonides] of the *Moreh* [*Nevukim*] in the thirty-second chapter of the first part, nicely wrote that there is a limit to the perception of human intelligence, just as the bodily faculties are limited. Therefore, it is appropriate that every investigator investigate subjects based on proof and research; that they accept gracefully and rely on the tradition of the prophets and first patriarchs [i.e., the rabbis] for those matters which cannot be proven. This was the level of R. Akiva, who entered his investigation in peace and left in peace. However, if you try and investigate that which is beyond your capacity, you will return to the level of Elisha [ben Abuya] 'the other.'[4] Not only will you fail to rise in your understanding; you will descend and return to what was after you. The force of your imagination will overpower you daily, an evil spirit will disturb you so that you will become another person.[5] I have told you this, my son, so that you will heed our words in order that they will be a shelter[6] from [the] evil thoughts that matter [brings] to the kidneys [i.e., conscience] of man and [which] incites him to think meaningless ideas. Such is the case regarding [the insolvable question about] the *sefirot* that stand before you on the wall:[7] How are they united with the *ein sof* without [engendering] multiplicity [within God's essence]?

[47] "The proof and analogy regarding them [the *ein sof* and the *sefirot*] is the human soul, which is one [entity] although multiple functions are

---

(1982): 89–111; H. Tirosh-Rothschild, "Sefirot as the Essence of God in the Writings of David Messer Leon," *Association for Jewish Studies Review*, 7–8 (1982–83): 409–25; J. Ben Shlomo, *Torat ha-Elohut shel R. Moshe Cordovero* (Jerusalem, 1965), pp. 100–169; and Ruderman, *Kabbalah, Magic, and Science*, chap. 9. See also below, sec. 140.

[1]Cf. Job 8:10.
[2]Cf. Ecclesiastes 5:7.
[3]Cf. B. T. Hagigah 13a (quoting Ben Sira); *Bereshit Rabbah*, 8:2.
[4]Cf. B. T. Hagigah 14b.
[5]Cf. 1 Samuel 10:6.
[6]Cf. Isaiah 4:6.
[7]The woman perhaps refers to one of the walls of the heavenly palace upon which Yagel eventually will gaze.

derived from it, depending on the organ which receives an emanation from it.[1] Indeed, the activity of the hand writing in a book with ink, that of the foot moving in dance, that of the ear listening, or the eye seeing—each is different from the other but, nevertheless, all receive their potency and unique power from this one entity. Thus the rabbis likened her [the soul] to the Holy One, blessed be He, in a number of places, as [for example] what they declared in the first chapter of *Berakhot:*[2] 'Behold, the expression "Bless [the Lord] O my soul" appears five times.[3] To whom did David declare it except the Holy One, blessed be He, as well as the soul, etc.' Also in *Midrash Tehillim*[4] [regarding the same verse] 'Bless the Lord O my soul,' [they ask]: 'Why did David command his soul to praise the Holy One, blessed be He? Just as the soul fills the body, so does the Holy One, blessed be He, fill the earth, etc.' Other similar examples abound.

"Thus if you read the words of the prophets or sages, [you will see] that they attribute nothing, not even a small thing, to God—not corporeality, nor affection, nor deficiency. Know that [such apparent descriptions] are there to make the hearer better understand what he is capable of hearing and to teach wisdom and morality with respect to man's behavior with his Maker, with himself, or with other people.

"It is similar to what R. Joshua ben Levi said in the passage that we mentioned above:[5] 'For seven days, the Holy One, blessed be He, mourned for His world before the flood came to the earth.' [48] The passage meant that [God, through] His blessed providence, did not hasten to bring punishment to His world until He had warned the inhabitants with one warning after the next. They likewise stated in [chapter] *Ḥelek:*[6] '[regarding the verse] "And on the seventh day [the waters of the flood came upon the earth],"[7] the Holy One, blessed be He, changed the orders of Creation for them [humanity] so that the sun rose in the west and set in the east [to induce them to repent]. Another explanation of "on the seventh day" is that He [God] established a small amount [of time] after a large amount of time for them, etc. [to provide one last opportunity for repentance].' In

---

[1]This is one of the analogies used by Moses Cordovero (among others), mentioned above. Cf. Ben Shlomo, pp. 127–35. For an overview of discussion on the *sefirot* in kabbalistic theosophy, see Idel, *Kabbalah: New Perspectives* (New Haven and London, 1988), pp. 136–53.

[2]B. T. Berakhot 10a.

[3]Cf. Psalm 103: 1, 2, 22; 104:1, 35.

[4]*Midrash Tehillim,* on Psalm 103: 4, with slight modifications.

[5]*Bereshit Rabbah,* 27:4.

[6]B. T. Sanhedrin 108b.

[7]Genesis 7:10.

another place,[1] the rabbis declared that during the entire period that Noah sat and built the ark, he warned them [his generation], telling them that the Holy One, blessed be He, was going to bring a flood to the earth. For He [God] is blessed and His mercy is upon all His works.[2] It is not His desire that a man should die; rather that he should turn back from his [evil] ways [and live].[3] At his death, it is as if God mourns for him, so to speak, and that the *sefirah* called 'the lower mother,'[4] hovers over her children as if she mourns and weeps. It is like what R. Joshua ben Levi states, so to speak, that He mourned for his world for seven days. This also indicates the seven lower ones [*sefirot*] hinted at by the seven days of rotation; furthermore, they teach us good conduct, as I have stated above.

"It is appropriate for everyone to pay attention to every sorrow and tragedy that happens to a person, to examine one's actions so that by his repentance and good deeds, strict justice will be transformed into mercy. By good deeds and by the good [cosmic] awakening which rises from below, the queen [i.e., the *shekhinah,* the lowest of the *sefirot*] will return to happiness and goodness so as to permit and to generate the flow of blessing and praise. This was also their [the rabbis] intention in that story that I have mentioned in which they interpreted [the verse]: 'But if you shall not hear it, my soul shall weep in secret,'[5] that is, I will hide My face from you, causing you to weep. This is [the meaning of] 'Its name is secret, etc.'[6]

"But, God forbid, should we attribute weeping to the Holy One, blessed be He, because it is an affection and any affection is a deficiency? Rather, let us add to what I have said above, that the author of this passage intended to hint at the following: 'But if you shall not hear it,' to return and seek God[7] with repentance and good deeds, 'My soul will cry in secret,' that is, I will hide My face from you, causing you to weep. This is [the meaning] of, 'Its name is secret.'

"But someone might raise an objection:[8] 'But is there any sadness or

---

[1]*Tanḥuma Bereshit,* 1:25.

[2]Cf. Psalm 145:9.

[3]Cf. Ezekiel 18:23.

[4]*Malkhut,* the lowest *sefirah,* also called the *shekhinah.* The *sefirah binah* was called "the higher mother." Cf. G. Scholem, *Pirke Yesod be-Havanat ha-Kabbalah u-Semaleha* (Jerusalem, 1977), pp. 288–89, on its place in kabbalistic thought.

[5]Jeremiah 13:17; see above.

[6]See above, Part II, sec. 34. What follows is a full explanation of the passage in Ḥagigah already quoted.

[7]Cf. Job 8:5.

[8]A further explication of the aforementioned passage in B. T. Ḥagigah 5b, quoted in sec. 34 above.

weeping in the presence of the Holy One, blessed be He? For, behold, R. Papa said: "There is no grief [in the presence of God], etc.,"' that is, evil does not descend from above, for only good can come from good. Moreover, the Lord is good to all and His mercy is upon all His works,[1] whether his creatures are good or bad. One could respond: 'There is no contradiction. The one case [where there is no grief in God's presence refers] to the inner chambers [of the kingdom of heaven]; the other case [refers] to the outer chambers,' that is, 'the inner chambers' from which blessing comes to the world [even] when [God] hides His face and Israel causes the cessation of the [heavenly] outpouring to the whole world. There is never any sadness since strength and beauty are in His sanctuary [i.e., His inner chambers].[2] Thus the ministers of all the kingdoms of the nations take the outpouring in such a way and empty it on all the inhabitants of the world.

"The questioner might respond: 'Thus there is [also] no grief in the outer chambers. Yet, indeed, it is written: "My Lord God of hosts summoned on that day to weeping and lamenting, etc."[3]; that is, all the ministers among those people did not receive the [heavenly] outpouring which burst forth at that moment as they formally had received it. They were also scorched in the coals of Israel.

"He [the respondent] could answer: 'But the destruction of the Temple is different, for even the ministering angels wept [over it], as it is said: "Hark! The Arielites cry aloud,"[4] that is, the force of [God's] hiding His face was so powerful at the time the Temple was burned, that there was no one to look after the ministers of the other nations. [49] The rabbis likewise interpreted in *Sifre* [the verse]:[5] '"It is a land which the Lord your God looks after." Does He look after her [Israel] alone? But doesn't He look after all the other nations, as it is written: "To rain down on uninhabited land, etc."?[6] What does "It is a land which the Lord looks after" mean, but that He [God] looks after, so to speak, her [Israel] alone? However, by the merit of looking after her, He [also] looks over the nations with her, etc.' However, at the time of the destruction of the Temple, there was not enough [divine] involvement and good influence; rather, [God was] hiding His face and there was bad influence; thus He gave strength to the demon

[1]Cf. Psalm 145:9.
[2]Cf. Psalm 96:6.
[3]Isaiah 22:12, describing the destruction of the Temple, as it appears in the passage in Ḥagigah 5b.
[4]Isaiah 33:7, as it appears in the passage in Ḥagigah 5b.
[5]*Sifre Devarim*, beginning of 40, on Deuteronomy 11:12.
[6]Job 38:26.

of destruction to harm.[1] The numerous angels of peace who [minister] over the rest of the nations wept bitterly[2] since they were unable to receive their portion from the essence of that [divine] providence.[3]

"The meaning of [the verse]: 'And my eye shall drop . . . these three tears, etc.,'[4] is that [God's] great hiding of His face, which engendered the angels of peace to be afflicted, happened only three times. 'One is for the First Temple; and one for the Second Temple; and one for [the children of] Israel who have become exiled from their place.' It is similar to what the rabbis said at the end of *Sotah:*[5] 'There is no day which does not have a curse. [50] Raba said: "And the curse of each day is severer that that of the preceding one, etc." How, in that case, can the world endure? Through the doxology recited after the scriptural reading[6] and the [response of] "May His name [be blessed!]" [which is uttered in the doxology] after studying *agadah* [rabbinic homily], etc.'[7] They intended to indicate by this [passage] that the world endures only because of the doxology of the scriptural reading. In other words, the Holy One, blessed be He, wanted to establish His world created in the order of six days so that on the seventh day, He said: '[And the heaven and the earth] were finished,' which is the great doxology.[8] Thus, because of the benefit of the Torah, the Holy One, blessed be He, created the world, as it is written: 'As surely as I have established My covenant with day and night and appointed the laws of heaven and earth, [so I will never reject the offspring of Jacob, etc.,]'[9] [but] the world was unable to stand because [God] did not watch over the land of Israel.

"But others say: 'One [tear] for the neglect [of the study of] Torah, etc.,'[10] [with respect to] the creation of this man. One of the pillars upon

[1]Cf. *Mekhilta,* Bo, 11.

[2]Cf. Isaiah 33:7.

[3]I have omitted an additional line that appears in the margin of the manuscript.

[4]Jeremiah 13:17, as found in the aforementioned rabbinic text in Ḥagigah 5b.

[5]B. T. Sotah 49a. The same passage was quoted by Yagel in Part I, section 20.

[6]*Kiddushah de-sidrah,* "the doxology of the order," now recited at the conclusion of the morning service, which begins: "And a redeemer shall come to Zion." Cf. I. Abrahams, *A Companion to the Authorized Prayer Book* (New York, 1966), pp. 82–83.

[7]The response is found in the *kaddish* prayer (also a doxology), which originally functioned as a concluding prayer to the public aggadic reading.

[8]Cf. Genesis 2:1. The *kiddushah rabbah,* "the great *kiddush,*" refers euphemistically to the minor version of the benediction over the wine recited on the morning of the Sabbath or festival. Cf. B. T. Pesaḥim 106a. However, Yagel clearly refers here to the principal Friday night version, which includes the passage from Genesis. Note how Yagel and the passage from *Sotah* bring together the doxologies of three distinct prayers: the *kedushah,* the *kaddish,* and the *kiddush.*

[9]Jeremiah 33:25.

[10]Referring back to the same Ḥagigah passage.

which the world stands is the Torah. And notice that when the Temple was destroyed, the associates [i.e., those who fully observed the law] and freemen were ashamed and covered their heads; and the sages began to look like synagogue servants.[1] If the first [sages] are likened to men, [then] we are like donkeys but not [even] the donkey of R. Pinḥas ben Yair.[2]

"[This person just identified as 'others say'] truly stated that this third tear, that is, [the result of God's] turning away His face, as I said, should be attributed to the neglect [of the study] of the Torah instead of [the children of] Israel who were exiled from their place. On whom should we rely? Furthermore, the matter of neglect of [the study of] the Torah comes with the authorized support [51] of the rabbinic teaching regarding the three things for which the Holy One, blessed be He, cries each day:[3] 'over he who is able to study Torah,' which is the tree of life, 'but does not' (for what good is money in the hands of a fool?),[4] 'over he who is unable to study Torah but does' (This is fair since everyone was created to fulfill this [responsibility], so that out of his duress, he studies Torah. The rabbis similarly declared: 'The whole world is sustained by [the merit of] my son Ḥanina [ben Dosa, first century, C.E.] and Ḥanina my son subsists on a *kav* [a small measure] of carobs from one week to the next'[5]); and 'over a leader who domineers over the community for no reason.'

[52] "[In the case of the latter, it is] because the leader's only status is derived [from serving] the community, just as the king's status is derived from the people [he serves], as it is written: 'In a multitude of people is the glory of a king.'[6] A leader who domineers over them is like one who shows that his status over the community is like that of a shepherd over his flock. He does not realize that this arrogance in his heart comes for no reason since the two [the status of the leader and the shepherd] are not analogous. It is fitting that the shepherd should take pride in his flock since they belong to him and he can do with them as he wishes; so too, with the cattle who walk at the feet of their masters. However, the leader appointed over the community is only like a head of a flock, a part of its parts. He does not rule over them and does not do as he wishes with them, for God is their king and He appointed him [the leader] over them in the same way He appointed

---

[1]This is borrowed, with changes, from the additions to Mishnah Sotah 9:15.

[2]Based on B. T. Shabbat 112b. The donkey of Pinḥas was alleged to be so pious that he only ate feed that was tithed. Cf. B. T. Ḥullin 7a–b.

[3]This is the last part of the passage in Ḥagigah 5b, which is quoted above.

[4]Cf. Proverbs 17:16.

[5]B. T. Berakhot 17b.

[6]Proverbs 14:28.

the head over the rest of the organs. What would happen to the head if it were separated from the body for [even] one day? Similarly, what would happen to the leader who separates himself from the community?

"Thus the Holy One, blessed be He, mourns and cries for this [person], so to speak; that is, He hides His countenance from him so that he is ready prey; many evils and troubles shall befall him[1] and He humbles him to the ground.[2] So he perishes like his dung.[3] Rabbi hinted at this [thought] at the end of that [aforementioned] passage where it stated that his book [of Lamentations] fell from his hands. He declared: 'It fell from a roof so high to a pit so deep!' [53] Likewise, it will happen to a leader who domineers over the community; he will fall from heaven to earth.

"They [the rabbis] illustrated this fact for us by interpreting these passages that came only into our possession. They have taught us good conduct, as I initially have stated—how a person should conduct himself in good and bad times, since there is a time for every experience.[4] As Ecclesiastes stated: '[There is] a time for weeping and a time for laughing.'[5] [54] The rabbis similarly stated in *Bereshit Rabbah,* chapter 27, regarding the response of R. Joshua ben Karḥa to that gentile who asked him if the Holy One, blessed be He, foresees the future. He answered: 'He [God] knows that every living thing is doomed to be destroyed on the earth; because of their evil, God brought a flood upon them.' [The gentile then asked]: 'So why was it written in His Torah:[6] "And His heart was saddened," as if it [man's wickedness] was a novelty previously unknown to him?' The sage then responded with a lovely analogy and concluded [with the words]: 'Rejoicing in the time of rejoicing and mourning in the time of mourning.'[7]

[55] "I informed you of all this in order to guide you in the paths of righteousness.[8] Don't let the scholars among the philosophers and astronomers, the disciples of my sisters, entice you by declaring that if the [heavenly] decree is true, diligence is false and one cannot accomplish anything himself. Their words are only true [in one respect]: A person will

[1]Cf. Deuteronomy 31:17.
[2]Cf. Isaiah 26:5.
[3]Cf. Job 20:7.
[4]Cf. Ecclesiastes 3:17.
[5]Ecclesiastes 3:4.
[6]Genesis 6:6.
[7]*Bereshit Rabbah,* 27:4. The rabbi had asked the gentile whether a son had ever been born to him and whether he had rejoiced at that moment. When the man replied affirmatively, the rabbi responded, "Yet did you not know that he must die some day?," followed by the above rejoinder.
[8]Cf. Proverbs 4:11. The third sister's justification for her long homiletic digression.

not sink to Sheol with that grief[1] until he abandons his trust in God. But, on the contrary, he should think to himself that his iniquities entrapped him like an evil person and he was caught in the snares of his sin and depravity. If he returns to Shaddai [God], asks for forgiveness, and banishes his iniquity and evil from his tent,[2] God, as a compassionate one, will accept his repentance. He will notice his tear because the gates of tears are never closed.[3] He will remove His [chastising] hand from him and will favor him as a father [favors his] son.[4]

"So, my son, accept instruction from my mouth; lay these words which are mine in your heart.[5] Regard treasure as dirt;[6] [likewise] silver and gold, which are all on the same level, since none of them offers perfection to the soul. With the stones of the wadi,[7] abandon the evil thought which constantly entices you to neglect your soul's perfection in order to pursue the vanities of this world and its devices. Instead of these, hold up the design of goodness and happiness, [which is] to love the Lord your God with all your heart, with all your soul, and with all your might.[8] Then Shaddai will become your treasure,[9] that is, the good and the desire to pursue spiritual things will come to you, because one who comes to purify [himself] is assisted by Heaven.[10] In this manner, you shall seek the favor of Shaddai and lift up your face to Him. You will pray to Him and He will listen to you; you will decree and it will be fulfilled.[11] He fulfills the wishes of those who fear Him; He hears their cry at all times and at every moment.[12]

"But the time of the singing has come[13] at midnight when we go and listen to the lessons about those laws renewed in the heavenly academy[14] beyond the curtain [of heaven].[15] It is on the high mountain opposite you, which is called 'the mount of myrrh.' On the top of this mountain is a hill called 'the hill of frankincense.'[16] There all the flocks are rounded up[17] from

[1]Cf. Genesis 44:29, 33.
[2]Cf. Job 22:23.
[3]Cf. B. T. Berakhot 32b, Babba Meẓiah 59a.
[4]Cf. Proverbs 3:12.
[5]Based on Job 22:22.
[6]Cf. Job 22:24.
[7]Cf. Job 22:24.
[8]Cf. Deuteronomy 6:5.
[9]Cf. Job 22:25.
[10]Cf. B. T. Shabbat 104a; Yoma 38b and elsewhere.
[11]Cf. Job 22:26–28.
[12]Cf. Psalm 145:19.
[13]Cf. Song of Songs 2:12.
[14]Cf. B. T. Babba Meẓiah 86a.
[15]Cf. B. T. Ḥagigah 15a.
[16]Cf. Song of Songs 4:6.
[17]Cf. Genesis 29:3, 8.

the sciences and the fields of learning, flock by flock.[1] Turn over every stone and every monument upon which you will stand from the mouth of the well[2] of sciences. Intelligence will not move from there until every doubt is refined and purged[3] through it. Now let us go in the direction opposite you. You and your father who made you[4] will come slowly since I have been aware that you are held captive in the tresses[5] of matter and are unable to fly or to live like one of us."

## The Women's Departure and the Father's Further Instruction

[56] When this important woman completed her words, I turned here and there and noticed that the three women arose and stood in one line on the mount of myrrh which was in front of us. It was higher that all the mountains of Ararat. In one moment, they reached the hill of frankincense, which is at its summit. I and my father remained alone at the foot of the mountain. I then asked my father about these three sisters [and about] their activities and their natures, and he responded to me:

[57] "Know that the first woman who initially spoke to you was the science of philosophy.[6] She generates a philosophic emanation upon all the scholars who investigate and seek her. Her clothing [is represented] in the same manner [as she is], that is, her actions and inquiries are hinted in them. The letter 'tav,' written from right to left, signifies the 'tav' of *tiḥeyeh* [you will live] and the 'tav' of *tamut* [you will die]. This hints at the man clothed in linen whom Ezekiel the prophet saw in a prophetic vision. He placed a mark on the foreheads of the men who moan and groan.[7] The man with a mark of ink on his forehead would live and the one with a mark of blood would die. The rabbis stated in chapter *Bemah Behamah:*[8] 'Why does it teach "tav"?' R. Joseph said:[9] ' "tav," you shall live; "tav," you shall die.'

[58] Thus it will be good for the person who takes from the words of philosophy, (which is called by the author [Isaac Arama] of *Akedat Yiẓḥak*

---

[1]Cf. Genesis 32:17.
[2]Cf. Genesis 29:3, 8.
[3]Cf. Daniel 12:10.
[4]Cf. Deuteronomy 32:6.
[5]Cf. Song of Songs 7:6.
[6]This woman, as we have stated, is clearly Boethius's Lady Philosophy with certain "Jewish" modifications. For a further discussion of this woman and the other two sisters, see the introduction above, pp. 45–50.
[7]Cf. Ezekiel 9:3–4.
[8]B. T. Shabbat 55a.
[9]The statement is attributed to Rav in the standard edition of the Talmud.

the tree of knowledge of good and bad, the exalted things,[1]) and separates the food from the refuse. A 'tav' of *tiheyeh* will be upon him. This is similar to what the great eagle Maimonides did [when he] found a pomegranate, ate its center, and discarded its peel in the manner of R. Meir.[2] The things that a person will take will taste as sweet as honey to him[3] in comprehending the words of the sages and their riddles and in knowing what is obscure in some of their utterances. With this principle, they [the words of philosophy] will enlighten his eyes in a dark and gloomy place, [enabling him] to preach in public, to inform the multitude [about] the Torah and the commandments, and to place it [the Torah] in their mouths as teachings reconcilable with the mind and acceptable to the intelligence.[4]

"However, this is contingent upon the fact that a person will not sink in them [in philosophic teachings] lest he deviate from the [right] intention and become an agnostic or a heretic, God forbid. Then the 'tav' of *tamut* will be upon him as it happened to Elisha [ben Abuyah] *aher*, [another person][5] who was seen with heretical books which fell from his bosom.[6] Similarly, they [philosophical teachings] enticed Gersonides, to a certain extent, although the Lord forgave him, since from the time that Maimonides died, no one has risen in Israel comparable to him [Gersonides] in wisdom, intelligence, good taste, and righteous words. But his wisdom is shameful when interpreting the verse: 'I will go down to see,'[7] and in so many other interpretations found in his works. [59] But he does deserve credit because when he spoke of these matters, he spoke as a philosopher.

[1]Isaac Arama, *Akedat Yizhak,* vol. I, sha'ar 7, p. 59b.

[2]B. T. Hagigah 15b, in reference to his studies with his heretical teacher, Elisha ben Abuyah.

[3]Cf. Ezekiel 3:3.

[4]Yagel's formulation is interesting here not only in stressing the positive function of philosophic knowledge in comprehending "the sages and their riddles," but also in educating the masses with this knowledge. This position is reminiscent of that of Yohanan Alemanno, of the late fifteenth century, who both integrated "Greek" learning with rabbinic learning and made this the focus of an educational program for the Jewish community. This view was in opposition to that of his contemporary, Elijah Delmedigo, who argued for the separation of this elitist learning from the masses. Cf. M. Idel, "The Study Program of Yohanan Alemanno" (in Hebrew), *Tarbiz,* 48 (1979): 303–31.

[5]The second-century C.E. Palestinean rabbi who later renounced Judaism. On his designation as *aher,* see B. T. Hagigah 15a.

[6]On this tradition, see B. T. Hagigah 15b.

[7]I have used the edition of Gersonides' commentary on the Torah published in Venice, 1546–47, p. 27a. Gersonides, in interpreting Genesis 18:21, explicitly denies the possibility of God's descent to the earth and explains this verse allegorically as written "in the language of men."

However, he was possessed by a different spirit in his thinking which was different from what the rabbis and every divine philosopher of the Torah believed. This is the case in his introduction to his book *Milḥamot Adonai*.[1] Nevertheless, you should realize that his words are intelligent and pure and have enlightened the eyes of students. From them, the more recent scholars, R. Isaac Arama and R. Isaac Abravanel, dug up food [for thought]. Nevertheless, he would be able to complain about them saying: 'I reared children and brought them up [and they have rebelled against me].'[2]

[60] "What you have seen torn on the extremities of the woman's garment was torn by scoffing men, sects of common people, who arose after the death of Plato and Socrates, his teacher.[3] They too expected to be called philosophers like those once famous on earth.[4] However, they [merely] stole several ideas from their [teachers'] exalted words, since one stone in a pitcher cries out: 'rattle, rattle.'[5] They were surrounded by empty and fickle-minded people. They magnified their own importance before the public with a [mere] chain of granules [i.e., a mere chain of random thoughts] from the words of the philosophers which they recited. Thus they became proud and arrogant,[6] thinking that they were like the ancients and even better than them. But they never knew nor understood that if the ancients were like angels, they [themselves] were like donkeys.[7]

"Moreover, they conceived false thoughts regarding the secrets of nature and creation and wrote down their fantasies in books. Thus they split up those few ideas taken from the ancients that we mentioned [and made them into] base silver laid over earthenware.[8] Consequently, the confusions of the sects of the Stoics and Epicureans emerged, as well as the sect of the Mutakallimun, mentioned by Maimonides in the *Moreh* [Ne-

---

[1] Yagel's thoughts on Gersonides should be seen in the context of a bitter polemic against the philosopher's views, especially those on divine providence and creation, instigated by Judah Messer Leon and his son, David, at the end of the fifteenth and early sixteenth centuries. For a summary of this polemic on Italian soil and additional bibliographic references, see Ruderman, *The World of a Renaissance Jew*, pp. 112–14. In contrast, Yagel's attitude to Gersonides is relatively mild and tolerant. Cf. also Part I above, p. 217.

[2] Isaiah 1:2. Yagel understates Arama's and Abravanel's strong critique of Gersonides. Cf. M. M. Kellner, "Gersonides and His Cultured Despisers: Arama and Abravanel," *Journal of Medieval and Renaissance Studies*, 6 (1976): 269–96.

[3] Cf. Boethius, *Consolation of Philosophy*, I, 3, p. 143 (Loeb ed.).

[4] Cf. Psalm 49:12.

[5] Cf. B. T. Babba Meẓiah 85b. The proverb refers to one scholar from a family of fools who becomes famous because he is the only stone in the pitcher and makes a lot of noise.

[6] Cf. Proverbs 8:13.

[7] Based on B. T. Shabbat 112b.

[8] Cf. Proverbs 26:23.

*vukhim*], and the students of the Magians [i.e., the Zoroastrians]—who conceived of an independent influence of good and one of evil—along with other errors and the prattle of their ideas found in their books.

[61] "Don't think that the ancients thought like them with their blunders, for in the case of Plato, one doesn't even have to acknowledge that most of his words are true.[1] If this is not apparent to you, go back to them [his words] again and connect each word to the other so that its end is inherent in its beginning. Then you will see that a righteous person would utter [the words] of his [Plato's] mouth[2] most of the time since the Torah of Moses was available to him [Plato] and he listened to its teachings interpreted by the priest and prophet, Jeremiah, may his memory be blessed.[3] He drank his words with thirst, as Augustine mentioned in the seventh chapter of the *Confessions*.[4] [62] If many vilified him by arguing that he claimed that the world had no beginning, that it has no purpose, and that it is coeternal with its creator, their efforts were in vain, for they really did not penetrate his true intention.

"There is a big difference between things limited by time and things unrelated to it, as in the case of the Lord God. Thus we cannot call Him 'Ancient God,' God forbid, since He is unrelated to any measure of time. [He can only be described] in the simplicity of the nature of His essence. This is so described by Boethius at the end of book five of his *Consolation of Philosophy*.[5] Plato hinted at this very fine philosophic distinction in his writings. Yet it is also true that he considered the world to be created and not eternal as the Creator, God forbid.[6] However, it [the world] lacks a final end [for him], which is like the view of Maimonides in the *Moreh* [*Nevukhim*][7] and of [Isaac] Arama[8] and is [also] similar to what is written:

[1]Yagel's appreciation of Plato was shared by a number of Italian Jewish thinkers, especially Yohanan Alemanno. Cf. Idel, "The Magical and Neoplatonic Interpretations of the Kabbalah in the Renaissance." However, Yagel's esteem of ancient philosophy and its truths far exceeded that of his Jewish contemporaries. Cf. Ruderman, *Kabbalah, Magic, and Science*, chap. 9.

[2]Cf. Psalm 37:30.

[3]On the theme of Plato studying with Jeremiah in Jewish writing of this period, see M. Idel, "Kabbalah and Ancient Theology in Isaac and Judah Abravanel" (in Hebrew) in *The Philosophy of Leone Ebreo*, eds. M. Dorman and Z. Levy (Haifa, 1985), pp. 98, 101, nn. 21 and 30.

[4]The passages cited by Idel, pp. 100–101, also quote from Augustine but, in contrast, refer either to *The Christian Doctrine* or to *The City of God*.

[5]*Consolation of Philosophy*, V, 6, p. 427 (Loeb ed.).

[6]Cf. Maimonides, *Moreh Nevukhim*, 2:13, where Maimonides denies this assertion, stating that Plato held that the world came into existence through generation from some other being.

[7]Cf. *Moreh Nevukhim*, 3:13.

[8]On the contrary, Arama criticized Maimonides' view and held that the final goal of

'One generation goes, another comes, but the earth remains the same forever.'[1]

[63] "It is also true from the perspective of the nature of the world, the science of the stars, and the tradition of our sages, that the world will return to chaos as it was before Creation, to an absolute nothingness.[2] The naturalists understand that the four elements actually share one common matter and are only distinguishable in form. The scholars also explain that by knowing the nature of a single human being, no matter what kind, one can adduce evidence for the entire human race. Thus when we fathom the nature of one species from the various kinds of essential matter, we learn the nature of everything, since there is nothing in the individual except what is in everything, and the nature of the part is in the whole.

"We know from experience that the land, which is part of the [eternal] formless matter, loses its strength when we plant on a part of it, year after year, for five or six years, until it no longer yields the fruit that it naturally yields. Even if we would add more effort than this in planting and working it [the soil], its strength would cease completely despite the incessant labor. For the nature stamped on a part is equally stamped on everything.

"This analogy in itself [is true] with respect to all the other elements since matter is common to them all and every material thing is subject to deficiency and weakness. But [this condition] arises by virtue of the matter in it, not [by] its form. Accordingly, the analogy is the same for all the elements. Since they share the same matter, they, by necessity, share the same nature. Just as one generally finds a varying degree of strengths, one necessarily encounters a similar variety of weaknesses [in any thing], following the analogy of the earth's nature which is a part of matter. Therefore, it is impossible not to locate in this common matter, through which being and passing away revolve, a nature of weakness. Subsequently, it is possible that its strength slowly diminishes, until in time, according to the natural law of weakening with which it was potentially endowed at the

Creation was man. See S. H. Wilensky, *R. Yizḥak Arama u-Misnato ha-Pilosofit* (Jerusalem and Tel Aviv, 1956), pp. 109–12.

[1]Ecclesiastes 1:4, a text that Maimonides felt obliged to interpret since it ostensibly indicates the world's eternity. Cf. *Moreh Nevukhim*, 2:28.

[2]On the context of the discussion that follows, see S. Feldman, "The End of the Universe in Medieval Jewish Philosophy," *Association for Jewish Studies Review*, II (1986): 53–77. Yagel's discussion of the naturalists' views closely parallels those of Isaac Abravanel in his *Mifalot Elohim* (Venice, 1592), bk. 8, especially Abravanel's understanding of the general weakening of the elements from which all bodies, including human ones, are composed. Yagel clearly goes beyond Abravanel in soliciting the testimony of the astrologers and kabbalists to argue for this world's termination. As we have seen already, Yagel arrives at his conclusion on the basis of integrating the knowledge of the three worlds—the natural, astral, and spiritual.

beginning of its creation, its existence will end at a specified time. [This] is similar to [the case of] the part [of the land] that weakens in a short time due to the incessant labor [upon it] which takes it out of its natural course.

"This [situation] is also analogous to that of man who is called a microcosm by all the sages,[1] who will sprout like grass,[2] [and] will become larger and yield fruit from above. But in time, his powers will diminish and his strength will weaken slowly until he dies and is gathered to his kin.[3] The condition that affects the microcosm also is possibly very close to what happens to the nature of this macrocosm, as we have said. Thus you have proof from the nature of the world that it must return to absolute nothingness and death.

[64] "From the perspective of the science of the stars, some of the scholars also uphold the view that the world will necessarily become nothingness as it was before Creation. [This is so] because of the well-known fact regarding the changes in [celestial motions], that when an astral conjunction occurs, changes [also] occur among the inhabitants of the earth, according to the nature of the sign of the conjunction. Since the independent motion of the ninth sphere is completed every 49,000 years, they [the aforementioned scholars] thus declared that the firmament deteriorates every 49,000 years and returns to its original state of existence a second time. Since the self-motion of the eighth sphere is 7,000 years, they state that the land and its creatures will come to an end and expire every 7,000 years either by fire or by water or by eruptions[4] in the heart of the ocean as a result of earthquakes or hurricanes or something else. This condition will remain until the big jubilee, which is the year 50,000, at which time all the weary[5] will return, each man to his family and possession.[6]

[65] "A similar thought is expressed by our sages, which is their tradition, that the seven days of Creation allude to one revolution [of the world]. So R. Katina hinted in his statement:[7] 'The world exists for 6,000

[1]Cf. *Tanḥuma*, Pekudei, 3, and elsewhere.

[2]Cf. Isaiah 44:4.

[3]Cf. Genesis 25:8, 17; 35:29.

[4]Meaning not certain.

[5]Cf. Job 3:17.

[6]Cf. 2 Chronicles 31:1. Cf. Abraham bar Ḥiyya's *Megillat ha-Megalleh* (Berlin, 1924), ed. A. Poznanski, p. 11, where a similar idea regarding cosmic cycles is mentioned on the authority of unnamed "philosophers." Cf. G. Scholem, *Kabbalah* (Jerusalem, 1974), p. 120. Even closer to Yagel's formulation is that of Isaac Abravanel in his *Mifalot Elohim* (Lemberg, 1863), p. 51b. On this subject, see I. Weinstock, *Be-Ma'aglei ha-Niglah ve-ha-Nistar* (Jerusalem, 1970), pp. 215–21; B. Z. Netanyahu, *Don Isaac Abravanel: Statesman and Philosopher* (Philadelphia, 1953), pp. 132–35; M. Idel, "Kabbalah and Ancient Theology in Isaac and Judah Abravanel," pp. 87–89.

[7]B. T. Rosh Ha-Shanah 31a, Sanhedrin 97a.

years and is destroyed in the next millennium, etc.' He thus indicated that the world would be destroyed, [emptied] of all humans and animals that work and care for the land. However, the time would remain as it had been. This is exemplified by the six days of Creation and the seventh day, which is a day of rest to God.[1] Thus you should let the land lie fallow of all work. In every *shemittah*[2] there is a *sefirah* from the seven lower *sefirot* so that at the completion of seven cosmic cycles, which are in the end 49,000 years, the glorious crown[3] will be renewed afterward. The Lord will create the new heavens and the new earth[4] as in the beginning. According to the will of the *ein sof* [the transcendent aspect of the Deity], blessed be He, the fiftieth year is the great jubilee. [At that time] all the greatness of God's acts will return to the sun with the strength [of the letter] 'nun' [which equals fifty], as it is written: 'The eyes of all look to You expectantly and You give them their food when it is due,'[5] that is, their continuity, as the author of the *Sefer Ma'arekhet [ha-Elohut]* explains in the seventh gate as well as in [the commentary of Judah] Ḥayyat there.[6]

[66] "We have already wandered from the intention of the speech with which we began, which was to ask why the clothes of the woman were torn. [This was] because scoffing men[7] ripped them, a dull and witless people[8] who don a foreign vestment[9] before the eyes of the common people. They [the scoffing men] told them [the common people]: 'We are the sons of wise men and ancient philosophers.' But their words caused harm for generations and [bequeathed] a bad name to their master because they hung their 'stench' on him. You indeed can see that even Epicurus, upon whom so much asps' venom[10] has been written, that he only believed in

---

[1]A parallel is drawn between the days of Creation and those of the world, conceived as a great cosmic week, which "rests" (i.e., is destroyed) at the end.

[2]Literally, the sabbatical year, as described in Deuteronomy 15. Yagel refers again to the kabbalistic doctrine of *shemittot,* the cycles of creation, found in the *Sefer ha-Temunah* (c. 1300). According to this doctrine, the seven apprehendable lower *sefirot* are emanated from the *sefirah binah*. Each of these *sefirot* influence the specific nature of one *shemittah* or creation-cycle which lasts for 7,000 years. In the seventh millennium of the cycle, the world returns to chaos. At the close of the seven *shemittot,* the "great jubilee" appears when everything is reabsorbed into *binah*. See Scholem, *Kabbalah*, pp. 120–21, and idem, *Origins of the Kabbalah*, pp. 460–75, and see above.

[3]Cf. Isaiah 62:3, Ezekiel 16:12 and elsewhere.

[4]Cf. Isaiah 66:22.

[5]Psalm 145:15.

[6]*Sefer Ma'arekhet ha-Elohut* (Mantua, 1558; reprint, Jerusalem, 1963), chap. 13, p. 187a.

[7]Cf. Isaiah 28:14 and elsewhere.

[8]Cf. Deuteronomy 32:6.

[9]Cf. Zephaniah 1:8.

[10]Cf. Job 20:14.

[the testimony] of the senses and in only one world, [was not like this at all]. You will not observe this in the words and writing of Seneca, his student, who quotes his words and sayings, which truly have in them wreaths of gold with spangles of silver.[1] In fact, his students were small foxes who inflicted injury by not using them [his teachings] properly. Therefore, the disciples of the ancient philosophers were mistaken [in understanding] their [masters'] words and they learned to lie from them [the words]. Accordingly, the woman's torn clothing is meant to allude to them [these disciples]."

[67] "In like manner, the rabbis hinted at the end of *Berakhot:*[2] 'When the heretics corrupted [the liturgy] by stating that there was only one world, etc.' In my modest view, 'heretics' in this passage allude to those changing sects who considered themselves philosophers but were actually heretics [*minim*], from the same root [as the expressions] 'trees of every kind bearing fruit,' 'seed-bearing plants of every kind,' and 'every kind of living creature,'[3] and other similar passages. When the heretics corrupted [the liturgy] by saying there was only one world, the sages ordained that they should say: 'From this world to the next.'[4] In their [the sages'] using [the expression] 'When they corrupted' they meant to indicate that prior to the corruption, it was proper, for one does not call something distorted or corrupted unless it previously had been in proper condition but now was corrupted. And this alludes to those philosophers who truly deserve that appellation [of being proper, uncorrupted], such as Plato, Pythagoras, and the ancients, who were believers, but their descendents afterward were deceived as I have stated.[5]

[68] "The second woman is the science of astronomy,[6] who pours out emanation on all the astronomers and learned scholars. You can see that her clothing alludes to the heavens and its hosts since the blue is like the sea and the sea is like the firmament. Those sparkles of light that appear on her clothing allude to the stars, which are like pegs hanging on them [the

[1]Cf. Song of Songs 1:11. Yagel's positive view of Epicurus, in contrast to that of his later followers who misrepresented Epicurus's thoughts, is consistent with his positive attitude toward the other ancient philosophers, including Hermes, Orpheus, and Pythagoras. Cf. Ruderman, *Kabbalah, Magic, and Science,* chap. 9.

[2]B. T. Berakhot 54a, Mishnah Berakhot 9:5.

[3]Genesis 1:11, 12, 24.

[4]Or "from everlasting to everlasting," translating *olam* as eternity rather than world (the continuation of the same passage in *Berakhot*).

[5]A further example of Yagel's search for correlations between general (i.e., Boethius) and rabbinic knowledge. Note how Yagel refers to the ancient philosophers as "believers," and compare my remarks in this regard in Ruderman, *Kabbalah, Magic, and Science,* chap. 9.

[6]Or astrology. For Yagel, the two were interchangeable and were both "scientific."

heavens] [and] which will not fall from there. That part of the sphere[1] that is dense and not translucent is prepared to receive the light of the sun more than the other parts which cannot contain the light since they are translucent. It is just like the air, which is incapable of receiving light when the sun shines on the earth; thus the sun shining on it is unrecognizable. This is not the case, however, when it [the sun] shines on the earth since the earth is dense and not translucent like the air.

[69] "The small ladder in her left hand[2] indicates that the science of astronomy is all set on the ground[3] from which it ascends to the divine wisdom, being a shadow of God. This is the way known to the ancients, the patriarchs of the world, as we found in the case of Abraham, our father, who was a great astrologer as the rabbis declared in the first chapter of [Babba] Batra:[4] [70] 'Abraham our father had a great expertise in astrology since all the kings of the East and the West would get up early [to gather] at the entrance [to his home], etc.' They likewise stated, regarding [the verse]: ' "Who never gave a thought to the plan of God,"[5] that [this refers] to one who knows how to calculate the seasons and gematriot [the method of disclosing the hidden meaning of the biblical text by reckoning the numerical equivalent of the Hebrew letters] but doesn't reflect [on it; i.e., doesn't apply this knowledge].'[6] They also declared [regarding the verse]: ' "This is your wisdom and understanding in the eyes of the nations,"[7] what is the wisdom [esteemed] in the eyes of the nations? It is the calculation of the seasons [and constellations].'[8]

[71] "I also found in a history book of the gentiles that Moses, our teacher, was a great astrologer. When he acquired the Cushite woman in the land of Ethiopia (as explained in his history book [The Chronicles of Moses] and quoted in the Yalkut [Shimoni] in the portion of Shemot),[9] he made two coins fashioned under the constellation of Gemini. One had a

---

[1]There may be a gap in the narrative at this point since this line seems unrelated to the previous one.

[2]Yagel had previously indicated that the ladder was in her right hand. See above, p. 223.

[3]Cf. Genesis 28:12.

[4]B. T. Babba Batra 16b, somewhat misquoted.

[5]Isaiah 5:12.

[6]B. T. Shabbat 75a, misquoted. Instead of mazzalot (constellations), Yagel inserts gematriot.

[7]Deuteronomy 4:6.

[8]B. T. Shabbat 75a.

[9]Yalkut Shimoni, I, 168. On the story of Moses and the Cushite woman in the Chronicles of Moses, see A. Shinan, "Moses and the Ethiopian Woman, Sources of a Story in the Chronicles of Moses," in Studies in Hebrew Narrative Art Throughout the Ages, ed. J. Heinemann and S. Werses (Jerusalem, 1968), pp. 66–78.

special property of love, and the other, the praise of love. The first he gave to his Cushite wife so that she would love him and so that he could do with her kingdom as he wished. The other he took for himself in order that she would be unable to entice him with her words and cause him to sin with her.[1]

[72] "The stars are truly the shadow of [divine] light, as we have said and as the rabbis stated: 'The sphere of the sun is an inferior variety of the light from above'[2] God also made one to correspond to the other so that through them [the stars], a woman's child among us will be able to look and see the intellectual, internal, hidden forms which are opposite our eyes, as the holy sage, R. Joseph Gikatilia wrote and was quoted by the author [Shem Tov b. Shem Tov, c. 1400] of *Sefer ha-Emunot:*[3] 'Indeed the sun and the moon are circular witnesses which teach us the form of the secret and hidden higher beings. Without the quality of the sun and the moon, we would be unable to enter the secrets of the upper chariots. Moreover, this is the secret [of the verse]: "God made the two great lights, etc."[4] The great lights were truly to enlighten the earth, to enlighten our eyes [for those] who dwell on earth so as to comprehend the secret of the hidden higher beings in the order of spiritual ascents and beyond them, the secret of the *sefirot,* and the secret of the reality of the Divinity, may He be blessed, and His unity. Indeed, all the higher and lower qualities, hidden and revealed, are all examples of the secrets of the high chariot. From what we can feel and understand, we are capable of comprehending and knowing those secrets and hidden things. So this is the secret [of the verse], "Lift your eyes to the heavens and see etc."[5]'

[73] "The seven steps of the ladder signify the seven sciences which one must climb as a preliminary stage before reaching the reality of the higher wisdom.[6] They are all introductions to it and auxiliaries of wisdom,[7] as R.

[1] I could not locate the precise source of Yagel's story here but the general context is clear. Yagel's portrait of Moses as an astrological magician is similar to that of Yohanan Alemanno, the Jewish thinker of the Renaissance whose writings deeply influenced him. See Idel, "The Magical and Neoplatonic Interpretations," p. 203. On the portrait of Moses as a magician in the ancient world, see J. Gager, *Moses in Graeco-Roman Paganism* (Nashville and New York, 1978), pp. 134–60.

[2] *Bereshit Rabbah,* 17:5. For Yagel's interpretation of a line similar to this one, see M. Idel, "Prometheus in Hebrew Garb" (in Hebrew), *Eshkolot,* n.s. 5–6 (1980–81): 119–27.

[3] Shem Tov ibn Shem Tov, *Sefer ha-Emunot* (Ferrara, 1556), sha'ar 4, chap. 19, p. 47a.

[4] Genesis 1:16.

[5] Isaiah 40:26.

[6] On the seven sciences, see generally H. Wolfson, "The Classification of Sciences in Medieval Jewish Philosophy," in *Hebrew Union College Jubilee Volume* (Cincinnati, 1925), pp. 215–63.

[7] Cf. Avot 3:18.

[Isaac ibn] Latif wrote in his book *Rav Pe'alim:*[1] 'The eye looks after seven shells and sees the stars of the eighth sphere after the seven spheres. The human intelligence fathoms the reality of the higher wisdom after the seven sciences. This is the approximate meaning of the secret of the rabbis when they stated: "How many virtues were in the ladder? Seven, etc."'

"Those letters and flowers which are at each step [of the ladder] indicate the other sciences and crafts that emerge from each [major field] [74] [and] which add up to a total of sixty. The instructional science called, in Latin, *mathematica* is included in all of them. One is only entitled to be called a mathematician who knows them [the sciences] all, who is expert in them and their terminology. However, ignorance and pride freely bestowed on man have created a situation whereby a person who understands a little about one of these fields will not only act contemptuously by calling himself [a master] of that name [of one of the fields of wisdom] as the ancients did, but will desire to be called a mathematician, which is the generic title for all [the sciences], as if he is accomplished and an expert in all of them.

"This is the situation today among many of the leaders of our people who grant permission to teach and to adjudicate to anyone in the Jewish community. One who calls himself *resh* or *ḥaver* [the titles of rabbi] mocks himself since students today are now inappropriately designated by these titles. But *resh* is a title that distinguishes a scholar from a common person, [75] as Isaac Abravanel explains in [his] book, *Naḥalat Avot,* chapter 6 [Abravanel's commentary on Avot 6:2]. And there are [even] those who wish to be called *rav, rabban,* and *gaon,* which are titles reserved for those who are ordained. They did not bother to realize that there can be no ordination [of rabbis] outside the land of Israel, as the rabbis stated at the end of *Sanhedrin*[2] and [as] quoted by Maimonides in his *Sefer Shoftim,* chapter 4 of the laws of the Sanhedrin.[3] R. Isaac Abravanel wrote there: 'It was the custom in all of Spain that as long as the leaders of the exile were in power there, no person was given ordination. However, after coming to Italy, I noticed that the custom spread to ordain one another. I saw its beginning among all the Ashkenazim who granted and received ordination and [were considered] rabbis. I did not know the origin of this permissive act except for the fact that they were jealous of the ways of the gentiles who grant doctorates, so they did likewise. If only they would ordain suitable candidates as rabbis! The great scholars of these times already wrote that a

---

[1]Isaac ibn Latif, *Sefer Rav Pe'alim* (Lemberg, 1885), no. 47, p. 15a.
[2]B. T. Sanhedrin 14a.
[3]Maimonides, *Mishneh Torah,* Sefer Shoftim, Hilkhot Sanhedrin, 4:6.

person who is proficient in three orders [of the Talmud]: *Mo'ed, Nezikin, Nashim,* can be called a "wise expert"; if he also masters the order of *Kodashim,* he can be called "rabbi"; and if he masters *Zera'im* and *Tehorot* as well, he can be called a *gaon.* How then can they ordain one who is not even proficient in [one tractate] of the *Gemarah,* etc.?"[1]

"I also heard that [the word] *gaon* is equivalent by *gematria* to [the number] sixty. This stands for the sixty tractates of the six orders [of the Talmud]. Only a person proficient in all of them is worthy of being called a *gaon,* according to what the rabbis wrote, as we have mentioned. Perhaps the honorable rabbis have been accustomed to grant ordination at this time even to those unworthy [of it] in order to arouse their minds [to acquire] wisdom so that they would learn as Rabbi did with regard to R. Yose, the son of R. Eleazar, the son of R. Simeon, as related in chapter [*Ha-Sokher Et*] *Ha-Po'alim.*[2] Also in [chapter] *Elu Kesharim:*[3] 'R. Yohanan said: "Who is a scholar who is appointed a leader over the community? He who is asked a question of the law in any place and answers it, even from the tractate *Kallah.*" R. Yohanan also said: "Who is the scholar whose work is the duty of the town's people to perform? He who abandons his own interests and engages himself in religious affairs, and that is only to provide his bread."' They [the rabbis] also state there [in the *Shabbat* passage]: 'If [he is well versed only] in one tractate, he can be appointed in his own town, if in the whole [field of] learning, [he can be appointed] as the head of the academy.'

"Note that they [the rabbis] established three categories regarding the status of a scholar. The first: If he is an expert in all the Talmud and is engrossed in its discussions, he is worthy to be a head of an academy as they had [during the period of] the patriarchate. The second: If he is an expert in one tractate [of the Talmud], that is, in the laws of one area, such as the laws of forbidden and permitted things, of property, or of women, he is then appointed in his locality to adjudicate [cases regarding] the laws of the Torah. [Such cases] come before him through questions posed to him by the members of his community, depending on the nature of the [Talmudic] tractate and the subject of his specialization. The third: If he is a person who

---

[1]On the institution of the Ashkenazic ordination, see M. Breuer, "The Ashkenazic Ordination" (in Hebrew), *Zion,* 33 (1967–68): 15–46. On the controversy over this institution in Italy and the background of Abravanel's comment, see Bonfil, *Ha-Rabbanut be-Italyah bi-Tekufat ha-Rabbanut,* pp. 23–66.

[2]B. T. Babba Meẓiah 85a. Rabbi ordained Yose a rabbi prior to his becoming a great scholar.

[3]B. T. Shabbat 114a.

abandons his [earthly] interests to pursue heavenly ones in an area in which the community needs him, whether to teach them the [proper] way to follow or to teach their children. Then the members of his town are required to perform his work like those sages who went to adjudicate and who would leave their work for others to perform so as not to neglect [the Torah], etc. Examine [the comments] of the *Tosafot* there and in the chapter *Ha-Ish Mekadesh*.[1]

[76] "The form of the globe which turns by itself in the left hand of the woman signifies that, with respect to her wisdom, no investigation can resolve [the question] whether the spheres turn by themselves or whether they have a propellant, whether an angel or a separate intelligence. The latter is the view of Avicenna, who wrote that the spheres have propellants and that out of every separate intelligence, in its generating a form of itself, another separate [intelligence] or sphere is launched until [reaching] the tenth intelligence. The latter is called the 'active intellect,' which stands under the concavity of the lunar sphere. It operates in this lower world and distributes the influence it receives from the stars to all creatures.[2]

[77] "However, from the perspective of the science of the stars, it is unnecessary to state that any separate intelligence propels them. Rather, they [the spheres] move by themselves in a natural beginning, established for them by their Creator, by which all their parts move toward a special place. It is as if you would say that the parts of the diurnal sphere [move] toward the western point and every part of the sphere, when it is away from that position, will naturally move toward it. So the stone moves toward the center [of the earth] when the stone is away from it. However, any one part can never rest there since every part of the sphere is joined together and each runs as well to reach that place. Thus by way of its circuitous course, each sphere pushes that part which has already reached that place, compel-

---

[1]The Tosafot on B. T. Shabbat 114a cite the reference to tractate *Kallah* in B. T. Kiddushin 49b, to which Yagel also refers.

[2]According to Avicenna's and Averroës' interpretations of Aristotle, there is a plurality of movers called "intelligences," transcendent beings existing apart from the spheres, that impart motion to the spheres as final causes. Avicenna, in particular, argued that the intelligences form a series of successive emanations. Each intelligence is the cause of another intelligence which emanates from it, and only God is an uncaused cause. Harry Wolfson called this view "the imposition of a Plotinian concept of immaterial emanation upon the Aristotelian view of the plurality of immaterial movers of the planetary spheres." See H. Wolfson, "The Plurality of Immovable Movers in Aristotle, Averroës, and St. Thomas," in *Studies in the History of Philosophy and Religion: Harry Austyn Wolfson*, ed. I. Twersky and G. H. Williams (Cambridge, Mass., 1973), vol. I, p. 12. See also J. Weisheipl, "The Celestial Movers in Medieval Physics," *The Thomist*, 24 (1961): 286–326.

ling the [previous part] to remove itself from that location until the time it will return and displace another part [of the sphere]. In such manner, this rotation continues,[1] eternally [contingent] only on the will of He who spoke and [for whom] the world came into being and who did not say 'enough!' But when He wishes, He can say to the sphere and [the] movement 'enough!' and then it will revert to chaos.

"This view verifies the words of Plato and anyone else who maintains that the world has no final end, and as it is written: 'But the earth stands forever.'[2] So blessed is the One who knows the truth and the only truth that we possess is the words of our sages, the kabbalists. They hold the secret of God and no mystery baffles them,[3] either small or great.

[78] "The center in the middle of the globe signifies the earth, which is in the middle of the sphere even though it is known from the science of the stars that the spheres emerge from a center that is not the earth. These are alluded to [in the representation of the globe] by the lines that radiate from it, establishing another center. Because of this [uncertainty], the naturalists were divided, because, on the basis of their knowledge, it was not possible to locate any sphere that emerges from a [different] center. However, the astronomers agreed about this matter and established this concept as a centerpiece of their learning and as a true principle, in order to verify and to discover a cause for the changing appearances of the sun and stars [that vary] from large to small and in height and depth, depending on the difference of times.[4] And even they acknowledge that when we conceive

---

[1]The entire paragraph is copied from Isaac Arama, *Akedat Yizḥak*, sha'ar 2, pp. 30b–31a. On the context of the debate whether the celestial spheres were naturally endowed with circular motion or not, see H. Wolfson, *Crescas' Critique of Aristotle* (Cambridge, Mass., 1929), pp. 77–78, 118–20, 535–38, where the sources of the natural view of Arama, Crescas, Ha-Levi, and others are discussed. The same passage of Arama was also copied by Isaac Abravanel. See Wilensky, *R. Yizḥak Arama*, pp. 54, 113–17; idem, "Isaac ibn Latif, Philosopher or Kabbalist?" in *Jewish Medieval and Renaissance Studies*, ed. A. Altmann (Cambridge, Mass., 1967), pp. 192–93.

[2]Ecclesiastes 1:4. See the previous discussion above, pp. 260–61.

[3]Cf. Daniel 4:6.

[4]Yagel here alludes to the fundamental disagreement between Aristotelian cosmology and Ptolemaic astronomy regarding the configuration and arrangement of the celestial spheres. Aristotle assumed a series of concentric spheres each moving with a natural, uniform, and circular motion in a fixed direction, and sharing a common center, the earth's center. Ptolemy, on the other hand, employed eccentric and epicyclic circles to represent planetary motions in order to account for the variations in the differences of the planets' motions as seen from the earth. Thus a planet's motion might be represented by an eccentric circle whose center was not the earth's. Medieval astronomers eventually effected a complex compromise between the two positions, saving the foundation of the Aristotelian system. For a succinct summary of the subject with bibliography, see E. Grant, "Cosmology," in *Science in the Middle Ages,* ed. D. C. Lindberg (Chicago and London, 1978), pp. 280–84.

and draw them all together, they appear in relation to each other as onion skins whose center is the earth.[1]

[79] "The third woman with a scepter in her hand is the divine science, the Torah which God gave to His chosen people upon which it is said: 'I was with Him as a confidant . . . rejoicing before Him in all times.'[2] Thus the Holy One, blessed be He, occupied Himself and created His world. If it were not for this, His covenant, He would not have established the laws of heaven and earth.[3] You can see that the beauty of her appearance and her garments allude a little to her attributes, which are superior to all other matters and sciences that God created in the world. [80] Thus, all the other sciences have a limit depending on their subject, and were created like the sea, which is unable to surpass its border because of the sand [enclosed] around it. However, it is stated in the Torah: 'Your commandment is broad without measure.'[4] Alternatively, [we might explain] that the naturalists only investigate what is on the earth and what is related to its inhabitants; the astronomers limit their inquiries to the heavens and what they generate; [81] but the Torah sage sits in the company of God,[5] knowing what is in the heaven above and on the earth below, as well as what is beyond them, reaching the Creator of everything. He begins to learn from Him, always placing God opposite him and in everything. Subsequently, he will attain knowledge from above like a man who sits at the top of a watchtower looking at what is before him and in back of him, glancing easily in a manner unavailable to one who sits at its bottom. When the latter person gazes above himself, the power of his vision is weakened and his efforts are in vain as those of all the philosophers and astronomers who requested to ascend the ladder of seven steps but never left the earth. They were only capable [of fulfilling] half their desire. Even regarding the little they attained with difficulty, they vacillated.[6] One said this and another said something else.

"This is not the case for the divine Torah sage who knows everything and who understands that which is above and below through the [holy] names of God. The diadem on her forehead alludes to this, with the four

[1]An allusion to the compromise solution in saving the Aristotelian cosmology mentioned in the previous note. For the common metaphor of the spheres as onion skins, see Maimonides, *Mishneh Torah, Sefer ha-Madda,* Hilkhot Yesodei ha-Torah, 3:2; *Moreh Nevukhim,* 1:72.

[2]Proverbs 8:30.

[3]Based on Jeremiah 33:25.

[4]Psalm 119:96.

[5]Cf. Jeremiah 15:17.

[6]Literally, "yes and no were weak in their hands." Cf. B. T. Kiddushin 65a and elsewhere.

letters of God's name engraved on it. These four letters enlighten her eyes as a beam lit in a dark and gloomy place. This is the secret of the letters, their alternating combinations and *gematriot* utilized by the kabbalists by which they engender signs in heaven and on the earth. They [the kabbalists] will demand that nature, the sun, and the stars be silent and do their [literally, 'our'] will and the latter will obey [the kabbalists] just as the slave obeys his master. In their recalling [the letters] in an appropriate fashion, the kabbalists will know how to direct the allusion to which they hint, to activate the effluvia and spirituality from the source, to clothe that spirituality in those letters, and to make wonders, as it is written: 'He will satisfy the will of those who fear Him.'[1] Anyone who wants to see a lovely discussion on the science of letter combinations and *gematriot* should look at the *Pardes* [*Rimmonim* of Moses Cordovero], gate 30, where the author elaborates [on the subject] and is deserving of praise.[2]

[82] "The scepter in her right hand signifies that dominion will come to her.[3] The scepter in her hand and the large golden crown are all [made] from fine gold without impurities because all her words are few but pure.[4] The gold is from *parvaim*,[5] producing fruit in this world and an eternal fund for the next[6] in which all is lasting,[7] as it is written: 'In her right hand is the length of days.'[8] The cup in her left hand is like the verse: 'In her left hand, riches and honor.'[9]"

## On the Correct Interpretation of These Women Figures

[83] I then said to my father: "My master, if you find me agreeable, tell me whether these women appear as allegories in the manner in which the ancient gentile writers often used them rhetorically in their poems as a mirror of everything? Are they to be understood similarly as teaching devices whose lesson is hinted at? Or rather, should we not pay attention to the allusion? Should the wise-hearted accept their command and instructions while the weak-tongued struggle to understand whether they are like

[1]Psalm 145:19.
[2]Moses Cordovero, *Pardes Rimmonim* (Jerusalem, 1962), 2, pp. 68b–72a.
[3]Cf. Micah 4:8.
[4]For the expression, see B. T. Erubin 62b.
[5]Cf. 2 Chronicles 3:6.
[6]Cf. Mishnah Pe'ah 1:1.
[7]Cf. B. T. Kiddushin 39b.
[8]Proverbs 3:16.
[9]Proverbs 3:16.

their image and likeness in the manner that I, not another, saw with my own eyes[1] this night? [Scripture states that] dreams come with much brooding.[2] Or are these three wise women actually noblewomen and masters of all the sciences and fields of learning, or creatures or kinds of forces or spiritual beings appearing in the form of these ladies? Do these women playing before us look like angels that appear to human beings? Give me understanding that I might live."[3]

[84] My father responded: "You asked a hard question and it is difficult for me to say. If it were not for our sages who have opened this gate, I would not speak about it either briefly or at length. However, I have supported you [as your guide and teacher] in standing erect with as much strength as there is until your body returns to the earth. Thus [I will allow] the light of your intelligence and spirit to enable you to see with mirrors[4] the secret and hidden things before your eyes. So now wait a little and let me hold forth[5] and I will teach you wisdom.[6]

"Know that some wise men are of the opinion that just as everything below has a constellation in heaven which strikes it and says 'grow,' as the rabbis stated regarding the verse: 'Did you know the rules of heaven, etc.,'[7] so, too, there is a separate spiritual being for every science and craft who influences and bequeaths to every person what he desires to eat in the garden of that science. That spirituality is created from the stars [and] is renewed and formed in the air of the firmament in the same way that a shadow is related to a body. This happens in the manner described by [Abraham] ibn Ezra, who wrote in the *Sefer ha-Azamim*[8] on the subject of the creation of spirits, demons, and on bringing down the emanation from above to earth. These [creatures] are the *maggidim* [celestial spokesmen or angels], the teachers of [the] sciences and crafts that are found among soothsayers.[9] Among the latter, there are those who make an incantation,

[1]Cf. Job 19:27.

[2]Cf. Ecclesiastes 5:2.

[3]Cf. Psalm 119:144. For the significance of this discussion, see the introduction above, p. 54.

[4]Cf. Exodus 38:8.

[5]Cf. Job 36:2.

[6]Cf. Job 33:33.

[7]Job 38:33; *Bereshit Rabbah*, 10:6.

[8]*Sefer ha-Azamim* (incorrectly attributed to Abraham ibn Ezra), ed. M. Grossberg (London, 1901), p. 16, and generally pp. 12–17.

[9]On the phenomenon of *maggidim* as revelatory spokesmen in the Jewish community of the sixteenth century, see L. Fine, "Maggidic Revelation in the Teachings of Isaac Luria," in *Mystics, Philosophers, and Politicians, Essays . . . In Honour of A. Altmann*, ed. J. Reinharz and D. Swetschinski (Durham, 1982) pp. 141–57; M. Idel, "Inquiries on the Doctrine of the Author of *Sefer Ha-Meshiv*" (in Hebrew), *Sefunot*, n.s. 2 (17) (1983): 201–43; R. J. Z. Werblowsky, *Joseph*

lock a spirit in a room, and dress him in the form of a teacher sitting at a desk. He then teaches one or two persons a particular science or investigation for several days. I even heard of someone who saw and heard its [the *maggid*'s] words.

"Now, regarding this subject, before their wisdom went stale and their counsel had vanished from the prudent,[1] the ancients knew this order and custom by which a person would become proficient in any science. He would cleanse himself, dress in gentile clothing, make ready and prepare himself to receive the spirituality emerging and pouring down from the star in heaven which is appointed over that specific science. He would request from Him [God] that an emanation of blessing and praise would appear to him and that he would succeed in the study in which he was to involve himself.[2] For example, when a secret spirit of the devil [literally, "the left side"] is created in the manner we have said, a secret holy spirit 'of the right side' also is created from those sparks that shine. This [latter] spirit comes to fortify a man of holiness and influence him with a spirit from on high, for if one is willing to be purified, he will be assisted.[3]

[85] "The rabbis alluded to this matter in their interpretation of the verse: 'There are sixty queens and eighty concubines.'[4] They said that the sixty represent the tractates [of the Talmud] which have queens. Each tractate has a queen appointed over it.[5] [86] This is known to us from what is written in the *Tanḥuma* regarding a pious man who had only mastered the tractate *Ḥagigah* during his lifetime. At the time of his death, a figure of a woman came to him, crying and mourning for him, uttering: 'A pious man, a modest man!,' until men and women gathered around her to mourn for that pious man. Thus they payed him honor at the time of his death, etc.[6]

"They claim that the eighty concubines constitute the eighty forces of

---

*Karo: Lawyer and Mystic* (Philadelphia, 1977); G. Scholem, "The 'Maggid' of R. Yosef Taitaẓak and His Circle, Its Nature and Its Form of Inquiry" (in Hebrew), *Sefunot*, n.s. 11 (1971–77): 67–112; S. Pines, "Le Sefer ha-Tamar et les Maggidim des Kabbalistes," *Hommages à Georges Vajda*, ed. G. Nahon and C. Touati (Louvain, 1980), pp. 333–69.

[1]Cf. Jeremiah 49:7.

[2]Compare Yohanan Alemanno's technique for performing miracles which also requires external cleansing and spiritual purification. Cf. Idel, "The Magical and Neoplatonic Interpretations," pp. 198–99.

[3]Cf. B. T. Yoma 38b. The last two lines are written in Aramaic, in the language of the *Sefer ha-Zohar*, and most likely were written to imitate the latter.

[4]Song of Songs 6:8.

[5]Cf. *Bamidbar Rabbah*, 18:21, *Shir ha-Shirim Rabbah*, 6:9, and elsewhere.

[6]This is an abbreviated version of a story that appears in Isaac Aboab's (late fourteenth century) *Menorat ha-Me'or* (Jerusalem, 1961), third candle, kelal 8, pt. 3, chap. 5, p. 443. The mourning woman in the story is the personification of the tractate *Ḥagigah*. Aboab also quotes

impurity and derive from the world of making [the lowest of the four worlds conceived by the kabbalists]. Each one has power over some science. 'And damsels without number'[1] [signifies] the other crafts created for the benefit of the political community. All of them have a constellation and [a force] appointed over them in heaven. The damsels are unlimited in number, just as the practical crafts are unlimited. These include all the thirty-nine categories of crafts which the rabbis explained in chapter *Kelal Gadol*.[2] Everything is influenced from the [fifty] gates [of wisdom], from the intention known to Moses as the rabbis stated on [the verse]: 'That you have made him a little less than divine.'[3] [87] It is written in a work of R. Mattathias:[4] 'The study of Torah will bring you the reward of divine compassion [*ḥesed*] since the word "Torah" is mathematically equivalent [to the phrase] *gemilut ḥasadim* [acts of loving-kindness].[5] The efflux of intelligence is that reward which will pour upon you. God will bestow upon you strength and power to receive that emanation by way of the known pipelines and by the known devices.'

[88] "Another text that supports us in the view that these spirits are found in everything concerns the incident the rabbis relate in *Yoma*, chapter *Ba Lo* and in chapter *Arbah Mittot Beit Din*.[6] The men of the great assembly wanted to kill the evil desire of idolatry; so they killed it. Afterward, they asked for mercy from the tempter to evil [another evil spirit] and he was handed over to them. They were told by a prophet: 'Realize that if you kill him [the spirit], the world will be destroyed.' They put out his eyes and let him go, as it is written there.

[89] "Likewise, you will see that the gentile rhetoricians drew a cupid, the minister of love, with his eye closed.[7] They did this for many reasons, as they explain. Perhaps the secret in the mind [literally, "eyes"] of the ancient

*Tanḥuma* as his source, but the story is not found in the versions now available (cf. p. 443, n. 36).

[1]The continuation of Song of Songs 6:8.

[2]Cf. B. T. Shabbat 69a.

[3]Psalm 8:6. Cf. B. T. Rosh Ha-Shanah 21b, Nedarim 38a, and elsewhere: "Fifty gates of wisdom were created in the world and all were given to Moses except one, as it is written: 'That you have made him a little less than divine.'"

[4]Probably Mattathias b. Solomon Delacrut, the sixteenth-century commentator on astronomical works as well as on Joseph Gikatilia's *Sha'are Orah* and other kabbalist writings. I was unable to locate this specific reference.

[5]The *gematria* of each is 611.

[6]B. T. Yoma 69b, Sanhedrin 64a. Yagel paraphrases and condenses the story. The evil desire of idolatry is cast into a leaden pot. The tempter to evil was first imprisoned for three days before his eyes were put out.

[7]On the motif of the blind Cupid, see E. Panofsky, *Studies in Iconology: Humanistic Themes in the Art of the Renaissance* (Oxford, 1939; New York, 1967), pp. 95–128.

rhetoricians was actually the incident the rabbis related.[1] Perhaps cupid was seen by one of the men with the same form of a closed eye. Don't be surprised by what I have said since it is based on observation and may have appeared to one of the common folk. In fact, I have seen oaths and magical phenomena where, because of love, people swear on a cupid in the company of several noblemen. If a person's effort in taking that oath is not in vain, then the believer should not allow his intelligence to deny the fact that such things actually exist. If for every blade of grass there is a constellation in heaven, how much the more so, for a science or a craft! Anyone who thinks that all this happened allegorically, that the ancients drew him this way to teach the hidden secrets of wisdom and its mysteries, and that they grasped the gate[2] of investigation and science regarding this subject, thinks like any philosophic investigator who has not deepened his thought and investigation. Rather, he understands only the books of Aristotle and his associates who only appeared recently, of whom the ancients never imagined.[3]

"But it is no loss since the truth will follow its course and blessed is the One who knows the truth. All the secrets are revealed to God alone since He created and formed them in a straight and fitting order before Him and He created [everything] for His honor, even the world and its vanities. [90] He gave to the heart of man the desire for wealth, lust, and honor, without which he would not discover the product that God made from beginning to end. All things are wearisome and man is unable to speak [about them], for his days [i.e., his life] are either in the shelter or not in the shelter of a tree [i.e., they are precarious]. And during those few days, he will complete his days and years in a world that is not his, and [he will] gather up the wind in the hollow of his hand.[4] One who adds to those vanities will add pain on his shoulders and is set on a path of no good[5] to rob people while showing himself off to be pure. He will invent every deformed judgment that emerges[6] before him, engraved on tablets. Despite every strength and effort, a passing wind that does not return[7] will carry him away. The One

---

[1] Another example of Yagel's inclination to correlate rabbinic and pagan ideas and motifs.

[2] Cf. Job 18:20; Yagel changes *sa'ar* (horror) to *sha'ar* (gate).

[3] Elsewhere, Yagel argues in a similar fashion against the philosophers who deny the existence of demons despite their "verification" by eyewitnesses. See Ruderman, *Kabbalah, Magic, and Science,* chap. 3.

[4] Cf. Proverbs 30:4.

[5] Cf. Psalm 36:5.

[6] Cf. Habbakuk 1:4.

[7] Cf. Psalm 78:39.

who sits in judgment and despises robbery with a burnt offering,[1] who tests the righteous and examines the heart and the mind,[2] will take revenge against him. With the measure that he measured others, they will measure him.[3]

## The Son Relates the Final Part of His Life Story

"But now let us take the path that leads to the hill of frankincense, the place where the three sisters whom you saw dwell. On the way, it will be good for me to hear what happened to you up until now and how the affair [in which you were involved] developed. I had left you, during the first time that I had come to you, in the prison in Luzzara. How did you get out of there and how were you brought to the city? So, now, open your mouth and let your words enlighten [me]."

[91] I responded to my father: "My master knew how I was brought to prison initially. You shall see even more terrible abominations[4] of which the nations will be dismayed.[5] All the laws of heaven that have existed from former times of yore[6] for [all] those [people] who dwell from here to the rivers of Kush called Barbary are equivalent to the evil deeds that those men did to me. Maimonides expressed this well in the *Moreh* [*Nevukhim*], [part 1], chapter 34, [when he declared] [92] that this perfect human form that does not protect its [divine] image in seeking to reach perfection might [also] utilize intelligence to cause evil, an evil worse than that of the animals of the forest. Everything that is diminished tends to its opposite and the opposite of complete good is complete evil. Therefore don't be surprised about the people of Israel. As long as they do not observe the divine commandments, when they are aroused, their intelligence will despise their image[7] and will be overturned in materiality to a quality worse than that of all peoples and cultures. The intelligence and thought that was capable of reaching perfection but will not reach [it], will be employed for all kinds of evil devices. While sitting at the table together, each person will lie to his neighbor[8] with a slippery, deceitful and false tongue. [All this] instead of

[1]Cf. Isaiah 61:8.
[2]Cf. Jeremiah 20:12.
[3]Cf. Mishnah Sotah 1:7.
[4]Cf. Ezekiel 8:6, 13, 15.
[5]Cf. Jeremiah 10:2.
[6]Cf. Isaiah 23:7.
[7]Cf. Psalm 73:20.
[8]Cf. Daniel 11:27.

the [acts of the] remnant of Israel, which shall do no wrong and speak no falsehood.[1]

"My master, you shall now see what happened to me with my accusers. So now it is fitting to inform you that after [the] ninety-one days of my first imprisonment had passed (which is equivalent to the time it takes for a woman to leave the jurisdiction of her first husband and become available to marry a second, thus distinguishing [if she gave birth] after seven [months of her second marriage] by the first husband or after nine [months] by the second[2]), my opponents acceded to grant the request of several important people to release me from prison as long as it was appropriate for these people to offer guarantees. They [my enemies] did this with guile and deceit in order to prepare another net for my feet and to satisfy their thirst by putting me in the fortress in Mantua.

"I was a fool, without knowledge[3] of this net which they prepared for me. I [assumed] that I would go out of prison and stand on the lookout with continuous hope that the distinguished R. Azariah Finzi and Judah Colonia would settle the matter, since I had placed it on their shoulders. Two months elapsed but these perfect men among us accomplished nothing. The days of [the holiday of] Purim [literally, "lots"] approached and these men [his enemies] cast a lot that sealed my fate in placing me in the net they had prepared for me during these days of Purim.

"In the same week, an official decree was sent to me, ordering me to report to the authorities [in Mantua]. Upon receiving this order, I girded my strength, rode in a passenger carriage, and came to Mantua in the company of a Christian man from Luzzara who also had to make the journey to Mantua. We arrived in the city in the evening after dark. It already was a late hour to find lodging and I did not know where to sleep for the night. Moreover, my companion pleaded with me to go to his place of lodging. So I accepted his suggestion and went with him to the home of a distinguished Christian man. I ate bread and dried figs at his table that night. However, at midnight, Eliezer, alias Lazzarino [Lazzaro], the eldest son of the Almagiati, arrived with the men of the cardinal. They arrested me and took me to the prison, locking me up in my misery and in iron. I still did not know the reason this evil had happened to me. Nor did I fear the *civilo* [civil authorities] because of the guarantees I had been given. I only knew that I had done rightly.

---

[1]Cf. Zephaniah 3:13.

[2]Cf. Mishnah Yebamot 4:10; B. T. Yebamot 42b; Maimonides, *Mishneh Torah,* Hilkhot Gerushim, 11:18; *Tur-Shulḥan Arukh Eben ha-Ezer,* 13:1, 4.

[3]Cf. Psalm 73:22.

"I thus stood all the night, thinking evil and mischievous thoughts until the morning at breakfast time. Then, the 'satyrs' came for me and brought me chained[1] before the chief judge, the head of the court. He questioned me about the place where the 'satyrs' had found me the previous night. I stated the specific place and the name of the specific person in whose company I had been.

"He continued to ask: 'Did you eat at the same table in the company of Christians and with the master of the house?'

"I answered: 'Yes, I had eaten, but not at the same table since I was only near the man.'

"He then asked: 'What did you eat?'

"I replied: 'Bread and dried figs.'

"[He further asked]: 'And what did they eat?'

"I answered: 'Fish which I did not taste.'

"He then asked: 'Didn't you realize that Hebrews cannot eat bread with Christians under the same roof by order of the duke and his officials? How could you imagine yourself ridiculing the decree of the duke and his officers?'[2]

"I replied: 'I was not aware nor had I heard of the law until now. In our city, which is under the jurisdiction of this exalted ruler, there has been no such decree upon us. What I did, I did because the hour was late and I did not know where to turn to find a place to sleep.'

"He responded: 'Your words will do you no good because it was announced publicly throughout this city and even the deaf and the fools who are impaired from obeying the law heard it. Now you must return to your place so I will consider what to do to you.'[3]

"So I returned to the closed fortress. No one was allowed to speak with me there for fifteen days until the judge [first] issued my release on bail for [a payment] of fifty *meginim* [literally, bucklers] until the time of his final verdict regarding this matter. So I paid the fifty *meginim* and the additional expenditures of the salaries of the scribes and guardians of the court, which totaled more than thirty *meginim*. Look and see, my master, and write this as a memorial in a book; put it in the ears of the later generations that will come after us!

[1] Cf. Song of Songs 7:6.

[2] The judge apparently referred to the proclamation of Duke Guglielmo of 1 March 1576, which was intended to distance Jews from Christians. Among other things, Jews were no longer allowed to purchase Christian property, nor could they socialize in Christian homes on festive occasions and celebrations. Cf. Simonsohn, *Mantua,* pp. 113–14.

[3] Cf. Exodus 33:5.

"Furthermore, when I had exited the gates of the prison after paying a small amount of the bail—having gone only a short distance of four cubits—the gatekeepers approached me a second time and returned me to jail, [this time] at the request of Lazzarino Almagiati on account of an illicit monetary matter. Indeed, I already had offered them guarantees and everything had been handed over in a pledge, a sum much larger than what they had paid me [for my bank]. I thus remained at the courthouse and they perverted and distorted justice with the power they possessed for satisfying their thirst. The slander this man Lazzarino had spread regarding my eating with Christians was not sufficient. He also added everything,[1] raising again the matter [of the earlier fiscal arrangement], while the woman dwelling in Mantua, Madame Rina, the wife of R. Jacob de Lacairo supported him [regarding my imprisonment] in jail. This time, however, she did not go toward 'snakes' [apparently, to the Almagiatis] but let others handle her affairs. She never accused me publicly, as she had done the first time, in order to clear her tracks and to state: 'Look, I am innocent!' Instead, she removed this veil and with her words, held up the crown of Israel's glory so that all would still remember the name of Israel. She did as observant Jews do; when there is a dispute between them, they turn to a rabbinic court and approach its leaders, authorities, and judges. Accordingly, she was unwilling to go with them [the Almagiati]. So they [alone] went with all their affairs and grievances to the [gentile] courts, where they [the courts] adjudicated on these matters two or three times, in any case, favoring our enemies' own estimation [of the controversy]."[2]

## The Appearance of Five Men and the Lessons of Their Lives

[93] As I was speaking these words to my father, and as we began to ascend to the hidden parts of the mountain leading to its summit, we came across five men who were approaching us, engaged in argument. They were questioning and interpreting the *beraita* [a rabbinic teaching of Palestine left out of the *Mishnah*] in chapter *Tollin:*[3] "R. Jose b. Elisha said: 'If you see a generation that is overwhelmed by many troubles, go forth and examine the judges of Israel, for all retribution that comes to the world comes only on account of the judges of Israel, as it is written: "Hear this, you heads of

[1]Literally, "the moist and the dry alike." Cf. Deuteronomy 29:18.
[2]Cf. Deuteronomy 32:31.
[3]B. T. Shabbat 139a.

the house of Israel, etc." It is also written: "Who build Zion with crime. . . . Her rulers judge for gifts, her priests give rulings for a fee."[1] They are wicked but they put their trust in He who decreed and the world came into existence.'"

One of them [the five men] asked his associate: "Was this *beraita* uttered and also heard 'at this time,' [that is,] after the judges and those responsible for justice [in Israel] had perished, since they no longer adjudicated fines in Babylonia. If one claims that it also was uttered 'at this time,' [there now appears to be] a suspension of the three punishments mentioned in that *beraita* which the Holy One, blessed be He, wrought to correspond to the categories of sin (which are: judging with a bribe, ruling for a fee, or divining for pay; the [corresponding] punishments wrought by God are: 'That Zion shall be plowed as a field, Jerusalem shall become heaps of ruins, and the Temple Mount a shrine in the woods').[2] Notwithstanding our present sins, none of these punishments have befallen us. What, then, does the Holy One, blessed be He, [now] bring upon the judges and upon Israel for the miscarriage of justice?"

His companion responded: "This *beraita* certainly refers 'to this time' since R. Jose, the teacher of this *beraita*, intended that it teach that whenever a generation experiences many tribulations, and [when] the reason for the punishment is obscure, nor is it clear what the iniquity of the generation was that caused it, we should then examine the [actions of] the judges of Israel. Every fault and accusation can be attributed to their utterances. They are her [the community's] heads and leaders who pervert justice, who support criminals, speaking arrogantly: 'Who sees us, who takes note of us?'[3] They say to themselves: 'Since there is no law on earth, so, God forbid, there is none in heaven.' [But this should not be so] since the heavenly court is punctilious [in its legal decisions] toward itself and with respect to its own behavior.

"Therefore, one should not complain about the tribulations that happen to an entire generation but about the judges of Israel who had the power to protest [against injustice] either by [the power] of royal authority or by 'the elusive twisting serpent,'[4] by which God would have heard their cry.[5] [94] For this reason, the Holy One, blessed be He, brings [punishment] to the world and to a [particular] generation corresponding to the

[1]Micah 3:9–11.
[2]Cf. Jeremiah 26:18.
[3]Cf. Isaiah 29:15.
[4]Cf. Isaiah 27:1, apparently meaning "by appeal to supernatural authority."
[5]Cf. Psalm 145:19.

three aforementioned categories of sin, as illustrated by the rabbi [Jose] following the prophetic statement. Thus the dear sons of Zion, who would never venture to set foot on the ground,[1] to enjoy themselves, and to be watered as this field plowed by the plower [was],[2] will go into slavery, as in the case of the many expulsions our forefathers experienced. The verse speaks of their sorrow: 'They shall call to the mountains, "bury us," to the hills, "fall on us."'[3] [Furthermore,] 'Jerusalem shall become heaps of ruins'[4] [indicates that] the daughters of Jerusalem, who were once valued as gold[5] at the beginning of this exile, now will go into captivity before the enemy.[6] And in the city and in the heaps of ruins, which constitute trampling and lawlessness in everything, their enemies will gloat over their downfall.[7]

[He further explained:] "'And the Temple Mount a shrine in the woods'[8] [indicates that] the mountain of our holiness and the glory of Israel, the small sanctuary, the place of our worship, the houses of our study and our assembly will become a shrine in the woods for that people [that is] likened to the beasts[9] and to the ass that is in the woods. Their nervousness will increase and there will be great distress in their complaints. Therefore the sons will hover over them as an eagle who rouses his nestlings,[10] having compassion for and taking pity on them. He will not spread his wings until the wicked judges and officers[11] of Israel will be destroyed, as it is stated: 'I will turn my hand against you and smelt out your dross as with lye.'[12] 'I will restore your judges as of old'[13] who will not show favoritism to any person and will despise iniquity in judgment. Then 'Zion,' the children of Zion 'will be redeemed with justice'[14] and the haughty and the magicians shall cease to exist,[15] as it is written: 'I will smelt out your dross as with lye, etc.'[16]

[1]Cf. Deuteronomy 28:56.
[2]Cf. Jeremiah 26:18.
[3]Hosea 10:8.
[4]Cf. Jeremiah 26:18.
[5]Cf. Lamentations 4:2.
[6]Cf. Lamentations 1:5.
[7]Cf. Lamentations 1:7.
[8]Cf. Jeremiah 26:18.
[9]Yagel apparently confuses *behamot* (beasts) with *bamot* (shrine).
[10]Cf. Deuteronomy 32:11.
[11]Cf. Deuteronomy 16:18.
[12]Isaiah 1:25.
[13]Isaiah 1:26.
[14]Isaiah 1:27.
[15]For the expression, see B. T. Sanhedrin 98a.
[16]Isaiah 1:25.

Then the wicked judges and the managers of the houses will be destroyed. The Lord will annul the judgment against you and sweep away your foes."[1]

[95] When the five men coming toward us noticed us, they quickly became silent long before we approached them. We greeted them and bowed before them. We then asked the oldest of them about what he and the other four men with him represent, as well as why they did not ascend that good mountain toward the location of the hill of frankincense.

He responded: "Know that I will answer you regarding what I and the [other] men arguing over this [passage] with me represent and why we were incapable of ascending the mount of myrrh, each one for a different reason than that of the other. I stood in this place because I saw divine men ascending from it, hosts of angels in headlong flight.[2] All of their homilies and expositions are like the words of God, being very, very fine."

He then asked: "Is there anyone who has touched the secrets of the God of Jacob with impunity like these men? As the head of the sages [Solomon], who eternally was bestowed with peace, said: '[The secret of] what happens is elusive and deep, deep down; who can discover it?'[3] It is also written: 'And how can wisdom be found?'[4] I learned the preliminary teachings that were taught to me concerning the way I was to ascend. For this purpose, all the investigations were placed on the wall before me. But I could not understand the difference between my right hand and my left as a man who does not know how to swim and imagines that his lips are [to be used] to remove the pearls from the bottom of the sea. Not only will his efforts be in vain but he will sink in deep waters since he cannot accustom himself to swim unless he regularly has learned to do so. The reason my associate who stands in second place next to me was denied this honor was because he truly had potential perfection which was never actualized due to his meager intelligence and understanding. For not every brain can become intelligent; moreover, it is not the aged who become wise.[5] The dough is poor which at its beginning was intended for spongy-cakes and in the end was used for spongy-cakes; it is inappropriate for dough-offering.[6]

"My third associate, upon seeing the magnitude and quality of specu-

[1]Cf. Zephaniah 3:15.
[2]Cf. Psalm 68:13 where "kings" is replaced by "angels."
[3]Ecclesiastes 7:24.
[4]Job 28:12.
[5]Cf. Job 32:9.
[6]Cf. Mishnah Hallah 1:5. On the dough offering, see Numbers 15:18–21. The Mishnah actually reads that this kind of dough is exempt from dough offering. Like certain dough, certain human beings lack the ability to realize their potential.

lation, strongly aspired to realize the [ultimate] purpose and to become wiser than any man instantaneously, without the prior mastery of introductions and necessary principles. He said to himself: 'One should degrade these fields [of learning]'; so he made fun of so much wearying of the flesh. He gave himself [only] to reflection rather than to the wearying of the flesh. But God wrought this evil thing [i.e., the wearying of the flesh] to afflict him. Furthermore, he did not take heed of the fact that without the connections of the sciences, one to another, the ancients would not have placed them [in perspective].

[96] "This is what the rabbi [Maimonides] wrote in the *Moreh* [*Nevukhim*], in part 1, chapter 36, that there is no way to understand God's existence except [by understanding] His acts. They explain His reality and what one should believe about Him, that is, what can be attributed to or denied Him. One therefore is obliged to examine all created things as they exist before Him. From every category, we should take true and correct principles that will be beneficial to us according to our divine demands. One may take some principles from the nature of numbers and from the special properties of geometrical forms that will provide us knowledge. Their distance from God will also indicate to us their distance from many objects. Similarly, there are many other disciplines for which the human intelligence must accustom itself and acquire the ability to establish proof and knowledge of the truth essential to it. Accordingly, one will discard the distortions that exist regarding most views of those who investigate them. It is therefore impossible, as I stated, for a person to gain human perfection without first studying the sciences that constitute the basic principles leading to perfection. This poor man wearied his intelligence with some of these subjects but disregarded others, thinking that they were not helpful or useful to him. So he turned to wingless 'sea monsters' to fly in the sky. But he fell prone on the ground.[1] Even what he possessed was taken from him. So he remained without hope and unsuccessful, as you can see.

"My fourth associate possessed a natural disposition from birth that prevented his intelligence from reaching perfection. [97] In fact, he had a temperament that was the opposite of one appropriate to a person attempting to acquire perfection. One who aspires to perfection requires a pleasurable and harmonious personality to learn good qualities, to control his passion, and to be satisfied with what he has.[2] [He also requires] other good qualities connected to this: humility, courteousness, etc. All of them

[1]Cf. 1 Samuel 28:20.
[2]Cf. Avot 4:1.

[these qualities] can be found, [albeit] with difficulty, in any man who initially was of such poor character that his nature tended to one of its four [extreme qualities], as in the case of this person. His heart was heated, he had a strong nature and constitution, and he learned to hunt the prey of man. But because of his anger and explosiveness, smoke came out of his nostrils, the condition of his eggs was moist and hot, and the forces of the [bodily] structure and the pockets of semen produced so much that it was very difficult for him to guard from sinning in [not showing] reverence to his Creator. His lust was enhanced, and although a thief is not held in contempt for stealing to appease his hunger, [he is still punished].[1] This [condition] became a cause of stumbling and of faltering sin[2] [and prevented] his ascent to the good mountain and the hill of frankincense.

"My fifth associate was also born in poverty; moreover, the sins of his wife and children overwhelmed him. He was so degraded and his house was so empty that he had no opportunity[3] to go to the houses of study. In fact, if one would have weighed his time, he would have remained without any at all, by which he might have been able to reach perfection in something. He was even poorer than Hillel. Rather, he enhanced his desire for the vanities of wealth and emersed himself in them. Out of his desire for what was necessary, he sank into what was unnecessary. He relinquished his trust in God on high so that when he died, he remained totally isolated. Whatever profit he gained from the vanities of the world, it amounted to a flower pot with holes. He even discarded this pot [i.e., the little profit he had gained] for the woman he later married. His widow and orphans begged for food but did not find it because of the toil of their father, who had lost everything. Since he did not have compassion, measure for measure, the orphans also did not find compassion."

Some time later, we turned away from them and we went up the slope [of the Mount] of Olives,[4] facing in the direction of the north. [98] My father then declared: "Know my son, Abraham, there are two ways to ascend the summit of this mountain. One is short and one is long. The short cut was discovered by the Ancient of Days [God] with the covenant of His treasured possession, the remnant of His inheritance [Israel], whereby no one will sin, nor speak falsely, nor desire to drink with thirst from the words

[1]Cf. Proverbs 6:30.
[2]An emendation of 1 Samuel 25:31.
[3]Cf. Ecclesiastes 9:11.
[4]Cf. 2 Samuel 15:30. This is Yagel's first mention of his approach to the Mount of Olives; previously, he had referred only to the ascent of the mount of myrrh and the hill of frankincense.

of the philosophers and from alien customs.[1] Rather, they will satisfy their thirst by approaching the living waters, as the verse states: 'Ho, all who are thirsty, come for water,'[2] and 'water' [in this context] signifies Torah.[3] They will receive willingly and without hesitation the words of our revered sages and their riddles, which Moses received on Sinai.

"In this manner, no one will interfere with them as long as their hearts are [turned] toward heaven. Whether one [studies Torah] much or little, he is rewarded as long as his intention is directed to heaven.[4] Our holy Torah possesses this perfection with the special virtue of the Creator, who bestows perfection in general to all who occupy themselves with it [the Torah]. So the rabbinic expression goes:[5] 'God wanted to benefit Israel; thus He increased for her the Torah and the commandments, as it is said: "The Lord desires His [servant's] vindication [that he magnify and glorify Torah]."'[6]

"If these five men whom we have met had occupied themselves with it [Torah] and had not involved themselves with other theses in order to ascend to the summit of the mountain, they would have succeeded. Consider the first man, who realized the depth of things but feared to approach them. He would not have experienced what happened to him if he had read and studied what the children in the academy of Raban studied: The [Talmudic] Orders of *Mo'ed, Nashim,* and *Nezikin* and the like. With these, he would have acquired perfection for his soul, one step after the next. Thus he would have learned how to swim in the depths of the great sea which God created in order to enliven and save our souls from death. [99] Even if he had not emersed himself deeply in the secret of *halakha* [Jewish law], [he would have saved his soul], as the rabbis already declared regarding the verse: 'His banner of love was over me, even if he mocked me with love, etc.'[7] This line refers to him. He would have learned much as long as his intention had been [directed] toward heaven.

"If he had gone out and learned from the saint [about] whom I spoke to you, [who was] mentioned in *Tanḥuma* [and] who only studied the [Talmudic] tractate of *Ḥagigah,* he would have gained much profit from only this [exposure].[8] The rabbis accordingly taught in the Jerusalem

[1]For the expression, see Isaiah 2:6.
[2]Isaiah 55:1.
[3]Cf. B. T. Babba Kamma 17a.
[4]Cf. B. T. Berakhot 5b.
[5]B. T. Makkot 33b.
[6]Isaiah 42:21.
[7]Song of Songs 2:4. Cf. *Bamidbar Rabbah,* 2:3: "Even if a man sits and occupies himself with Torah and skips over one law to the next, the Holy One, blessed be He, says he is loved by Me."
[8]See above, Part II, sec. 85.

Talmud *Berakhot*[1] regarding the verse: 'A worker's sleep is sweet, whether he has much or little to eat, etc.'[2] The rabbis also stated explicitly and not by implication in *Avot:* 'It is not for you to finish the work, etc.'[3]

[100] "Even the limited knowledge of men is not initially a hindrance to learning, since you can find people whose minds are like that of those men. The Torah contains this perfection which, first and foremost, makes the fool wise, as it is written: 'The testimony of the Lord is true, making wise the simple.'[4] We can learn from R. Eliezer the Great, who went up to R. Yohanan ben Zakkai after the morning plowing to study Torah and learned, as it is mentioned in the first chapter of his chapters.[5] For is there any person, whatever his nature, who is incapable of understanding a verse or a saying either from a book or by word of mouth? And anything, whether insignificant or great, can provide much perfection. Note to what extent our sages emphasized this fact when they declared in [chapter] *Ḥelek:*[6] 'The child, when he is able to answer "amen," enters the next world; for with this, they acquire so much perfection for their souls that it brings them to the next world.'

[101] "The length of the premises [of a given field of study] also should not hinder someone from ascending the mountain of God [to reach] the lands of the living. What the philosophers know in their investigations and casuistry—regarding the creation of the world, its nature, and its character, who created it and how much water was created—even after their toil and effort, will amount to nothing. Who among them has stood in the council of the Lord?[7] The Jewish child who goes to school is taught by his father: 'In the beginning, God created [the earth], and in six days He made His world. On the seventh day, He rested.' He also knows His purpose and capacity and His providence [over everything] from buffalo's horns to gnats.[8]

"The rabbis similarly declared:[9] 'A small one among them knows how the Holy One, blessed be He, created His world, etc.' [102] It is like the incident when R. Joshua struck the shoulder and head of the philosopher

[1]J. T. Berakhot 2:8.
[2]Ecclesiastes 5:11.
[3]Avot 2:16.
[4]Psalm 19:8.
[5]*Pirke de R. Eliezer,* chap. 1.
[6]B. T. Sanhedrin 110b.
[7]Cf. Jeremiah 23:18.
[8]For the expression, cf. B. T. Avodah Zarah 3b. Compare a similar formulation of the entire paragraph in M. Idel, "The Sefirot above the Sefirot," *Tarbiz,* 51 (1982): 279.
[9]*Shemot Rabbah,* 30:9.

who had asked him, on the basis of his investigation and experience: 'How long is the birth of a serpent?' R. Joshua immediately learned [the answer] on the basis of a verse where it is written: 'You are cursed from among all cattle and from among all the beasts of the field.'[1] Now if [the serpent] was cursed [to go with young for a period] longer than cattle, [how much] longer must this have been than that of the beast? So [the object of the verse is] to tell you [the following]: Just as the cattle is cursed [to go with young] longer than the beast in the proportion of one to seven, (What is [an example of] this? An ass which [goes with young longer] than a cat), so [the serpent] is cursed [to go with young] in the proportion of one to seven [in relation to the cattle], which is seven years, etc.[2] Look as well in *Bereshit Rabbah*.[3]

"Thus the philosopher left dispairing, since R. Joshua found an argument, based on interpreting one verse of the Torah, more useful than all the experience [of the philosopher]. You will find similar examples with even greater potency and strength regarding the wisdom and morality of our sages over those of the nations [of the world], as the Talmud explains in several places [103] and especially in tractate *Bekhorot,* in the first chapter regarding that incident of R. Joshua ben Hananiah.[4] [The latter] declared before the emperor that he was wiser than the sages of the Athenian school. Thus he followed his own wisdom and brought them [his proofs] to him [the emperor], as is mentioned there. Based on this [one] act, you will then appreciate his wondrous statements and accomplishments among the sages of the Athenian school that surpass the limit of all the sciences.

"Likewise, the rabbis mentioned in chapter *Kol Ha-Yad:*[5] 'Ifra Hormiz [a gentile woman who observed some Jewish ritual], the mother of King Shapur, once sent some blood to Raba when R. Obadiah was sitting in his presence. Having smelt it, he [Raba] said to him [R. Obadiah]: "This is the blood of lust." "Come and see," she remarked, "how wise the Jews are." "It is quite possible," he [R. Obadiah] replied, "that he [Raba] hit upon it like a blind man on a window." Thereupon she sent to him sixty different kinds of blood and he identified them all, etc.'

"From these accounts and others like them, which are very numerous, you may understand the great wisdom, either natural, mathematical, or

---

[1]Genesis 3:14.
[2]Cf. B. T. Bekhorot 8a–8b.
[3]Cf. *Bereshit Rabbah,* 28:3; 78:1.
[4]Cf. B. T. Bekhorot 8b.
[5]B. T. Niddah 20b.

divine, that was in the minds of our fathers, the sages. [104] They learned everything in a manner different from that of the philosophers. The latter spend their lives finding evidence and proof for one fact which afterward is taken as a premise or an assumption to understand something else. This fact is then accepted as correct by scholars and students and appears to them as a first premise without [further] effort on their part. But the premises stated by the man, which are taken from mathematics, geometry, and other such fields, are unnecessary for our sages in order for them to train their intelligence and to acquire wisdom. They can understand and learn much from the order [of the Mishnah] *Zera'im* [*Seeds*], from the laws of forbidden mixtures in the orchard or in weaving, or regarding the laws of boundaries and measurements that contain [principles of] the science of geometry and mathematics, things that train their minds in wisdom and establish the truth. Don't we learn in the argumentation of students accustomed to study the Talmud and the order of damages [in particular] what the rabbis declared in chapter *Get Pashut:*[1] [105] 'He who would be wise should engage in the study of civil laws; for there is no branch in the Torah more comprehensive than they are, which are like a bubbling spring'? Similarly, the author [Isaac Arama] of *Akedat Yizhak* expressed the thought in a beautiful homily in gate 46, where he explains well the advantage of the Torah and its study over all the other sciences. He substantiates all of this with true and correct proofs.[2]

"Notice as well the natural preparation that causes the temperament of man to become imbalanced as he fulfills the desire of his heart and neglects study, as in the case of the fourth friend whom we met. But the study of Torah, which is called salvation,[3] weakens a person's vitality so that he is saved like a deer out of the hand [of a hunter].[4] If, therefore, his heart within him will burst, [he will be protected by Torah study] as the rabbis emphatically[5] declared: [106] 'If this repulsive wretch [the evil inclination] assails you, lead him to the schoolhouse.'[6]

"Who is a lustful person? He who desires one of the things for which the biblical text demands: 'Turn away and don't do it!' Because of the iniquity tied to the heel of the sinners and the punishments which befall them, the warnings in the Torah were issued so as [for them] not to go

[1]B. T. Babba Batra 175b.
[2]Isaac Arama, *Akedat Yizhak,* II, pp. 117a–129b.
[3]Cf. *Pirke de R. Eliezer,* chap. 3.
[4]Cf. Proverbs 6:5.
[5]Meaning not certain.
[6]Cf. B. T. Succah 52a; Kiddushin 30b.

astray. If a person sins, since no one is totally righteous on the earth,[1] he should repent immediately to God. And if he does this, he need not worry. Who is the man who would not tremble and make a guilt offering[2] upon hearing the annual call of the ram's horn awakening the sleepers and arousing the slumberers, calling them to repent of their wicked ways?[3] On Yom Kippur, when everyone fasts and sits as divine angels, there is no opportunity for Satan, the evil inclination which is the angel of death, to bring charges [against humanity]. It is a day for a person to afflict his soul and to bow down his head like a bulrush.[4] He should not be afraid lest he think [bad thoughts]; rather he should prepare his soul to repent so that he will hear [God's] voice.

[107] "Torah study should not inhibit activity related to material needs. It is not our responsibility to finish the work.[5] Moreover, the rabbis declared explicitly and not by implication:[6] 'Excellent is Torah learning together with a worldly profession.' We find that most of the sages of Israel were also craftsmen and artisans as, for example, R. Joshua, who knew that R. Gamaliel was a charcoal burner [upon seeing] the walls of his house.[7] Abba Hilkia worked in the field[8] and R. Joseph[9] and many among the great scholars toiled at their labor and studied the Torah.

"For the Torah has ten hands[10] exceeding all the other sciences, as we have said, in everything and in every way, and particularly in this respect: All the other sciences require the participant to give up his other activities and to devote himself exclusively [to them]. If he does not, he will fail to succeed, since wisdom and [the pursuit of] an occupation are entirely unrelated. They are opposites which cannot stand together in one subject.[11] However, since the Torah is the beginning of God's ways[12] and the beginning of everything, and that everything is found wherever one goes and in every act one does, a person should thus take heed of the commands of the Torah. Accordingly, [the instructions on] how a person should seed

[1]Cf. Ecclesiastes 7:20.
[2]Cf. Isaiah 53:10.
[3]Cf. 2 Kings 17:13; Ezekiel 33:11.
[4]Cf. Isaiah 58:5.
[5]Cf. Avot 2:16.
[6]Avot 2:2.
[7]Cf. B. T. Berakhot 28a.
[8]Cf. B. T. Ta'anit 23a.
[9]According to B. T. Menahot 82a, he was a winegrower. Cf. also B. T. Babba Batra 22b–23a.
[10]For the expression, see 2 Samuel 19:44.
[11]For the expression, see Maimonides, *Moreh Nevukhim*, 1:15.
[12]Cf. Job 40:19.

his field will not leave his mind but will always stand before his eyes. Thus he will remember not to seed forbidden mixtures and will reflect on all the laws related to this commandment. If he is a refined person or better, he will devote himself to certain aspects of a field of wisdom that he is capable of understanding, to the reasons why things are forbidden and permitted, and, [for example], why the rabbis stated:[1] 'There is no prohibition of forbidden mixtures in the vineyard until one sows wheat with barley or with a pomace of kernels by throwing seed, according to the view of R. Josiah.' [He might understand] why one man may not flank a field of grain, mustard, or safflower, but one may flank a vegetable field.[2] Thus one can observe scrupulously every detail of the laws of forbidden mixtures and seeds, giving a good reason for them all.

"To the extent a person is able to augment and elevate these things, he should do [them]. For the sages did not count these things fortuitously like those who count up spices,[3] but rather they said this and not that [with good reason]. Similarly, one who builds his house should recall the commandment of fixing his openings and windows so they are not opposite the courtyard of his neighbor. For the damage of overlooking is a substantial one.[4] It is like the evil Balaam's statement. When he came to curse Israel and saw that each tent among the tents of Israel did not have an opening opposite another one, [he declared]: 'How goodly are your tents, O Jacob, etc.'[5] Thus one gains from the wisdom of these good practices. If damage of overlooking is forbidden, how much the more so for other damages and their causes! If a man is a craftsman or an artisan, he should remember the verse when making a parapet: 'If a man falls from it [his roof]'[6] and its [rabbinic] explanation that he was predestined to fall, etc. [thus the owner is not responsible].[7]

"One can thus generalize that in all man's dealings and to everything [to which] he turns and does, he should be wise and remember the words of the Torah. God's commandments and statutes should always be before his eyes, even at the times when he is not doing them, in order to provide a good reason and explanation, as we have stated. If a man who works as a laborer in the field is accustomed to read on a regular day in the evening, he

---

[1]Cf. B. T. Ḥullin 82b.
[2]Cf. Mishnah Kilayim 2:8.
[3]For the expression, see Mishnah Terumot 11:2.
[4]Cf. B. T. Babba Batra 2b–3a.
[5]Numbers 24:5.
[6]Deuteronomy 22:8.
[7]Cf. B. T. Shabbat 32a, which actually reads: "It is appropriate that this [man] fall."

should read. If he is accustomed to study, he should study. He should establish set times for Torah study[1] and should be careful to complete his portion each day. He should do what R. Nahman bar Isaac stated in chapter *Ha-Dar:*[2] 'We are all day workers. R. Aḥa b. Jacob borrowed [from the day time] and repaid [it in the night].' Thus one should be able to involve himself in Torah and in his work and the needs of earning a living for his household. In all his ways, he will come to know his Creator and His ordinances. He will eat of the fruit of his labor in this world and the fund will be placed and guarded for his soul in great perfection in the next.[3] How glorious is this treasure to those who revere the Lord and esteem His name![4]

"Thus you see, according to these words, that if the five men had traveled this short route, they certainly would have reached the top of the mountain of myrrh. If they would not have been able to enter into the houses and the ascents in the palace before me and you—for every person is not meritorious of this, as the rabbis stated:[5] 'I have seen the sons of heaven, and they are but few'—nevertheless, they would have entered the palace and sat there, from the oldest in the order of his seniority to the youngest in the order of his youth,[6] each according to his station. [108] Thus the rabbis taught:[7] 'Every member [of the people] of Israel has a portion in the world to come and your people are all righteous, etc.' They further stated:[8] 'Every righteous person has a station according to his honor. Everyone will be burned by reason of [his envy of the superior] canopy of his friend,' just as the ability to see is impaired by looking at a translucent and illuminating body. Every person will be differentiated from another, each according to his power and the strength of his gaze.

"One who finds it difficult to understand these five men and considers that human perfection is dependent on a particular wisdom or field of learning other than the divine Torah, shall fall into evil and remain at the bottom of the mountain, isolated from all sides and from every good thing in this world and the next. [109] Accordingly, both in this world and the next, when a person experiences illness, expulsion, pain, or old age, and

---

[1]Cf. B. T. Shabbat 31a.
[2]B. T. Eruvin 65a.
[3]Based on B. T. Shabbat 82a, Mishnah Pe'ah 1:1.
[4]Cf. Malachi 3:16.
[5]Cf. B. T. Sukkah 45b.
[6]Cf. Genesis 43:33.
[7]B. T. Sanhedrin 90a.
[8]B. T. Babba Meẓiah 53b.

thus cannot accomplish his work or study, he must die of hunger or be obliged to wander for bread and ask forgiveness. However, one who involves himself in the Torah does not share such a fate. The Torah stands by his side in his hour of need and gives him a future and a hope in his old age, as it is written: 'Those who believe in God will renew their strength.'[1]

"The rabbis similarly taught at the end of *Kiddushin:*[2] 'R. Nehorai said: "I abandon every trade in the world and teach my son only Torah, for man enjoys the reward thereof in this world while the principal remains for him in the world to come. But all other professions are not so, etc." ' Moreover, at a time of misfortune when the wheel turns, it is like what the rabbis stated in chapter *Sho'el:*[3] 'It was taught that R. Eleazar [Ha-Kappar] said: "Let one always pray to be spared this fate [of poverty], for if he does not descend [to poverty] his son will, and if not his son, his grandson, for it is said: 'In return for [*bi-gelal*] this thing, etc. [for helping the poor, God will bless you].'[4]" The school of R. Ishmael taught: "It is a wheel [*galgal*] that revolves in the world, etc." It is held there [as a tradition in this text] that a rabbinical student does not suffer poverty. He does not engage in begging.' Rather his food is available to him because of [his] honor and it was always the case that he sat at the front [of the academy] and was the first to enter while everyone heeded his voice."

[110] Subsequently, I asked my father: "What was the reason that these five men whom we met were interpreting the aforementioned *beraita?*"

He responded: "If they had interpreted another *beraita,* you would have similarly asked me. Nevertheless, I shall give you a reply[5] for it is impossible to discharge you with nothing. I realize that above everything else, they interpreted this *beraita* for two reasons. First, for themselves. For if the judges of Israel and her leaders in every generation had supervised the children of the house of Raban and their fathers; and if they had rushed to send them to the house of study and obliged the rich to supply provisions to the needy and to those whose homes were empty; and if they had hired a teacher to train their children as David and Hezekiah, the kings of Judah, had done [111] (as the rabbis indicate in chapter *Helek:*[6] 'Search was made from Dan to Be'er Sheba and no baby boy or girl was found who was not versed, etc.' It is also stated there: ' "And the yoke shall be destroyed because

[1]Isaiah 40:31. The last three lines are based on the Mishnah of B. T. Shabbat 82a.
[2]B. T. Kiddushin 82a.
[3]B. T. Shabbat 151b.
[4]Deuteronomy 15:10.
[5]Cf. Job 35:4.
[6]B. T. Sanhedrin 94b.

of the oil."[1] [This means that] the yoke of Sennacherib shall be destroyed on account of the oil that Hezekiah burnt in the synagogues and schools, etc.'), [if they had done all these things], what did happen would not have happened, whereby they [are obliged] to stand at the bottom of the mountain without the ability to ascend and reach the hill of frankincense.

"Second, perhaps [they interpreted this *beraita*] because they heard your words regarding the horrible things done to you by your opponents. There was no teacher among them, just as there was no God in Israel. These five men were incensed at the judges and rabbis of that region on your account, since they [the judges] were able to protest but did not. If initially they had corrected the matter,[2] it would not have evolved to the extent that thousands of gold dinars of the Jewish community were wasted, as it happened, so that by an act of God,[3] it came about that these men were the cause. All [the members of] the Jewish community there were like silent ones and mutes. They did not protest the matter so that justice could not collect its due from the guilty parties. For the Lord is a just God[4] and does not punish without cause."[5]

[112] I responded: "My master, your thoughts are correct. What is most difficult for me is this affair and even more difficult for me is their devious talk[6] in which they spoke maliciously about me. Especially the great man among giants like a tower of David, Zuaro [probably "Lazzaro," Eliezer Almagiati], wrote bitter things against me and vengeful things against my departed brother,[7] claiming that I was the instigator of many quarrels and other charges that wrought sin, anger, and agitation. With all due respect to him, he was not accurate in his charges for two reasons. [As the rabbis declare:] 'Our teacher was mistaken in his teaching and he must reverse it.'[8] First, being a father to many and an old man who had acquired wisdom, with gray hairs here and there upon him,[9] he should have offered proof, if I had sinned according to his view. He should have spoken to me directly and if [then] I had committed an iniquity, I would not do so again.[10] [He should have] pointed out the way before me to Goshen, [to

---

[1]Isaiah 10:27.
[2]Literally, "made repairs." Cf. 2 Kings 12:6 and elsewhere.
[3]Cf. Exodus 21:13.
[4]Cf. Lamentations 1:18.
[5]For the expression, see B. T. Berakhot 5b.
[6]Cf. Proverbs 4:24.
[7]I cannot identify him by name or determine the time of his birth or death.
[8]B. T. Ketubbot 84b.
[9]Cf. Hosea 7:9.
[10]Cf. Job 34:32. The original has *avel* instead of *avon;* both terms mean "iniquity."

reach] God[1] and the ways of repentance taught in the verse: 'You shall surely rebuke your neighbor and not bear sin because of him.'[2]

"Second, he judged me in isolation. He did not consider that a judge is required for my case to hear the charges of both parties. [The verse that states: 'The ordinances] which you shall set before them'[3] suggests that the judge should hear both parties speaking together, for if he listened to only one party, the first [one he heard] would be acquitted in his quarrel. He also did not ask that his neighbor come [as a witness] so that he could examine him. There are many more complaints and bitter remarks made regarding Abraham [myself] that are made without confirmation. First [among these is] that I have no right to complain against him since he did me no wrong. He harmed neither my body nor my property but only spoke words [against me]. But words spoken in private or in the public domain[4] are inappropriate for a man like him; nor will they bring him honor but [rather] will make him appear as a slanderer, God forbid.

"But I, in my innocence, went along. When those who paid him attention told me of his words, I told them to keep quiet and not to be informers[5] regarding this man since he could not have spoken these things. They could never have crossed his mind and you [they] murmur lies about him. Even when I saw his own writing to my departed brother, filled with baseless and evil words from one end to the other, I still decided to be silent and restrain myself,[6] since I am a young man in comparison with him, and the truth would follow its course. Perhaps a means of proof could be established.

"Furthermore, I would not question his words lest, God forbid, the young man would appear to bully the old.[7] I would bear the indignation of God[8] since I would have sinned against Him. If the Lord has incited him against me, let Him be appeased by an offering. But if it is men [who are responsible], may they be accursed before God[9] because they made me objectionable[10] in the eyes of the civil authority[11] for no offense of mine

[1] Based on Genesis 46:28.
[2] Leviticus 19:17.
[3] Exodus 21:1.
[4] Literally, "in my inner or outer chambers." Cf. B. T. Ḥagigah 5b.
[5] For the expression, see B. T. Gittin 56a and elsewhere, and see the autobiographical sections above, where it is also used.
[6] Cf. Isaiah 42:14.
[7] Cf. Isaiah 3:5.
[8] Cf. Micah 7:9.
[9] Cf. 1 Samuel 26:19.
[10] Cf. Exodus 5:21.
[11] Literally, "officer."

and for no transgression.¹ From the day I was born, I never had appeared to him [Almagiati] as a trickster,² doing anything that was unpleasurable to him. But now, for no reason, he pursues me with his words like one hunts a partridge in the mountain.³ [113] So please listen, my master! Do you think these troubles that I encountered were atonement for some of my iniquities and will they rescue my soul, to some extent, from the punishment of that [i.e., the next] world?"

He [my father] responded: "Undoubtedly, when a person experiences either a few or many tribulations he should accept each of them for the sake of Heaven and should submit to the divine judgment. When he prays to God, He [God] will remove these afflictions from him; what he received will be an atonement for all his sins. Then these afflictions will cleanse his sins and transgressions,⁴ and this is certainly the case for such tribulations whereby your flesh and blood was diminished and the disgrace clung to your soul. When it is stated concerning a person who receives lashes: 'Then your brother will be dishonored before your eyes,'⁵ this indicates that since he received lashes, he is like your brother.⁶ Certainly, in your case, where you repeatedly received lashes and where your opponents did not spare anything in what they inflicted upon you, as long as you ask forgiveness for your sins, the Holy One, blessed be He, will heed your cry.⁷ These things will then be an atonement for all your iniquities.

"Look at what the rabbis declared in *Eruvin* in chapter *Mi She-Hozi'uhu*:⁸ 'Three kinds of persons do not see the face of Gehenna. They are: [one who suffers from] oppressive poverty, one who is afflicted with bowel diseases, and [one who is in the hands of] the *reshut*.' Rashi interpreted *reshut* [in that passage] to mean one who has creditors. There they simply spoke of a person who has creditors but did not refer to a person like you who is victimized by the cruel acts of his creditors. The judgment you received was not [meant] to be for one who committed an intentional crime. Therefore, if you cry about the retribution received due to your many sins and seek compassion from God, He will bring healing to you⁹ in this world and cure you of your wounds in the next. Then you shall stand

---

¹Cf. Psalm 59:4.
²Cf. Genesis 27:12.
³Cf. 1 Samuel 26:20.
⁴For the expression, see B. T. Berakhot 5a.
⁵Deuteronomy 25:3.
⁶Cf. B. T. Sanhedrin 10b and note the similar usage above.
⁷Cf. Psalm 40:2.
⁸B. T. Eruvin 41b.
⁹For the expression, cf. Jeremiah 30:17 and elsewhere.

before Him as you previously did, your house will be established as in former times, and He will punish all your oppressors."

### The Encounter with the Mother of All Languages and Her Discourse

[114] In the meantime, we ascended to the ascent of [the Mountain of] Olives,[1] opposite the path leading to the north. When we reached the summit of the mountain, a woman approached us, projecting the image of a noblewoman, beautiful as the moon and radiant as the sun.[2] She was dressed in black and flowing a black [color].[3] But her head was like crimson wool and the lock of her hair was like purple,[4] giving her a beautiful appearance. We recognized that she was a virgin because her head [literally, hair] was disheveled.[5] Moreover, her two breasts were like two fawns, twins of a gazelle[6] [that were] beautiful in appearance. From these two wells flowed fresh water that surged and became more powerful until the water swelled into a gushing stream that could not be crossed[7] except by a powerful boat.

On both banks of the river were babes sitting and playing, drinking with great thirst from the waters of the river which were as sweet as honey in their mouths.[8] From these waters, they obtained their vitality and nourishment. The river flowed around a castle that was on the hill of frankincense. Near the same castle on both banks of the river sprouted all kinds of pleasant and beautiful trees whose fruit is good to eat, whose leaves will not whither nor their fruit fail, but will yield new fruit daily.[9] So from the breasts of the woman they [the waters] flow, while on the banks of the river roses and other flowers bloom, whose good fragrance can be scented from a distance, spiced with the perfume of oranges in the field, like aloes planted by the Lord.[10]

[115] I then asked my father about this woman and about the powerful

[1]For the expression, see 2 Samuel 15:30.
[2]Cf. Song of Songs 6:10.
[3]Meaning uncertain.
[4]Cf. Song of Songs 7:6.
[5]Cf. Leviticus 13:45.
[6]Cf. Song of Songs 4:5 and 7:4.
[7]Cf. Ezekiel 47:5.
[8]Cf. Ezekiel 3:3.
[9]Cf. Ezekiel 47:12.
[10]Cf. Numbers 25:6.

waters running from her two breasts which provided food for the several thousand and tens of thousands of children who sat on the banks of the river. He answered me:

"This woman is the science of language who speaks correctly in every one of the seventy languages.[1] This is the entrance to the reception room whereby a person is able to know and understand every science. When a person drinks with thirst from the waters of this river until he is able to understand how to speak clearly and with beguiling words, it will then be easier for him to comprehend every science, and what he will learn, he will retain. It is similar to what the rabbis stated in *Eruvin* chapter [*Kezad*] *Me'abrin:*[2] 'R. Judah said in the name of Rab: "The Judeans who cared [for the beauty of] their language [were rewarded], for the Torah was fulfilled in their hands; but the Galileans who did not care [for the beauty of] their language [were not rewarded], so the Torah was not fulfilled, etc."' Thus anyone who studies any book or science should concentrate and be exacting regarding its language and should lay down signs [i.e., mnemonics] as it is written: 'Erect markers.'[3] It is also written: 'And call understanding [i.e., of language] a kinswoman.'[4] Thus you will succeed in any particular science.

"If a person fails to understand the purity of a particular tongue and [fails to penetrate] a language that can be interpreted from many perspectives, how can he utilize it with precision since his words will be like those of a sealed document[5] which hides its sayings from him in the future, [including those] regarding the law of messianic times?[6] However, he who tends a fig tree will enjoy its fruit.[7] What is [the meaning of] this fig tree? Whenever a person touchs it, he finds figs; similarly for one who knows a language precisely, anytime he acquires a book in that language, he finds in it good taste and knowledge. This science will be a loving doe and a graceful mountain goat[8] to him for all times."

We came closer to this important woman and bowed to her from afar. She responded to us gently and clearly in the holy language. She also prostrated herself on the ground and declared: "peace." [116] We then asked

---

[1]Compare the description of "Grammatica" in Ripa, quoted in the introduction, p. 56, n. 173. On the entire discourse on language, see the introduction above, pp. 56–60.

[2]B. T. Eruvin 53a.

[3]Jeremiah 31:21.

[4]Proverbs 7:4.

[5]Cf. Isaiah 29:11.

[6]Cf. B. T. Sanhedrin 51b.

[7]Cf. Proverbs 27:18.

[8]Cf. Proverbs 5:19.

her which language she was teaching the babes who were nursing from the waters flowing from her two breasts.

She responded: "I teach them from all the seventy languages, to each person according to his own language and according to the particular way he writes."

We then asked her: "How is it possible that from only one river such an ever-changing suckling can be dispersed?"

She answered: "Know accordingly that God created man upright from his beginning,[1] bestowing on him the spirit of life, a spirit of words,[2] and a language with which heavenly angels address him, which is the holy language. For the world was created with the holy language, [117] as the rabbis declared in *Bereshit Rabbah*, chapter 18: '[regarding the verse] "For from man she was taken."[3] From this you can learn that the world was created with the holy tongue. Have you ever heard them say [in Greek or Aramaic]: "gina, ginia, etc."? No. But one may say in Hebrew] *ish* [man] and *isha* [woman] since one form corresponds to the other [both masculine and feminine forms are found in the same word].'

"This holy tongue is the most perfect of them all, not only because one discovers in it correspondences of word forms, as I have mentioned, but also because it is the top of the citadel of all languages. All the world's languages take from her while she never takes from them. Her special virtues and words are so numerous that one who writes to praise her will weary. Furthermore, one who enuciates [this language] with his lips and with flowery expression surpasses the beauty of any other language. From the location of [the *sefirah* of] *binah*, this 'higher mother' was hewn.[4] Thus it is an inheritance to the remnant of the children of Israel, for she [the holy language] takes compassion on her children and all of the good qualities return to her. She is thus called repentance [*teshuvah;* literally, "returning"] as well as a stream, as in the verse: 'Sending forth its roots by a stream.'[5]

[1]Cf. Ecclesiastes 7:29.

[2]Cf. Daniel 7:11; Targum Onkelos on Genesis 1:7.

[3]*Bereshit Rabbah,* 18:4; 31:8 on Genesis 2:23. Note that this passage, along with several others below, is also found in Azariah de' Rossi's *Me'or Enayim* (Vilna, 1864–66), Imrei Binah, p. 453 (de' Rossi's discussion of the antiquity of the Hebrew language). It seems clear that Yagel consulted this chapter, along with several others, and was familiar with de' Rossi's recently completed book, although he never mentions it by name. On de' Rossi's work, see R. Bonfil, "Some Reflections on the Place of Azariah de' Rossi's *Me'or Enayim* on the Cultural Milieu of Italian Renaissance Jewry," in B. Cooperman, ed., *Jewish Thought in the Sixteenth Century* (Cambridge, Mass., 1983).

[4]Yagel earlier had referred to *binah* as "the mother of the world." See above, p. 173, and see Scholem, *Kabbalah,* p. 120.

[5]Jeremiah 17:8.

[118] "Similarly, in the future, all the other languages will return to what they originally were as naught, but the holy language alone will remain, as Zephaniah the prophet wrote: 'For then I will make the peoples pure of speech, etc.'[1] The *gematria* of 'pure speech' is equivalent to that of 'holy language' with the addition of two particles besides the one. The latter is the material of the number that is all bound together and is not [considered] a number.[2] So it was from the beginning of the world's creation when all the earth had the same language and the same words,[3] and as Rashi interpreted [this verse], 'the same language' refers to the holy language. The numerical value of the one ["the same language"] is equivalent to that of the other[4] ["the holy language"] with one additional letter.[5] Thus the Jerusalem translator rendered [Genesis 11:1]: 'When the whole earth was one language and one speech and one opinion,' which is the holy tongue with which the world was created from the beginning.

"Likewise, the author of the *Tanḥuma* wrote at the end of the portion of Noah[6] that the first language that men spoke was the holy tongue, and with this language the world was created. Thus it [the world] will return to its original state, for what was, will be in the future. But because of the sin of the world in the generation of divisiveness, when human beings requested to build a tower, God confounded their tongues.[7] He then divided them into seventy languages and each took something from it [the holy language].

"The sages already know that from the quality [of the *sefirah*] *binah*, the suckling divides up into the seven others [the seven lower *sefirot*] which each include ten [languages] which totals seventy. [119] So don't be surprised if I am able to nurse different peoples and nations with one suckling, for God spoke once at the station of Mount Sinai and He divided this speech from its natural state into seventy languages. Just as you can find that when God watches over the land of Israel, the other nations nurse, (as the rabbis explained in *Sifre* regarding the verse: 'A land that the Lord your

---

[1] Zephaniah 3:9.

[2] The *gematria* of *safa berura* is 798; *lashon ha-kodesh* is 795. Yagel thus acknowledges the discrepancy of two particles and disregards the third.

[3] Cf. Genesis 11:1.

[4] For the expression, see J. T. Berakhot 2 (5a).

[5] For this same *gematria*, see de' Rossi, p. 455. It is also mentioned by Jacob b. Asher in *Perush la-Torah* on Genesis 11:1, and by Profiat Duran in *Ma'ase Efod*, chap. 3. See also A. Halkin, "The Medieval Jewish Attitude Toward Hebrew," in *Biblical and Other Studies*, ed. A. Altmann (Cambridge, Mass., 1963), p. 241, n. 37.

[6] *Midrash Tanḥuma*, parshat No'aḥ, 19. This paragraph in our text appears on the side margin of the Cincinnati manuscript.

[7] Cf. Genesis 11:9.

God looks after, etc.'¹), so it is similar regarding the afflux that falls on me in order to nurse the children with the holy tongue. The other nations nurse from the same influence.

"You also should know what is written: 'A river goes out from Eden to water the garden and from there it divides into four streams.'² All the other streams of the world are nursed from these four streams. Thus from the river of emanantion going out from Eden, the garden of [the *sefirah*] *binah* that irrigates the holy tongue, there is a division into four languages, which are the principal ones for all the seventy tongues of the world; from them, the suckling of everything emerges. These four languages are those mentioned by the rabbis in the Jerusalem Talmud, in the first chapter of *Megillah* and also in the Midrash of Esther, at the end of chapter 3, which reads:³ 'Four languages came into the world to be used by it: the vernacular [*la'az*] for singing, Roman for warfare, Syrian for lamentation [*ileya*], and Hebrew for conversation.' The term *la'az* signifies Greek since in *Megillah* the rabbis declare that the Greek vernacular is good for all peoples.⁴ The rabbis also expanded on this [in interpreting] the verse 'God enlarged Japheth.'⁵

"Roman is Latin, which is used by the residents of Rome. The meaning of 'for warfare' is to speak publicly, as it is explained in *Sukkah*⁶ and in *Shir ha-Shirim Rabbah* [when interpreting] the end of the verse:⁷ 'Who is this that comes up [out of the wilderness]. . . .' [What is the meaning of] 'with all the powders of the merchant' there? This means that he [Solomon] was learned, being also a liturgist and poet [and thus a public speaker].

"Syrian is the Aramaic language, as the rabbis declared in chapter *Ha-Merubah*:⁸ 'The Syrian language is given its glory in the Torah by the expression: *yagar sahduta* [the heap of witness]⁹ or by the phrase in the prophets: "Thus shall you say unto them, etc." [which is spoken in Aramaic].¹⁰' The meaning of *ileya* is to respond with the sound of feeble crying¹¹ and dirges. Furthermore, *ileya* is taken from the word *yelala* [wailing].

¹Cf. Rashi on Deuteronomy 11:12.
²Genesis 2:10.
³J. T. Megillah 1 (71b); *Esther Rabbah*, 4:12. This entire section is also found in de' Rossi, pp. 462–63.
⁴B. T. Megillah 18a.
⁵Genesis 9:27; Cf. B. T. Megillah 9b.
⁶I could not find this reference but compare *Pesikta de Rav Kahana*, 179a.
⁷*Shir ha-Shirim Rabbah*, 3:5 and *Vayikrah Rabbah*, 30:1 on Song of Songs 3:6.
⁸Tosafot on B. T. Babba Kamma 83a.
⁹Genesis 31:47.
¹⁰Jeremiah 10:11.
¹¹Cf. Exodus 32:18.

"The last [language] is the dearest,[1] Hebrew, that is, the holy language, which is the inheritance of the children of Eber [and] which is beautiful for conversation. What greater goodness and beauty can there be than that it was natural to Adam when he emerged from his mother's womb [i.e., he spoke it immediately and spontaneously], the mother of all the living? It is the most perfect of them all, being the body of the river that goes out from the Garden of Eden, as I mentioned. The ministering angels speak it to each other, as it is stated: 'Each called to each other and said: "Holy!"'[2]

[120] "It was not for naught that it was called a holy tongue since it is the holiest and most perfect of them all, as the author [Judah Ha-Levi] of the [*Sefer*] *Ha-Kuzari* declared:[3] 'The holy tongue was not established through human consensus with respect to all the particular meanings of its words like the rest of the languages. Rather, it was created and fluent on his [man's] tongue[4] from the moment he was given a living spirit, a spirit of words.'[5]

[121] "Maimonides, in the *Moreh* [*Nevukhim*], part three, chapter 8 wrote:[6] 'Don't think that our tongue was called the holy tongue for the sake of our pride or because of a mistake; rather it is actually a holy language. No one will find in it words for the male or female organ of copulation, nor for sperm, urine, or excrements, except by allusions. Don't let the word *shegel* [sex] fool you because it is a name of a female slave prepared for copulation.' See also the words of R. Shem Tov [in his commentary] there in the aforementioned chapter.

"Know that from the science of the stars, we can understand its [Hebrew's] greatness along with that of the other three languages that we mentioned which possess greater vitality and strength than the other languages. [We can also understand] how all [the rest] of them receive the emanation from them [the four] and in the manner we mentioned. You can understand this subject from this diagram before you."

I turned and saw the diagram with the form of the constellation called "the zodiac" of the constellations [*afudat ha-mazalot*][7] with the twelve of

[1]For the expression, cf. *Bereshit Rabbah*, 78:2.
[2]Isaiah 6:3.
[3]*Sefer Ha-Kuzari*, 2:66, 4:25; de' Rossi, p. 458.
[4]Cf. Psalm 15:3.
[5]Cf. de' Rossi, p. 458.
[6]Cf. de' Rossi, p. 463.
[7]For the expression, see J. Klatskin, *Ozar ha-Millim Ha-Pilosofi'im* (Berlin, 1928), vol. 1, p. 64.

them divided into four quarters like this and in the manner that I shall explain.[1]

[122] "It is known to the astronomers that Aquarius is the constellation of the Jews since it is set apart from the houses of Saturn and is the constellation of Israel. It receives emanation from [the *sefirah*] *binah,* as the kabbalists explain and as R. Abraham b. David elucidated in his commentary on the *Sefer Yezirah.*[2] They thus declare that with *binah*'s ascent, our forefathers went out of Egypt [*mi-Mizrayim*], as it is written: 'In distress [*min ha-mezar*] I called on the Lord.'[3] It is also written: 'Now the Israelites went up armed [out of the land of Egypt].'[4] Don't read it as 'armed' [*ve-hamushim*] but as 'fifty' [*ve-hamishim*], a hint at the fifty gates in which and from which the emanation came to the constellation of Aquarius, which draws water from it [*binah*] and disseminates it among all the other constellations. Furthermore, it is known that *binah*'s nature is to disseminate goodness to [the people of] Israel at the time when they observe the ordinances of the Torah. If they do not, it is stated: 'I will hide my face from them, etc.'[5] 'They shall be ready prey, etc.'[6] Then all the other nations will rule over them, even the son of the slave girl who is behind the millstones.[7]

"It is similarly the case with the holy language, for initially prosperity existed in all the world with [respect to] the holy tongue until the generation of divisiveness [of the tower of Babel] sinned,[8] and then [God] turned His face away. Consequently, there was no one in the world to use it [the holy tongue]. The emanation remained only for the slave and his family who were incapable of reaching that height. Thus the Hebrew language and all the other languages of the nations were called counterfeit with respect to the nature of the star that emptied on them. This [condition was engendered] by means of the constellation Aquarius, which provides vitality to all according to the potency of its influence, as we mentioned, so as to arrange words correctly or not, according to each nation's order and grammar which initially had been established for them. By so doing, the

[1]There is a space for the diagram in the Cincinnati manuscript but it has been left empty.
[2]The actual author of this commentary was Joseph b. Shalom Ashkenazi (Spain, fourteenth century). See [pseudo] Abraham b. David on *Sefer Yezirah* (Jerusalem, 1962), pp. 102–3. Cf. Part I, p. 171 above.
[3]Psalm 118:5.
[4]Exodus 13:18.
[5]Deuteronomy 32:20.
[6]Deuteronomy 31:17.
[7]Cf. Exodus 11.
[8]Cf. Genesis 11.

various cities and states were formed and it became possible for any person to understand the language of his neighbor with respect to particular words. Then people wrote books and stories on the basis of this [situation], with the exception of the holy tongue. [123] But these grammar books, which were composed by newcomers, had never been anticipated by the ancients, who had not conceived of them because they had no need for them. But the moderns did this because the times required it.[1]

[124] "Since the sphere is divided into four parts so that each constellation is located in one of the four parts, the kingdoms under them rule throughout the entire world. The language used by their nations is the choicest of them all. This is so for two reasons. First, because of the nature of the stars. Just as a star's strength is great and provides an emanation of blessing, vitality, and power to its [respective] nation to bear fruit above and to rule over its enemies around it, so too will its strength also be great in providing it with a language that speaks with lofty and subtle words.[2] The second reason is the totally accepted proposition that in any place where wealth and honor is found, in any state or kingdom, [125] the citizenry and nobility will also seek wisdom because this is the natural inclination of every man, as the philosopher stated.[3] They will also travel to other states as Ptolemy, the king of Egypt, did gathering all the books he could acquire from one end of the world to the other. Wise men, knowledgeable in science, expert in the study of language and the science of astronomy, came from distant lands to her [Egypt]. Thus they constantly added strength and vitality to that language.

[126] "See what happened to the Roman language called Latin.[4] It initially was impoverished when the ancients discovered it and were seized with horror[5] [regarding its condition] in the time of Janus and Saturn,[6] the

---

[1]Literally, "it is time to act for the Lord." Cf. Psalm 119:126.

[2]Cf. Job 15:5.

[3]Maimonides, *Moreh Nevukhim*, 3:54, expresses a similar idea.

[4]This entire section is based on Isidore of Seville, *Etymologiarum sive Originum*, ed. W. M. Lindsay, 20 bks. (Oxford, 1911), bk. 9, chap. 1, titled "De Linguis Gentium." Isidore's encyclopedia circulated widely in the Middle Ages and was printed throughout the fifteenth and sixteenth centuries. Yagel may have consulted the Venetian editions of 1493 and 1510 or the Basel edition of 1577. Among Renaissance humanists, Battista Guarino relied on the same chapter in his writing on the origins of Latin. See M. Tavoni, *Latino, Grammatica, Volgare: Storia di una questione umanistica* (Padua, 1984), p. 230. De'Rossi quotes Isidore on two occasions (*Me'or Einayim*, pp. 133, 138), but not in this context.

[5]Cf. Job 18:20.

[6]Isidore, *Etymologiarum*, IX, 1, 6: "Prisca est, quam vetustissimi Italiae sub Iano et Saturno sunt usu, incondita, ut se habent carmina Saliorum." On the description of the gods of Greek and Roman mythology as mortal men who initially ruled Rome (the so-called medieval

kings of ancient Italy. The language was very counterfeit, both in the form of its writing and in its pronunciation, as anyone who desires can observe from the laws and customs of the cities of Sicily, called by them 'bucolic,'[1] and from their writings. That language was called 'early'[2] and it existed at the time the Greeks conquered the city of Tarentum in the reign of the king Latin, the king of Italy, which is [also called] Latin. He corrected the form of this language to some degree, invented words, and gave it some order. They named this language in his name, Latin, and with it, they wrote the twelve tablets containing the rules and mores which Solon bestowed on the citizens of the city of Athens and which the Romans later sent for in order to confiscate them.[3]

[127] "These constituted the root and essence of the laws and statutes by which all the regions of Europe are ruled until this very day. This is because the emperors in each generation established further limitations and appended new laws and rulings depending on the need of the people of their lands and the exigencies of each generation. Afterward, when they expelled the kings from the city of Rome, wise men then arose, like Ennius, Plautus, Ovid, Vergil, and Marcus Tullius [Cicero],[4] who invented many words of the language, gave them a right, attractive and corrected order, and had grammar books written in that language. Subsequently, they named it 'Roman' and this is the Roman language mentioned by the rabbis in the Jerusalem Talmud that we indicated. Many books of wisdom and morality were composed in this language and it is the language of discourse of their scholars to this very day.

[128] "When the government of this nation eventually became strong and its fame was known in all countries, people of every nation and language came to live in Rome, including the Italian Goths. They were a people scattered and dispersed[5] among the nations. The majority was a mixed multitude who went up with them[6] and lived in Italy for close to

---

euhemeristic tradition), see H. J. Erasmus, *The Origins of Rome in Historiography from Petrarch to Perizonius* (Assen, 1962), pp. 40–41. On Azariah de' Rossi's identification of Janus with Noah, who was supposed to have visited Italy, see J. Weinberg, "Azariah de' Rossi and the Forgeries of Annius of Viterbo," *Aspetti della storiografia ebraica* (Rome, 1987), p. 42.

[1]*Bucolica,* pastoral.

[2]*Prisca,* as in Isadore in the aforementioned line.

[3]Isidore, *Etymologiarum,* IX, 1, 6: "Latina, quam sub Latino et regibus Tusci et ceteri in Latio sunt locuti, ex qua fuerunt duodecim tabulae scriptae."

[4]Ibid., IX, 1, 7: "Romana, quae post reges exactos a populo Romano coepta est, qua Naevius, Plautus, Ennius, Vergilus poetae, et ex oratoribus Gracchus et Cato et Cicero vel ceteri effuderunt."

[5]Cf. Esther 3:8.

[6]Cf. Exodus 12:38.

seventy years. During this time, they give birth to sons and daughters, being fertile and multiplying in all the land.[1] In order that one person understand the next, a language was conceived among them, one mixed of all the languages which is called corrupted.[2] This is the same language found today in all the regions of Italy. It has now been perfected like the Roman language as we mentioned. Scholars arose who corrected and organized it and removed all impediments from it until it now has become as beautiful and as exalted as Latin. It also did not take long before all the books of the sciences and riddles that had been translated from Greek to Latin were now translated from Latin to this Italian, just as they have begun and continue to do with growing intensity.[3]

"What we have said regarding the example of Latin, of which you are familiar, can be exemplified in the case of all four languages from the four quarters of the globe which the rabbis praised in the aforementioned passage. They similarly reached perfection and eminence, with the exception of Hebrew, which, from the time of its inception, stood fully developed in its scent and taste[4] when God bestowed it to the first man in its [full] stature and character.

"However, its [Hebrew's] script was not given forever,[5] as Rabbi taught in *Sanhedrin,* chapter *Kohen Gadol:*[6] 'It was taught that Rabbi said that with this script, the Torah was given to Israel. But because they sinned, it was changed into *Ra'az* [the form of Samaritan type],[7] as in the meaning of the verse: "shatters the foe"[8] so that they forgot it.[9] Because they repented, he restored [it] to them, as it is said: "Return to Bizzaron you prisoners of hope, etc."[10] Why was the language called Assyrian [*Ashurit,* i.e., the square modern form of Hebrew type]? Because its characters are

[1]Cf. Genesis 8:17.

[2]*Mista, mixta.* Isidore, *Etymologiarum,* IX, 1, 7: "Mixta, quae post imperium latius promotum simul cum moribus et hominubus in Romanam civitatem inrupit, integritatem verbi per soloecismos et barbarismos corrumpens."

[3]Perhaps this line is an indication of Yagel's awareness of the extended debates in Italy between proponents of the Italian and Latin languages. See, for example, R. A. Hall, "The Italian 'Questione della lingua': An Interpretative Essay," *University of North Carolina Studies in the Romance Languages and Literature,* 4 (Chapel Hill, N.C., 1942).

[4]Cf. Jeremiah 48:11.

[5]This passage and the one following are additions appended to the bottom of the Cincinnati manuscript, fols. 81b–82a.

[6]B. T. Sanhedrin 22a; cf. J. T. Megillah 1 (71b).

[7]Cf. de' Rossi, p. 467.

[8]Exodus 15:6.

[9]The last phrase is Yagel's expansion of the Talmudic passage.

[10]Zachariah 9:12.

substantial [*me'usheret*]. R. Simon, in the name of R. Eleazar ben Parta who spoke in the name of R. Eleazar ha-Moda'i [declared]: "This script has not changed one iota as it is said: 'The hooks of the posts.'[1] Since the posts did not change, neither did the hooks."[2] This means that just as their language is like a strong post of the speech of everything and it never changes, so it is with their script which is like the hooks of the posts; its pegs are connected and do not change. So it was said: 'To the Jews in their own script and language.'[3] Just as their language did not change, neither did their script. Note how Rabbi explained [the phrase] 'with two hands' in the [aforementioned] *beraita* as the change in script. [The opinion of] the person who explained why the language was called Assyrian because it went up with them from Assyria [can be disregarded] since it is [only] the view of one individual.[4]

"If, because of the sin [of the generation of divisiveness], the majority of the people forgot it [the Hebrew script], for God then confounded their language[5] so that they spoke in a debased tongue, the Torah scroll in their possession was not changed because of this, God forbid. For many[6] of those who remained faithful to God had in their possession, sealed up in their storehouses,[7] the beauty of the language and the script [as established] by Ezra and the tribunal who received [the Torah text] from Barukh, the son of Neriah, his teacher, [and who had received it] from prophets going back to Moses. Subsequently, closer to the time of our forefathers, during the exile of Judah and Benjamin, the language began to be changed to *Ra'az* because of the sin and the exile. Thus their tongues were confounded and they spoke Roman, German, and Spanish, depending on the region to which they were exiled. But this factor did not change the text that was studied and that was in the possession of the leaders of the community, the holy ones and sages. They spoke it like Rabbanu [Judah], the holy one, who wrote the Mishnah and established his teaching in the sight of the nations. They noted the beauty, dignity, and splendor of this composition which is still called today: 'A praise to the living God.'

[129] "If, because of the exiles, they [the Jewish people] forgot it, our holy teacher who composed the *Mishnayot* arose and reconstituted it.

---

[1] Exodus 27:10, 11.
[2] Cf. de' Rossi, p. 467.
[3] Esther 8:9.
[4] Cf. B. T. Sanhedrin 22a.
[5] Cf. Genesis 11:9.
[6] Cf. Nahum 1:12.
[7] Cf. Deuteronomy 32:34.

Today, we may praise the Creator and Maker of man's breath within him[1] that the script and the language exist and its perfection is as it was from the beginning of time. It is a sign of a great thing and a good sign for Israel since it is their natural language. The time approaches when all the peoples will write in a pure tongue and with the same words.[2]

"However, the other languages of the nations, besides the three we mentioned, cannot be smelt nor scented from afar as these [three] because the strength of their [the other nation's] constellations is not as powerful as theirs [the three] nor do they [the other nations] ascend to their heights. This is because of the two conditions that we mentioned, that is, the reason related by the rabbis for the exalted position and the perfection of the languages.

[130] "But, in truth, the Arabic language (which is the Arabian) is most praiseworthy because of the scientific books written in it. However, it is a corrupted translation and is like the aforementioned Roman language which divides up into four good languages as I have indicated. Likewise, the Syrian divides into many dialects more than any other language. However, the root and choicest of them all is rabbinic Aramaic, which is the Babylonian version utilized by the sages of Babylonia. It is the clearest and most praiseworthy of the Aramaic dialects, as Rabbenu Tam mentioned in chapter *Merubah*.[3]

[131] "Similarly, Greek divides into five dialects that are called: Commune, Attic, Doric, Ionic, and Aeolic.[4] Each shares something of the other for they have a common root. Besides these languages which we have mentioned, the three languages—Syrian, Greek, and Roman—can be divided into many other dialects and languages until one reaches the sum of seventy. For example, from the dialects of Roman, even though they are unrelated to it, one can derive German, Spanish, French, Polish, and Russian. From Greek emerges the Slavic[5] and the languages of those islands and countries, each with its own script and speech. [One can also derive the language of] the Persians and Medes and [that of] the other

---

[1]Cf. Zachariah 12:1.

[2]A combination of Zephaniah 3:9 and Genesis 11:1.

[3]Cf. Tosafot to B. T. Babba Kamma 83a; cf. de' Rossi, p. 463 (the passage was also quoted above).

[4]This is also taken from Isidore, *Etymologiarum,* IX, 1, 4–5. The same five dialects are mentioned by Abraham Portaleone in his *Shilte ha-Gibburim* (Mantua, 1612; reprint Jerusalem, 1970), p. 9a, in his own discussion of languages. Cf. also Claude Duret, *Thresor de l'Histoire des Languages de cet Univers* (Cologne, 1613), pp. 690, 775.

[5]*Schiavano.*

islands in the lands of those nations, each with their own language, each according to its own family and nation.

"The aforementioned Persian and Medean [languages] are derived from Japheth, as the rabbis described in the first chapter of *Yoma:*[1] 'How do we know that the Persians derive from Japheth? Because it is written: "The sons of Japheth: Gomer, Magog, etc."[2]' From Syrian the languages of the *Targum* are derived and all the other languages used by the people of the East since it is the first of them all with the exception of Hebrew. Thus it [Syrian] spread among all the countries of the East since human settlement began there and from there, Egyptian and the [languages] used by the peoples of India, Cush, and Put emerged. Finally, seventy different languages are found in all the world. But the four we have described are the best of them all for the reasons I have mentioned.

[132] "Nevertheless, some of the other languages do possess beauty and stature for the reasons already stated, as, for example, Spanish. It even surpasses the limits of the [languages of other] nations in beauty, eminence, and flowery speech. This is because the kings of Spain grew in honor and wealth in comparison to what they initially had been. What happened to the Roman language (which we mentioned) also happened to their [language]. This is also the case with German, which always was most distorted, lacking any order among the languages of the nations. But recently, men arose who composed grammars, writing words both in relation and not in relation to each other, distinguishing between past and future tenses, plural and singular forms, as with other languages. Now it [German] is not inferior to any of them. This is due to the kingdom of German emperors. This same situation is true for all the languages that I have described that were initially corrupted and disorganized until wise men of each language arose to repair the breach [133] with the exception of the holy Hebrew tongue which never received any order or repair from any person and does not allow any compound words. On the contrary, Hebrew's influence is in all of the languages since all of them took words and expressions [from her]. This is explained to the wise because she [Hebrew] is the top of the citadel to which all [the others] turn."

[134] I then asked: "Why can one find in Hebrew some words that appear to have been formed from another language, as you might say *pilegesh* [concubine] which is similarly called in the Greek and Latin languages as *pellex*, or *meretrix*, which also appears in the Roman language? I

[1]B. T. Yoma 10a.
[2]Genesis 10:2.

heard from the sage the honorable Rabbi Elijah of Melli, a resident of Mantua about several [Hebrew] words that are spoken in foreign languages.[1] He claimed that they were derived long ago from the holy tongue. They are: *ospedale* (in Hebrew, *osef dalim* [a gathering of the sick]); *piolada,* a woman who gives birth, from the Hebrew *efah yolda* [I will scream like a woman in danger];[2] *miracoli,* from the Hebrew, *mi ra'ah ka'eleh* [who ever witnessed such events?];[3] *mirabile,* from the Hebrew phrase [*mi*] *barah eleh* [who created these?];[4] *spalla,* the shoulder, from the Hebrew words *noseh sabal* [porter];[5] *sale,* salt, from the Hebrew word *selah* [forever], for the salt lasts forever, as the rabbis declare regarding the covenant of salt;[6] *ambasceria,* from the Hebrew word *besorah* [good tidings]; and *misura* from the Hebrew word *mesorah* [measure]."[7]

She answered: "So it is. It appears that the Hebrew language took these words from another language but [in fact] it is like the aforementioned words of the rabbis [who stated that] they were actually derived and appropriated from the holy tongue itself. For Hebrew is the root of all the other languages prior to the time when God confounded the languages of all the earth. It thus would have been impossible for some words not to have remained in the possession of the nations. This is similar to what the sage [Profiat Duran] the Efodi wrote in chapter 3:[8] 'There is no doubt that when the nations agreed on seventy languages, they employed some nouns and verbs from the language to which they had been accustomed previously.'

[135] "Know that some gentile sages reckoned that the total number of languages equals seventy-two.[9] But the rabbis disagreed when they declared in *Pirke de Rabbi Eliezer,* chapter 24:[10] 'Seventy angels for seventy

---

[1]According to Simonsohn, *Mantua,* p. 719, there was a rabbi named Elijah ben Abraham Melli who lived in Mantua in the fifteenth century. Perhaps Yagel meant Pinhas b. Elijah b. Zemah Elijah Melli of the sixteenth century. Cf. Simonsohn, p. 720. De' Rossi similarly offers a list of Hebrew words supposedly found in foreign languages, quoting David Provenzali's now lost work, *Dor ha-Pelagah,* which contained 2,000 such words, according to de' Rossi. The existence of two separate lists, those of Melli and Provenzali, testify to the great interest in this subject of comparative philology among Mantuan Jewry. Cf. Roth, *Renaissance,* p. 331.

[2]Cf. Isaiah 42:14.

[3]Cf. Isaiah 66:8.

[4]Cf. Isaiah 40:26.

[5]Cf. 1 Kings 5:29.

[6]Cf. *Sifre, Bamidbar,* Korah, 119. Rashi on Leviticus 2:13.

[7]I have omitted a short comment added in the side margin of the Cincinnati manuscript.

[8]*Ma'aseh Efod* (Vienna, 1865), chap. 3, p. 31; Cf. de' Rossi, p. 456.

[9]Cf. de' Rossi, p. 455, who explicitly mentions Augustine, Annius, and Tostado.

[10]Cf. de' Rossi, p. 456.

nations and to each nation its own script and language.' And in *Bamidbar Rabbah,* chapter 13, they declared:[1] 'Why was the weight of the one silver vessel seventy [shekels]? To correspond to the seventy nations from one end of the earth to the other.' Jonathan ben Uziel translated the verse:[2] 'The Lord scattered them from there' as 'The word of God was revealed concerning the city and its peoples, seventy kingdoms, each corresponding to seventy peoples, each with the language of its people and with a copy of their script in its possession; so they were scattered from there.' And in *Pesikta de Rav Kahana,* cited in the homilies of Avkir and Abba Gurion, in an ancient book I saw in the study of the noble Isaac Fano, a citizen of Ferrara,[3] on the passage titled 'The festival of booths,' they reckoned there seventy nations, one after the other. They declared that Japheth had fourteen; Ham had thirty; Shem had twenty-six, which totals seventy, etc.[4] The reason they mistakenly considered the number to be seventy-two was because they included Assyria and Philistia. But we don't consider this so because these two families came out of the rest that are included in the seventy.

"Now I shall inform you of something new on earth[5] in the discussion regarding languages.[6] How is it that the holy tongue is the choicest of them all and [the language of] the sweet melodies[7] of the hosts above and below? It is because all the other languages are destined to be lost while it [Hebrew] will stand [forever] because all came from it and all will return to it. [136] How beloved is Israel on whom [God] bestowed this holy language as an inheritance! He imposed it as a decree upon Joseph.[8] Just as all the other languages will wither and pass away, as they have done until this day—one language disappears while another appears according to the changing situations of the nations—nevertheless, the holy tongue will remain forever from the time it was created by the originator of the universe. While all the other nations will be like fruit that has become refuse, the people of Israel,

[1]*Bamidbar Rabbah,* 13:18; de' Rossi, p. 456.
[2]Genesis 11:8; Cf. de' Rossi, p. 455.
[3]He is mentioned by de' Rossi in his discussion of the earthquake of 1571. This is taken word for word from de' Rossi, p. 455, and is explicit proof that Yagel copied from de' Rossi's chapter.
[4]Cf. S. Buber (*Pesiqta de Rav Kahana* [Lyck, 1868], p. xxiii, n. 22), who could not find this precise reference.
[5]Cf. Jeremiah 31:22.
[6]Yagel seems to imply that what preceded was not novel but was based on de' Rossi's discussion.
[7]Cf. 2 Samuel 23:1.
[8]Cf. Psalm 81:6.

all of them righteous, shall possess the land for all time. They are the shoot that God planted, the handiwork in which to glory.[1] They shall never be ashamed nor embarrassed[2] if they await His deliverance. For God formed this people[3] and bestowed upon them an inherited law, the perfect Torah of God and a holy tongue, [as it is stated:][4] 'This language was a help to them.' In their deeds and with the words of their mouths, the higher [Hebrew] words fully adhere to the higher [worlds] and draw the spirit down upon them from the divine heavens. So the entire hosts of heaven hear their voices, especially when they are in the Holy Land, the fairest of all lands,[5] built and established in a land knit together[6] in the heavens and in the heavenly heavens.

"This secret was hinted at in the Jerusalem Talmud *Shekalim:*[7] [137] 'It was taught in the name of R. Meir: "Whoever lives in the land of Israel and eats ordinary food with purity, speaks at length in the holy tongue, recites the recitation of the *Shema* [prayer] in the morning and in the evening, and is ritually fit, so it will be for him in the next world, since eating ordinary food in purity is called holy and gives perfection to the soul." ' And by living in the land of Israel, one always finds the watchfulness of the Ancient of Days [God], as the verse states: 'The eyes of the Lord are upon you from the beginning of the year until the end.'[8] The rabbis also declared:[9] 'All who live outside of Israel are like one who has no God.' Similarly, speaking in the holy tongue gives great perfection to a person's soul. The advocates [of a person speaking Hebrew], so to speak, will need him to borrow his strength, and to bring his prayer [on their behalf] from behind the curtain [of heaven].[10] So it was established that whatever men utter below in the holy tongue, all the hosts of heaven understand and take heed of, while any other language they do not understand, as the great man, R. Simeon bar Yoḥai, pointed out regarding the verse: 'And the Lord said: "If as one people with one language, etc."[11]' The creator of comforting words[12] will

[1]Cf. Isaiah 60:21.
[2]Cf. Isaiah 45:17.
[3]Cf. Isaiah 43:21.
[4]The language is adapted from *Sefer ha-Zohar,* 1:75b.
[5]Cf. Ezekiel 20:5, 15.
[6]Cf. Psalm 122:3.
[7]Cf. J. T. Shekalim 3:4 (47c).
[8]Deuteronomy 11:12.
[9]B. T. Ketubbot 110b.
[10]Cf. Exodus 26:33.
[11]Genesis 11:6; Cf. *Sefer ha-Zohar,* 1:75b, on which the language of the previous line is based.
[12]Cf. Isaiah 57:19.

fulfill His request. He will remove the speech of anyone else with a crooked and perverted tongue, one slanderous and defamatory, sinful and of idle talk. He will bear fruit above and will create unchanging worlds with a line of chaos and with weights of emptiness.[1] The rabbis hinted to the recitation of the *Shema* prayer in the morning and evening so that a person would have the right intention regarding the heavenly unity to bring the Holy One, praised be He, toward him, preparing his heart before Him. When he supplicates himself, a spirit from heaven will appear before him, a spirit of knowledge and intelligence[2] to know the wonders of his Creator and His activities so that he will follow His laws and observe His statutes. But enough of this for you. [138] And if you shall desire to enter the palace before you, I will show you this short path through me, as long as you are careful to stay on it and not stray to the right or to the left."

## Entrance into the Heavenly Palace and an Explanation of Its Secrets

The woman came with us [and] showed us the land and the passageway by which we could enter the palace. We left her with shouts of "beautiful, beautiful"[3] with respect to all her words. We also were zealous in following the path she indicated. We passed a small stream called "the passage of love" and this was its nature: When a man with passion and desire crossed it, he would tread over it with his feet instantaneously; the water would become shallow so he would not feel it. However, a person lacking passion and desire would find its appearance like mighty waters, and even a powerful ship would not [be able] to cross it. When I crossed the stream, we heard a pleasant and fine voice singing from the music of Solomon and the land was like the Garden of Eden before us. We approached the palace built in the middle of the hill of frankincense on the path the woman had shown us.

When we arrived at the great and beautiful palace, whose pillars were silver with latticework of gold, with all of the building's walls of translucent marble, and whose splendor was like that of the sun and the moon, a small opening appeared to open by itself before us. There was a banner [hanging] on it whose height and length were ten [spans], and upon it was written: "This is the gate of the Lord; the righteous may enter it."[4] [139] When we entered the gate, the third woman whom we initially had seen dressed in

[1]Cf. Isaiah 34:11.
[2]Cf. Isaiah 11:2.
[3]Cf. Zachariah 4:7.
[4]Psalm 118:20.

royal garments and [with] a great golden crown approached us. She was clothed with strength and splendor[1] and she comported herself with majesty and greatness before us.

We bowed down before her and the woman turned to us and said: "See that the hand of God has done this.[2] Come with me so that I might show you the concatenation of the worlds and their interconnection[3] in my treasure house and how man is like the example of this great building. He is fitting and ready with respect to his form to receive a good emanation of all the worlds so long as he acknowledges that his ways are according to the Torah, through which God instructs him. In this manner, he will become a living creature through his own resources, loved above and pleasing below,[4] and greater than the ministering angels. During his lifetime, when he is still imprisoned in the tresses of matter,[5] he will behold God while still in his flesh.[6] All creatures will listen to his voice when he commands them to go out. He will be able to tell them to stand quietly, and they will accept and carry out his orders, like a slave before his master.

"Likewise, at his death, his mind, spirit, and soul will ascend, breaking the knot between one [the soul] and the other [the body]. He will also ascend to cling to eternal life and become before Him [God] like that same youth whose name is like his teacher's, who declared in his youth: 'I have been young and am now old [but I have never seen a righteous man abandoned, etc.'[7] But he cannot see[8] everything and every request [he wishes to make] cannot pass by the ford of the Jabbok[9] into the innermost place[10] where the asker of the question and [maker of the] request who is there might be provided [an immediate response]. Rather, all the honest scales and balances[11] stand to weigh the acts of man and his cleverness, whether he is worthy of fulfilling his desire according to the example of the earthly or heavenly kingdom."

We followed this distinguished woman until we entered a large room

[1]Cf. Proverbs 31:25.

[2]Cf. Job 12:9.

[3]As the narrator reaches the culmination of the ascent, the reader is again reminded of this fundamental insight, so critical and central in all Yagel's writings. Cf. the introduction above.

[4]For the expression, cf. B. T. Berakhot 17a.

[5]Cf. Song of Songs 7:6.

[6]Cf. Job 19:26.

[7]Psalm 37:25.

[8]Cf. Job 34:32.

[9]Cf. Genesis 32:23. Man is not given eternal life without proving worthy of it.

[10]Literally, "into the inside of the inside." Cf. B. T. Babba Meẓiah 16a.

[11]Cf. Proverbs 16:11.

of pure marble.[1] There I saw riddles on the wall of the house opposite the entrance, [painted] in a color close to the blue like this form.[2]

I turned to the right and to the left and saw riddles on the right wall [and] the image of a man whose head reached the roof of the ascent while his feet led to the floor. His hands were outstretched and reached the two ends of the wall. Changeable letters which I did not know how to combine emerged from him. This was because some [were written] in Hebrew, others [in] Assyrian, Aramaic, Hittite, or Ammonite. The general principle, as the woman later explained to me, was that they were from all the seventy languages of the nations, and riddles were [written] there in [each of] their scripts. On the head [of the man] was a kind of diadem and large gold crown. A seal [with the words] "Holy to God"[3] was engraved upon it.[4]

On the second wall opposite it was inscribed the form of a very high tree in the midst of the ground. Its foliage was beautiful and its fruit abundant. There was food for all in it[5] without complaint since all the fruit that God created during the six days of Creation was drawn and engraved upon it along with every kind of bird. Letters and words emerged from the branches of the tree and from the mouths of the foul, sayings [so numerous] that they would weary anyone trying to write them down since they had no end or limit. Just as it is impossible to count the sand of the sea, it is likewise impossible to count the sayings and aphorisms written there.[6]

The fourth wall containing the entrance in the middle was smooth and contained no riddles and had nothing on it. However, it was so translucent that when a person stared at it, he could see anything placed opposite it. Consequently, all the aforementioned things engraved on the three other walls could be seen [reflected] on that wall as well as anything placed opposite it.

The woman perceived that I was immediately frightened as [I tried] to understand what I saw. I declared that wisdom is far from me[7] since these things are so exalted that I cannot comprehend or fathom their underlying meaning.

[1]Cf. B. T. Ḥagigah 14b.

[2]There is a space left in the manuscript for a picture that obviously was not completed.

[3]Exodus 28:36; 39:30.

[4]The figure seems strangely reminiscent of a Jesus-like portrait.

[5]These two lines are based on Daniel 4:7, 9.

[6]Note that Yagel omits mentioning the third wall here. It is described below, p. 335, as the wall with the tree, the second wall in this description. Likewise, on p. 332 below, Yagel describes the wall with the image of man as the second wall, not the first. Apparently, Yagel failed to describe a third wall, other than the three mentioned here.

[7]Cf. Ecclesiastes 7:23.

## The Third Woman's Discourse on the Harmony of the Universe

[140] She thus said to me: "Don't be frightened by your thought if you do not understand them since these things are closed and sealed off to either an empty or wise man. However, wait a little and let me hold forth[1] and I will inform you about what you are capable of understanding. I will offer you the chapter headings to provide you with the intention of the artist who designed this house and ascent. So make your ear like the hopper,[2] pay attention with your mind, and listen to all that I shall tell you. Know faithfully that from the source of [the *sefirah*] *binah* they were hewn. All of this came from the counsel of wise sages, the exalted scholars of Israel who possess the divine secret, as it is written: 'The secret of God is to them who fear Him.'[3]

"Now know that the Creator, exalted and blessed is His name, provides a measure of His goodness to influence and benefit creation with an emanation of blessing and praise, so that all creatures can enjoy the splendor of that emanation. That influence is bestowed according to the nature and ability of the person who receives it. It is unlike the light of the sun that blinds the eye of the beholder because of the large quantity of light and [because of] its splendor or because of the diminution or deficiency of the strength of the beholder. Nor is it like the heat of fire from which man cries when he gets too close. Accordingly, God desired to benefit the world[4] and thus he requested to make, to form, to create, and to emanate many heavenly and earthly hosts. He created everything for His honor to inform His creatures about His accomplishments. How plentiful, how great and how mighty is that what the mouth is unable to relate nor the ear [able to] listen to! For who has stood in the council of the Lord[5] and who has fathomed His true meaning?

"However, a man who sees, investigates, and listens will know that the lower creatures are dependent on those higher than themselves, and the latter, on those higher than themselves. For one high official is protected by a higher one, and upon them still higher ones.[6] Man will also fathom that God created everything together perfectly[7] with the goal of perfection. His acts are perfect without deficiency although we see that this world that He

---

[1]Cf. Job 36:2.
[2]For the expression, see B. T. Hullin 89a.
[3]Psalm 25:14. The highest wisdom is that of the kabbalists.
[4]For the expression, see B. T. Makkot 23b, Avot de R. Natan 41:27.
[5]Cf. Jeremiah 23:18.
[6]Cf. Ecclesiastes 5:7.
[7]Cf. Psalm 33:15.

gave to humanity is transitory, filled with many vanities, nonsense, and [the] toil of the flesh from one end to the other.

"Therefore, the ancient philosophers reliably said, without any doubt, that [our material] reality is not the primary one that the exalted God made since the perfection of the activity indicates the perfection of the agent. Rather, the genus of those creatures [on earth] was first. The latter is superior to the former [for it is] not subject to any addition or subtraction. Moreover, by its agency, with His [God's] infinite power, lower forms of creation come into being and, similarly, still lower forms. In this manner, an agent and cause [emerge], one that influences and one that is influenced.

"These scholars agreed that these processes developed, spread, and expanded out of nothing. All that descended was thus shortened and thickened until they reached the center of the earth, which is like a grain of mustard as the center of everything. They also agreed that all of His creatures are found on four levels, one higher than the next, and every level is divided into ten parts. Each part has a unique property and shares from the property of its neighbor in its likeness, as, for example, the four elements, whose nature is known and famous in the world. Each of them [the elements] has a unique property but at the same time possesses a property shared by its neighbor. I do not mean to describe by this the subject of the qualities of which each [element] has two while one is mixed up with that of its neighbor. I mean to indicate instead that not one [of the elements] is either simple or mixed; in each is included the power and property of the four, as the philosophers explain.

"Similarly, [one conceives] of the matter that is called *sefirot,* which are like ten changeable vessels, different in kind, each from the other. The emanation and the light that reaches them from the *ein sof* is one, and from the latter's perspective, there is no plurality. However, the beholder notices and conceives the actions that come out [of it] as if it were divided into ten parts, as we have stated. It is like ten glass vessels, each different in coloring. A well of clear, fresh, and pure water passing through them makes the ten different colored vessels appear to change so that they look like ten wells. This is so since the water passing through each vessel looks different from the outside, depending on the coloring of the vessel [through which it passes]. In reality, the water passing through all of them is one. From the perspective of the water's essence, it comes from one coloring and does not change its essence. Only because of the appearance of the glass, does one view it from the outside as if it changes, which is not what actually happens.[1]

[1]This discussion reveals Yagel's awareness of a major controversy among kabbalists

"In a similar way, the emanation from the divine unity proceeds through these ten vessels. From the perspective of their variety—the judgment and mercy that emanates from them—they are called vessels. But from the perspective of the great emanation that peers on them and illumines them, one calls it His [God's singular] essence. It is like saying that, from the perspective of the strength the soul provides the hand when writing in a book with ink, this strength is called the essence of the soul, for without it, one could not raise his hand. However, from the perspective of the material action that proceeds from it in moving the pen and in writing, it is called the activity of the hand and not that of the soul.

"From this example, you might understand how a person can comprehend the essence of the *sefirot,* which I have mentioned, and how the kabbalists sometimes refer to God's essence, from the perspective of the strength and emanation in them, and [sometimes] to the vessels, from the perspective of the activity that comes out of them. The emanation that passes through these *sefirot* will be seen as not coming from one place because of the conflicting activities emerging from these aforementioned *sefirot,* just as one sees the water in the glass that we described. Each seems different from the other because of the changing color of the glass. But this is not actually so since everything comes from one place, either judgment or mercy, or good or evil.

"When the exalted God wished to reveal the primary ten *sefirot* called *azilut* [the world of emanation],[1] [He established] the relation of the secondary [*sefirot*] to the primary ones as that of the body to God. From

---

regarding the nature of the *sefirot,* already referred to above (in Part II, sec. 44). Were they an intimate part of the divine essence itself or nondivine in essence, considered to be instruments in creating or governing the world, or vessels containing the divine influx, or divine emanations immanent within nature itself? The controversy primarily centered on the intra- or extra-divine status of the *sefirot,* a controversy noticeably reminiscent of the philosophical discussions on the existence of ideas within or outside the divine mind. On this controversy in the fifteenth and sixteenth centuries in Italy, see the articles of Idel and Tirosh-Rothschild referred to above, p. 248, n. 3.

Yagel's indebtedness to the sixteenth-century kabbalist Moses Cordovero is particularly striking. Cordovero tried to reconcile the two opposing views of the *sefirot* by maintaining that they were simultaneously part of the divine essence but also instruments perceived by human beings as being external to God. Yagel not only adopted this position but even borrowed some of Cordovero's analogies for illustrating this position, especially that of the sun and its rays and that of water flowing through colored vessels. For the source of these analogies, see Moshe Cordovero, *Pardes Rimmonim* (Cracow, 1591), p. 23b; J. Ben Shlomo, *Torat Ha-Elohut shel R. Moshe Cordovero* (Jerusalem, 1965), pp. 124–27.

[1]On the kabbalistic doctrine of the four worlds, see G. Scholem, *EJ,* 16 (1971): 641–43, and see above.

these secondary ones [of *beriah,* the world of creation] were revealed ten others called by the name of *yezirah* [the world of formation]. Those clothed in this [latter world] include [the angel] Metatron.[1] Their level in relation to [the world of] *beriah* is the same as that between *beriah* and *azilut.* From the levels of this [world of] *yezirah* emerge boundaries, changes, absence, and limit. Thus you can see all the processes from potentiality to actuality, except for the fact that they are not completely activitated by themselves until we include the fourth [of the four groupings] of ten additional levels. These are called the *sefirot ha-asiyyah* [the *sefirot* of the world of making], which approach corporeal and material things and include the *kelippot* [shells, the cosmic forces of evil] as well as the ten spheres, the elements, and all the composites of them. The ten spheres are outer garments of the ten *kelippot* and they also are divided into ten levels from which emerge the forces of holiness called *ofannim* [angels], so as to distinguish the holy from the profane.[2]

[141] "Know that the wisdom of the astronomers and philosophers reaches to this point; they never surpassed the world of *asiyyah.* They [the kabbalists] also declared that for every one of the ten heavenly spheres there are two forces—one good and one bad—each corresponding to the other that God made. So that opposite 'crown' [*keter*] is 'destruction' [whose last two letters are reversed to yield *karet*], and opposite 'joy' [*oneg*] is 'trouble' [*negah,* also formed by a letter reversal]. Know accordingly that all that the astronomers declared regarding the heavenly spheres—those that go out from the center and the circuitous ones, the changes in the stars, and the forms and movements—all are a kind of shadow and reflection of the ten *sefirot* that have no substance or essence.

"Just as they declare that the first sphere [the *primum mobile*] revolves daily, that it has no variety, and that, through its great strength, all the rest of the spheres revolve beside it, so it is the case for the first *sefirah,* called the high *keter* [crown] which constitutes complete mercy [unmitigated by justice].[3] It has no coloring of justice, as it is written: 'And the Ancient of

[1]On Metatron in Jewish thought, see Scholem, *Kabbalah,* pp. 377–81.

[2]According to the *Massekhet Azilut,* a pseudoepigraphic treatise of the fourteenth century, the world of *asiyyah* included the whole range of angels known as *ofannim* through the ten spheres to the material world. Cf. Scholem, *Kabbalah,* p. 119.

[3]Here begins Yagel's tour de force of speculation on the *sefirot,* demonstrating once again that every process in the highest level of creation has its analogue in the lower levels as well. Yagel's lengthy elaboration of the correlations between the various levels of creation, man, and the parts of the body was obviously presented by the author as the ultimate knowledge the narrator was to gain from his spiritual ascent. For other attempts to relate the ten *sefirot* with each of the spheres of the medieval cosmos, see Pico's forty-eighth kabbalistic

Days took His seat. His garment was like white snow.'[1] All the forces of justice strongly desire the emanation that comes out of it [*keter*]. It is the cause and bestower of emanation to everything, like the aforementioned diurnal sphere.

"Just as they stated that the second *sefirah* is also simple mercy and called 'nothingness' [*ayin*], indicating the hiddenness and absence found in the deeper recesses of hidden thought, so too the astronomers declared that the second sphere [the *stellatum*] is simpler than any star; it is translucent and its purpose is totally hidden. It is conceived as 'nothingness,' since because of its movement as it drives a wheel of the exalted chariots, it is unrevealed. Due to the forms inscribed there, it is unrecognizable since it has no picture.

[142] "I discovered that one of the philosophers wrote that from the power of the movement of this sphere and corresponding to the thirty-two sparks of light that scatter from the light of this *sefirah*'s essence, called the thirty-two paths of wisdom,[2] are scattered thirty-two changes in one orbit.[3] All the philosophers might turn and focus their attention on this phenomenon but, nevertheless, [they] will remain ignorant of its cause. He [God] removes kings and states instantaneously;[4] where they are, nobody knows.[5] Observe wonderously that the word 'path' suggests the hidden and concealed, as in the verse: 'And a path through mighty waters,'[6] or 'no bird of prey knows the path in it,'[7] and in similar examples. So too, the reason for the changes [in the orbit], whether for evil or good intention, is hidden from the philosophers so that the kingdoms will listen, take notice, and repent of their evil ways. In this regard, I am inclined to follow the words of the one who said that the thirty-two paths of wisdom are red colored because of the secret of the [red] coloring of justice that is hinted at by the thirty-two [times] God is mentioned in the act of creation.[8] And in every [one of the thirty-two] places, God is known [for his quality] as a judge.

---

conclusion, quoted and discussed in F. A. Yates, *Giordano Bruno and the Hermetic Tradition* (London, 1964), pp. 100–101, and Agrippa, *De occulta philosophia*, pt. 2, chap. 10.

[1] Daniel 7:9.

[2] For an elucidation of the thirty-two paths of wisdom in kabbalistic thought, see the introduction of [pseudo] R. Abraham b. David's commentary on *Sefer Yezirah* (Jerusalem, 1962), pp. 19–23.

[3] A further illustration of Yagel's penchant to locate correlations between kabbalistic and astronomical thought.

[4] Cf. Daniel 2:21.

[5] Cf. Nahum 3:17.

[6] Isaiah 43:16.

[7] Job 28:7.

[8] That is, in the thirty-two times the word *Elohim* appears in the first chapter of the book of Genesis.

[143] "Perhaps all that we have said is alluded to by the liturgical poet in the poem: 'They will bear witness and tell,'[1] a dear glorious song which the holy community of *Lo'azim* and *Sephardim* are accustomed to recite at the daily morning prayer service. They declare: 'Thirty-two paths are Your course for anyone who understands their foundation. They will tell of Your greatness,' that is, thirty-two are the paths of wisdom to anyone who understands their foundation, and from ancient times, they will tell of the greatness of the Creator of the world. Through them, they will recognize that everything is Yours through [Your] consequential activities, that is, every creature above and below is reviewed, each one from the thirty-two changes we mentioned, by the One who removes and installs kings, states, and kingdoms.[2] They will recognize and realize that everything is from the Holy One, blessed be He. As the rabbis interpreted the verse: 'He revealed to his people his powerful acts'[3] of the creation of the world in order to bestow on them the kingdom of the nations. They will not say it was stolen with their hands.[4] For, in truth, the Most High is sovereign over the realm of man, and He gives it to whom He wishes.[5] He delivers and saves, and performs signs and wonders in heaven and on earth,[6] as he wishes. For judgment is rendered in favor of the holy ones of the Most High, for the time has come.[7]

"You will understand from this [thought] the good taste of the holy congregation of the *Lo'azim* regarding their custom of reciting this prayer immediately after the 'Song of the Sea' [Exodus 15: 1–19]. Just as the great change of the splitting of the Red Sea and the exodus of the children of Israel from Egypt with great signs and wonders, surpassing the laws of nature, was a strong testimony that the world is not eternal but rather created by the will of God who can do according to His will—'For He split apart the Red Sea and made Israel pass through it, and hurled Pharoah and his army into it,'[8] and this belief is a basis and foundation for the entire Torah that depends on it—so, too, do each of the thirty-two changes alluded to in this hymn signify a sign and wonder regarding the exodus from Egypt. So the song ends: 'Everything is from You, which we will recall, etc.'

[1] The opening of the *piyyut* entitled *Kol beru'ai ma'alah ve-matah* (All creatures above and below). Cf. I. Davidson, *Thesaurus of Medieval Hebrew Poetry* (New York, 1929), 2, p. 402, n. 3136.

[2] Cf. Daniel 2:21.

[3] Psalm 111:6.

[4] Cf. *Bereshit Rabbah*, 1:2.

[5] Cf. Daniel 4:14, 22, 29.

[6] Cf. Daniel 6:28.

[7] Cf. Daniel 7:22.

[8] Cf. Psalm 136:13–15.

"The third *sefirah* is called *binah* [intelligence], which from its own essence and from the emanantion it receives from [the *sefirot*] *keter* and *hokhmah* is 'mercy.' [This is ascertained on the basis] of what it releases to the extremities that nurse from it since most of them incline toward [the quality of] 'mercy.' Nevertheless, qualities of 'justice' are joined to her [*binah*] since [the *sefirah*] *gevurah* [power; also called *din*] emanates from her [*binah*'s] essence. As long as the emanation from her descends to *gevurah* from her [*binah*'s] special channel (since the higher windows were thought to be seen through lower beings), then the powers of *din* [justice] will be joined [to *binah*] and *gevurah* will become powerful.

"Corresponding to *binah* is the eighth sphere called the zodiac of the spheres. It is third from top to bottom in the celestial order within which the spheres are capable of emanating a blessing onto the world. None of them [the spheres] when dwelling alone in its proper place, fails to exert a good sprinkling. However, when one experiences difficulty because of the changes in motions or change in place from the houses and ascents [of the sky], each of them will form a conjunction with the planet Mars in harmful places [in the sky], which corresponds to the *sefirah gevurah* that I will explain. Then the pillars of heaven will tremble before it;[1] the land will shudder[2] and become very bare.[3] Several killings and wars will occur in the world, as the astronomers explain, all because of the changes of places and aspects and not because of the simple character of the stars of that sphere.

[144] "Just as *binah* has fifty gates,[4] so too can one find forty-eight formations in this sphere. Know that they are lacking two formations. However, these two were hidden from the ancient astronomers, as [pseudo] R. Abraham b. David testified in his commentary on the *Sefer Yezirah*.[5] Know that, in this time, the seamen discovered stars and new formations in the horizon of the lands of Peru, [and they were] more numerous that those on this horizon. These were not mentioned by the ancient astronomers nor [are they found] in their books. It is appropriate that these two formations that were hidden from these astronomers were discovered in order to complete the number fifty. These formations were also alluded to by R. Eliezer the great in his chapter 7, where he wrote:[6] 'All the great luminaries

[1]Cf. Job 26:11.
[2]Cf. Proverbs 30:21 and elsewhere.
[3]Cf. Isaiah 24:3.
[4]Cf. B. T. Rosh ha-Shanah 21b, which are all given to Moses excluding one; *Sefer ha-Zohar*, 2:115a; 3:216a.
[5][Pseudo] Abraham b. David, commentary on the *Sefer Yezirah* (Jerusalem, 1962), p. 14.
[6]*Pirke de R. Eliezer*, chap. 7.

were given in the south except for the revealed ones located in the north, etc.'

"The fourth *sefirah* is called *gedullah* [greatness]. It has the quality of Abraham and is thus called 'mercy' [*ḥesed*], for his propensity was to act mercifully. In its domain is *ḥokhmah,* as the rabbis hinted: 'A person who wants to become wise should face south.'[1] Also [in its domain] are love, graciousness, and mercy in the presence of great people, as well as the element of water and all white things.

"Corresponding to it is the planet Saturn, which is the most important of all, in whose domain lie the elements of water, wisdom, and philosophic investigation. The philosophers who use talismans know that when it [Saturn] is successful, straight from the south with its house in the middle of the heaven, it yields gracefulness and mercy in the presence of great people and represents gold to nobility. It is stationed over buildings and over first fruit and its secret includes prophecy and dream visions. It is the constellation of the Jews and was the constellation of Abraham, our father, the head of the Israelite nation.[2]

[145] "It is known that when the Jews do the will of God, a good emanation will flow on them with cheerful countenance. No one in the world is [then] their superior in wisdom, wealth, honor, and in victory over [their] enemies. When they sin, the emanation turns away from them and God looks down from His holy height[3] with an evil glance. The good influence is then reversed, as in the case of Saul, the king of Israel, who was terrified by an evil spirit when God turned away from him.[4]

"See the wonders of this planet's nature which [Pseudo] ibn Ezra described in the *Sefer ha-Aẓamim.*[5] When an iniquitous priest falsely requests to cling to it and to bring down its spirituality to him but does not watch his guard, this planet will then turn on him maliciously, for evil and not for good, not leaving him alone until it kills him. This will not happen to the rest of the iniquitous priests who turn away from their [evil] worship. You are able to grasp from this [example] the nature of this star appointed over the Jews. As long as there is an awakening from below, from the sweet fragrance of the actions of the children of Israel, it will ascend above and continue the good influence from the quality of mercy surround-

---

[1] B. T. Babba Batra 25b.

[2] On Saturn as the planet of the Jews, see the aforementioned essay of E. Zafran (Part I, p. 171); see also Idel, "Magical and Neoplatonic Interpretations," p. 209.

[3] Cf. Psalm 102:20.

[4] Cf. 1 Samuel 16:15.

[5] *Sefer ha-Aẓamim,* pp. 18–21.

ing the planet. Then they will present a burnt offering[1] and none of the other nations will be above them. However, when the good turns away from them, because of the nature of this aforementioned planet, they will descend to the bottom depth, to the lowest tier of hell, and there will be no other nation more despised as a reproach and a curse than them.[2]

"The next *sefirah* is called *nezah* [lasting endurance], which is [located on] a right line with *hesed*. The planet Jupiter whose mighty and great power exerts an influence of greatness and mercy is a branch of it. Moreover, the glory [*nezah*] of Israel does not deceive.[3] [146] What the rabbis declared, that Abraham has a sphere, as it is written: 'Who has roused a victor from the East; he calls to his service *zedek* [Jupiter],'[4] should not contradict what we have said, that his sphere was Saturn since both [interpretations] are correct.

"*Nezah* is the branch of *hesed* and what is in the branch is also in the root. This is alluded to in the verse: 'He calls *zedek* to his service,' that is, the sphere Jupiter was not its main and essential sphere but a branch of it. Therefore, he said: 'to his service.' Note also that according to the rhetoricians of the nations, Jupiter is called the son of Saturn, indicating that he is a branch of the latter, just as a son is like a leg of his father. The great constellation belonging to *nezah* is called by the astronomers *fortuna major*. It will bring eternal blessing to a home, and will look down with a good gaze. Moreover, it is appointed over all laws and statutes. Thus we find in the case of Abraham, our father, that he observed God's commandments as it is written: 'Inasmuch as Abraham obeyed Me and followed My mandate, etc.'[5] Just as *nezah* is the treasure upon which life depends to bring life to the world, and it derives from two arms [the *sefirot, hesed* and *gevurah*] and it is on the right [side], so too the planet Jupiter is appointed over life because blood is in its strength, which is the soul and giver of life to all living creatures. Therefore, all the beloved members in his household will live long lives upon the earth. This planet is one of the two *fortunas,* the larger and the right one. It is also *yakhin* [the right column of the portico of Solomon's Temple],[6] by whose word the nobles and the mighty are supported and established in peace.

"The next *sefirah* is called *gevurah* [power], which is on the left side and

[1]Cf. Jeremiah 14:12.
[2]Cf. Jeremiah 24:9.
[3]Cf. 1 Samuel 15:29.
[4]Isaiah 41:2. Cf. B. T. Shabbat 156a–b.
[5]Genesis 26:5.
[6]Cf. 1 Kings 7:21; 2 Chronicles 3:17.

from whose domain emerges the element of fire and all red things, the increase in the forces of justice, and the emanation of the influence of wealth and rain. The rabbis hinted at this [idea] in relating the increase of rain to the awakening of excitement regarding the desire for sexual intercourse between a man and his wife.[1]

"The planet Mars corresponds to it. From its domain emerges the element of fire, which causes the earth to become inflamed, [producing] a vapor that ascends from it and waters the face of the land. [147] The naturalists thus declared that when the great and mighty heat breaks its limit, this is a sign that the heavenly windows are about to open up, to pour a rain cloud on the earth. The scholars explain that this [planet] bestows power through victory over one's enemies. It is appointed over the nation of Esau, the son of Isaac, who is Edom [i.e., red], and its officers are Edomites. He [Esau] possessed the fear of Isaac. Furthermore, all the brave things he accomplished were because of his fathers' blessing and good quality.

"The excitement in sexual arousal is also known and explained naturally for it is derived from an increase in the force of fire within men. Moreover, all red-haired men with pretty eyes love women and [enjoy] sleeping with them. This is also explained in the writings of the astronomers. They declared that this planet is despised by the others, except for Venus. On the contrary, the two of them are compatible. The rhetoricians of the nations also alluded to the companionship of Mars and Venus in their riddles. [148] The master of Venus named Vulcan came and tied them together in an iron net in order to show them off to the rest of the heavenly host. Even though this riddle has other allusions and hidden secrets [in it] for the naturalists and the astrologers, and this is not the place to explain them, at least we can better understand this. [Accordingly,] Mars, which is hot and dry, has a love relationship with the planet Venus, which is hot and moist, since the master of Venus, that is, its agent which is heat, tied them in a net and they were compatible with each other. This corresponds to the quality of *gevurah* that is tied to the quality of the [*sefirah*] *hod* [majesty], which is under it in the left line. The latter is a branch of it and receives emanation and power from the known channel that comes to it, as I shall explain below.

"The next *sefirah* is called *tiferet* [beauty] to which all the channels of the structure [of the ten *sefirot*] are connected and influence it [since it is in the center]. They receive influence from it and from its vitality emerges all

---

[1]Perhaps Yagel alludes to *Bereshit Rabbah*, 13:13.

the emanation of glory, magnificence, and majesty, the influence of anger, the secret of the thirty-two combinations of God's name, and that of the [the number] four and of twelve months. It [*tiferet*] radiates its light and influence to [the *sefirah*] *malkhut* [kingdom] who is like its young man. Through it [*malkhut*], blessing, influence, and outpouring come to the rest of the worlds, for it receives from this lord [*tiferet*] as a wife secretly receives from her husband in the deepest chambers and afterward, [*malkhut*] discharges with a loud voice, as the rabbis explain in *Berakhot:*[1] 'There is no fruit in the stomach of a woman that is blessed except from the fruit of the stomach of a man.'

"Corresponding to it [*tiferet*] is the sun which goes out from his bridal canopy like a groom. It is the light of the world and a glimmer of the light from above, from that of the aforementioned *sefirah*. It is also in the middle of the seven spheres like a king in the middle of his armies. It divides and bestows light and vitality to all the heavenly host according to the words of [Abraham] ibn Ezra.[2] From its power and special property come glory, majesty, splendor, and the influence of [having] children, like the statement of the philosopher: 'Man together with the sun induces procreation,'[3] that is, the heat generated from its vitality aids in insemination in nature stamped by the Creator.[4]

"Due to the sun's annual course in the region of the spheres, the twelve months of the year are constituted, as described by the verse: 'They will serve as signs for the set times—the days and the years.'[5] It also radiates its light to the moon; the first [the sun] is called the great light and the second [the moon] the small one. One bestows and the other receives, like the example of the male and female. Moreover, it is known that the quality of *tiferet* includes both justice and mercy and is called 'truth.' This is Jacob's quality, as it is stated: 'You shall give truth to Jacob,'[6] hate robbery and iniquity, and not show favoritism in judgment. Likewise, the nature of this star is to diffuse its emanation, as the rabbis declared in chapter *Mi she-Hihshikh:*[7] 'He who is born under the constellation of the sun will be a distinguished man; he will eat and drink of his own and his secrets will lie

[1]B. T. Berakhot 51b.
[2]I could not locate the exact reference, but compare [pseudo] ibn Ezra, *Sefer ha-Azamim*, p. 32.
[3]Following the reading in the London manuscript, fol. 120b. Cf. Aristotle, *Generation of Animals* (Cambridge, Mass. and London, 1942), 716a15.
[4]This last line appears in the side margin of the Cincinnati manuscript.
[5]Genesis 1:14.
[6]Micah 7:20.
[7]B. T. Shabbat 156a.

uncovered. If a thief, he will have no success, etc.' Thus it is appropriate for kings in the sun's domain, rulers and judges of the earth, to pursue justice and truth, for all to be fair in judgment, and to despise robbery, injustice, and bribery. One who takes a bribe will not succeed because he will become blind, as the rabbis declare at the end of *Pe'ah:*[1] [149] 'Any judge who takes bribery and perverts justice will have his eyes become dim, as it is stated: "You shall not take bribes"[2] for bribes blind the clear-sighted, etc.' Furthermore, a man born under its [the sun's] dominion [will be affected] either all for his good or all for his bad. The reason for this is that light and darkness [together], that is, justice and mercy, were created on account of it.

[150] "The astronomers declared that if a person's horoscope shows the sun in the middle of the firmament while the rest of the nebulous stars or most of them around it are in good aspect, he will become a general of an army or a king or prince. If it is in the middle of the heaven without other stars [around it] and it wanders alone, that is, the constant aspect called *pellegrino* [wanderer] by the astronomers, this person will be [like] an ensign to nations hanging from a tree. Notice how in one situation it [the sun] can emanate [some] good or bad or all good or all bad, light or darkness. [151] From this [situation], you can understand what the scholars know from experience, that any creature hanging from a tree always turns its back toward the sun and will never be seen facing it. This is because the hanging is attributable to it [the sun]. It is as if wise nature was embarrassed by its master who punished him in judgment. So this star is the reflection of the *sefirah* which is made up of justice and mercy. I would be able to relate to you many more words and pearls of such quantity; however, the time does not allow us. The proof from the righteous Joseph's dream is sufficient. He saw the sun and moon bowing down before him.[3] It is known that the sun alluded to his father who was his stem and that this represents its [the sun's] quality.

"The next *sefirah* is called *hod* [glory], which is a treasure upon which the spheres depend. It is the branch of *gevurah* and therefore is composed of justice and mercy. The planet Venus corresponds to it which influences all the earth's inhabitants with all kinds of precious things, food, and produce. It is called a small planet in the same way that Jupiter, which stands in a right light in relation to it, is called a great one.

"Because it [*hod*] is a branch of *gevurah* and the latter alludes to Mars,

[1]Mishnah Pe'ah 8:9.
[2]Exodus 23:8.
[3]Cf. Genesis 37.

you can understand the relationship of the various planets to it as I have mentioned above. One influences while one receives influence, just as the quality of *gevurah* influences while the quality of *hod* receives the influence. And just as the quality of *gevurah* has two forms—one for the quality of *hod* and one for the quality of Torah study—so too the planet Mars has two relations: one with the sun, since it is also hot and dry (for a like quality enjoys its likeness), and one with Venus, because of the heat in her. Just as *hod* possesses justice and mercy, so too does Venus, which has a good influence that is straight and a bad influence in reverse. In place of 'delight' [*oneg*] comes pain [*negah*].

[152] "This is what the scholars of [the constellation] of Phoenix suggested with its two houses. The first is called 'the cheek bowl' whose name is known for goodness and mercy, while the other is called 'mammon goes out.' Its name indicates fear and evil, as the scholars explain from experience.[1]

"The next *sefirah* is called *yesod* [foundation], in which all the forces and processes array themselves. It is a branch of *tiferet* that carries influence from the latter to *malkhut*. It is called the 'holy cherub,' like the example of the covenant which is the light that brings the influx of all the male body to that of the female. It has within it processes that reflect all the *sefirot* and it pours out its emanation on *malkhut*.

"It [*yesod*] corresponds to the star called, in the language of the sages of Israel in chapter *Mi she-Hihshikh*, 'the sun's scribe' [Mercury].[2] It never distances itself from its course and in its motion from the sun. It is called the 'messenger of the gods' in the interpretations of the ancient philosophers since it is the messenger of all the spheres and it carries their force, influence, and special property to the moon. It mixes with everything, it is in everything, and everything is in it. Thus it is good with good forces, magnifying their strength, and bad with bad forces, to the utter ruin of everything.[3] One finds two forms in the quality of *yesod:* the first to extract good emanantion and the second to extract the surplus which is food to the *kelippot* [the evil forces]. Similarly, one finds two holes related to ritual circumcision: the first from which semen ejaculates, coming from the brain, from every choice piece of the body,[4] thigh, and shoulder, and the second

---

[1]This last paragraph appears oddly out of place. There is also an empty space after this paragraph in the manuscript.

[2]B. T. Shabbat 156a.

[3]Cf. Deuteronomy 29:18.

[4]Cf. Ezekiel 24:4.

from which urine is emitted, which is natural excess. So nature excretes it to the outside in this manner.

"Know that the ancient astrologers declared that the stars have dominion in two places in the body. First, in the place of the circumcision as I have said, and second in the mouth. From this they conceived of the secret of the kiss. [153] Just as every desire of union between male and female involves the discharging of his strength into her, so too is the desire of a kiss, since he gives her some [influence] through the kisses of his mouth. Everything that goes out of him mixes up in her by way of the same place [the north] ruled by Mercury, in the same manner that it rules in the place of circumcision. Thus they call it 'the messenger of the spheres.'

"The tenth *sefirah* is called *malkhut* [kingdom]. It is the high cherub who receives all of the influx of the upper *sefirot* and emanates it to the rest of the worlds by way of those pipes that go out from it. It is like the female who is impregnated by the male [and] stores it [the discharge] until his order comes for it to go out to the air of the world. The moon corresponds to it since it receives the influx from all the spheres through Mercury, as I have mentioned, and empties it afterward on all the world, as the sages explain. Besides its influence and special property, the moon is known by all humanity with respect [to its impact on] their bodies, illnesses, and even [their] irreligiousity, more than the rest[1] of the stars and spheres. This is so because all of their influence comes through it since it is closer to the world than all of them.

"The moon and the sun are the great luminaries, male and female, [which represent] the divine secret that is not spoken as it is written [i.e., God's name]. Its [the moon's] quality is [called] 'dry land' and 'sea' by the kabbalists since, by itself, it is a dry land. So, like its example [of being a dry land], the moon is a dark, demeaned body that has no light of its own but receives it from some other body. But it is [also] a 'sea' since it is the great sea in which the emanations of all other qualities are gathered. So the emanation of the other stars collect on the moon, as I have stated. Besides, it has the power to turn back the great sea, as explained by sailors and sea travelers. I would be able to adduce many images about it regarding its changing names and words, but this is sufficient for our purpose. Besides these images that I have mentioned, one might find thousands and ten thousands of meritorious examples in the spheres of the heavens. Just as the

---

[1] A comment added on the bottom of the manuscript page, but which interrupts the flow of the passage, is omitted here.

rabbis declared in the *Sefer ha-Zohar:*[1] 'There are seven stars to correspond to seven firmaments, etc.,' so are you able to understand the way things work from their foundation and origin.[2]

[154] "Even in this lower world, whose foundation is in the dust,[3] there is nothing that does not have its reflection above, as the rabbis explained regarding the verse:[4] '"Do you know the laws of heaven, etc."[5] There is not a blade of grass below that lacks a constellation in heaven which strikes it and tells it to grow.' If they claimed that everything has a constellation in the heaven and that all the heavenly constellations and stars are reflections of what is above [them], thus everything that is on earth is also a reflection of what is above [it]. This is the meaning of the verse: 'Our days on earth are like a shadow.'[6] Observe well that all the reality of the lower world, whose foundation is dust, is divided into ten parts corresponding to the ten spheres and to the ten *sefirot,* and they are the following:

"The first part is nature, which binds and bestows strength to processes that are in a state of potential being so as to actualize them; for without it, they would not 'raise their head,' as the philosophers explain. It corresponds to the tenth sphere called the 'diurnal sphere,' which makes utterance day to day.[7]

"The second part is primal matter, whose essence is still not understood by the scholars. It desires and detests form like the adulteress who eats and cleans her mouth [and says I have done no wrong].[8] It is the void described by Naḥmanides upon which man reflects to understand its essence.[9] It corresponds to the ninth sphere, which is unknown to the scholars, as I have said.

"The third part is the element of fire. It corresponds to the heavenly sphere, for just as the former drives all things, the heavenly sphere gives strength through its light to work and to produce. According to the sun's course in it, there are changes in time and modifications in the world.

---

[1]*Sefer ha-Zohar,* 1:34b.
[2]Two additional comments on the bottom and side of the manuscript page have been omitted.
[3]Cf. Job 4:19.
[4]*Bereshit Rabbah,* 10:7.
[5]Job 38:33.
[6]1 Chronicles 29:15.
[7]Cf. Psalm 19:3.
[8]Cf. Proverbs 30:20.
[9]Cf. Naḥmanides on Genesis 1:2, which does not fit precisely Yagel's quotation. Cf. also Rashi on the same verse, which fits more closely.

"The fourth part is the element of water, which corresponds to the sphere of Saturn in whose domain lies water. Many have written about it, for its secret is 'the high waters.' The sage R. Shabbetai [Donnolo], the physician, in his commentary on *Sefer Yezirah,* said that it was the terrible crystal that Ezekiel [the son of] Buzi saw.[1]

"The fifth part is the element of air corresponding to the sphere of Jupiter, which is hot and moist, just like the nature of air and blood. Therefore, when there is mold in the air, blood is moldy and blisters appear in meat.

"The sixth part is the element of earth, which corresponds to the sphere of Mars. It is dry like the dry and dusty earth.

[155] "The seventh part is mineral, corresponding to the sun, which encircles all minerals in the clefts of the rocks. By its power, a moist and thick vapor rises from the land but is unable to ascend since the rock hides it. This vapor turns into mercury, which is the mother of all the minerals. There it hardens according to its nature and [because of] the sulfur in it. Depending on the heat it receives from the sun, it turns into some metal or into partial metal as the scholars explain. They also declared that all metals are potentially gold because the latter is the most perfect of them all. It is the nature of the world to strive to produce and create the most perfect thing possible if external causes don't diminish it. It is also known that gold was called by the name of 'sun.' Therefore, it is appropriate to relate the minerals to the sun.

"The eighth part is vegetable, corresponding to the planet Venus, which causes every tree that is pleasing to the sight and good[2] to grow, as well as all plants and grass, as understood by the naturalists.

"The ninth part is animal, corresponding to mercury, as the scholars explain that all that moves is found in its dominion. Thus its name is like its part, 'living silver' [mercury], and all living things are according to its kind.[3]

"The tenth part is human, which is man, corresponding to the moon. Just as it [the moon] receives heavenly emanation as I have described, so too man, who is called in the secret language of the sages 'small world' [microcosm], is worthy of receiving all the emanation of the worlds in the context of his form and honorable image. This is so hinted by the wise man who drew the walls of this room. So we interpreted for you the short path,

[1]Cf. Ezekiel 1:22. I could not find the exact reference but compare *Il Commento di Sabbatai Donnolo* (in Hebrew), ed. D. Castelli (Florence, 1880), pp. 40–41.

[2]Cf. Genesis 2:9.

[3]Cf. Genesis 1:24.

which is the inscription imprinted on the first wall: the secret of the concatenation of all the worlds, their connection to each other, and that one is like the shadow of the other.[1]

[156] "The divine sage R. Simeon bar Yoḥai similarly wrote in the *Midrash ha-Ne'elam* in many places and especially in the portion *Lekh Lekha,* which reads:[2] 'Melchizedek' is the latest world and 'king of Salem' is the higher world which are joined one to another inseparably. The two worlds are like one and even the lowest world is also the whole, and the whole is one.

[157] "Know, turn your ear, and listen regarding the intent of this second inscription on the second wall,[3] which is the figure of the man who is called 'small world,' as I have said. Examine the [writings] of the sages of Israel, what R. Simeon bar Yoḥai wrote in many places, and especially in the book of *Tikkunim, tikkun* 70, and in *Midrash Ḥazit* on the verse: 'A small city, etc.'[4] The great eagle Maimonides in the *Moreh* [*Nevukhim*], part 1, chapter 72, and all the Greek philosophers who similarly refer to him by name, call him in their language 'microcosm,' that is, small world. Many of them even divided up his parts to correspond to the parts of the general material world.

"The astrologers also attempted to locate a sprinkling of the twelve spheres and the seven nebulous stars in every part of man and his limbs, as the sage Haly Aben Ragel mentioned in his book and the sage [Henry Cornelius Agrippa] in his *De occulta philosophia,* part 1.[5] Not only this, but our sages elevated it as an image of the high chariot and also divided its parts to correspond to the ten *sefirot.* [158] If you would like, you can see how this division is made in their books. Take a look at the *Sefer ha-Zohar* and in other kabbalistic works and especially in the *Sefer Marot Elohim* of Meir ibn Gabbai.[6] But we will not be a mule who carries books [i.e., supplying excessive book titles], and in a place where one asks to shorten [one's explanation], it is impossible to expand since the time does not allow us. Already three quarters of the night has passed and the time of singing

[1] Yagel had previously described the first wall as that with the image of man.

[2] Cf. Genesis 14:18; *Sefer ha-Zohar,* 1:87a.

[3] This was earlier described as the first wall.

[4] Ecclesiastes 9:14. I could not find a reference to the verse there but compare *Kohelet Rabbah,* 9:15.

[5] *De occulta philosophia,* bk. 1, chap. 22. On Yagel's use of Aben Ragel's work, see above, Part I, sec. 57.

[6] Cf. Meir ibn Gabbai, *Sefer Avodat ha-Kodesh* (Lemberg, 1857), ḥelek ha-yiḥud, chap. 18, pp. 22a–23a.

has come[1] when each one of us will turn to go his way to his special place and will leave his companion.

"I will only inform you that we shall add to the words of the former rabbis and show you a sign that, just as the universe generally consists of four parts based the secret of the four worlds [*azilut, beriah, yezirah, asiyyah*], as I have stated, so too, in the human body, one can find a hint to all the worlds from the perspective of its construction and form. This is suggested by the verse: 'He made you and established you.'[2] The rabbis also wrote: 'The Holy One, blessed be He, and His tribunal are appointed over every limb and restore it to good.'

"So notice that first one finds ten special things in the head, three of which are hidden. Those in the brain are divided into three parts: the picture in the front part of the head, the thought in the middle part, and the memory in the back part. The potency and special property that emerge from them flow to the seven revolving forces. The latter are the two eyes, the two ears, the two nostrils of the nose, and the mouth, which total seven, corresponding to the seven last *sefirot* that also receive emanation and light from the first three secret worlds [i.e., the three higher *sefirot*]. Moreover, the head is also the shape of a ball without a top or bottom, which is the most praiseworthy shape of all, [159] as the engineers explain. Note that this part corresponds to the highest world of *azilut,* the most important one of all.

"The second part is divided into ten parts, all of which are hidden from our eyes. They are the heart, liver, lung, the food pipe, windpipe, stomach, abdomen, intestines, spleen, the organs producing semen in man, and the womb of the woman. They correspond to the second world of *beriah,* which is also secret and hidden and known only by way of the kabbalah and from the activities that emerge from it. Our rabbis in *Midrash Kohelet* counted ten inner organs in man and called them ten rulers in the city.[3] Perhaps they hinted at this secret that I have described, for they correspond to the hidden and secret world of *beriah.* However, it is the ruler of the worlds of *yezirah* and *asiyyah* that activates their processes from their potential state.

"The third part is the ten fingers of the hand, five opposite five, which correspond to the world of *yezirah*. The intelligences activate the emanation and light from their potential state originating in the two higher worlds and

---

[1]Cf. Song of Songs 2:12.
[2]Deuteronomy 32:6.
[3]Cf. B. T. Nedarim 32b; *Kohelet Rabbah,* 7:19, interpreting Ecclesiastes 7:19.

empty them on whomever is inclined to receive them [emanation and light]. It is the same with the ten fingers of the hand by which a human being works and produces and activates potential things which he conceived in his brain and upon which he decided in his heart.

"The fourth part is the ten toes of the feet, five opposite five. They carry and move man from one place to another and provide a means to complete his activities. They are situated at the bottom level more than anything else and correspond to the fourth world, the world of *asiyyah,* which is also the last of everything. The secret of the nails and hair is [well] known. They hint at the *kelippot* and other things that you can fathom yourself and imagine their creator from the form which the wise artist hinted at (by way of a small example)[1] with those Hittite, Hebrew, and Ammonite letters that he inscribed and drew on [the figure of] the man engraved on the second wall. This is to indicate the agreement of all the sages of the nations and languages regarding the fact that man is the image of the world in general and is worthy of receiving the emanation and sprinkling by way of the nature of the form and number of his organs. A wise craftsman shaped them with wisdom, understanding, and intelligence in order to elevate man, according to his abilities, to one of the [four] worlds, so that he cannot be kept banished[2] [from them].

[160] "The rabbis hinted at this [idea] in saying that every righteous person is a world unto himself[3] and each is built from the marriage canopy of his neighbor.[4] In truth, according to the nature of retribution and that of [one's] actions, one man appears to cling to the higher world, while another appears to be connected to it, while another is satisfied with [reaching] the pillars of God and dwelling in His sanctuary in the rest of the [four] worlds. The conclusion is that everything exists according to the ability [of a person's] awe, knowledge, and action.

### Final Revelations on the Secrets of the Palace

"In order [to show] that it will not be difficult for man—for how can he, born from a woman, ascend these great and steep steps since God did not create wings for him to fly in the heaven, and the bad inclination is tied to the heel of Jacob?—the wise artist thought it fitting to display the world

---

[1] The phrase is an addition to the text.
[2] Cf. 1 Samuel 14:14.
[3] *Shemot Rabbah,* 52:3.
[4] *Bamidbar Rabbah,* 21:20.

before him by which man can ascend to the heavens and the heavenly heavens. Through it, he can also discover the paths among those who stand eternally, so there in the lands of the eternal life, his image and form will not mock him. On the contrary, he will be a warrior and head to them all, commanding them and acting in the image of the high chariot, as the rabbis declared:[1] 'The fathers are the chariot.' Therefore, the artist drew on this third wall a tree which is the Tree of Life.[2] He who eats of its fruits will live forever in the world in which all is well-balanced and good.[3]

[161] "This tree is cast in the image hinted at [by the rabbis] in the secret of the ten *sefirot* of *azilut, beriah, yezirah,* and *asiyyah,* and it is similarly suggested by the body of man, as I have stated. It is situated opposite him so that all his parts will be able to receive the emanation of blessing and praise from all the worlds and, by virtue of the action of this tree, he will be able to bring down an influence to every part and to the creatures of this world and the next. Then God will say to him: 'You are my son; I have gathered you this day.'[4]

"Notice that [the message of] this tree should be in your mouth and heart to do [its injunctions]. One is not deemed righteous by ascending to heaven or by dwelling at the ends of the earth, or by doing anything else. Rather this thing [message] is close to you,[5] which is to observe all the words of the Torah which God gave to his people on Sinai. It is called a tree of life, as it is written: 'It is a tree of life to those who grasp it, etc.'[6] For in it, one will discover the positive and negative commandments corresponding to the organs and parts of man. Many commandments will be found in the part of the head and brain that corresponds to the world of *azilut,* as I have stated, such as knowing God, [162] as it is written: 'Know therefore this day and keep in mind,'[7] and repeated by the prophets: 'But only in this should one glory, in his earnest knowledge of Him,'[8] and repeated again in the writings: 'And you, Solomon, my son, know your God, your father, etc.'[9]

"Knowledge is the root and principle of everything, as the rabbis declared:[10] 'Whenever there is a man with knowledge, it is as if the Temple was built in his days.' They further said [there]: 'Knowledge is great which

[1]*Bereshit Rabbah,* 82:7; 47:8.
[2]Earlier, Yagel had designated this as the second wall.
[3]Cf. B. T. Kiddushin 39b.
[4]Psalm 2:7.
[5]Cf. Deuteronomy 30:14.
[6]Proverbs 3:18.
[7]Deuteronomy 4:39.
[8]Jeremiah 9:23.
[9]1 Chronicles 28:9. A comment in the side margin has been omitted.
[10]B. T. Berakhot 33a.

is set between two names and what are they? "[The Lord] is an all-knowing God."¹ Maimonides wrote in the *Moreh* [*Nevukhim*], part 1, chapter 54: 'One who knows God will be acceptable in His sight just as the head of the prophets [Moses] declared: "Show me now Your ways so that I may know You in order that I may find favor in Your sight."² With these words, [he indicates] how God, may He be exalted, is known through His attributes. When one knows these ways, he will know Him, for he [Moses] said: "In order to find favor in Your sight," which indicates that one who knows his Creator will find favor in His sight. Not merely one who fasts or prays, but anyone who has knowledge of Him is favored and permitted to come near Him, whereas anyone who does not know Him will anger [Him] and be kept far away [from Him]. For His favor and wrath, His nearness and remoteness, are proportionate to the extent of a man's wisdom or ignorance.' His unity, love, and fear, the love of those who love Him, hear His voice, and cling to Him [all] emerge from it [knowledge].

[163] "Who is compassionate? One who acts compassionately with other human beings as a father has compassion for his children.³ He should not be excited, God forbid, nor affected with his compassion, for this will be a defect in his character, as I have explained, and as the rabbi [Maimonides] explained in that aforementioned chapter. You too should be so compassionate to be like Him, to act with the quality of compassion and love without the excitement of the soul, since all passions are evil. Rather guard yourself from them to the extent of your ability, as the author [Moses Maimonides] of the *Moreh* [*Nevukhim*] commanded the leaders of the state to do in that same chapter, as well as what is gracious along with the other good qualities. You too should do likewise.

[164] "The conclusion is that just as the emanation and light come from the world of *azilut* to all the worlds, so, too, man comes to observe the rest of the commandments related to the other parts [of his body] from the commandments dependent on that part related to knowledge. Accordingly, many commandments are dependent on the hands, such as giving charity, weighing with honest scales and honest *hin* [a liquid measure],⁴ putting on phylacteries [and] the priest's observance of the sacrifices and his lifting his hands in blessing, etc. Many [commandments] are dependent on the heart,

---

¹Cf. 1 Samuel 2:3. The word "all-knowing" is between the words "Lord" and "God." The line is somewhat misquoted.

²Exodus 33:13.

³Cf. Psalm 103:13.

⁴Cf. Leviticus 19:36.

such as 'You shall not take vengeance nor bear any grudge.'[1] In every place where Scripture declares: 'And you shall fear your God,'[2] [the commandments are dependent on the heart], as the rabbis indicated. [This is also the case regarding one's proper] intention in prayer and loving your neighbor as yourself, which is a major rule of the Torah,[3] and upon which all the polity and all the laws and customs are built. The heart is the principal part of the body, as it is written: 'More than all that you guard, guard your heart, for it is the source of life.'[4]

"Likewise, many commandments are dependent upon other internal organs and upon the sexual organs, [such as the commandments] to be fruitful and multiply, to do what is permitted for the perpetuation of life alone, to observe the ritual of circumcision, and not pollute oneself with forbidden sexual acts. Some commandments are dependent on the feet, such as 'do not go about as a talebearer among your fellows and do not stand upon the blood of your neighbor,'[5] and run to the synagogue and to the house of study, and be swift of foot as Asahel[6] to go every place where commandments and good deeds are performed, as King David did, as it is written: 'I have considered my ways and have turned back to Your ordinances.'[7] From your own intelligence, you can combine and establish one thing to correspond to another from all the specific commandments to each organ.

"Know surely that this is the way to ascend to the heights, as the rabbis wrote: 'A ladder [sulam], that is Sinai.'[8] The numerical value of the letters of one is equivalent to the other. It is like what the kabbalists declared, that all the Torah commandments are divided into right and left, front and back, above and below, a good and a bad depth, white and red. [165] Anyone who observes one commandment receives goodness from above since, through that commandment, he causes power to be exerted above from 'the nothingness of thought.'[9] It is as if he actually lends stability, as it were, to a part of the Holy One, blessed be He, if it is permissible to speak in this way. Regarding this [thought] it is stated: 'And He said to me: "You are my

[1]Leviticus 19:18.
[2]Leviticus 19:14, 32; 25:36, 43.
[3]*Bereshit Rabbah*, 24:7.
[4]Proverbs 4:23.
[5]Leviticus 19:16.
[6]Cf. 2 Samuel 2:18.
[7]Psalm 119:59.
[8]*Bereshit Rabbah*, 68:16.
[9]The expression refers to the *sefirah keter*. Cf. G. Scholem, *On the Kabbalah and Its Symbolism* (New York, 1960), p. 125. My thanks to Professor Moshe Idel for the reference.

servant Israel in whom I glory."[1] [God] will receive a supplement of influence from the source until it is discovered that due to its cause and because of it, out of love, the blessings from above and below will increase and spread out.'[2]

"The rabbis declared in the homily of R. Simeon bar Yoḥai:[3] 'Observe this. The commands of the Torah are exalted essences on high. Whenever a person fulfills one of the commands, that command presents itself, all adorned, before the Holy One, blessed be He, saying: "So and so fulfilled me and I proceed from him." Accordingly, that person, as he stimulated that command below, similarly caused a stirring on high and brought about peace on high and below. So the biblical verse states: "But if he holds fast to My refuge, he makes peace with Me; he makes peace with Me."[4] He makes peace with Me on high and below. [Thus, happy is the portion], which is all from God, of the person who observes the commands of the Torah.'

[166] "Know that besides the great perfection that man bestows on his soul by observing the dictates of the Torah and the commandment, he also learns from it all the virtues of the good qualities and the intelligent and wise concepts that the philosophers of the nations tried to write down for memory after their deep investigations and efforts. He will see [this] in the Torah and the general principle will be inscribed in it since there is nothing that is not written in the Torah, as it is stated: 'I, wisdom, live with prudence; I attain knowledge and foresight.'[5] [167] This is because every recent scholar who writes a book has a variety of great intentions, some revealed, some secret, some which he will reveal to his admirers, and some which he will keep to himself and not publicly disclose in that composition. Thus if man is so, what should He who has all wisdom act and do? For God is the source of everything: he gives wisdom to the wise and understanding to those who know.[6] And in this composition which He gave as a present to His people, there is not a word and letter lacking a higher secret and without multiple meanings, as it is written: 'Behold, my word is like fire . . . and like a hammer that shatters rock,'[7] as the rabbis interpreted.

[1] Isaiah 49:3.
[2] Yagel's source is Menahem Recanati's *Ta'amei ha-Miẓvot* (Basel, 1581), 3a. It is quoted by Scholem, *On the Kabbalah*, p. 125, and by M. Idel, "A Commentary on the Ten *Sefirot* and Fragments from the Writings of R. Joseph of Shushan ha-Birah" (in Hebrew) *Alei Sefer*, 6–7 (1978–79): 83.
[3] *Sefer ha-Zohar*, 3:118a.
[4] Isaiah 27:5.
[5] Proverbs 8:12.
[6] Cf. Daniel 2:21.
[7] Jeremiah 23:29; see also B. T. Sanhedrin 34a, Shabbat 88b.

"This is what this recent scholar alluded to in drawing the tree in the midst of the land with foul and birds flying on the branches. From their [the birds] mouths, peace goes out, riddles and words of wisdom and morality. This suggests that the person who meditates on the Torah all day long will have words as sweet as honey in his mouth.[1] New moral insights will be renewed for him, which he will understand from the study of the words and riddles of the sages. There is nothing hidden from the King of Kings, the Holy One, praised be He, which was not inscribed in the Torah. If you speak of or see with your own eyes what is not found [there], then it was misunderstood by you, as the rabbis wrote:[2] 'If it is thin for you, turn it [the Torah] and turn it over again, for everything is in it.'

[168] "The fourth wall has no riddles upon it and nothing is drawn on it since it is translucent. All the things that will appear opposite it will be drawn instantaneously on it to suggest the next world, which is the world of retribution connected to the tracks of death, since it has no [independent] activity. However, one who wearies, labors, and achieves [something] in this world, all of it will come with him in that [the next] world because he will eat the fruit of his labors.[3] Just as the reflection of everything that appears opposite this world can be seen immediately, so too will every activity and every action that you do in the world of being and absence be inscribed and written before you in that world. Therefore, happy is the one who comes here with teaching in hand."[4]

### The Conclusion of the Heavenly Tour

Afterward, my father and I left this exalted room and entered a great parlor. When we entered it, the two women whom we had initially seen came out from a small opening in front of us. They approached us and wanted to speak with us but the important woman [the third woman] addressed [us instead]: "Leave them and go and don't be late. The way is long and it has already reached the end of the third watch [of the night] when the wife speaks with her husband and the infant nurses the breasts of his mother. You will see them and their treasure houses on another occasion. I will also finish speaking with you about the subjects of the worlds and the soul of man for I still have said nothing to you except for a little about the body and

[1] Cf. Ezekiel 3:3.
[2] Avot 5:25.
[3] Cf. Jeremiah 17:10; 32:19.
[4] Cf. B. T. Pesahim 50a; *Kohelet Rabbah*, 9:8.

its shape and the form of its organs. Even the small amount that I spoke is like a drop in the bucket and like a drop of water in the sea."

In the meantime, while this woman spoke these words to me, I turned from side to side to see my father, but lo and behold, he disappeared completely from my sight. I rose to ask for him, for I was afraid to stand there alone in that place. I called him with a loud voice but there was no answer until my throat became parched because of the shouting and I awoke. I saw myself on my bed in jail as [I had been] before. I looked and, alas, the day had arrived and it was already time for the recitation of the *Shema* [prayer] of the morning service.

# Indexes

## Biblical Passages

| | |
|---|---|
| 8:2 | 135 |
| 12:6 | 294 |
| 17:13 | 290 |
| 24:14 | 159 |

ISAIAH
| | |
|---|---|
| 1:2 | 259 |
| 1:5 | 226 |
| 1:25 | 282 |
| 1:26 | 282 |
| 1:27 | 282 |
| 2:6 | 286 |
| 3:5 | 295 |
| 3:10 | 215 |
| 4:5–6 | 154 |
| 4:6 | 249 |
| 5:1 | 88 |
| 5:2 | 88 |
| 5:4 | 88 |
| 5:7 | 88, 89 |
| 5:12 | 93, 265 |
| 5:25 | 202 |
| 6:3 | 302 |
| 6:10 | 238 |
| 7:4 | 226 |
| 7:17 | 167 |
| 8:10 | 162 |
| 9:5 | 100, 187 |
| 10:27 | 294 |
| 11:2 | 313 |
| 11:7 | 94 |
| 13:21 | 177, 202 |
| 14:23 | 186 |
| 14:26 | 121, 135 |
| 14:27 | 137, 170 |
| 14:32 | 117 |
| 17:6 | 73 |
| 20:2–4 | 189 |
| 21:1 | 71 |
| 21:2 | 108 |
| 21:16 | 100 |
| 22:12 | 243, 252 |
| 22:17 | 96 |
| 23:7 | 277 |
| 23:13 | 166 |
| 23:18 | 75, 230 |
| 24:3 | 322 |
| 24:17 | 228 |
| 24:23 | 172 |
| 26:4 | 214 |
| 26:5 | 255 |
| 26:20 | 94 |
| 26:21 | 128 |
| 27:1 | 75, 191, 281 |
| 27:5 | 338 |
| 27:8 | 199 |

| | |
|---|---|
| 28:14 | 263 |
| 29:4 | 109, 135 |
| 29:8 | 177 |
| 29:11 | 298 |
| 29:13 | 78, 84 |
| 29:15 | 281 |
| 30:33 | 110 |
| 31:5 | 94, 177 |
| 33:7 | 243, 252, 253 |
| 33:21 | 189 |
| 34:11 | 97, 225, 313 |
| 34:13–14 | 225 |
| 35:6 | 94 |
| 35:10 | 182 |
| 38:5 | 104 |
| 40:25 | 247 |
| 40:26 | 266, 310 |
| 40:31 | 229, 293 |
| 41:2 | 324 |
| 41:16 | 214 |
| 41:24 | 110 |
| 42:14 | 109, 295, 310 |
| 42:21 | 286 |
| 43:16 | 320 |
| 43:21 | 312 |
| 44:4 | 262 |
| 45:3 | 235 |
| 45:17 | 312 |
| 48:22 | 222 |
| 49:3 | 338 |
| 49:9 | 205 |
| 50:4 | 245 |
| 52:7 | 99 |
| 52:8 | 76 |
| 53:2 | 109 |
| 53:3 | 225 |
| 53:9 | 203 |
| 53:10 | 290 |
| 55:1 | 286 |
| 55:9 | 247 |
| 57:13 | 219 |
| 57:19 | 312 |
| 58:5 | 290 |
| 59:1 | 174 |
| 59:2 | 174 |
| 59:10 | 133 |
| 59:16–17 | 174 |
| 59:19 | 174 |
| 59:20 | 175 |
| 60:21 | 312 |
| 60:22 | 174 |
| 61:8 | 204, 277 |
| 62:3 | 263 |
| 62:5 | 219 |
| 63:9 | 117, 158 |
| 63:10 | 247 |

# Classical and Medieval Non-Hebrew Sources

## General Index